An Introduction to Camp Administration

5th Edition Basic Camp Management

Armand & Beverly Ball

American Camping Association®

Dedicated to Kathy and Robin,
who found a love of people
and of the world outdoors while growing up at camp.
The Staff of YMCA Camp Widjiwagan,
St. Paul, Minnesota, 1963-1974,
who will always be a part of our lives.

Copyright 1979, 1987, 1990, 1995, 2000 by American Camping Association, Inc.
Available in Russian from the Union of Children Associations of St. Petersburg.
Previous editions have been translated into Russian and Japanese.

Printed in the United States of America

American Camping Association, Inc.
5000 State Road 67, North
Martinsville, Indiana 46151-7902
765-342-8456 American Camping Association National Office
800-428-CAMP American Camping Association Bookstore
www.ACAcamps.org

Library of Congress Cataloging-in-Publication Data

Ball, Armand B., 1930-
    Basic camp management / by Armand and Beverly Ball. — 5th. ed.
        p. cm.
    Includes bibliographical references (p.) and index.
    ISBN 0-87603-165-3
    1. Camps — Management.   I. Ball, Beverly H., 1927 – .   II. Title.
GV198.M35B34 2000
796.54'068 — dc21
                                                            99-41510
                                                            CIP

Contents

Preface vi

1 The Tradition of Camping 1
Historical Overview 1
Types of Camps 5
What Is Camp? 7

2 What Is the Camp Director's Job? 13
Job Description 13
Leadership Styles 15
Camp as a Community 18
Ultimate Responsibilities 18

3 Where Does Program Begin? 21
Developing a Philosophy 22
Statements of Purpose 23
Purpose 24
Goals 25
Outcomes/Objectives 26

4 The Participant 31
Determining Your Target Population 31
Understanding the Participants: Growth and Development 34
Preparation of Participants 49

5 Designing the Program 53
Steps of Program Development 54
Program Design 56
Elements of Program Organization 59
Pacing/Flow 63
Program Emphases in the Summer Camp 64
Program Design Beyond Summer 66
Specialized Clientele 67
Specific Program Activities 69
Operating Procedures for Program 71

6 Personnel Organization and Recruitment **75**
Staff Organization 76
    Supervisory Lines 78
    Elements of Job Descriptions 82
    Personnel Policies 87
Recruitment 90
    Applications 94
    References and Background Checks 97
    The Job Interview 103

7 Staff Orientation and Training **113**
Orientation 113
Precamp Training 116
In-Service Training 124
Staff Meetings 125

8 Staff Supervision and Performance Appraisal **127**
Functions of a Supervisor 127
Guidelines in Supervision 128
Legal Negligence and the Supervisory Process 130
The Supervisory Process: Counselors 132
The Supervisory Process: Noncounseling Staff 140
Stress and Camp Staff 142
The Supervisor and Termination 145

9 Selection, Development, and Maintenance of the Site **149**
Physical Facility as an Asset 149
Selection 150
Development of an Owned Site 151
Maintenance 154
Winterization 160

10 Risk Management **165**
Definitions 165
Legal Aspects 166
Identification of Risk Exposures 167
Regulations 168
Management of Risks 169
Recordkeeping 178
Accreditation 183

11 Operation and Supervision: Central Administrative Services **187**
Health Service 187
Food Service 203
Transportation 211

12 Marketing **219**
Customers and Consumers 219
Market Analysis 220
Developing a Marketing Plan 226

13 Business and Finance   241
Accounting Practices 241
Budgeting 247
Operational Systems 253
Camp Store and Camper Bank 256
Recordkeeping 261
Fund-Raising 264

14 Volunteers   271
Legal Ramifications 272
Volunteers as Staff 274
Volunteer Committees and Boards 275
Other Roles 278

15 Evaluation and Reporting   281
Evaluation 281
Reporting — The Judgment Phase 293

16 Becoming a Professional   297
Camping as a Profession 297
Expanding One's Education 300

Appendixes   305
Sample Job Descriptions 305
Risk Management Checklist for Camp Personnel 308
Organizational Resources 312
International Resources 318
Governmental Resources 319
ACA Code of Ethics 330
Precamp Training Topics 332
Sample Personnel Hiring Log 334
Outdoor Living Skills 336
Selected Resources 338

Index   343

Preface

The idea of the first edition of *Basic Camp Management* was to provide a manual for the very new camp director and to keep the volume short and simple. With each revision, additional information and topics have been added, changing it from the rather elementary volume we had originally visualized. One factor in that change has been the growing complexity of the management of camps and conference centers. The second has been the continued use of the book as a text in college courses and the American Camping Association's Basic Camp Director Courses, where additional information needs to be provided. Hence, this volume is not quite as short and simple as we would like it to be.

TERMS

Throughout this book, terms have been used that should be thought of in their broadest sense. Here are some brief explanations.

The term *camp* has been used throughout as the comprehensive term describing all types of operations; it can also be interpreted as a camp, a camp that also rents its facilities for conference/retreat use, a conference/retreat center, or an environmental education program. It may be a program using a rented site, a site that rents facilities, or a site that encompasses its own program.

The term *director* is used to refer to the administrator of the camp, conference/retreat center, or program who is present on the site the majority of the time. (Although there are some organizations that operate multiple camps and may have an administrator in the central office who supervises several directors, this pattern is not the most common.)

The term *operator* or *owner* is used to designate the entity (whether an individual, a partnership, or an organization) that owns the operation. In some cases, the ownership involves the property and site and/or the program operated on the site. In other cases, it involves only the program operated on a rented site.

Rather than using the term *he* as the universal gender denoting both male and female, we have used the rather awkward form *he or she* (in the tradition of John Ledlie), to assure equal billing for the many female camp directors and staff members, as well as the numerous Mr. and Mrs. partnerships of directors and staff members in the field.

The term *independent* camp refers to a camp ordinarily organized for profit, sometimes identified as a private-independent camp.

The term *nonprofit* is used to identify camps that are operated either under a 501(c)(3) Internal Revenue Service classification or by a government body. This would include agency, organizational, public, and religiously affiliated camps, as well as a number of camps that were at one time private-independent camps and now operate under a board of directors in compliance with 501(c)(3) regulations.

The term *core areas* refers to the fourteen topics that make up the body of knowledge for the camping profession. All of the core areas are addressed in the book. Since this is an introduction, you will want to pursue a more in-depth study of each as you gain experience. The core areas are:

- Leadership
- Target population and diversity
- Mission and purpose
- Participant development and behavior
- Program design and activities
- Human resources
- Risk management
- Health and wellness
- Business and finance
- Marketing
- Site and facilities
- Food service
- Transportation
- Strategic planning

Listed at the end of each chapter are references to the American Camping Association's *Accreditation Standards for Camp Programs and Services*, the self-assessment tool "Additional Professional Practices" that are part of that volume, and *Standards for Conference and Retreat Centers*. Though these are modern documents, they have been developed through a professional review process over fifty-plus years.

Similarly, the quotations at the beginning of the chapters come from a variety of publications dating back some years and further illustrate the continuing effort of many directors toward professionalism.

We wish to express our thanks to the staff of the American Camping Association, Ed Schirick, Linda Ecerg, and David Gray for their assistance in reviewing relevant materials. We also wish to express our appreciation to Connie Coutellier for her leadership in revising the Basic Camp Director Course curriculum which, to a large degree, we are trying to parallel in the outline of this edition. Finally, we wish to thank the training team that helped refine this course.

We hope that this book will be a practical help to persons entering the field as well as to the experienced director and will inspire *better camping for all*.

Armand and Beverly Ball
Sanibel Island, Florida
February 1999

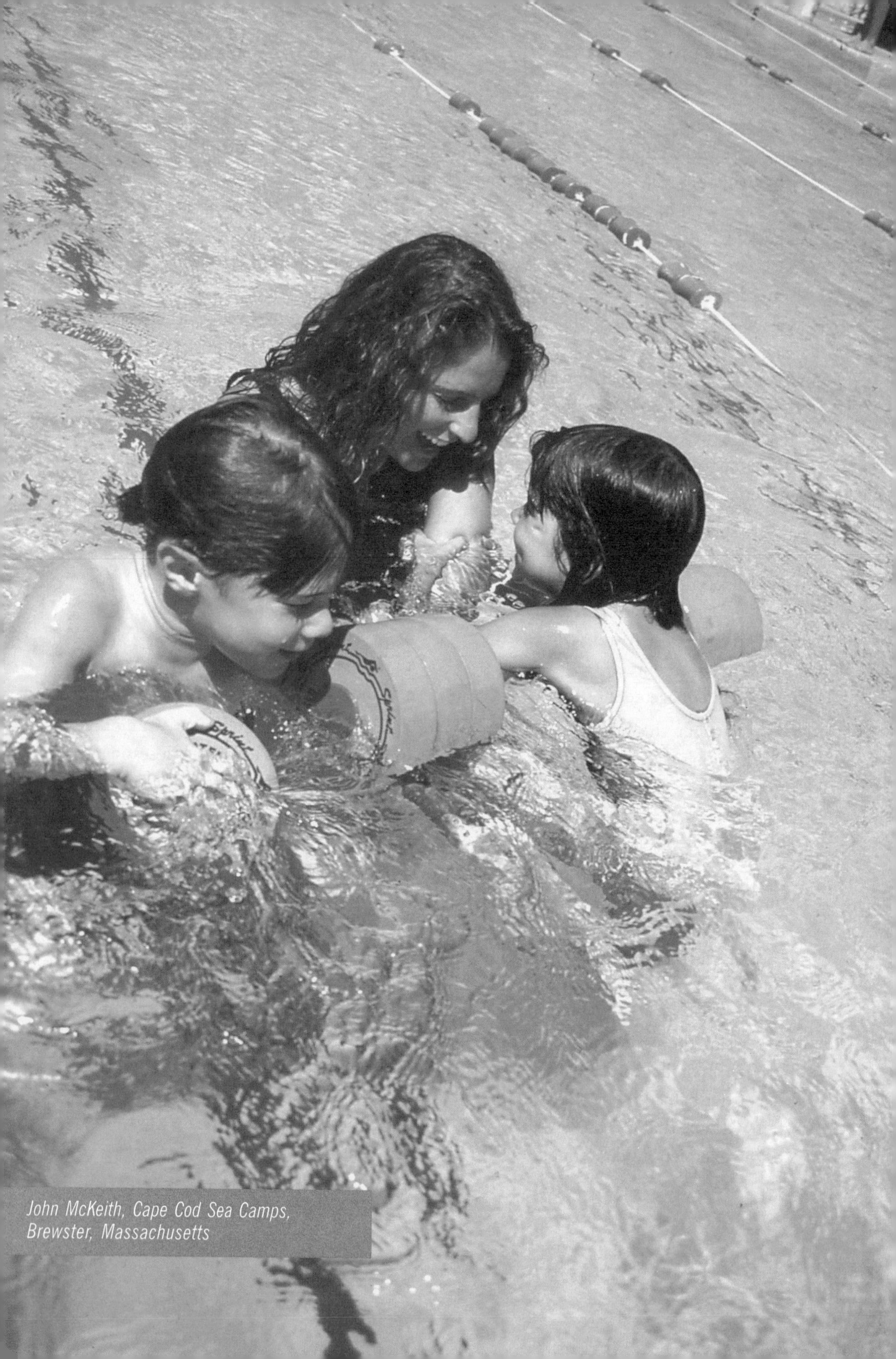

John McKeith, Cape Cod Sea Camps,
Brewster, Massachusetts

1

The Tradition of Camping

Camping needs the imaginative, the picturesque, the romantic; needs it for its own attractiveness and for the sake of young America, for whom the imaginative will be the only enduring type of play . . . The . . . camp, if it is worthy, is one of the greatest socializing, humanizing, civilizing factors which can enter the life of a boy or girl.[1]

Organized camping began in North America in the mid-nineteenth century. No accurate record exists of the exact location of the first actual camp. To gain a better understanding of the growth of the organized camp movement during its first one hundred years, one should read *History of Organized Camping: The First 100 Years* by Eleanor Eells and *Blue Lake & Rocky Shore* by the Ontario Camping Association. However, it may be helpful to offer a brief summary of that history as a background for the person new to the field.

HISTORICAL OVERVIEW

The Beginnings

The Ontario Camping Association Committee reports that in 1840 a church camp group met for summer camping under canvas at Hogg's Hollow (since renamed York Mills), just north of Toronto's present city limits. It appears that other camps did not come into existence in Canada until the late 1800s.

The first recorded organized camp experience in the United States occurred in 1861, when Frederick William Gunn, the headmaster of the Gunnery School for Boys, Washington, Connecticut, led a group of students on a forty-mile trek to Milford on Long Island Sound. After the two-day hike, the boys camped out for ten days and then hiked back to the school. This experience was stimulated by the interest of youth at that time in the Civil War, and the encampments and campfires common to the soldiers of that

---

[1] Bernard S. Mason. 1930. *Camping and Education*. New York: The McCall Company.

day. A plaque commemorates that camp at Welch's Point near Milford. Mr. Gunn continued to offer such camp experiences until 1879.

In 1876, the first private independent camp was organized by Dr. Joseph Rothrock, a practicing physician in Wilkes-Barre, Pennsylvania. The camp was designed to improve the health of children, and there was emphasis on physical fitness and health; the camp was short lived. In 1880, Camp Chocorua for boys aged twelve to sixteen was organized on Asquam Lake, New Hampshire, by Ernest Balch. This camp continued for eight years and centered around sports activities and the actual daily living chores of cooking, cleaning, and dishwashing. A decidedly spiritual emphasis was given to the camp. In both of these camps, fees were charged to cover the costs. These fees were, however, not very realistic because both camps closed with deficits.

The first camp run by an organization was founded in 1885 by Sumner F. Dudley as a YMCA camp near Newburg, New York. The camp, which still bears his name, later moved to Lake Champlain near Westport, New York, and is the oldest continuously operating camp in the United States. The oldest camp continuously operating on the same site is Keewaydin Camps, operated by the Keewaydin Foundation, and founded as an independent camp in 1894.

All of these camps were camps for boys; it was not until 1892 that an independent camp, called Camp Arey, reserved a summer session for girls. By 1902 three camps exclusively for girls began: Kehonka in New Hampshire, and Wyonegonic Camps and Pinelands Camps in Maine. This delay in camping for girls was due to some degree to the Victorian attitudes toward young women's dress, decorum, movement, careers, and education.

During this same period, organizational camping was growing rapidly, with the development of Fresh Air Camps, designed to serve inner-city youth. These camps sprang up in Connecticut (1886), Wisconsin (1887), and New York City (1892), as did Life Camps (1887) in Connecticut and New Jersey. The YWCA opened a vacation camp in Asbury Park, New Jersey, in 1874. Settlement houses sprang up during this period and established camps related to such urban centers as Boston, Pittsburgh, New York City, and Chicago (1898–1908). A camp for children with disabilities began in Chicago in 1899–1900. National youth organizations came into being in the early 1900s with their own camping programs: Boy Scouts of America (1910), Camp Fire Girls (now Camp Fire Boys and Girls) (1911), and Girl Scouts of the U.S.A. (1912).

Camps throughout this period of history primarily focused on getting young people out of the city into a healthy, rural environment and providing recreational activities. However, much of the experience was related to activities necessary to daily living (e.g., cooking, cleaning). Boys' camps tended to place value on rugged outdoor living. Girls' camps also included hiking and aquatics, with a great strength in the creative arts. There was a strong spiritual emphasis, often with Bible study, in most of the camps of this era. Moral or character development was a key element. Camps were often small during this period, quite rustic, and with much emphasis placed on small group living.

The emergence of national youth organizations and local social service organizations and the continued growth and success of independent camps stimulated growth of camps in a number of areas. Camps began to spread westward, with camps springing up in Pennsylvania, West Virginia, Illinois, Missouri, and California. Local governments started camps in Los Angeles in 1914, Detroit in 1915, and Kansas City in 1920.

With the expansion of camps from around 1910 onward, a more open emphasis on the educational values of the camp experience is seen. Activities such as arts and crafts, music, and dancing were added to the curriculum. The progressive education movement began to make its philosophy felt during this period. The training of camp staff began to be accepted as a necessary part of camp planning. By the 1920s, many camps were much more structured with greater emphasis on competition, awards, and scheduled activity. Good character, spiritual attainment, and a good personality were stressed. Natural sciences became part of the instructional activities in many camps.

International Expansion

The greatest expansion of camps into other countries occurred through the efforts of several youth organizations in the United States and Canada that were international in scope, as well as missionary efforts by various Christian denominations. The world headquarters of various international youth organizations such as Boy Scouts, Girl Scouts (Girl Guides in most other parts of the world), YMCA, and YWCA provided some guidance to develop camp programs in their movements in other countries.

Missionaries from various Christian denominations simply replicated the camp model utilized in the United States of America, as they were prone to do with church, church school, and educational programs. These camps were not always successful in meeting the needs of the people indigenous to other countries, but gradually models adapted to the needs and culture of the people emerged.

At least two countries developed models which were utilized by their respective governments to provide services to youth in their country: in France, where camps began in the late nineteenth century, and in Russia, where camps began in the early 1900s. In Russia, camps were primarily operated in canvas tents prior to World War II. After that war, camps began to spread and to upgrade their facilities, and by the 1980s Russia represented the largest camping movement in the world.

In Japan, camps began in the early 1900s. In Australia, camps began in the 1940s and developed primarily as facilities for schools to conduct outdoor education. Camps began in Venezuela in the mid-1900s.

Professional Associations

As camps grew in numbers early in the twentieth century, camp directors began to meet together to discuss common problems and to learn from each other. A professional association for directors of boys' camps, the Camp Directors Association of America, was begun in 1912. By 1916 an association of directors of girls' camps, the National Association of Girls' Private Camps, emerged. These merged in 1924 into the Camp Directors Association, and published a new journal, *Camping*, in 1926. Concerns about health and safety were emerging, and directing a camp began to be taken more seriously as a profession, such as teaching or social work. Conventions or training conferences began for camp directors during this period. Camp directors in Ontario and Quebec were also attending many of the professional meetings in the United States. In 1933, the Ontario Camping Association was formed, and for a period became part of the American Camping Association.

The emphasis on structured or regimented education in camp began to lessen in the thirties as the White House Conference on Child Health and Protection, coming at the beginning of the Great Depression, focused the camp's attention on youth and health. "One of the significant findings of that conference was the demand for an inclusive national organization to . . . articulate the needs and interests of the growing camping movement in the United States."

The next several years led to the reorganization in 1935 of the Camp Directors Association (CDA) into the American Camping Association (ACA), with locally operated sections based upon geographical boundaries. This organization began to evolve a set of health and safety standards, which eventually became the set of accreditation standards accepted throughout the United States. The American Camping Association remains today the only professional organization for directors of all types of camps and the nationally recognized accrediting body for all types of camps.

The Canadian Camping Association (CCA) was formed in 1947, and it included the Ontario and Quebec Camping Associations, as they moved out of the American Camping Association. Gradually each Canadian province formed associations as part of CCA.

Camps Increase

Following World War II, there was a rapid expansion of camp paralleling the increased population of youth in the country. There was wide acceptance of camp as the appropriate summer experience for youth. The numbers of camps and campers expanded rapidly. As Nelson Wieters, then of George Williams College, pointed out, many camps with generally global objectives began because of that broad acceptance and a ready marketplace, while other camps began for very specific purposes, either philosophical or instructional in nature. The latter objective led to the specialty camp boom in the sixties. More and more questions were raised by parents and educators about the specific impact of the camp experience on character development, improvement of physical skills, or spiritual growth.

School camping or outdoor education began to come into its own in the early 1940s. Large programs were begun in Michigan, under the auspices of the Kellogg Foundation, and in Tyler, Texas, and San Diego. Though early efforts began in the early thirties, it was not until the fifties that rapid growth came about. Colleges and universities began teacher education programs in this field. The Outdoor Education Council of the American Association of Health, Physical Education, Recreation and Dance (AAHPERD) began during this period and gave leadership to much of the professional development in this field.

Camps for very specific spiritual objectives grew beyond church-sponsored camps to interdenominational and nondenominational camps and conference settings, many privately operated. Out of this growing segment of camp emerged Christian Camping International (CCI) in 1963, which initially required the signing of a statement of personal Christian faith for membership. Its national offices are in Colorado Springs, Colorado.

In the past twenty years, there has been a growth of experientially based outdoor programs, primarily involving adventure and stress/challenge activities. The growth of this type of program accelerated greatly with the establishment of Outward Bound, an adventure program which began in England and spread to the United States and other countries. Variations of the Outward Bound methods have spread to use in many settings, including work with youth-at-risk, adjudicated youth, and even business executives. In 1972, the Association for Experiential Education (AEE) began as a professional organization to bring together persons interested in this discipline.

Camps and camping associations are now operating around the world. There are national camping associations in at least eleven countries: Australia, Canada, Colombia, Greece, Japan, Malaysia, Mexico, Russia, Taiwan, United States, and Venezuela. With the help of the Canadian Camping Association and the American Camping Association, three international conferences were held: in Toronto in 1983; in Washington, D.C., in 1987; and in Toronto in 1994. In 1987, an International Camping Fellowship was organized to provide information sharing among individuals interested in international education and exchange. This group publishes a newsletter and promotes international events. The 1997 International Camping Congress was held in St. Petersburg, Russia, with another Congress scheduled for Tokyo, Japan, in October 2000.

TYPES OF CAMPS

Camps are almost as varied as people; but, basically, there are two types of camps: day and resident. The day camp operates only during a portion of the day, typically morning and afternoon, usually for five successive days of the week, Monday through Friday. However, there are day camps which operate only three days a week, others which operate in the evening hours, and many which include at least one overnight experience as part of their camp period. Resident camps are those which bring participants to a setting in which housing is provided for a period of days. The typical resident camp provides lodging and meals. However, the resident camp experience may also take the form of travel or trip camping, in which the housing may be tents, shelters, or hotels and motels, and the campers move every day. Camp sessions vary in length from three to sixty days.

The camp program is operated and staffed by the camp, and supervision of individual campers is a camp responsibility. Camps may be operated with paid or volunteer staff, or a combination thereof. Many camps operate twelve months a year, involving a more typical summer camp experience, as well as school camps, conference groups, retreat groups, and adult education groups. A camp may also be a program operated by a given group for only one or two weeks a year on property owned by an individual, public park, or another camp. Camps may serve youth, adults, senior adults, or families.

Camps are generally recognized as for-profit or nonprofit. The for-profit camp or entrepreneurial camp may be operated by an individual, partners, or a corporation to return a profit to the owner, including some return on the capital investment made in property and facilities. While for-profit camps are commonly known also as independent camps, some nonprofit camps also use the term "independent" because they are not connected to any national organization.

The nonprofit camp may be operated by an organization such as the YMCA, the Girl Scouts, a settlement house, a health-related association, a religious entity, or a government body. Public camps are those operated by a government body, such as a parks-and-recreation department, school systems, 4-H, etc. Funding comes from fees and tax dollars. They may be owned by a private tax-exempt corporation or foundation. In all of these cases, the camp has a tax exemption under article 501(c)(3) of the federal tax code or is operated by a governmental body. In the last two decades, a number of independent camp owners have moved from for-profit to nonprofit corporations and secured 501(c)(3) status from the federal government. The camp is owned by a corporation and is provided tax breaks, and the camp is preserved for the future. This is especially true when second or third generations of the family are no longer interested in running the camp.

The goals of many nonprofit camps and for-profit camps are parallel. The facilities in some nonprofit camps may, in fact, be more expensive than in some for-profit camps, because they have the advantage of securing tax-deductible contributions for that purpose. The for-profit camp generally charges higher fees for many reasons, including the need to recover income from the capital investment made by private parties, as well as being subject to many taxes nonprofit camps do not have to pay. Therefore, the for-profit camp's clientele tends to come from a socioeconomic level that can pay such fees. Both types of camps may provide financial assistance for those who cannot afford the fee and to provide a more diverse camper group. The for-profit camp has most often offered longer sessions (three to eight weeks) than the nonprofit camp, though many have changed to shorter sessions in recent years. Nonprofit camps have tended to have shorter sessions (one or two weeks) than have for-profit camps, though there are some camps which offer four- or eight-week sessions to offer special programs or address child-care needs.

There are few generalizations that can be made about one type of camp or the other concerning wages, clientele, program, goals and objectives, and facilities. Peter Drucker suggests that "The task of the nonprofit manager is to try to convert the organization's mission statement into specifics." The task of any camp director is to try to bring the camp's purpose/mission into practical accomplishments, and that purpose/mission may be very similar in a for-profit camp and a nonprofit camp.

In both cases, it is essential that the camp operate in a fiscally sound fashion and that the director earn a decent living. In the nonprofit camp and in some independent for-profit camps, where the owner is director, the director receives a set salary. In other independent for-profit camps, the director receives a bonus or a portion of the profit (if any) as salary. A nonprofit camp may have a hard time offering a competitive salary; however, it will be difficult to retain a good director if the salary is not consistent with other like professions. The camp cannot long continue to operate in today's competitive climate (however lofty the stated purpose or mission of a camp is) if it does not have as a parallel purpose to be financially accountable.

One of the growing complexities of the camp world is the increase in camps providing a variety of services and serving a variety of audiences. Many camps operate twelve months a year, a portion of which is devoted to the more traditional camp experience, and the other portion to short-term programs run by the camp or by rental or user groups. These include weekend retreats, school environmental education classes, parent-child programs, etc. When a camp is accredited, the public assumes that all programs on the site are accredited. In 1998, the American Camping Association, addressing this trend and perception, changed its standards to affect all the camp-related programs and services of the organization throughout the year. There is a separate set of standards for conference/retreat centers; however, many of the principles in the management of camps, short-term and year-round programs, and conference centers are the same. This text identifies some of the differences wherever possible.

WHAT IS CAMP?

The early camps were primarily directed toward getting youth out of the city into a healthy and moral environment, and little energy went into defining a camp. By 1929, a special committee of the New York Section of the Camp Directors Association reported the essential functions of the camp as being "education for: physical health, emotional integration, an understanding of primitive processes, enlightened social participation, the acquisition of tastes and appreciations, and spiritual growth."

The "primitive processes" referred to outdoor experiences. By the late forties, Hedley S. Dimock identified that the "characteristic elements, blended together in the right proportion, of an organized camp included: 1) persons, 2) outdoor life, 3) living in groups, 4) a camp community, and 5) leadership and conditions designed to satisfy personal needs and interests, and to stimulate wholesome personal, social and spiritual development."

He goes on to underline the importance of experiences that are "indigenous to group living in the out-of-door setting." The American Camping Association offers as its definition: "A sustained experience which provides a creative, recreational and educational opportunity in group living in the outdoors. It utilizes trained leadership and the resources of the natural surroundings to contribute to each camper's mental, physical, social, and spiritual growth."

With all of the words that have flowed from experts, it is still difficult to draw narrow lines around what a camp is and what a camp is not. There is substantial support for the basis that a camp provides a group living experience, with trained leaders who facilitate that group and community experience and utilize the outdoor surroundings to accomplish the mental, physical, social, and spiritual goals of the sponsoring body or owner.

As Bernard Mason suggests in the opening of this chapter, camps must be imaginative to interest individuals in the outdoor experience. Camp owners and directors have not always been the best source for interpreting the value and meaning of the camp to the general public, but have more often relied upon the voice of previous campers to propagate the camp.

The commonalties among all types of camps, resident or day, for-profit or nonprofit, are far greater than the differences. The basic similarities are easily discovered when the directors of camps take the opportunity to sit down together, get to know each other, and get beyond labels, terminology, and preconceptions. Regardless of the type of camp and program, the similarities bind camps together because they all work for an ultimate developmental experience for each camper.

Generic Values of Camping

If one reviews the literature in the camp field concerning how others perceive the value of the camp experience, the lists will be varied and idealistic, as camp directors tend to be idealistic persons. There are, however, several values that one would find on almost any list.

Understanding the Outdoor Environment. The environment of camp should be a key factor in determining program and objectives. Being outdoors is one of the distinctive features of the camp experience, and youngsters have few other opportunities to learn about the natural world and recognize their responsibility as stewards of its resources.

A Group Living Experience. The learning experience of living in a group of one's peers provides opportunities for teachable moments not easily encountered elsewhere.

Fun. Camp should be fun. Play is a natural growing experience of children and a lifelong need of adults. Gaining leisure skills and attitudes that can be used throughout life is a valuable experience.

To these, Betty Lyle would add:

Experience in Democracy. "With campers from various backgrounds, children may for the first time have an opportunity to live in a really democratic community . . . ."

Participation in Program. ". . . related to the interests and needs of the camper" and "campers must have an active share in planning what the camp life and program shall be."

Understanding and Guidance. "The relationship with a counselor is a new kind of relationship with an adult for most campers . . . a good counselor (is) one who likes his campers, understands them as individuals, helps, suggests, listens, guides."[2]

Reynold E. Carlson would add to that list:

Experiencing Individual Growth and Development. "Camp should offer children a chance to discover their own potentialities, to exercise their personal initiative, and to earn respect for what they do as individuals."

Practicing Health and Safety. In camp children should be ". . . practicing . . . good personal health habits . . . (and) practicing rather than talking about health and safety."

Developing New Skills and Interests and Perfecting Old Ones. "Many of the camp activities have a high carry over value into later years."

Developing Spiritual Meanings and Values. "Many of these insights are caught as well as taught."[3]

James C. Stone, in a 1986 study, found that "campers made a statistically significant gain overall, and increases in the following characteristics:

Responsibility. Skill in being accountable for one's own behavior.

Decision Making. Skill in thinking for one's self.

Self-concept. Skill in getting along with others.

Interpersonal Relations. Skill in making friends and being accepted.

Citizenship. Skill in respecting the rights of others.

Environmental Concern. Skill in appreciating one's natural surroundings." [4]

What Are Conference/Retreat Centers?

As camps have moved to year-round operations and facilities designed and improved for multiseason use, many have had to reevaluate their purpose. Most operations that desire to provide programs or lease facilities to other groups for camp-style programs focus primarily on *outdoor* and recreation activities, and the improved facility allows the operation to provide year-round services. Some camps design multipurpose facilities and may operate a conference/retreat center along with other camp-style programs. Designing one facility that serves both a camp-style group and an adult-conference group and that focuses primarily on *indoor* meetings utilizing the outdoors for release from the thought process is a challenge. Many operations that desire to serve both groups have both kinds of facilities on one piece of property. As a camp moves into more year-round use and

[2]Betty Lyle. 1947. *Camping: What Is It?* Martinsville, IN: American Camping Association. pp. 4–5.
[3]Reynold Carlson. 1975. *The Values of Camping*. Martinsville, IN: American Camping Association. p. 4.
[4]James C. Stone. "Kids Learn Responsibility." *Camping Magazine* Vol. 59, No.1, September/October 1986. p. 21.

develops its statement of purpose, and subsequent goals and objectives, these client and usage differences should be kept in mind.

The American Camping Association defines a conference/retreat center as "a residential facility designed for adults and other groups who come together for meetings, training sessions, and educational or inspirational programs. Such a facility generally operates at least three seasons of the year and is designed to minimize outside distractions. It provides dedicated meeting space, food service, hospitality and support services, access to facilities and natural environments for release and diversion, and housing styles appropriate to the target clientele."[5]

Kathleen M. Trotter illustrates these conceptual differences in an article for *Camping Magazine* and through her camp consultancy firm, KALEIDOSCOPE, Inc. The myriad of camp and conference center programs for persons of all ages takes place in a variety of natural settings and styles of accommodations. Notice in illustration 1.1 that the spectrum from rustic camps to refined centers is, indeed, wide, and it is sometimes difficult to see common ground among these diverse facilities and programs.

Facilities and program styles differ because of what we want to accomplish. We increase our effectiveness with our clients and with each other when we remember that we share similar values but offer different environments in order to implement our various programs.

"All of us as camp and conference center leaders strive to positively influence our clients in holistic ways so that they leave camp healthier, stronger, more skilled, and mature. Some of us facilitate this process by designing *educational activities* for our campers or guests.

Others among us provide the context for the experience by creating comfortable, caring *residential environments* that free campers or guests to fully engage in learning and growth. Regardless of the focus, the very nature of our enterprise calls for two essential ingredients: some kind of structured experience, usually called a *program*, and the group living accommodations, which can be referred to as *hospitality services*. Neither of these is dispensable if we are to truly accomplish our mission."[6]

There may be specific goals and objectives that deal separately with each type of operation. Both operations should contribute to the overall purpose of the camp and/or conference center.

As long as the decision concerning facilities and program styles is a conscious part of the planning process and is consistent with the mission, there should be few problems that cannot be worked through. However, to slip into one style or the other for expediency in meeting number, dollar, or other goals without being a part of the purpose of the camp can only lead to severe problems in setting priorities and serving clientele. There are additional considerations about budgeting for a year-round operation in the chapter on business and finance.

---

[5]American Camping Association. 1993. *Standards for Conference and Retreat Centers*. Martinsville, IN: American Camping Association. p.5.

[6]Kathleen M. Trotter. "Getting Out of the 90-Day Mentality." *Camping Magazine* Vol. 61, No. 7, May 1989. pp. 28–29.

1.1

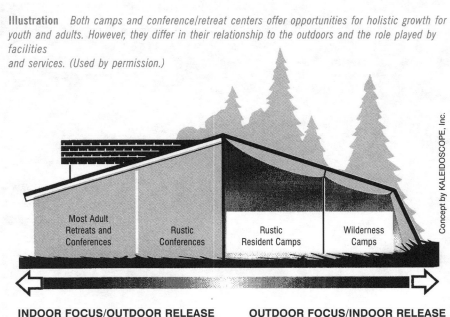

Illustration *Both camps and conference/retreat centers offer opportunities for holistic growth for youth and adults. However, they differ in their relationship to the outdoors and the role played by facilities and services. (Used by permission.)*

Concept by KALEIDOSCOPE, Inc.

Most Adult Retreats and Conferences | Rustic Conferences | Rustic Resident Camps | Wilderness Camps

INDOOR FOCUS/OUTDOOR RELEASE

- "Home-like" comfort and convenience prevent distraction of learning
- Personal, private space helps facilitate comfort, study, and reflection
- Learning usually begins conceptually and then is applied "experientially"

OUTDOOR FOCUS/INDOOR RELEASE

- Rustic accommodations help teach simplicity and creativity
- The outdoors becomes a focal point of the curriculum
- Facilities and activities are designed to foster community participation and group interdependence
- Learning usually begins experientially, then is conceptualized

CHECKPOINTS

1. Compare your camp history to the historical overview of camp.
2. What are the overall generic values of camps and how do your camp values compare?
3. How would you determine if the camp is for-profit or nonprofit?
4. What are some of the differences between camps and conference/retreat centers?

Related Standards

Listed at the end of most chapters are references to specific standards from the American Camping Association's *Accreditation Standards for Camp Programs and Services* and *Standards for Conference and Retreat Centers*. These are the accepted industry standards. References are also made to the "Additional Professional Practices," a section in the *Accreditation Standards for Camp Programs and Services*.

Standards for Conference and Retreat Centers: II-1

Bill Harwood, Camp Counselors U.S.A., Camp Seafarer in Arapahoe, North Carolina

2

What Is the Camp Director's Job?

The philosophy under which a camp functions, the morale of staff and counselors, the contributions the camp makes to the lives of youngsters, the adequacy of physical equipment — all are reflections of the insight, character, and competency of the camp director. His/her executive ability, together with a sense and appreciation of justice, needs to be at a high level. He/she needs insight, a world of patience, physical stamina, and ability to command the respect as well as the friendship of those associated with him/her in the camping enterprise.[1]

If you were to line up ten experienced camp directors and ask them what the job of a camp director is, you would probably get ten different answers. To survive, a camp director must possess a smattering of many skills and must combine many roles: cook, bookkeeper, plumber, minister, teacher, nurse, electrician, mechanic, risk manager, salesperson, lawyer, politician, corporate executive, naturalist, and eternal optimist. Every camp director will discover new dimensions to the job each summer.

JOB DESCRIPTION

A new camp director's first task, if a thorough job description is not supplied, should be to develop such a description, in consultation with various people at the particular camp. Each camp owner will have different expectations. For example, in one camp, the bookkeeping may be handled entirely by a centralized organization office while, in another, the bookkeeping may be part of the director's job. A summer day camp director's duties and concerns will differ from those of a year-round residential camp director. Therefore, it is difficult to outline one model job description for a camp director.

However, there are aspects of the job in any camp that are somewhat uniform and require specific duties depending upon the administrative situation. A camp director's job might include all of the following responsibilities:

[1]John A. Ledlie, ed. 1961. *Managing the YMCA Camp.* NY: Association Press (Y.M.C.A. of the U.S.A.).

- Develop and implement the mission/purpose, goals, and objectives of the camp and/ or year-round operation.
- Determine the constituencies or target populations to be served by the camp.
- Design a program based upon the goals, objectives, and various constituencies to be served.
- Develop and implement a risk management system to protect the participants, the camp, and the staff.
- Develop and implement a marketing plan for the camp. Recruit participants.
- Design and implement a staff organization based upon the program and target population; develop job descriptions and personnel policies.
- Design and implement a plan for the development and maintenance of the camp site and facilities.
- Develop and implement a health care plan that provides for the health and safety of the campers and staff.
- Develop and implement a nutritious and sanitary food service program.
- Develop and implement a safe transportation system to meet the needs of program, maintenance, and safety.
- Design a financial development program that includes not only fund-raising, but also a sound business plan and budget which is monitored regularly.
- Recruit and train staff.
- Develop and implement an evaluation system that allows campers, parents, staff, etc., to assess program facilities, operations, the staff structure, and youth development outcomes.
- Develop a plan for supervision of staff including training for supervisors, staff structure, expectations for behavior, job responsibilities, and dealing with performance issues.
- Maintain relationships with the local community near the camp and the broader community served by the camp.
- Maintain the director's own professional growth through study, peer relationships, and conferences.
- **For Nonprofit Camps Only.** Serve as the principal staff member to the managing board or committee, working to ensure the strongest, most effective board or committee possible, and provide the staff support to help that group define the philosophy and policies governing the operation.

Once a job description is created, it is vital for a new director to have a clear understanding with his or her supervisor about the priorities of the job. All things are not possible immediately so the supervisor's expectations need to be clarified. The plan of work for the upcoming months should reflect the priorities of both the supervisor or the camp owner and those of the camp director.

Administrative Roles

The camp director is an administrator and needs a clear understanding of the principles of administration which shape the day-to-day jobs that are encountered. Here are some of those principles.

Developing Goals and Objectives. This will be discussed in more detail in chapter 3.

Planning. This is a matter of securing facts about the present operation, looking ahead to what is predictable based on those facts, and examining the unusual or unpredictable events that could occur. With this information, a short-term and/or a long-range or strategic plan for action should be developed. In the nonprofit camp or conference center the long-range or strategic plan may be incorporated into the organization plan and approved through the board of directors.

Organizing. One can't do everything simultaneously, even if one has the time. The plan should be broken into units of work and delegated to persons who are given clear tasks and time tables with adequate physical support and supervision.

Developing and Managing Resources. This means pulling together anything that is needed to accomplish the plan you have organized: people, materials, and finances. It also involves maintaining those resources for the future whether it is land, buildings, staff, campers, or contributors. This will probably be the most time-consuming of the administrative roles.

Directing. Once the plan is in place and delegated to people with adequate resources, the administrator must become the overall resource for implementation and keeping the plan on course. This involves consultation, supervision, communication, coordination, and decision making. An aspect of directing is the control of the overall plan, making sure the goals and objectives are being met. This is where the day-to-day supervision comes into play.

Evaluating. This is actually the first step in beginning over, for here you examine whether goals and objectives were met, whether there need to be adjustments in the goals and objectives another time, and where to begin again.

Reporting. In the nonprofit camp, one aspect of evaluation is reporting to the board or committee and the constituency of the organization.

The camp director must gain skills in each of these administrative areas. It is far more important that these skills be mastered than that he or she become certified in aquatic skills, learn medical information, or be an expert in building repair. The director is a manager and management is complex and demanding. Success in camp management is built upon being a generalist in a community of specialists and generalists.

LEADERSHIP STYLES

Beyond asking what the job is, it may be more important for the new director to determine what kind of director he or she wishes to be. The attitude with which a director begins work may well affect his or her ultimate job performance. Only careful thought can prevent a new director from being cast in stereotypic roles like the following ones.

- **Joe Doer.** He is the only one who knows how a thing is to be done and, consequently, he does *everything*. Others may assist him, but ultimately, he must be in the forefront and *do it*.
- **Jane Delegator.** She delegates everything. Everyone else does the work; she simply makes assignments and gives out gold stars.
- **Happy Mary.** She wants to make everyone happy and cannot operate if anyone is unhappy with her or does not like her decisions.
- **Mike Fix-It.** He loves to fix anything that goes wrong: plumbing, locks, typewriters, motors, cars. He leaves the program and other areas of camp to the rest of the staff.
- **Alice Waterfront.** She was always a great swimmer and directed waterfront when she was a camp staff member. You will always find her at the waterfront; she personally plans the water carnival.
- **Uncle Henry.** He is the father figure of camp. Everyone calls him Uncle; he loves to sit by the fireplace and spin tales.
- **Office Sam.** He spends all day in the camp office, signing checks and letters and writing parents. He lets the program directors walk over camp and check on activities, the kitchen, or the health service. You know where to find him anytime you need him — behind his desk.
- **Easy Millie.** What do *you* want to do? The decision is *yours*. Do it in whatever way you would like. Any way suits her, and she seldom expresses an opinion.
- **Bossy Mac.** He will tell you how to do it. He makes the ultimate decision on anything in camp — from where the hiking trip is going, to when camp is having roast beef. There is no question about who is boss.

It is hoped you will not be any *one* of these directors, but they do exist.

Select Your Own Style

There are three areas of skill which, in combination, make a leader effective. To select your own leadership style as a camp director, you need to take a look at the three areas: technical skills, interpersonal skills, and conceptual skills.

1. Technical skills. A camp director plans, implements, and evaluates programs and services — and is also responsible for logistics, safety, and legal issues, and office routines.
2. Interpersonal skills. These are techniques that involve working with people. A camp director needs to understand the dynamics of a group and to be able to resolve conflicts. To accomplish this, he or she also needs to value and respect every individual and be able to communicate with infinite varieties of people.

3. Conceptual skills. These skills are probably the most difficult to develop, but are key for a successful director. They involve evaluative thinking, problem-solving skills, and an ability to see the whole picture. Central to the leadership role of a camp director is the conceptual ability to relate a camp's philosophy to program and to see its impact upon his or her style of leadership.

In an article in *Camping Magazine*, Debra Jordan describes six styles of leadership: democratic, benevolent autocratic, consultative, participate, laissez-faire, and coaching. She also points out the importance of understanding the appropriate style of leadership necessary for different situations.[2]

Being a Leader or a Manager?

As one examines leadership styles, the differences between being a leader and a manager begin to appear. A director is employed to be a manager and is consciously evaluated on the results of managing. On the other hand, a camp director is also expected to be a leader and many times is unconsciously evaluated on his or her ability to lead staff or volunteers. The administrative roles identified earlier in this chapter align with managerial responsibilities in that they lead a director to:

- Confine discussion to current problems and options
- Focus on outcomes and accountability
- Control change and evolution
- Monitor staff uniformity according to known procedures
- Determine actions and decisions based on rules and policies
- Plan for the future

A leader will also move to:

- Investigate and discuss diverse ideas openly
- Focus on people to obtain outcomes
- Strive to make change happen
- Empower others and encourage decision making
- Build actions and decisions around values
- See the future and make plans to attain it

Being a good manager can be learned by study and evaluation. Being a leader comes with self-examination and observation of others in leadership roles, and is more natural for some than for others. The two are not mutually exclusive, and the most successful directors are able to blend the two.

---

[2]Debra Jordan. "Leadership Styles, Which One Is Right for You?" *Camping Magazine*, Vol. 68, No. 4, March/April 1996. pp. 19–21.

CAMP AS A COMMUNITY

One of the unique aspects of administration in the camp setting is that the camp is a community. Hedley S. Dimock points out that:

> the camp community possesses most of the elements of a normal community, but in a simplified form. Here may be found the functions of government, home, health, employment, recreation and religion. Because of the relative simplicity and immediacy of the camp community, these basic functions can be concretely visualized, participated in, and shared by the camper. Here, further, may be found in concrete, visible, and manageable form the inner and informal aspects of community life common purposes and aspirations, traditions, customs, cohesiveness, and control.[3]

Although many businesses or institutions develop a sense of family among their employees, the opportunity for developing a community relationship does not exist. This can be a distinct advantage of the camp setting and experience. However, it can also create problems and tensions for the camp administrator that would not ordinarily arise in other situations. The camp community is interdependent and to some degree isolated from the outside. There is little opportunity for relief from the twenty-four-hour-a-day intense environment. Building on the sense of community can have great educational benefits, as well as develop the sort of relationships and loyalty that endures for many years.

In this context, one of the primary tasks of the camp director is to be an enabler. In her book, *Social Group Work: A Helping Process*, Gisela Konopka characterizes the leadership role as one of enabling, trying to discover the way in which one can enable others to achieve their best performance.[4] To be an enabler, one has consciously to outline the goals an individual wishes to attain and to analyze that individual's abilities and capacity to reach those goals. Where a person's abilities are inadequate for the task, an enabler must consider what he or she can do to help that person accomplish that task?

To be an enabler requires confidence in what the person can do or become. Often, one must look beyond an individual's immediate abilities or failures to see his or her potential for future accomplishments. The effective enabler sees potential and seeks to provide opportunities for the individual to grow and fulfill that potential. Such an approach to leadership will necessarily cause some disappointments but may also provide many moments of shared pleasure.

ULTIMATE RESPONSIBILITIES

There are some aspects of camp life for which the director cannot escape responsibility. These are *ultimate* responsibilities which belong only to the director and cannot be totally delegated to anyone else. However, in some situations the owner, executive, or

[3]Hedley S. Dimock. 1948. *Administration of the Modern Camp.* New York: Association Press (Y.M.C.A. of the U.S.A.). p. 29.

[4]Gisela Konopka. 1983. *Social Group Work: A Helping Hand.* Englewood Cliffs, NJ: Prentice Hall.

camp administrator may keep the responsibility and not delegate it to the on-site camp director. The director's ultimate responsibilities include the following.

- Adhering to the mission
- Maintaining the goals and objectives and camp policies
- Setting the standards for operation and health and safety
- Relating to the committee or board, if there is one
- Handling legal obligations
- Protecting the investment in property, reputation, and assets
- Managing the bottom line financially
- Supervising personnel administration

To make sure that these ultimate responsibilities are met, the camp director must understand the basics of every area of camp life. He or she must observe these areas firsthand at regular intervals and use check points to help evaluate performance. The supervision of areas in which the director has expertise can easily be delegated and checked informally. Areas in which the director has little experience require employment of persons with skills and experience in those areas and close supervision from the director until he or she is sure that the essentials are being covered.

Certainly the camp director should enjoy and be fulfilled by his or her job. If a director is skilled in a particular area, there is no reason why he or she should not utilize those skills as long as he or she does not neglect the director's ultimate responsibilities. On the other hand, if staff and campers are to feel that all parts of the camp program are equally valid, the director must exhibit an understanding and appreciation of all areas of camp life.

A camp director, by the very nature of his or her responsibilities, cannot readily avoid being the key person in camp. However, many tasks may be delegated or responsibility shared, and the director's role will change as his or her comfort level and experience increases. For the camp director to be such a dominant figure is not necessarily undesirable, but the ultimate effect of such dominance will depend on the role the director takes on and his or her ability to enable other staff to reach their greatest potential.

CHECKPOINTS

1. What are the administrative roles of the camp director?
2. What are the ultimate responsibilities of the camp director?

Related Standards

Accreditation Standards for Camp Programs and Services: HR-1
Standards for Conference and Retreat Centers: II-31–33

Edwin Ulanoff, Crane Lake Camp,
New York, New York

3

Where Does Program Begin?

In no other educational enterprise can the child have such continuous exposure to approved leadership, experience living closely with a small group of people where qualities of cooperation and consideration for others are the type of behavior that pays off, and be exposed to young adults who serve as models for the development of positive ideas and attitudes.[1]

After gaining a clear notion of the requirements of his or her new job, a director's next step should be to learn as much about the current operation of the camp as possible and, particularly, about the camp's philosophy, purpose, and goals. Though not necessarily recent or accurate, old camp literature can give a clue to the expectations of the parents of previous campers and, it is hoped, to the intentions of previous administrators.

Vision, philosophy, purpose, mission, goals, objectives, outcomes, outputs, targets, values are common terms used in almost any organization. Strategic or long-range planning adds another set of terms (including strategic goals, operational plan, checkpoints, benchmarks, action plans, etc.) that are or should be intertwined with the first set. However, these terms' definitions and their uses vary greatly depending on the organization, trends in youth development, funding sources, etc. The American Camping Association Standards require the camp to establish a written statement of program goals and outcomes/objectives with written strategic planning materials.

The process of reaching consensus on goals and outcomes/objectives is more important than how they are defined. To help sort through these, the following terms and definitions will be used in this book:

- **Vision** — a mental image of what the organization will look like in the future.
- **Philosophy/Values** — the critical examination of fundamental principles on which the camp desires to operate and an analysis of the basic concepts in the expression of those principles.
- **Mission/Purpose** — a statement of the essential reason for the existence of an organization and/or camp.

[1] Alice Van Krevelen. "Camp as a Fresh Start." *Camping Magazine* Vol. 51, No. 3, February 1979. p. 9.

- **Goals** — statements that define the specific elements that contribute to the accomplishment of the mission/purpose; more precise than mission/purpose statement.
- **Outcomes/Objectives** — ways that the accomplishment of a goal is to be measured; the desired results or benefits that contribute to the achievement of an overall goal.
- **Evaluation/Indicators** — the measure of success in reaching outcomes/objectives, used to adjust targets, goals, and outcomes/objectives for the remainder or next period of time.
- **Strategic Planning** — a process to periodically evaluate the camp's philosophy and mission, and to design a comprehensive or long-range plan outlining goals for that future period of time.

DEVELOPING A PHILOSOPHY

A camp must determine for itself which values will be its focus. This determination is often spoken of as the *philosophy* of a camp. *Webster's Third New International Dictionary of the English Language* defines philosophy as "the critical examination of the grounds for fundamental beliefs and an analysis of the basic concepts in the expression of such beliefs."[2]

By its nature, philosophy is theoretical and difficult to measure. Despite its abstract nature, the philosophy is the overall operational grounding of how one works with people in the camp setting. In the context of this book, the term philosophy is used to encompass the stated purpose, goals, and outcomes/objectives. It is a question of why the camp or conference/retreat center exists and what it hopes to accomplish. It is more than a physical setting. That philosophy should be determined by the camp's owners, if owned by an individual or group of individuals, and by the camp's board or governing committee, if owned by a corporation.

A camp director may have his or her own philosophy or values about working with people in a camp environment. This is likely to be evident in his or her leadership style, and is likely to evolve over a period of time. If there is a major philosophical difference between the camp director's philosophy and that of the operator, it is well to discuss it with one's supervisor and, ultimately, with the operating committee/board. An operator should not be expected to change the philosophy of operation with the arrival of each new camp director. Such changes should really come only after experiences in operation or the marketplace can be used to document a need for change.

For a camp's philosophy to be meaningful in its operation, the philosophies of the camp owner and the camp director must be compatible and symbiotic.

---

[2]*Webster's Third New International Dictionary of the English Language.* Springfield, MA: G & C Merriam Company. 1986.

STATEMENTS OF PURPOSE

Before a new camp director can move on to program, he or she must first find a way to put the basic philosophy or underlying reason for the existence of the camp into definitive terms. There should be a general overriding purpose or mission statement that can be broken down into several specific goals that express that purpose.

The basic philosophy or values of a camp rarely change. Most often a mission statement may change drastically because the mission or purpose has been accomplished. The language may be changed from time to time to make it clearer to the current generation, but the essence rarely changes. The changes most often take place in goals and outcomes/objectives which are more responsive to current trends, emerging youth-development needs, and demographics. To simply change the program activities and staff of a camp without carefully tying them to a written statement of purpose and goals can lead to considerable confusion on the part of staff and parents of campers.

The approval of the camp's purpose and goals in organizational-type camps may follow a time-consuming process of boards and committees, but it is an essential part of that board's educational and ownership experience. Though the owner/director of an independent camp has greater latitude to change its philosophy and stated purpose and goals more readily than organizational-type camps, he or she should give no less careful thought to developing purpose/mission statements.

The new camp director may need to research a variety of sources to discover a camp's purpose or mission statement. If not found in the camp's brochure, examination of other camp documents will be necessary. Perhaps an overriding purpose or some specific goals may have been defined by previous directors. If not written in specific documents, they may be discovered in a number of different places:

- In camp brochures
- In previous minutes, if the camp is operated by a board or committee
- In the articles of incorporation, if the camp is incorporated
- In conversation with a previous director or staff or with the executive of the organization or long-time board members
- In reports from previous summers
- In staff manuals

When the director has collected statements of purpose and various goals (whether verbal or written), he or she may find it useful to write them out as clearly as possible and then to examine them carefully. The director should examine them for clarity, appropriateness to current community patterns and attitudes, and for consistency with the operator's expectations. He or she should examine these statements with a supervisor to see if that person interprets the purpose in a similar fashion. If possible, the director should also examine them with an operating committee or board, the executive committee, or another small responsible group from the board.

When he or she clearly understands the stated purpose as it was defined in the past and as it is now perceived by the operator (committee, board, executive), the camp director should determine if there are any parts of the purpose which are in conflict with his or her own personal philosophy. Regardless, it is wise for the new camp director to operate under the stated purpose for at least one summer before making or suggesting any significant changes. Operation is a test of the validity and relevance of a camp's purpose and goals. A director should never hesitate, however, to seek clarification of the meaning of purpose or outcomes/objectives.

PURPOSE

The *purpose* or *mission* states the essential reason for the camp's existence and may not necessarily be easily measured. The purpose along with its clarifying goals brings the more intangible philosophy of the camp into more concrete terms. Here are some examples:

- **Camp A** — The principal purpose is to help young people of all backgrounds to grow into responsible maturity through the application of Christian principles in an outdoor setting.
- **Camp B** — The mission of the camp is to provide an outdoor setting for group living where people can design programs to meet their group's needs and to provide a regular opportunity for youth to gain a deeper understanding of their relationships to their fellow man and their natural environment.
- **Camp C** — The purpose of this camp is to help each individual camper gain skills that help him or her achieve a strong self-concept, self-responsibility, and an ability to get along with his or her peers.

The focus of each of these purposes is quite different. Camps A and C focus on the individual camper, but Camp A is directed more toward application of Christian principles and outdoor living where Camp C focuses on interpersonal and skill development. Camp B focuses both on the facility and provision of program, i.e., where a camp or conference center rents facilities as well as operates camp sessions.

To develop such a statement without consideration of the developmental needs of the age group to be served is unwise. One may not be able to address all developmental needs, but certainly many of them will be the foundation for the statement of purpose and goals. Human growth and development are discussed in more detail in chapter 4.

Peter Drucker states that "a mission statement has to be operational, otherwise it's just good intentions. A mission statement has to focus on what the institution really tries to do and then do it so that everybody in the organization can say: This is *my* contribution to the goal."[3] Therefore, the statement should be simple, clear, and concise

[3]Peter F. Drucker. 1990. *Managing the Nonprofit Organization: Practices and Principles.* New York: Harper Collins Publishers. p. 4.

— something others can remember and to which they can relate. A starting point is to write a statement, cut it to fifteen or twenty words, and then test it on others.

GOALS

The *goals* are more precise than purpose statements; they more clearly define specific things that will accomplish the mission or purpose in a given time period. Goals should be realistic and achievable. Some organizations set goals when they do strategic planning and through that planning process determine the length of time for the plan (usually five years or less). Some goals are renewed or continued through several planning periods. Here are some examples of goals relating to the purposes stated above:

- **Camp A** — The principal purpose is to help young people of all backgrounds to grow into responsible maturity through the application of Christian principles in an outdoor setting.
  Goals for Years 1–3
  - The camp will be recognized as contributing to a camper's awareness of himself or herself in relation to other members of a group.
  - The camp will help participants develop a better understanding and awareness of their natural environment.
  - The camp experience will help improve the awareness of the camper's spiritual dimension.

- **Camp B** — The mission is to provide an outdoor setting for group living where people can design programs to meet their group's needs and to provide a regular opportunity for youth to gain a deeper understanding of their relationships to their fellow man and their natural environment.
  Goals for Years 1–2
  - To provide a setting with comfortable facilities flexible enough for groups to carry out a variety of programs and activities of their own design.
  - To provide organized sessions when youth can come together and develop interpersonal relationships.
  - To provide a well-cared-for natural environment where activities naturally encourage a better understanding of, and responsibility for, the natural environment.

- **Camp C** — The purpose of this camp is to help each individual camper gain skills that help him or her achieve a strong self-concept, a sense of self-responsibility, and an ability to get along with his or her peers.
  Goals for Years 1-5
  - To provide activities and expert instruction to assist campers in gaining specific skills.

- To provide opportunities within the program for the development of interpersonal relationships and social skills.
- To design the living group and camp activities to help develop self-responsibility in each camper.

You will note that each statement of goals is further defining the stated purpose, but also is leaving room to more clearly define the specifics of the goal in measurable statements later. It is certainly possible to be more specific in the purpose. For example, in purpose three, the skills to be gained could be specified if the camp specializes in one or two areas.

OUTCOMES/OBJECTIVES

Outcomes/objectives are the ways in which the accomplishment of a goal is measured. The dictionary defines an objective as a "strategic position to be achieved," and an outcome as "the result or consequence." Combining these leads to defining the measurable result you wish to achieve in a given period of time. In each and every case, these grow out of a larger, more general goal and actually bring the goal into a defined entity.

Outcomes/objectives may be developed for a variety of purposes:

- Operation. These could deal with administrative areas such as completing facility construction, improving quality of food, lowering food costs, balancing the budget. These are primarily measured in quantities, deadlines, and quality.
- Hospitality. These come into play when a camp rents its facilities to other groups and becomes the host. They might deal with providing resources for the groups, developing facilities specifically for such groups, adding services, etc.
- Training. These would be developed for the precamp staff training week and, where there is year-round staff, for each person annually.
- Personnel Performance. These would be developed by a staff person in conjunction with his or her supervisor for a given time period and relate to the successful performance of job functions.
- Programmatic and/or Youth Development. These are the desired benefits to the camper during or after the experience at camp and they are measurable attainments for the camper.

The camp director will find it important to examine each of these purposes and determine how and when outcomes/objectives are to be developed and evaluated. For the purpose of illustration, discussion here will focus on the development of camp program and/or youth development outcomes/objectives. Here are some examples of outcomes/objectives relating to each of the previously stated goals.

- **Camp A** — The principal purpose is to help young people of all backgrounds to grow into responsible maturity through the application of Christian principles in an outdoor setting.

- Goal 1: To contribute to a camper's awareness of himself or herself in relation to other members of a group.

  Outcome/Objective 1: The camper, as a member of the group, will accept and attempt to carry out his or her idea for an activity or project.

- Goal 2: To develop an awareness of one's natural environment.

  Outcome/Objective 1: The camper will demonstrate minimum impact camping practices in removing his or her tent and cleaning up at the campsite.

- Goal 3: To develop an awareness of one's spiritual dimension.

  Outcome/Objective 1: The camper will express himself or herself about God in small group discussions.

- **Camp B** — The mission is to provide an outdoor setting for group living where people can design programs to meet their group's needs and to provide a regular opportunity for youth to gain a deeper understanding of their relationships to their fellow man and their natural environment.

  - Goal 1: To provide a setting with comfortable facilities flexible enough for groups to carry out a variety of programs and activities of their own design.

    Outcome/Objective 1: By May, 200_, a multipurpose program building will be completed.

  - Goal 2: To provide organized sessions when youth can come together and develop interpersonal relationships.

    Outcome/Objective 1: During the summer of 200_, the camp will sponsor at least two camp sessions for ages 9–16 emphasizing small-group living.

  - Goal 3: To provide a well-cared-for natural environment where activities naturally encourage a better understanding of, and responsibility for, the natural environment.

    Outcome/Objective 1: By May 200_, a series of three self-guiding nature trails will be established for use by individuals and living groups.

- **Camp C** — The purpose of this camp is to help each individual camper gain skills that help him or her achieve a strong self-concept, self-responsibility, and an ability to get along with his or her peers.

  - Goal 1: To provide activities and instruction to assist campers in gaining specific skills.

    Outcome/Objective 1: By the end of each session, each camper will perform at least three physical skills that he or she could not previously perform or perform them at a higher level than upon arrival at camp.

  - Goal 2: To provide opportunities within the program for the development of interpersonal relationships and social skills.

    Outcome/Objective 1: The boys' units will practice social skills by hosting the girls' units for a social event once during each session.

- Goal 3: To design the living group and camp activities to help develop self-reliance in each camper.

  Outcome/Objective 1: Each camper will complete daily assigned group living tasks.

As you review the outcomes/objectives you will note:

- Each is measurable.
- Each is specific to the goal and purpose.
- There are differences in the focus of the outcomes/objectives — Camps A and C focus on individual growth and experiences where Camp B focuses on hospitality to outside groups and provision of program to its own constituency.
- Each purpose and outcome/objective relates to the overall mission and philosophy of the camp in question.

Though a purpose will remain vague or idealized, the outcomes/objectives should be stated in specific terms which provide measurable targets for staff.

Evaluation/Indicators

After detailing the philosophy, goals, and outcomes/objectives of a camp, there must be some process for evaluating or determining the indicators of their success. Based on the evaluation of successful achievements, the camp can make adjustments to their operation and set new targets. There are a variety of methods to measure the successful

3.1

Illustration *Purpose, Goal, Outcome, Targets, and Evaluation Methods*

PURPOSE: To help each individual camper gain skills that help him or her achieve a strong self-concept, self-responsibility, and the ability to get along with his or her peers.

GOAL: To provide activities that will help campers develop new skills or improve their current skill level.

OUTCOME	ACTIVITIES	TARGET	EVALUATION METHODS
Each camper can perform at least three physical skills which he/she could not previously perform or performs them at a higher level than upon arrival at camp.	Outdoor living skills Swimming skills Archery target Arts and crafts Nature lore Horseback riding	All campers participate in at least four program areas. Seventy-five percent of all campers perform three physical skills which they could not previously perform or they perform them at a higher level than upon arrival at camp.	Discussion between counselor and camper Campers choose four program areas in which they would like to develop or improve their skills. Skilled activity leaders test skill learning needs at first activity session. Instruction is provided at the appropriate level for all campers. Campers are given a choice to practice skills during free time. Activity leaders test skills at the final activity session.

achievement of targets, including camper, staff, and parent written or verbal evaluations. Illustration 3.1 shows a pre- and post-skill test. Other methods for evaluation are in chapter 15. In terms of training and measuring the progress of staff, it is helpful to align specific target experiences with methods to accomplish the outcome/objective.

A checklist for each activity can be developed as an evaluation tool that can be marked for each individual both at the beginning and end of the camp session. This can provide a checkpoint both for any report to parents and for evaluating the accomplishment of the camp's goals at the end of the season.

At that point, the director and staff can then use the degree of success to determine adjustments or alterations, if necessary, to the goals and outcomes/objectives for the future. Once the process is in place, it becomes relatively easy to make adjustments in the target experiences and methods from year to year.

CHECKPOINTS

1. Do you have a written statement of the camp's purpose and goals?
2. Have you developed written outcomes/objectives under each of the goals specific to your camp?
3. Have you tested the purpose, goals, and outcomes/objectives with the operator (supervisor or committee or board)?

Related Standards and Regulations

Accreditation Standards for Camp Programs and Services: PD-2, 6, 7, 9; "Additional Professional Practices": 32–38

Standards for Conference and Retreat Centers: II-1

Regulations: Only those which may apply to the 50l(c)(3) status with the Internal Revenue Service (tax exempt status)

Kathy Buss, B'nai B'rith Camp, Mittleman Jewish
Community Center, Portland, Oregon

4

The Participant

The center of the camp is the camper. He is the only reason for operating the . . . camp. As the center about which all life revolves, we need to give our immediate attention to knowing him, to helping him learn to do things for himself, and to helping him learn to do things with others. The staff is in camp for that . . . purpose.[1]

E xchange the word *camper* for the broader *participant* and Ott's words from fifty years ago still underline the essence of what camp is about.

Lofty statements of purpose, definitive goals, and outcomes/objectives alone do not ensure the camp will endure or succeed in accomplishing those statements. However elaborate the program designed to support those goals, success is unlikely unless the persons to be served are matched with that program.

From the very beginning, the focus of the director and owner must include defining the participant or target population, the needs of that population generally and individually, and finally, the program design that will meet those needs and accomplish the goals of the camp. As you will see in chapter 5, "program" is everything that happens in camp, from activities to group living to the design of the food service.

DETERMINING YOUR TARGET POPULATION

Initially, it is helpful to describe the market areas for the participants you wish to serve. This information may relate to the camp's mission, purpose, and goals statements. Some camps by their sponsorship will draw campers primarily from the sponsor's sources (Girl Scout membership, a church or synagogue, a neighborhood, a specific disability) and that sponsor's mission will have given direction to the purpose and goals statements. Other camps may choose to look nationally and internationally for campers but may target families at a specific income level or age group.

Year round, it is not unusual for camps to serve a range of populations, often resulting

---

[1]Elmer Ott. 1949. *So You Want To Be a Camp Counselor*. New York: Association Press (Y.M.C.A. of the U.S.A.). p. 21.

from alternating the timing of sessions: summer for children and youth, weekends for family groups, weekdays for school groups or senior adult groups or adult conferences. In these instances, camps will need to identify target populations for each different program.

Make no assumptions about the population you have chosen to serve. For example, there may not be sufficient population in the geographic area you have chosen or there may be more groups trying to serve a given population than is economically feasible. This is particularly true for day camps, where daily transportation is an issue. So the analysis begins.

1. Camp market. Once the camp's market area is clearly defined (a county, a state, several states), a demographic analysis is essential. Gather demographic information about the population or area(s) you wish to serve; include age, gender, geographic area, economic and ethnic characteristics. If the camp's market is the membership of a sponsoring organization, it is important to secure the demographic breakdown of that membership. Whether the camp serves a specific membership or the entire country and international markets, it may be helpful to compare the actual composition of the camp's existing participants with the broader demographics of the country. Some indications of the limitations of the potential market can be gained from this comparison, especially for long-range planning.

   Analysis of the camp's potential market should include answers to the following questions. What is the population by ages, gender, socioeconomic groups, and ethnic groups broken down by geographic areas (zip codes, communities, counties) within the target market area? What have been the trends over the past five years? What is the projection for the next five years? Where is the largest concentration of prospective campers or groups? What are the economic ranges of the population in given areas? The U.S. Census Bureau's Web site provides regularly updated projections to its ten-year enumeration of the country's population giving age, gender, and ethnicity information by census tracts. The federal government also offers more statistics at an interagency Web site for The Forum on Child and Family Statistics. If the participant population is narrowed to include only persons with certain physical or mental disabilities, additional information may have to be secured through public or private organizations which provide services to those groups. The combined data provides a way to examine the various components of potential participants in your chosen geographic area.

   Even if the market is limited to the membership of the camp's sponsoring organization, a breakdown of the membership by age, gender, geographic, economic and ethnic characteristics should be secured. That breakdown should be compared to the similar population statistics of the geographical area covered by the membership and the organization's plans for membership expansion. Some indications of the limitations of the potential market can be gained from this comparison, especially for long-range planning.

2. Camp enrollment. Review the statistics from the camp's enrollment over the past five years; break out the statistics by geographic areas, age groups, socioeconomic groups, and ethnic groups for which you have secured demographic information. Has your camp's previous enrollment followed the trends in the general population for the same given period? How does your camp's enrollment match the demographics of the geographic areas you serve or wish to serve? How does it match the demographics projected for the next five years?

   It may be beneficial for your staff to reflect the diversity of your camper population. Review the composition of your staff over that five-year period. Overlay that with your camper composition and study how the two differ.

3. Camp diversity. If diversity of the participant population was not considered in the initial development of the mission statement, it is important and appropriate to consider that now. How diverse a population does the camp wish to serve? How diverse is the population of the market area, and what are the projected changes over the next five years? Do the goals and outcome statements illustrate a need to diversify the makeup of the participant population?

   Areas of diversity are shown in illustration 4.1. Each basic area of diversity should be considered first, followed by secondary ones. Basic areas are ones that are difficult to change and are most visible to others. Secondary areas are ones that are generally chosen or learned, and can often be changed.

   > *"Camps ought to be outdoor environments where differences and diversity are not merely tolerated, but appreciated and celebrated. Not all camps will address diversity issues in the same way, but the goal of all camp programs can be to strive toward developing multicultural organization where social oppression does not exist,"* states Dr. Karla Henderson.[2]

   In today's society, a camp that ignores the issue of diversity in its target market is also ignoring the growing diversity of the country's population and the importance of individuals learning to recognize and consciously deal with prejudice and stereotyping.

4. Camp competition. Identify your camp's competition and whom they are serving. Competition may come from other types of programs, other camps, schools, sports, and other types of activities that involve the entire family or segments of it.

   At this point, the goal should be to see if more programs with similar goals are serving the same population. Is the target population saturated with existing programs?

5. Once a director has compiled and thoroughly analyzed all of this data, it should be compared with the population the camp wishes to serve. Where is there overlap?

---

[2]Karla A. Henderson. "Unlearning the Isms." *Camping Magazine* Vol. 67, No.1, September/October 1994. p. 19.

4.1

Illustration *Areas of Diversity*

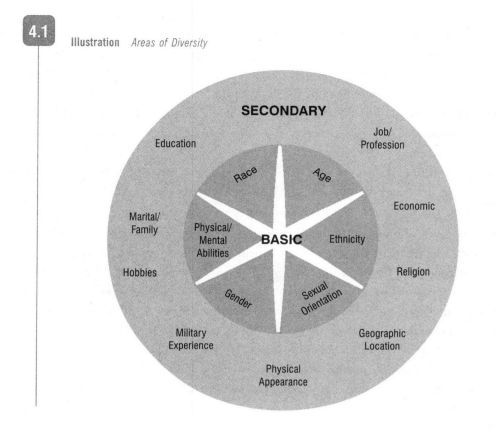

Where are there groups not being served by your camp or others? Where is there diversity?

6. The information should then be shared with others. Key staff who have long experience with the camp may have insights that will help. If the camp operates with a board or committee, that group should have a presentation of the information and an opportunity to react to it. Another camp director or mentor may be able to offer some observations. Often, outside consultants from the camping field can provide a clearer analysis of this data from a broader perspective, and help give guidance to the director, board, and committee in developing an overall market analysis and marketing plan.

7. At this point the camp should reevaluate and consider narrowing or broadening its targeted population.

UNDERSTANDING THE PARTICIPANTS: GROWTH AND DEVELOPMENT

Determining a target population is not enough. It is equally important that the director and staff be cognizant of the basic concepts of human growth and development and any special needs of the age groups being served.

Bob Ditter, a speaker and child and family therapist specializing in child and adolescent treatment, states in his book *In the Trenches*, "Today, as never before, camping is in a position to be a pivotal player in the growth and development of children. To realize this potential, camping professionals must become more aware of the social and emotional needs of both children and parents. We must be clear, articulate, and specific about exactly how the camp experience makes a positive impact on children and then practice the profession in a more conscious, consistent, and deliberate way."[3]

Parents have high expectations of camp, and it is important for directors to create a partnership with parents in the development of their child. This strategy helps the camp deal with both the developmental needs and problems of a specific child. It also reduces the exposure to risk when taking on the responsibility of children with behavioral problems or medical, physical, or psychological conditions.

Additionally, it would be ideal if the director and full-time program staff had completed courses in human growth and development during their college curriculum. However, this cannot always be the case, and it is not likely that many of the seasonal staff will have had exposure to such courses. A careful review of current literature in the field should be made once the target population is determined, and an overview of developmental needs is best included in staff training.

Developmental Needs

It is difficult to plan an effective developmentally appropriate program or even hospitality services unless one has an understanding of the particular characteristics and needs of the age group being served. Since, ideally, camp goals and outcomes are based upon meeting certain developmental needs, this is a starting point for a program.

An overview of varying age groups is shown in illustration 4.2 as a stimulant to learning more about the applicable groups. This material was originally developed by Jean E. Folkerth for the Project REACH Camp Staff Training Series and has been updated with information from the University of Connecticut.[4]

In examining the developmental characteristics in illustration 4.2, staff should be conscious of the varying conditions that could alter certain of those characteristics:

- Cultural differences
- Economic situations
- Environmental conditions (home, school, peers, etc.)
- Physical conditions (diet, disabilities, genetics)
- Current societal trends or issues that put children at risk (violence, drug use, sexual activity, technological changes, etc.)

These conditions may slow or accelerate certain elements of physical growth or behavior.

[3]Robert Ditter. 1997. *In the Trenches*. Martinsville, IN: American Camping Association.

[4]Connecticut Department of Human Resources and the University of Connecticut Cooperative Extension System. "Beyond Opening Day: Building Excellence in School-age Child Care Programs"; and Jean E. Folkerth. 1981. "Developmental Characteristics." *Perspectives on Camp Administration*. Dr. Elizabeth Farley, ed. Martinsville, IN: American Camping Association. pp. 26–28.

4.2   Illustration   *Developmental Characteristics by Age Group*

FIVE TO SEVEN YEAR OLDS

Physical
- mastering physical skills (physical activities)
- better control of large muscles than small muscles
- high activity level (restless and fidgety)
- working on eye-hand coordination

Social
- learning to be friends and have "best" friends
- becoming more aware of peers and their opinions
- beginning to experience empathy for others
- still family oriented (beginning to relate to non-family adults)
- becoming aware of sexual differences
- want to structure their environment as home is structured
- want assurance of an adult's presence

Emotional
- see fairness as being nice to others so they will be nice in return
- seek parent and adult approval
- behave in ways to avoid punishment
- developing modesty
- expressing feelings and emotions, upsets are usually short-term

Intellectual
- increasing attention span (activities best limited to fifteen to thirty minutes)
- more interested in process than product
- learning to sort things into categories and arrange in a series
- learning concepts of right and wrong, cause and effect
- handle well only one mental operation at a time
- can distinguish between reality and fantasy, but may be afraid of scary figures

Activities and Special Considerations
Provide opportunities for:
- experimentation using bodies, ideas, and material in different ways
- active, boisterous games, climbing and balance, rhythmic activities
- practicing skills in eye-hand coordination such as cutting, pasting, drawing, etc.
- practice in group cooperation, sharing, and good work habits
- freedom to do things for themselves (no longer babies) and use and develop their own abilities
- use of senses requiring use of ears, eyes, nose, mouth, and skin
- reenacting routines and events of their known world
- developing friendship skills of sharing, helping, taking turns, and working with others
- finding appropriate ways of channeling emotions and behaviors

EIGHT TO TEN YEAR OLDS

Physical
- experience steady increases in large muscle development
- increased strength, balance, and coordination
- active with boundless energy, often restless and fidgety
- boys and girls maturing at differing rates (boys are slower to mature)
- increasing in manual dexterity, eye-hand, and small muscle coordination

Social
- sees adults as authority
- follows rules out of respect for authority
- can be noisy and argumentative
- feels loyalty to friendship group, often with "secret" words
- identifies with same sex group
- expanded use of reasoning skills to solve problems, negotiate, and compromise

Emotional

- view right behavior as "obeying" rules set by those in power
- accepts parent/family beliefs
- admires and imitates older boys and girls
- developing decision making skills
- beginning to take responsibility for their own actions
- needs acceptance from peer groups
- emphasizes similarities between self and friends
- looks to adults for guidance and approval
- needs involvement with caring adult
- comparisons with the success of others difficult and eroding of self-confidence
- self-conscious, afraid to fail, sensitive to criticism
- feel they can do no wrong and are quick to correct others
- name-calling and teasing are methods for responding to being upset
- feel too "cool" for emotions

Intellectual

- quick, eager, and enthusiastic
- vary greatly in academic abilities, interests, and reasoning skills
- increased attention span, but interests change rapidly
- beginning to think logically and symbolically
- learning to use good judgement
- beginning to learn about moral judgments, applying principles of right and wrong
- wants to know how to, what, and why of things
- see things as "black and white" and "yes and no" and have difficulty with opinions different than theirs

Activities and Special Considerations

Provide opportunities for:

- using large and small muscles in activities
- organized team games and sports where everyone can be successful
- to work in groups in cooperative activities
- to use skills to explore and investigate the world
- assuming responsibility
- discuss other people's viewpoints
- to explore interests in collections and hobbies
- express feelings and imagination through creative writing or acting
- discussing reasonable explanations for rules and decisions
- interested in making and doing "real" things and using "real" tools, equipment, and materials

ELEVEN TO THIRTEEN YEAR OLDS

Physical

- exhibit a wide range of sexual maturity and growth patterns between genders and within gender groups (girls are about two years ahead of boys)
- rapid change in physical appearance
- growth of hands and feet, nose and ears my be faster than arms and legs and face causing concern for appearance
- may try experimental behavior to enhance sensory stimulation, e.g., drug and alcohol use

Social

- shifting from emphasis on same sex to opposite sex — girls develop interest in boys earlier than boys in girls
- looking more toward peers than parents, seek peer recognition
- seek acceptance and trust
- tend to regard sex in a depersonalized way
- search for adult role models and often identify with admired adult hairdos, dress, and mannerisms of popular sports and music stars
- question authority
- question family values
- willing to submerge self for benefit of group

4.2   Illustration   *Developmental Characteristics by Age Group continued*

- discipline can be a problem because of spirit of group
- friendship groups or cliques are often small but intense
- more realistic understanding of who they are and what they can do
- more interested in social activities

Emotional
- compare themselves to others
- concerned about development and emerging sexually
- see themselves as always on center stage
- conscious about bodily changes
- concerned about being liked by friends, social graces, grooming
- strive for independence, yet want and need parent help
- seek privacy from parents/adults
- want to be a part of something important
- aware of degrees of emotion and seek to find the right words to describe their feelings
- exaggeration and sarcasm are frequently used to describe subtle meanings

Intellectual
- need information for making decisions
- find justice and equality to be important issues
- think abstractly and hypothetically
- can solve problems that have more than one variable
- can imagine consequences
- ready for in-depth, long-term experiences
- have moved from fantasy to realistic focus on their life's goals

Activities and Special Considerations
Provide opportunities for:
- more structured and adult-like activities
- explore other cultures, foods, languages, and customs
- completing projects (emphasis on precision and perfecting)
- discuss issues and opposite sex with friends
- opportunities to making decisions
- fun, learning experiences
- interested in activities involving the opposite sex and learning to deal with opposite sex

FOURTEEN TO SEVENTEEN YEAR OLDS

Physical
- sexual maturity, with accompanying physical and emotional changes
- concerned about body image, may have complexion problems
- smaller range in size and maturity among peers
- tend to have realistic view of limits to which body can be tested
- desire to do things that give an adrenaline rush, or the extraordinary
- boys have enormous appetites; girls tend to watch weight

Social
- achieving independence from family
- tend to romanticize sexually, but moving toward more realistic understanding
- search for intimacy
- prefer to set their own goals rather than accept those set by others
- more accepting of differences
- makes and keeps commitments
- see adults as fallible
- renegotiate relationships
- want adult leadership roles

Emotional
- strong identification with admired adult
- desire respect
- beginning to accept and enjoy their own individuality, but still seek status and approval of peer group

- take on multiple roles
- are introspective
- can see self from the viewpoint of others
- can initiate and carry out their own tasks without supervision of others
- desire a role in determining what happens in their world

Intellectual
- beginning of occupational choice
- want their point of view heard
- enjoy demonstrating acquired knowledge
- develop theories to explain how things happen
- will lose patience with meaningless activity
- good problem solvers but are frustrated when not consulted
- can better understand moral principles
- idealistic view of adult life
- beginning to think of leaving home for college, employment, marriage

Activities and Special Considerations
Provide opportunities to:
- be a part of the decision making process
- be empowered to make a difference in what's happening
- show and value their individual differences
- take on responsibility for others
- be a part of coeducational activities
- apply leadership skills
- demonstrate self-expression
- discuss issues and values

ADULTS AND SENIOR CITIZENS

Young Adult Characteristics (18-26)
- becoming independent and making it on their own
- focusing on developing marketable skills and knowledge to earn a living
- rather idealistic view of adult life
- formulating values and developing a philosophy of life
- beginning to focus on choosing a mate
- interested in expanding base of experiences — travel, vocational experiences, etc.

Adult Characteristics
- achieving satisfaction in one's vocation
- assuming social and civic responsibilities
- developing skills that are family-centered
- becoming parents and raising children to become responsible and well adjusted
- learning to relate to (or care for) parents and older adults
- testing and refining values
- learning to cope with anxiety and frustration
- more financial pressures
- increased family and work-related stress
- expect housing that will provide some privacy and comfort

Senior Citizens' Characteristics
- adjusting to declining energy and physical changes of aging, i.e., decreased flexibility, balance, auditory and visual problems, less strength and endurance, slower reaction time
- building new relationships with grown children and grandchildren
- learning to relate again to one's spouse
- coming to terms with one's life goals and aspirations
- principled moral reasoning
- may have less financial pressure
- may have a more conservative outlook on life than younger adults
- expect housing that will provide privacy and accessibility

However narrow the age range served by a camp may be, the director and staff need a general understanding of all age groups since they may have ongoing relationships with other staff, parents of participants, board/committee members, etc., who may go beyond the age range of participants.

In examining the characteristics and developmental needs of various age groups, staff should also understand the basic competencies needed by a given age group. All of these should be clearly addressed in the previously developed stated goals and outcomes. In illustration 4.3, several youth development experts have identified these competencies for children and youth. Although the terminology may be different, there is general agreement among these experts about what competencies or attributes are essential to the health development of young people.[5]

In these examples, each relates to the way in which goals and outcomes are developed for children and youth in a camp setting. Second, these competencies materially affect the way in which program tools are used to accomplish outcomes. As one examines the basic concepts of human growth and development for a specific target population, one also needs to examine the viability of the stated goals and outcomes for that population.

Persons with Disabilities — Physical, Mental, Emotional

When participants have physical, mental, or emotional disabilities, an understanding of those specific disabilities is critical in helping participants gain the identified competencies. In some situations, a special camp or session is held for participants with a given disability or similar disabilities. This may provide some common starting points for these participants, but does not eliminate the varying developmental needs of individuals. Disabilities should be considered one of the physical/mental abilities of persons, as identified in the basic areas of diversity.

Camp directors need to consider the implications in the Americans With Disabilities Act of 1990 (ADA) to making programs available to all persons, regardless of disability. That Act requires that all camps, except those operated by religious groups and private clubs, make their programs and facilities accessible to individuals with disabilities. Religious groups and private clubs are exempted only when serving their own members and then only if they are not receiving any federal funding or food or milk commodities from the U.S. Department of Agriculture. Further detail on these implications is discussed in chapter 11.

Where integrating a camper with a disability into a living group, it should be clear that the goal is to provide a camp experience as close as possible to that provided to

[5]Peter C. Scales. 1991. "The Developmental Needs of Young Adolescents Today and Tomorrow." *Proceedings of a Symposium on Year-Round School.* Martinsville, IN: American Camping Association; and Basil J. Whiting. 1993. *Reweaving the Tattered Web, Socializing and Enculturating Our Children.* Kansas City, MO: Ewing Kauffman Foundation.

4.3

Illustration   *Child and Youth Development*

Competencies or Attributes Essential
to the Healthy Development of Young People

Center for Early Adolescence — Peter Scales, 1991
- positive social interactions with adults and peers
- competence and achievement
- structure and clear limits
- creative expression
- meaningful participation in families, school, and communities
- physical activity
- self-definition

Character Counts — Michael Josephson, 1996–98
- trustworthiness
- respect
- responsibility
- fairness
- citizenship
- caring

Reweaving the Tattered Web — Basil Whiting for Kauffman Foundation, 1993
- interpersonal and social skills
- basic academic skills and knowledge
- cognitive, creative, and mental skills
- emotional and psychological maturity and stability
- commitment to higher values
- vocational skills

40 Developmental Assets (in these seven categories) — Peter Benson, Search Institute, 1997
- social competencies
- commitment to learning
- boundaries and expectations
- constructive use of time
- empowerment
- positive values
- support
- positive identity

Desirable Youth Outcomes — Karen Pitman, International Youth Foundation, 1996
- social competence
- intellectual competence
- character (responsibility, spirituality)
- connection (safety, structure)
- membership and belonging
- civic competence
- physical and emotional health
- confidence (self-worth, mastery)
- cultural competence
- employability

A Matter of Time — Carnegie Council on Adolescent Development, 1992
- social
- cognitive or intellectual
- emotional
- cultural
- civic
- physical
- vocational

other campers. Helping the members of a living group to appreciate and understand each other is one goal of every camp living group, with or without members who have a disability. Counselors and activity specialists should be given as much information as possible about the disability of a camper who is being placed in a living group or program activity, including limitations, danger signals, medications, previous camp or outdoor experiences, and parental expectations. The more education and information given the staff, the better able they will be to work toward achieving the goals of the camp.

Behavior Management and Discipline

In camp, behavior management is a tone, an atmosphere in which a desired behavior is achieved without damaging relationships or hurting people. It is the director's responsibility to outline appropriate and inappropriate camper behavior, as well as appropriate and inappropriate consequences and staff responses to such behavior. These should be clearly outlined during staff training.

There are a number of positive ways in which camp leadership can encourage good behavior. One is to establish a caring relationship with campers by opening lines of communication and encouraging a camper to come to you if there is a problem. Praise is another effective way to encourage positive behavior. When counselors praise positive acts and ignore negative ones, the message is sent that campers must behave in a positive way to gain attention. Another way of encouraging good behavior is to create an atmosphere at camp that is full of cooperation and fun. Children are prone to imitate the behavior of those who are important to them, without judging whether the behavior is positive or negative. Staff members need to be sure that their individual behavior is worth being copied.

When dealing with a large number of youth from a variety of backgrounds and family patterns, in a setting where they can try new and different behaviors, there will be instances when those behaviors will be unacceptable and require discipline. "In every . . . camp, one of the major demands placed on directors and counselors is discipline. The key to handling this issue well is being prepared, which starts with having a plan and understanding different techniques that work."[6] The camp that enumerates a lengthy list of rules immediately upon arrival at camp invites the violation of those rules. Yet some rules are necessary in any community, and the method of educating youth about those rules and gaining their participation in setting and agreeing to those rules is critical to the educational purposes of the organized camp.

Staff training is a time to set guidelines for discipline and prepare counselors to deal with problem behaviors. The camp's policy on, methods of, and circumstances requiring discipline should be clearly outlined during this training. Time should be devoted to conflict resolution techniques, modeling behavior by staff, and the use of praise, I-messages, time outs, and other methods. Role playing a set of situations which require disciplinary action or group analysis may help staff gain a better understanding of the variable situations as well as appropriate disciplinary measures.

Discipline is sometimes regarded as an old-fashioned word; it is also a principle that helps subordinate selfish interests to the welfare of the whole group. Before discipline becomes an issue, there are some considerations that need to be understood and accepted by anyone dealing with children:

- A child has the occasional need to test the limits.
- A child cannot always manage self-control.
- A child has a strong tendency to the values of his or her peer group.
- A child has the right to make mistakes.
- A child has a right to be respected as an individual, regardless of unattractive attributes.

---

[6]Donnie Jackson. "Disciplining Campers." *Camping Magazine* Vol. 70, No. 4, July/August 1997.

When discipline is required, there are some guidelines that can be of help. Discipline should always be used sparingly to be effective — if you discipline constantly it becomes the accepted norm. Discipline should never be used vindictively or emotionally — never let a problem being dealt with put you off balance. Punishment, if any, should follow the deed as quickly as is possible. Using work as a punishment usually creates a poor attitude toward work; the exception might be when the punishable deed created work for others. Physical punishment is not acceptable, nor is verbal abuse, which can be as destructive as physical force. (It should be noted that physical punishment or verbal abuse of a camper by a counselor or another staff member may be symptoms of stress on the part of the individual.)

If initial attempts to control or change an unacceptable behavior have failed, these processes may help:

- Maintain the initiative and try to persuade the camper that it is better to conform.
- Avoid specific threats by using a broad warning of a possible course of action. Rather than saying, "if you do that again, you will be sent home," try "there are consequences for breaking camp rules or for not cooperating." A child may imagine far more fearsome punishments than you can suggest. A specific threat commits you to carry it out or back down and may even dare the child to try you out, whereas a general warning reinforces the idea that compliance will be better than defiance.
- Involve other campers in the process. An indication that peers may not like the behavior brings in a different aspect. (For example, in a situation where a group of boys were bullying a younger group, the camp director got the two groups together and, by asking questions, forced the older boys to face up to their actions. There were no threats or punishment, but the behavior changed.)
- Check age characteristics to assess the level of comprehension or the motivation for obeying authority.
- Review any punishment before setting it. Does it fit the offense? (For example, if one camper has peppered another's dessert, is it fair that the culprit goes without his dessert?) Is punishment necessary to deter a repetition of the behavior? Any persistently antisocial behavior should not be allowed to pass without some appropriate action. Some children respond better to negative consequences while others respond better to rewards or positive reinforcement.
- Look for causes. Avoiding difficult situations is much better than having to deal with them once they arise. Campers with too much energy can get into trouble; overtired campers are prone to react badly to provocation. If there is a camper more prone to negative behavior, try to start each day in a manner that will encourage proper behavior. Try to identify campers who might cause problems and have strategies in mind to deal with them; having a plan will keep the problems from seeming overwhelming.

Medical or Psychological Conditions and Inappropriate Behaviors

However well one understands human growth and development, there are special types of problems and situations that require some advance planning by the camp director. In an informal survey of camp directors conducted by Bob Ditter, the four major concerns most often mentioned were eating disorders, ADHD, increased aggressiveness and conflict among campers, and a surge in rudeness toward adults. The staff should be prepared to deal with these and other problems or conditions based upon training and information, rather than intuition. In addition to training on general behavior management, practical guidance should be given staff in dealing with special behavior concerns such as those listed below.

Abuse. Camp is often a place where abusive behavior (i.e., physical, sexual, psychological) that has occurred in the home environment comes to the surface, as youngsters find adults they trust and admire. Abuse by staff or other campers may also occur in the camp setting. (See chapter 6 for information on references and background checks.) Counselors can pick up signs of abuse in the living situation if they have been given appropriate training. For example, the observation of unusual bruises or scars as the counselor supervises youngsters changing clothes or in the shower should cause the counselor to discuss the potential of physical abuse with the camp nurse and director.

Symptoms of psychological abuse may be obvious but dismissed as other types of behavior: depression or withdrawal, lack of self-esteem, seeking approval endlessly, hostility, rigidity, an inordinate attention to details or constantly denigrating him or herself.

Symptoms of sexual abuse may also be dismissed or may be difficult to confirm. Some symptoms include abuse of animals, persistent or inappropriate sex play with toys or peers, and inappropriate understanding of sex for the child's age. Other symptoms have been identified by the National Center for Missing or Exploited Children:

- "Changes in behavior, extreme mood swings, withdrawal, fearfulness, and excessive crying
- Bed-wetting, nightmares, fear of going to bed, or wearing lots of clothes to bed
- Acting out inappropriate sexual activity or showing unusual interest in sexual matters
- Regression to infantile behavior
- A sudden acting out of feelings or aggressive or rebellious behavior
- A fear of certain places, people or activities, especially of being alone with certain people
- Pain, itching, bleeding, fluid, or rawness in the private areas"[7]

Staff should be given a clear understanding of the steps to be taken should there be any suspicion of abuse before or during camp. In most states camp staff have a legal obligation to report child abuse to the authorities.

---

[7]National Center for Missing and Exploited Children. 1988. *Camp Director's Guide: Preventing Sexual Exploitation of Children.* Washington, D.C.: Office of Juvenile Justice and Delinquency Programs, U.S. Department of Justice. Rhulen Agency in cooperation with the American Camping Association. p. 19.

Some of the sexual behavior identified as a normal aspect of human growth and development may become abuse when a camper exhibits that behavior with a younger camper or by force on a peer. Camper-to-camper abuse has been a growing concern at camp and what, in the past, may have been considered a prank or hazing is today considered abuse.

ADD/ADHD. Attention Deficit Hyperactive Disorder is a combination of symptoms that include inattention, distractibility, impulsiveness, and other difficulties associated with attention. Three to five percent of children in the U.S. have ADD/ADHD. Affected boys outnumber girls three to one.

Though most youngsters can be overactive at times, a child with ADD/ADHD may act impulsive and inattentive, race ahead, take chances, and will seldom persist in any activity or goal. Such behavior requires considerable supervision. The role of the counselor is to protect the child from his or her own actions and to try to get the child to participate in the normal activities. Some children will be on medication such as Ritalin for this condition; some parents take their children off the medication for the time away from home. In such cases, it is important that the health care manager and related counselor be alerted.

Aggression and Violence. Incidents in schools and elsewhere of violence, weapons possession, and threats against others have brought a heightened concern for these problems in camp. (See chapter 10 for a plan for prevention.) It is important that staff be trained to recognize warning signs that may precede acts of violence both in themselves and in others. Although there is no foolproof system for identifying potentially dangerous youngsters, The National School Safety Center identified some behaviors that could indicate a youth's potential for harming him or herself or others, such as engaging in tantrums and serious disciplinary problems, uncontrollable angry outbursts, name calling, cursing and abusive language and violent threats; having few or no close friends; being preoccupied with weapons; being bullied or bullying peers or younger children; preferring movies and reading materials dealing with violent themes or rituals; participating in a gang or an antisocial group on the fringe of peer acceptance; demonstrating significant mood swings; and threatening suicide.

AIDS. This is not a behavior, but awareness to persons having the condition can lead to behavior patterns. Persons with AIDS should be treated as normally as possible. Counselors should be prepared to deal with situations that might cause bleeding or where bleeding might occur, i.e., they should have rubber gloves available in the living quarters (or in first aid kits when out of camp) and be trained in universal precautions. Persons with AIDS ordinarily will understand the dangers to others. If the issue arises in the living group, counselors should be prepared to educate the group to the ways in which AIDS can and cannot be spread to alleviate the fears that some campers may have.

Eating Disorders. Anorexia Nervosa, Bulimia, and Binge (BED) are the three eating disorders that are most familiar to the general public. These conditions tend to be more a problem for girls and are closely associated with depression, low self-esteem, and stress. Adolescent girls who are concerned about weight gain often limit their food intake to a degree that can be problematic, or they may go on eating binges, followed by inducing vomiting to rid themselves of the food. These are not problems that can be solved at camp unless there is a staff person with understanding of and training in treating these maladies. Of all the behavioral difficulties a child might have, this is one that parents are extremely likely to deny, even if confronted with the facts. Because of this parent denial and the secretive aspect of these disorders, children often arrive at camp without the director being informed of the condition.

However, any counselor should be aware of what to do if he or she believes a camper is suffering with an eating disorder. The camper may react with embarrassment or become defensive or angry. Counselors should assure the camper that they will not discuss it with other campers or counselors, but because they really care about the camper and want the camper to be happy, they will report their concern to the director or camp health care manager. The camper should be able to sense acceptance from the counselor, not shock or disappointment. The counselor should encourage the camper to share feelings at any time he or she is disturbed or upset. (Directors should also be prepared to address a staff member who is suffering from an eating disorder.)

Encopresis. It is not unusual for younger campers to "soil" themselves in the process of play or excitement. The key to the situation is to avoid embarrassment or humiliation. The counselor may also help the situation by encouraging a regular time for a bowel movement or reminding the youngster about going to the toilet.

Enuresis. Neither is it unusual for younger campers to be faced with the embarrassing situation of bed-wetting in the resident camp setting. Bed-wetting is not a behavioral problem. No child wants to wake up in a wet bed. Camp is not the place to try to remedy the problem. The role of the counselor is to avoid embarrassment or humiliation of the camper before his or her peers. A procedure for handling the clothes and bedding should be developed so that counselors can deal with this quietly and sensitively without any punishment to the camper. Counselors can also help children by encouraging them to limit fluid intake after dinner and reminding all campers to go to the bathroom before going to bed. Counselors can also wake children in the night and walk them to the bathroom.

Homesickness. Nearly 95 percent of campers have some feeling of homesickness. Homesickness is defined as the distress or impairment caused by an actual or anticipated separation from home. It is characterized by acute longing and preoccupying thoughts of home and attachments to objects. One of the best preventive measures is to raise the campers' comfort levels right from the start. Make sure they feel welcome and know what will be happening on the first day. Many youngsters miss parents, friends, home, or pets and become despondent and tearful. Though involving the youngster in activity that helps one gain friends and forget home is one solution, many times it is not as easy as it sounds. Counselors need guidance during staff training about how to deal with this problem, how it may affect the living group, and when it would become necessary to consult with the supervisor or director.

Sexual Behavior. Young people often find camp an opportunity to explore or "act out" sexual behavior, given that they are in regular contact with peers and out of their home environment. This behavior may be aggressively heterosexual or homosexual in nature, and may be somewhat open in the group or secretive in nature. It is important to deal with sex honestly and openly without great moralizing and to help youth understand the normality of sex but also the accepted behavior patterns and the respect of others' rights.

Sleeping Problems. Sleepwalking or nightmares may occur, and if any campers have a history of either, the counselor will need to be particularly watchful of them.

Stealing. This problem may be best handled by discussing it with the group and exerting some peer pressure. When it is discovered that a youngster has stolen something, he or she should be confronted and faced with the responsibility of returning the item and apologizing. Some discussion with the affected group is important, but ostracizing the individual should be avoided.

Stress. Though this is a causal factor rather than a behavior, there is enough stress imposed upon youth in today's society that it is important to underline its consideration in staff training and supervision. Dr. David Elkind has probably been the most articulate voice about the stress on children in his book *The Hurried Child*. He states: "Children and teenagers are being hurried today as never before. Clock hurrying, [or] being asked to do or achieve too much in too little time, stresses children directly and gives rise to many stress symptoms such as eating, sleeping, and learning disturbances. Calendar hurrying, [or] being asked to do the wrong things at the wrong time, stresses young people indirectly by lowering self-esteem and thus rendering them more vulnerable to stress. The result is a dramatic rise in stress related behaviors in all age groups."[8]

The role of camp should be to relieve the stress of children rather than to create it. Helping staff understand their role in this endeavor is another step toward preventing problems or acting-out behaviors.

Substance Abuse. Camp is not isolated from alcohol, tobacco, or nonprescription substance use, consumption, or sharing among campers or staff. Certainly there is a high consciousness of substance abuse, and ample materials are available for the education of the director and staff. There are legal implications that need to be understood by the staff and director, as well as campers. Most important, the camp director must emphasize that it can happen at camp and provide adequate training before campers arrive. There should be clear statements in the literature distributed to campers and staff concerning the camp's position in this area, the consequences if violated, and the camp's policy on searching a camper's belongings.

---

[8]David Elkind. "The Hurried Child." *Camping Magazine* Vol. 58, No. 1, September/October 1985. pp. 25–26.

Suicidal Behavior. Society has become much more aware of the seriousness of suicide among youth. Suicide is the third leading cause of death for young people fifteen to twenty-four years of age. Counselors need to understand the signs of depression and the types of symptoms that often precede suicidal behavior. The warning signs you might notice at camp include a camper (or staff member) that:

- has sudden changes in behavior
- gives away prized possessions
- threatens suicide or talks about previous suicide attempts or suicide methods
- exhibits extreme or extended boredom
- demonstrates reckless behavior, carelessness, or self-destructive acts
- withdraws from friends and family and loses interest in activities
- is unusually sad, discouraged, and lonely, then suddenly calm and happy
- expresses feelings of hopelessness and/or worthlessness
- is preoccupied with death (perhaps evident in written expressions or artwork)
- makes statements about not being missed if he or she were gone
- has family or relationship disruptions, divorce trauma, ending of a romance
- demonstrates an unusually long grief reaction from death of a friend, loved one, or even a pet
- shows physical symptoms such as eating disturbances, sleeplessness, or excessive sleeping
- chronic headaches or stomachaches, menstrual irregularities, apathetic appearance

Any such behavior needs to be considered serious, not only by the counselor but by administrative staff as well. Make it clear that talking about thoughts and feelings is okay, express concern, listen attentively, be empathetic and not judgmental, don't promise confidentiality, stress that suicide is a permanent solution to a temporary problem, and remind them that there is help and things will get better. Most importantly, don't assume you can help them by yourself; know where you can get professional help in your area, i.e., mental health professional, crisis hot line, intervention team, minister, peer counselors, etc. A number of organizations offer Web sites that carry information about suicide statistics and prevention, such as: The Youth Online Club's www.soonet.ca/starla/suicide; the American Academy of Pediatric's www.aap/advoacy/childhealthmonth/prevteensuicide.htm; the American Academy of Child and Adolescent Psychiatry's www.suicide.mentalhelp.net; and the Center for Disease Control's www.cdc.gov/ncipc/dvp/suifacts.htm.

Vandalism. When personal or camp property is vandalized by campers, it may be a symptom of deeper problems. However, vandals should be dealt with directly and in a fashion that not only helps them gain an understanding of the seriousness of this behavior, but also requires them to have a role in restoring or replacing the vandalized property.

PREPARATION OF PARTICIPANTS

Individuals

Determining and understanding a camper or group population are only the first steps in building a positive growth experience that meets your camp objectives. Participants should be made aware of the camp's philosophy and expectations. Thorough preparation can eliminate or, at least, lessen some of the concerns identified earlier.

A camp director who begins or concludes enrollment of a camper with a personal interview will already have begun this preparatory process. In addition, after an interview, the camp director will have a better idea of who that camper is and how he or she will fit into the camp setting.

However, many camp directors are not able to interview every new camper, and thus it is most important to carefully prepare a plan for the orientation of campers. The first step is to mail confirmation of enrollment and receipt of the deposit with a welcome letter, indicating pleasure that the camper is coming to camp and when he or she might expect further information.

An information packet is usually sent to the camper and his or her parents at least two months before the camper arrives at camp. A number of items could be included in this packet.

- A sample clothing list should indicate the type and amounts of clothing needed. If special equipment, such as boots, riding gear, or a sleeping bag, is needed, specifications or details should be given about the type needed and potential sources for purchase.

  Information should be given about the appropriate marking of all possessions with the camper's name to assist in lost-and-found problems.

  Any restrictions about personal items such as radios, cell phones, knives, pets, or guns should be spelled out.

- Information about laundry should include whether the camp will arrange for service, whether the camper washes his or her own clothes, or whether quantities of apparel suggested are usually ample for the length of the camp session.

- Health examination information, including a form requesting information the parent needs to provide for a health history, should be included. If an examination is required, the form should specify information the physician needs to furnish, maximum length of time allowed between examination and camp opening, inoculations required, and health care available at camp. See illustrations 11.2 and 11.3 for samples of health forms. Special attention should be paid to ensure the health examination form is mailed early enough for parents to arrange for an appointment with the physician. The form should be explicit about the information needed in addition to the health examination, such as:

- Health history information — allergies, operations, previous illnesses, inoculations, disabilities.
- Medications that the camper is taking currently or was taking immediately prior to coming to camp along with written instructions from the doctor.
- A release signed by parents or guardians enabling the camp to provide a minor with routine health care and prescribed medications and to seek emergency medical treatment. Some hospitals now require notarized signatures.
- Health insurance information (if the parent's insurance is expected to cover any incidents at camp).
- Emergency addresses and phone numbers of parents or guardians.
- Any limitations on activity participation or living situation and any necessary medical attention.
- Information regarding transportation to camp. Will parents be expected to transport camper to camp? If group transportation is provided, list the times, fares, etc. If arriving campers can be met at air, train, or bus terminals, explain the procedure and any charges. For day camps, a schedule and times of the pickup and drop points for campers should be provided, as well as a plan for emergency arrangements.
- Visiting days, or times, if any.
- Information on the camp's mailing address; the use of fax, e-mail, or telephone for making or receiving communications; and the handling of mail and packages containing food items for campers.
- Information concerning religious services at camp and availability of services out of camp, especially if the family wishes child to attend special services.
- In day camps, an explanation of the plan for daily lunch, including what is to be brought by the camper and what is to be furnished by the camp.
- In day camps, if there is to be an overnight offered during the period, the plan and preparation for it.

When the majority of campers come from the same population center, a camp may have an orientation session or open house during April or May to answer any questions from campers and parents and to prepare new campers for their first year at camp. This session may include introduction of staff, slides or movies, and comments on what to bring to camp. It will also provide a chance for campers of the same age groups to get acquainted and for parents to gain a better understanding of the camp organization and policies.

Groups

Preparation of individuals who are coming as part of rental or program groups is no less important, but it does not require the same direct contact with the individuals since the group leader or organization has that responsibility. Since the information goes through that second party, it is even more important that the information be thoroughly and clearly written and mailed early with the confirmation of the reservation. Such an information packet could include the following items.

- A map of the camp property, as well as directions on how to get there
- A description of the sleeping accommodations and what bedding is furnished
- Rules and regulations that affect the activities and behavior of the group (e.g., alcohol, radios, firearms, drugs, skateboards)
- What health care, if any, will be available
- The camp telephone number for emergency purposes
- If the camp is responsible for any specialized programs, information about clothing or equipment that participants are expected to bring

When preparing the material indicated above, the director should assume that the persons reading it will know nothing about camp. The words and information should be checked for clarity. Every opportunity should be taken in the material to emphasize the potential fun, excitement, and value of the experience.

CHECKPOINTS

1. Identify your camp's participant population and describe efforts made to provide diversity in that population.
2. Review the developmental characteristics of the age group(s) served by your camp and devise a method of sharing these with the camp staff during precamp training.
3. In the precamp training schedule, outline how and where appropriate growth and development, as well as problematic behaviors, of campers is covered.
4. Examine the camp program and schedule in light of preventing unnecessary stress in the lives of campers.
5. Identify everything a new camper needs to know about camp before his or her arrival.
6. Organize, in chronological order, the steps parents of campers need to take before camp.
7. Identify what you would need to know and do as a leader of a group that is being brought to your camp for the first time.
8. Check your written materials to make sure they reflect the information in checkpoints 5, 6, and 7.

Related Standards

Accreditation Standards for Camp Programs and Services: OM-11E, 12, 19, 20, 21; PD-5, 8; SF-31–32; HW-6, 7, 8; "Additional Professional Practices": Items 9, 16, 17, 23, 27

Standards for Conference and Retreat Centers: II-1, II-6–4, II-19, II-20, III-21, 22, 23, 25

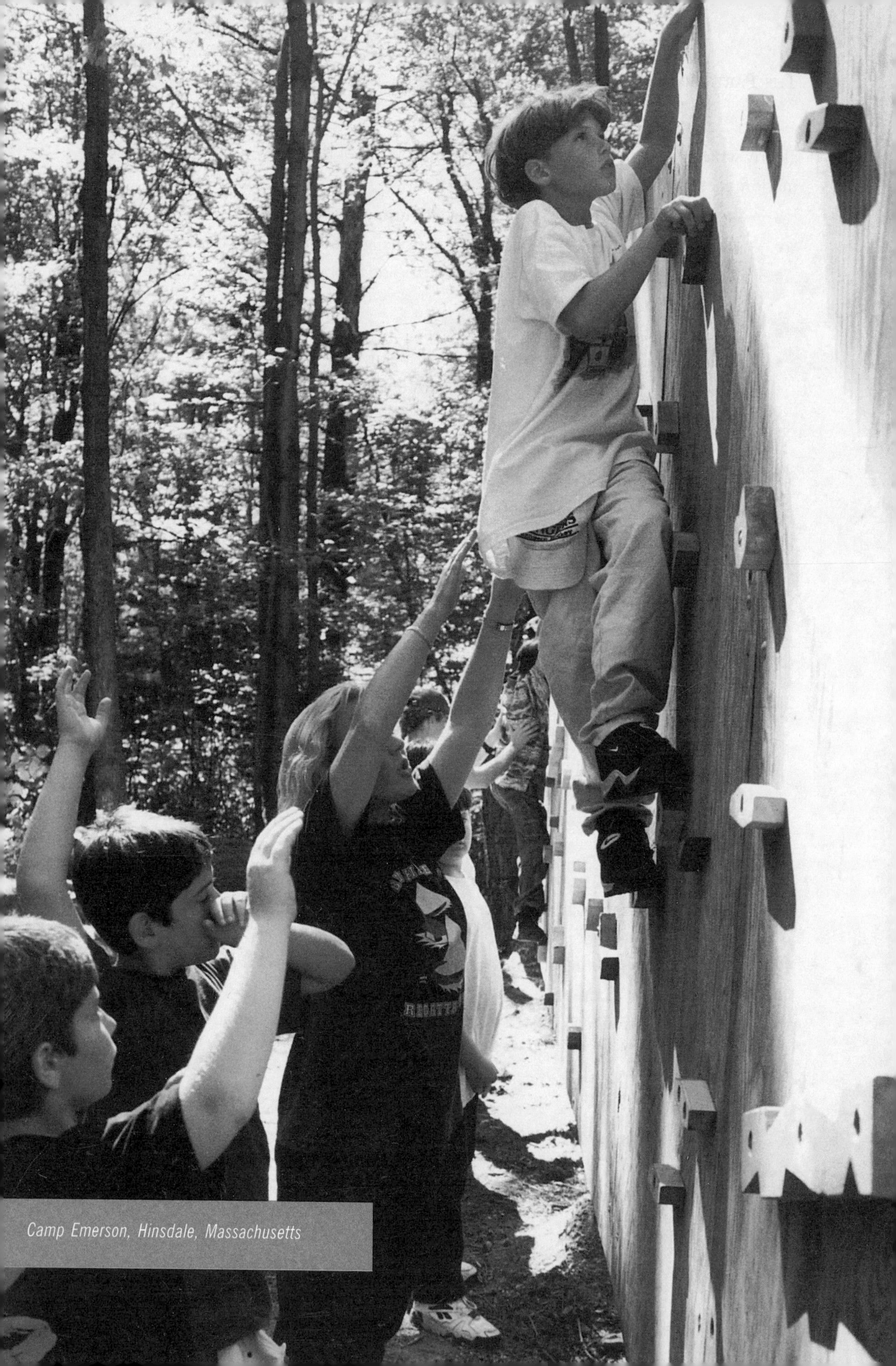

Camp Emerson, Hinsdale, Massachusetts

5

Designing the Program

And at each day's end a child should surely have experience with a small fire — sit close to it, tend it, feel its warmth and the warmth and security of her or his close-knit small family group gathered round; and in the wonder and magic of firelight be able to talk, in the semidarkness, of the problems that bother — begin to form attitudes, think out values, grapple for the ends for which he or she might live -— begin to put together the fragmented pieces of learning toward becoming a whole person.[1]

Program is, as we have already suggested, only a tool which grows out of the camp's philosophy, mission/purpose, and goals. To develop program activities without goals and youth development outcomes in mind is simply to provide a potpourri of activities, many of which may be just as easily available in the camper's home setting. Program is not just the activities, it is "all activities, conditions, and relationships that affect the camper: the planned activities as well as the unplanned; the subtle conditions that surround him as well as the more obvious conditions; the relationships that he has with other campers and with counselors; the counselor's attitudes toward him as well as the methods the counselor uses."[2]

If program is everything that happens in camp, it cannot be covered in this one chapter. But it is touched upon in many aspects of the living experience that are discussed from chapter to chapter: eating, sleeping, health care, staff, transportation, the camp setting, and, of course, activities.

In smaller camps, the director may give immediate supervision to the coordination of program activities; but, as the number of campers and the complexities of camp operations grow, the director will have to secure assistance or delegate this primary responsibility to a program director or coordinator. It is important that the ongoing responsibility be assumed by one individual so that the evaluation of the entire program rests with a single individual. That person needs a clear understanding of the camp's goals and

[1]Lois Goodrich. "A Time for Discovery." *Camping Magazine* Vol. 52, No.1, September 1979. p. 16.
[2]Hedley S. Dimock. 1948. *Administration of the Modern Camp.* New York: Association Press (Y.M.C.A. of the U.S.A.). p. 123.

desired outcomes, of the background of the target population, and of the age groups in camp, as well as the ability to maintain a working relationship with the staff. Regardless of the size of the camp, the director can never completely delegate supervision of the program.

The camp director and the program director must share a cohesive and collaborative approach to all of the elements of camp life to make the experience fruitful and monitor the camp's progress toward meeting its goals, and outcomes/objectives.

With the expansion of a summer youth camp into a year-round operation, the program may be different depending on the purpose of the expansion and any new target population. Therefore, this chapter has been subdivided to discuss not only the summer-camp approach, but some of the other types of programs and groups that may use a site in other seasons.

STEPS OF PROGRAM DEVELOPMENT

. There is a temptation to begin program development simply by determining the activities you want to offer. However, there are eleven steps in program development as shown in illustration 5.1. The first step in the development of program is to go back to the camp's *philosophy*, mission/purpose, and goals to identify one or more target populations or customer groups. Only with these clearly in mind is it safe to proceed in the planning process. Information gained in the program planning process may lead to the revision of the camp's philosophy or mission statement. When this happens it will be a conscious revision or change in direction.

The second step is to *assess your customers' interests* and developmental needs. This is a multifaceted assessment since, even if the camp serves solely youth, the parent and the camper are both customers, often with differing viewpoints. Many camps serve not only youth, but also adults, rental groups, and schools, as well as special populations within age groups, further necessitating an examination of each group's expectations and needs. Such assessments may take the form of questionnaires, individual interviews, or focus-type group interviews. Questions should be formulated carefully to avoid bias on the part of the author or interviewer, as well as to provide the type of information desired.

The third step, once the assessments are compiled, is to *review the camp's desired outcomes* to see if these are compatible with the needs and interests of the customers. In other words, can you really develop a program that will meet the interests and needs of your potential customers and also meet the camp's goals and outcomes? If not, this necessitates a reassessment of either the audience served or the mission, goals, and outcomes. There must be some alignment of these factors to expect the camp to be financially viable, and also have community support.

The fourth step is to *identify potential program activities* that will attract your custom-

5.1 Illustration *Steps to Program Development*

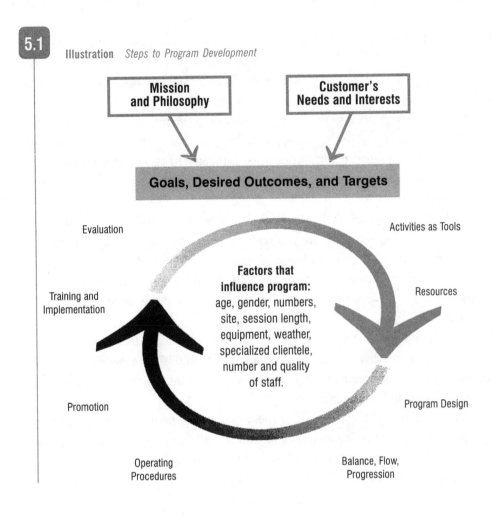

ers, pique their interest, contribute to their developmental needs, and help accomplish your desired outcomes.

The fifth step is an *appraisal of the camp's resources*, including the environment in which the program is to take place. A careful look, not only at facilities but at the natural environment, will be useful in appraising whether the type of program planned will fit in the environment. Will the program be inappropriate or counter-productive in the natural environment? Does the program take advantage of the natural resources at hand? What about staff? Can persons with the expertise and leadership skills required for this particular program be found? What about fiscal resources to initiate the program? What are the start-up costs? What is the cost effectiveness of the program?

The sixth step relates to *program design* and includes how the total camp experience is organized to fit together. See the following section for the overall program design.

Once the resources are appraised and activities identified, the director and key staff should begin the seventh step, the *refinement* of the specific program, outcomes, and activities. An effort should be made to create a balance between small-group and total-group activities, active and quiet times, and structured and informal times. In addition, the program should be age appropriate and provide progression during the session and from year to year. Progression will add to a camper's opportunity for challenge and success.

Operating procedures need to be determined for each program activity in the eighth step. Further emphasis is given to this process later in this chapter. Such procedures include eligibility requirements for participants, camper/staff ratios, appropriate equipment, safety regulations, emergency procedures, and the qualification of the staff supervising the activity.

Only when the program is clearly defined and outlined, and fiscal resources are committed to its accomplishment, are you ready to begin the ninth step, *promoting* it to prospective customers. A dry run with a small group of prospective customers is a good idea prior to broadly promoting the program. This information not only excites the potential participant but informs parents and/or organizations of the nature of the anticipated activities.

Having secured the customers and determined the staff needed, the next step is *training the staff* in the delivery of the program to accomplish the desired outcomes. Implementation of the program follows. Generally, participant training is integrated into the program design and implementation.

Both during and at the conclusion of the program, the final step should be implemented, that of *evaluation*. This process will lead to setting new goals, targets, and desired outcomes to improve the program before it is conducted another time. Evaluation is discussed in a later chapter.

PROGRAM DESIGN

After completing the first five steps, the director must begin designing the program to meet predetermined outcomes. The first part of this process is to make decisions about how program activities will be planned by individuals, by living groups, by staff, or by the central administration and whether the living group will carry out the activities or individuals will move into other groups for activities.

Historically, two different philosophies, *centralized* and *decentralized*, have evolved in camp programs. Under a *centralized* program philosophy, activities are carried out so that each individual camper may participate in activities with a variety of campers. These activities may be scheduled by one or more staff persons or by staff in collaboration with a camper council. By taking part in activity selection and scheduling, a camper learns to take responsibility for his or her decisions. The living group is usually a focus only for special events, sleeping, and sometimes eating. The emphasis in this type of camp tends to be on developing individual skills, as well as participating in occasional all-camp activities or unit activities.

When registering for or arriving at a camp with a centralized program, individual campers (or their parents) may sign up for specialized instruction sessions. Depending on the length of the sessions, it may be possible to change to other activities at various points in the camp session. Campers generally move from one level of instruction to another as the camper gains skills.

On the other hand, under a *decentralized* program philosophy, campers participate in activities with their living group, using a group work process. The group work process is a social work method which places its emphasis on "helping individuals to enhance their social functioning through purposeful group experiences and to cope more effectively with their personal, group or community problems."[3] The group work process began in the early part of the twentieth century as the basis of program in clubs, troops, and in settlement houses throughout the United States and found a natural home in many camps.

The group performs the planning function for their program. The group joins the larger camp community only for special events, common meals, and/or primary services such as health or acquisition of supplies. The emphasis here tends to be on the group relationships and on developing independence from the larger camp community, even to the preparation of certain meals. In this design, most scheduling is done within the living group. The central program personnel are consulted particularly as scheduling affects the use of central facilities or staff, or as the plan of one living group impinges on another.

In the original format as developed by Dr. L. B. Sharpe of Life Camp in New Jersey, a decentralized experience would consist of a living group which constructs its own camp site complete with cooking and toilet areas and shelters. The group would plan its own daily activities and prepare its own meals.

In reality, most camps do not operate a pure centralized or decentralized program. Naturally, it is possible to combine the two philosophies. In many camps, the camper's day is a combination of centralized and decentralized activities. This pattern can move along a continuum between centralized and decentralized. Where a camp's program design fits along this continuum should grow out of an analysis of the first five steps of program development: (step1) the philosophy and goals of the camp; (step 2) interest of campers; (step 3) desired outcomes; (step 4) program activities; and (step 5) facilities and staff of the camp. Illustration 5.2 identifies a variety of organizations' designs ranging from the pure centralized to pure decentralized.

Finding the camp's position along this philosophical continuum takes thought and experience. The place to begin is with the camp's stated goals and outcomes, the camp director's leadership style, the facility, and type of staff the camp has. In looking at these elements together, it is possible to examine several different ways of using the philosophies and to see which one can possibly meet the goals in the most effective manner.

---

[3]Giesla Konopka. 1963. *Social Group Work: A Helping Process.* Englewood Cliffs, NJ: Prentice-Hall. p. 20.

5.2   Illustration *Organizational Designs*

ORGANIZATIONAL DESIGN	CENTRALIZED	CENTRALIZED	COMBINATION	DECENTRALIZED	DECENTRALIZED
Camper/Staff Organization	as a whole camp	as a whole camp	half day as a whole camp and half day by unit or living groups	as units or cabin groups	as units or cabin groups
Program	designed and scheduled for individuals	individual choice by age or skill level	half day by individual choice and half day by living groups	planned and scheduled by staff for groups	planned and scheduled by small groups
Activities	specialized, standardized, familiar, skill development	specialized, individual skill development and options	specialized skill development half day and group activities half day	specialized, standardized, skill development as small groups	general guidelines, creative, group interaction
Motivation	individual competition, awards and rewards	competition is individual's choice, awards and rewards	individual skill improvement and group decision making and involvement	group competition or teambuilding, awards and rewards	group decision making, involvement, awards and rewards
Leadership	primarily specialists with counselors assisting	primarily specialists with counselors assisting	half day with specialists and half day with generalists	primarily generalists with some certified specialists	primarily generalists with some certified specialists
Evaluation	individual skill progress measured	individual popularity and quality of program areas measured	individual skill progress and quality of group interaction	quality of group interaction, some skill progress measured	quality of group interaction, some skill progress measured

With experimentation from summer to summer, one can soon reach the philosophy that seems to be most effective in that particular camp.

The program philosophy will naturally affect staff recruitment, organization, and design. Consider the following:

- Program specialists are most often the primary focus of the day's activities in a centralized program, while counselors are the primary focus in a decentralized program.
- Authority for program scheduling and supervision lies with program and administrative staff in a more centralized philosophy, whereas it resides with the living-group counselor and unit leader in a decentralized approach.
- The program specialists are more likely to determine program content and the schedule in a centralized design. Campers are often assigned program activity times by age or skill level, or program counselors may assist campers in selecting their activities and determining their individual schedule.

- When the living group is used as the basis of programming, program specialists need to be prepared to have campers with a variety of skill levels and ages participating at the same time.

Therefore, the more a camp program leans toward a centralized structure, the more important it is to employ persons with competence in specific skill areas and with good instructional abilities. Obviously, each instructor must know how to teach children and should have enough child psychology training to understand the tasks suitable for various developmental stages of children. A staff member with experience and skill in a program does not necessarily have the ability to teach that skill or apply it at the readiness level of different ages of children.

In a centralized program, program specialists often live in a camper living unit as a secondary counselor but usually do not assume the chief responsibilities of a counselor. On the other hand, the counselor in a living unit usually also assumes responsibility for assisting in a specific program area, since only a few hours of the day are spent in direct living-group activities.

A decentralized program requires counselors to have more general skills in a variety of program areas, since the primary authority for daily planning and scheduling lies within their group. Depending upon the degree of decentralization, counselors will need greater maturity and experience since they will be supervising campers nearly twenty-four hours a day. Under a decentralized program, there are usually fewer program specialists, and those are usually required to hold certifications. They may be available to lead activities for individual living groups at a group's request.

The location of living areas and physical facilities will influence a camp's ability to operate fully on either a centralized or decentralized basis. Though it is possible to make certain adjustments, the physical layout of the camp does have to be considered early in program planning. For example, a dormitory arrangement which has several camper groups occupying the same building makes it somewhat difficult to operate a truly decentralized program.

ELEMENTS OF PROGRAM ORGANIZATION

Program organization is essential whether the camp is decentralized, centralized, or some combination thereof. The schedule is one means of organizing the program, and enables the camp to use a variety of elements in its development. Scheduling and organization relate directly to the camp's program design. Many new directors and staff are more comfortable with a more structured centralized program. They know the schedule and where everyone is at all times. The same comfort level can be achieved with an unstructured decentralized program. In the process of developing the schedule, the director should look at many elements. The sample schedule in illustration 5.3 shows these different program schedules.

5.3   Illustration   *Sample Schedule of Centralized/Decentralized/Combination Programs*

CENTRALIZED	DECENTRALIZED	COMBINATION

7:30 am   Arise
8:00 am   Flag raising
8:15 am   Breakfast
            Cabin cleanup
9:30 am   Activity Period 1
10:45 am Activity Period 2
12:30 pm Lunch
            Rest period
2:15 pm   Activity Period 3
3:30 pm   Activity Period 4
4:45 pm   Open swim
            Other activities
6:00 pm   Dinner
7:00 pm   Free time
8:00 pm   Evening program
9:30 pm   Taps
	8:00 am Breakfast
	
	Activities that have been planned by
	living groups, which may include
	cabin cleanup, some program
	activity and lunch as a group or in
	central dining hall; some restful
	activity and time
	
	12:30 pm Lunch
	            Rest period
	
	Activities planned by living groups
	
	6:00 pm Dinner
	
	Activities in living groups or units;
	occasional all-camp activity
		7:30 am Arise
		8:00 am Breakfast
		            Cabin cleanup
		9:00 am Individual choice
		            of activities for
		            one-hour period
		10:00 am Same as above
		11:00 am Same as above
		12:30 pm Lunch
		            Rest period
		2:15 pm Activities planned
		            by living groups
		6:00 pm Dinner
		7:00 pm Free time
		8:00 pm All-camp planned
		            evening program or
		            living group activity
		9:30 pm Taps

Many new directors and staff are more comfortable with a structured program. They know the schedule and where everyone is at all times. The same comfort level can be achieved with an unstructured program. Campers, as individuals (centralized) or groups (decentralized), may sign up for activities at the beginning of a session, week or day and then a schedule is made so staff and campers know what activities they are participating in and how many will be there for that period.

The Living Group

In a decentralized program, the living group is the principal structure for the accomplishment of program. The only interaction with the total camp may be during meals and special activities or all-camp events. Even the all-camp events can be designed for participation by living groups.

In decentralized design, a living group and their counselor may tour camp and discuss program possibilities and then plan a schedule for their group. This schedule can be negotiated with other staff so that the things that require a specialist or a given number of campers at a time can be scheduled. A master schedule is created for coordination purposes. In some camps, groups may change their schedule based on "being considerate of others." For example, if they have told the cook they are cooking out on Tuesday night, it would be hard for the cook to count on having enough food if they changed their mind at the last minute. If they decide to work quietly on a craft in their cabin during their rest hour it probably won't affect another group, unless they are using all the scissors. A unit or living group may have a basic supply of tools and supplies so they are able to be more self-sufficient.

If the group doesn't plan their program until the morning or afternoon they expect to participate, they may then take their chances on getting a space. For example, only two groups can be at archery at a time since there are only twenty bows. A good comparison of this is a family on vacation; they may reserve a space at a popular tourist attraction before they leave home to make sure they have the space they wish.

In a centralized program, there is a place for the living group to have time to do things together, whether it is simply meals, cabin cleanup, bedtime chats, or specific activity period designated daily. Some camps use the living group in competitions with other living groups, whether in sports or other contests. However, too much competition at this level can be counterproductive to the real goals of group living.

The Individual

In centralized camps, the individual is given a choice of activities in set periods both morning and afternoon, and the program is tailored to that person's interests, skill level, and expressed needs. Choices are usually limited by eligibility requirements for certain activities, including a requirement that the camper stick with the activity for a minimum number of days. The camper is assigned a set of activities and given a schedule. In most cases, these are very skill-oriented camps, and there is an expectation of some degree of mastery in the skill or subject (e.g., some sports camps, science camps, performing arts camps, weight loss camps, or scuba camps, etc.).

Even in a camp where the camper has chosen specific activities in which to participate, there is an anticipation of improvement in the skill(s). In some less structured situations, older campers may be allowed to decide what they want to do in each time period and just show up. These campers may be limited by other factors. For example, if all the horses are taken for the ten o'clock trail ride for beginners, these campers will need to go to another activity and come back at another time.

In any program design, there should be opportunities for individuals to have some free time and to be able to do some things on their own. A camper may wish to spend time on a specific craft project or fish off the bank of the lake or simply lie on the hillside and watch the clouds or visit with friends.

Free time is, however, the time when the greatest number of accidents or incidents occur and should not mean unsupervised time. Campers should know where they can and cannot go. Staff should be stationed in program areas to assist and to be available where campers gather in case of a problem. Such a period should be followed by a meal or enrolled activity so that counselors can check their groups for the wanderer or lost child.

Interest Groups

There are advantages in having several living groups join together in a common interest for a given period. In some camps, participation in a joint activity is based upon skill as well as interest; for example, campers who have achieved a given skill level in canoeing can choose to go on a canoe trip. In other situations, it may be interest in a given project, such as an archaeology dig, or the building of a footbridge across a small creek that draws groups together. In another example, a camper council with representatives from various age or living groups may be formed for planning an evening program, recommending changes in the camp, or evaluating a project. The camp's ability to be flexible and provide staff support where needed can make interest groups an exciting dimension of camp life. This may also be an opportunity to combine centralized and decentralized structures for a period of the day, the length of a project, or for a special trip.

Some camps organize sessions by interest groups or by special theme; for example, the third session may be a "Western" theme and feature more activities and instruction time within the riding program. The camp may have an "international week" where activities or all-camp programs feature cultural experiences from the countries represented by their international staff. Session themes are promoted in camp brochures so that campers who are really interested in a theme may choose to attend a particular session.

Instruction

It is very common for camps to offer skill classes and for campers to move in and out of those classes as they achieve a certain level. For instance, swimming instruction is typically organized in this fashion. In a decentralized program, individuals from a living group may all attend swimming at one time, but once at the site, divide up by skill levels. In this design the plan and convenience of the group is more important to meeting the outcomes than having the schedule revolve around the activity specialists. In a centralized program, campers are normally assigned or sign up by the level of skill revealed in a test or an evaluation of their previous experience (e.g., a swimming test).

The Unit or Section

Several living groups usually form a unit or section in a camp. Often, evening programs are planned by the unit for all the living groups included, or one meal is cooked out daily within the unit. This works best where the living groups in a unit consist of campers of the same age range and maturity level.

All-Camp Activities

The enthusiasm generated by a well-planned all-camp event is not easily matched by any other type activity. This type of event can be more spectacular or exciting than a small-group activity, and often gives campers an opportunity to perform before others, as with a drama group presentation or a carnival where each living group designs a booth and takes turns leading the activity in their booth. All-camp activities often involve decorations or dressing up for the event.

Some long-term camps operate two or three days of all-camp activities around a theme near the end of the season. Some events may involve individual participation, while others involve living groups or units.

The wealth of program ideas usually generated by staff and campers may well replace a manual of operation. However, the perusal by staff members of various program resource books during staff training and throughout the summer can often provide the stimulus needed for staff and campers to generate variations or new ideas.

Bus Program

In day camps, campers are often transported daily by bus or van to the camp location. Resident camps, trip camps, and special field trips often involve transportation by bus, van, train, or boat. The time on the bus should be used as part of the program structure. Staff, other than the driver, should be aboard to give leadership and supervision. This is a period when new campers' anxiety can build or boisterousness can get out of hand. Some activities may be individual in nature, while others may be grouped by sections of the bus. Singing can provide an outlet as well as a group spirit-building exercise. The balance of maintaining enthusiasm and variety without distracting the driver will prove a challenge.

PACING/FLOW

The pacing of the day's activities is as important as the activities and structure. There should be plenty of physical activity to meet the energy and exertion needs of most children. On the other hand, there should also be time for quiet, relaxation, rest, and individual initiative. A midday break should be planned during which participants and staff can catch their breath by lying down, sitting on their bunks or under a tree, reading, or writing letters. The camper's age will dictate the logical approach for this break and its supervision. Younger children may need more regimentation or routine to get them to bed for rest; but once there, their bodies generally take over if the morning has been an active one. Teenagers will benefit from a more flexible approach; and of course, adults need this sort of flextime, too.

Varying the scheduled activities with those in which the camper has some choice, as well as varying living-group activities with instructional activities, provides more interest for the camper.

In a resident camp, evening also affords an opportunity for activities paced differently from those during the day. Evening activities are often broadened to include the unit or other portions of camp, if the day's activities have been in small groups. In camps where daily activities take place outside the living group, a more specialized evening can provide an opportunity for living-unit activities. Such activities should be paced so that the more physical or boisterous activity takes place earlier in the evening; a general slowdown in activity and noise level close to bedtime will help the counselor to quiet the living group for sleep in the resident camp.

PROGRAM EMPHASES IN THE SUMMER CAMP

A growing trend has been for some camps to focus their entire program or certain sessions on a narrow range of activities, which is then used as a marketing tool. This emphasis has ranged from overall sports to specific sports, such as basketball, golf, tennis, gymnastics, and from foreign languages to music, scuba, and canoeing. The appeal has often been to the consumer's interests as stimulated by schools or commercial sports and/or the customer's concern for his or her development of certain skills.

On the other hand, the majority of camps continue to offer a general program with a variety of program activities as well as a number of all-camp or all-unit activities. Many general program camps do provide more expertise and experience in certain activities than in others, e.g., providing a general program for younger campers and specialties for older campers. Often times, the geographic setting of the camp lends itself to certain specialties, e.g., mountain climbing, sea kayaking, lake sailing, and river canoeing. To argue that specialized or general programs are better or worse is a doubtful exercise, since the value of any camp experience is far more dependent upon the camp leadership and upon the rationale for the program design than it is on the specific activities.

Staff in the specialized camp or unit should be careful not to overemphasize skills in one sport or area at too early an age, or the child's experience will be too narrow. Even in a camp specializing in one area, there should be opportunities for other activities and experiences. More general program camps must recognize that to attract older campers a greater challenge in skill development and/or adventurous activity is needed. Similarly, in specialized programs, a staff member striving for greater experience and expertise should not be allowed to overshadow his or her overall counseling role. Although every staff member need not be a living-unit counselor in every camp, every staff member should have concern for the camper and be willing to deal with the needs and welfare of each individual.

Progression in Programming

In any camp program there needs to be an examination of the age groupings served to determine their human development and readiness level for certain experiences. The same program design and activities may not meet the needs of an eight-year-old and a seventeen-year-old. If there is not age-appropriate program design, there may be few returning campers at one end of the age spectrum or the other.

There has been a growth in the number of camps, especially day camps, that serve younger and younger campers. Almost simultaneously, as a marketing tool, camps have tended to expand their variety of program activity offerings. Unless there is careful program planning, this expansion can lead to campers perceiving that by age eleven or twelve, they have experienced everything that camp has to offer.

Developing outcomes/objectives for different age ranges based upon developmental needs and readiness can provide youth with a different experience at camp each year of his or her life right on through high school. This process requires enough study of human development to understand the social and coordination readiness of each age group. The camp manual should include a plan outlining developmental characteristics and needs for each age group. Identified for each age group should be each program activity and the emphasis corresponding with those age characteristics and needs (i.e., what five-year-olds do in swimming instruction should be very different than what fifteen-year-olds do even if neither knows how to swim). Not recognizing the age-appropriate program could mean the challenge and excitement of participating could turn to embarrassment and an unwillingness to try. Staff training should emphasize those differences and the philosophy of age-appropriate program progression.

Group Living

The day-to-day living experience should be as carefully considered as the scheduled activities. The interaction between campers, as well as between camper and staff in the living setting, is influenced directly by age-specific developmental characteristics and needs as is participation in activity skills. Especially in the resident camp setting, more actual hours of the day will be spent in living activities, such as eating, sleeping, and congregating in the living area, than in planned activities. In the day camp, certainly a significant part of the day is spent being transported to and from camp, moving from activity to activity, and gathering during lunch and rest periods.

It is critical that the leadership assigned to supervision of the living group during these times be as sensitive and mature as the leadership in charge of activity periods. Day-to-day activities present some of the most important teachable moments — when the right words, the tone of voice, the intervention or the nonintervention, a smile, or an arm around the shoulder, can make all the difference to an individual or group. These moments cannot be programmed, but staff can be educated and sensitized in the process of staff training and supervision to watch for and take advantage of them.

Mealtimes should be designed to reinforce camp goals and desired outcomes and to offer a learning and social experience. Providing this opportunity requires thought concerning the shape and size of dining tables, how table groups are formed, the way food is served, the role staff should play at the table, whether everyone comes and goes from the dining hall at the same time, and the agenda before and after meal service. Mealtimes, even breakfast, can easily become the high points of the day to campers and staff alike. Many camps use them as a time for singing, with program staff or counselors alternating as song leader. During this time tables and food can be cleared before campers are excused. This activity offers a wonderful opportunity to promote camp spirit with the singing of current and traditional camp songs.

Mealtime programming is as important in a day camp setting with sack lunches as it is in the largest resident camp with multiple dining rooms. The principles and opportunities are the same. To a large degree, this is also as true for the youngest child and the oldest adult participant.

For children, the use of the toilet/bath facility may be one of their first exposures to group use of such facilities. In any case, this is another area in which the living-group leader provides not only supervision, but also leadership in attitudes, language, sensitivity, and privacy. Responsibility for one's surroundings is taught in the care of facilities such as the toilet/bathhouse and the sleeping areas in a resident camp.

PROGRAM DESIGN BEYOND SUMMER

More and more camps are offering short-term program events beyond the summer. Such events for youth, by the nature of the school week, tend to be on weekends or during holiday periods. During the week a camp might work with one or more school systems to provide outdoor education opportunities for students. Being short term in nature does not lessen the attention that needs to be given to programming, planning, and staffing. In some ways, they are more important, for the camp has less time to reach its goals. The same steps in program development need to be applied in the planning process.

Certainly, the basic outcomes for a short-term experience need to be within reach for the time allotted. Therefore, outcomes need to be succinct, as well as clearly communicated to participants and staff. The experience provided by peer relationships, mealtimes, and nonscheduled activity is as important here as it is in the longer-term experience in the summer.

Nonsummer events for adults vary from weekend programs to week-long programs. The care and attention given to adult programming should be no less than that given to youth. Though it may require less staff, it requires no less development of goals and outcomes, and no less planning based upon the needs, interests, and human development characteristics of the particular age group being served. In fact, since many camp directors and staff are more experienced in working with children, it may require more time in the initial preparation and planning.

Providing outdoor or environmental education programs for schools allows the camp to share responsibilities with the classroom teachers involved. The development of the program will require teamwork and cooperative planning, but should use the staff and resources of the camp where it is strongest. Many camps have personnel with education and experience in environmental education beyond that of classroom teachers. Working to make those personnel available to classroom groups is an opportunity to expand the camp's services and impact more children.

In this conjunction, many camps have developed adventure and challenge courses which have added an exciting new educational dimension to the camp setting. However, these courses require careful construction after consultation with outside experts, and also need carefully trained leadership who can demonstrate both the skills and safety needed. There should be no assumption that a low ropes course will need any less capable leadership and safety precautions than a high course or a rappelling program. In a number of camps, these courses have opened the door to serving youth-at-risk and adjudicated youth. This exciting expansion provides service to a population that can greatly benefit from the camp experience. However, it requires careful planning and demands a mature and experienced staff to make it effective.

Many camps provide facilities and/or program activities for rental groups as their principal clientele in the nonsummer weeks. These camps are designed to be used by an organization's local group(s) year-round, or by other groups during the nonsummer months. If this use is one of the camp's principal goals, then its outcomes/objectives should be developed accordingly, following the program development steps. In this process, the camp becomes an enabling device to help others accomplish their goals. This requires a service-oriented staff and program philosophy; it should not be viewed as simply another source of income.

In this type of program, facilities become the primary focus and should be developed to meet the needs of the user groups. The assessment process is critical before expending considerable sums in facility improvement or development.

SPECIALIZED CLIENTELE

Many camps have been designed specifically to meet the needs of special populations while other camps use only part of their season to serve a special population or may mainstream special populations into regular program groups. Such clientele often have special physical or programmatic needs, and grouping with others who have similar special needs may provide a more comfortable environment for their first camp experience. Such groups include senior adults and youth-at-risk, as well as persons with similar physical conditions or disabilities (e.g., asthma, diabetes, cancer) or persons who have restricted mobility (e.g., persons who use wheelchairs or do not have sight). Some camps work in partnership with a hospital or organization that serves a particular special population and is willing to send medical personnel to camp with their clients.

For some years, there has been a growing effort by many camps to mainstream persons from certain special populations into the rest of the camp community wherever the particular difference does not prevent participation in the camp's activities or where facilities or special staff are not necessary. The passage of the Americans With Disabilities Act in 1990 underlines the greater obligation on the part of camps to accommodate individuals with disabilities. It dictates that any camp, except a religious camp which serves religious groups, may not exclude such individuals from camp program on the basis of a disability alone. Note: religious camps which serve the public, e.g., public schools, scouts, or other organizations, are not exempt from the ADA.

The entire camp community can gain greater sensitivity and learning from such integration, if there is a readiness on the part of all participants and careful planning. As Bedini, Bialeschki, and Henderson state in a *Camping Magazine* article: "People with disabilities often are overprotected by society, separated from others and given few participation options. Camp is a place where they could become fully functioning members of a community . . . . By integrating camp programs, camps will gain the opportunity to celebrate diversity and show how each individual, regardless of ability or disability, has something to contribute to the group's outdoor living experience."[4] To include the camper with a disability does not demand the elimination of any overall set of camp activities; this principle has been demonstrated again and again by creative and determined individuals who have adapted almost all possible activities in the camp setting.

The critical element in serving a special population is that the camp administration has researched any special needs and characteristics before agreeing to serve that special population. To quote *Camp Director's Primer*: "In a resident or day camp, the issue of program accessibility is of equal or greater importance as the issue of site accessibility. For a camper with a disability to be successful in an integrated program, careful planning is critical to every aspect of the camp operation."[5]

Staff will need additional training and understanding of any particular special population served. There may need to be additional medical staff, special menu considerations, or facility modification. The director of a camp seeking to serve a special population must be careful not to assume that certain things cannot be done, but rather must approach program with an enabling attitude and seek possible alternatives where the traditional approach does not work.

The *Camp Director's Primer* suggests that, in planning for the participation of the camper with a disability in the camp program, there are several guidelines which can be readily followed. One, adapt only on an individual basis. The program goal is to keep the camper's experience as realistic as possible; it is best not to automatically assume that a particular condition means problems with an activity. Consultation with the camper or his or her parents will highlight specific difficulties which need to be overcome in order to get him or her involved. Two, adapt only as much as is necessary. If unnecessary changes in the activity are made to accommodate the camper with a disability, he or she will stand out from his or her peers.

---

[4] Leandra A. Bedini, M. Deborah Bialeschki, and Karla A. Henderson. "The Americans With Disabilities Act: Implications for Camp Programming." *Camping Magazine* Vol. 60, No. 4, March/April 1992. p. 53.
[5] National Camp Executives Group. 1992. *Camp Director's Primer to the Americans With Disabilities Act of 1990.* Glen Allen, VA: Markel Insurance Company. p. 17.

In considering what form these adjustments or accommodations should take, there are three specific areas to be considered:

1. Materials or equipment adaptation. Some campers with disabilities may need special devices to function fully in a particular activity and temporary modifications may be necessary. A camper with little upper body strength may have difficulty with swinging a bat in a softball game (a good substitute is a whiffle ball and bat). Or, a child with paralysis in the lower body may want to wear socks in the pool to prevent abrading his feet on the rough surface of the bottom.

2. Procedural and rule adaptations. Through making minor changes in rules for the individual with a disability, success in participation for all can be achieved. For instance, if the general rule in archery is that each participant retrieves his or her own arrows, a fellow camper may be asked to pick up the arrows for a friend who uses a wheelchair.

3. Skill sequence adaptations. If a particular skill is being taught, it may be easier to adapt the process by breaking the skill down into smaller stages and working on each individual part.

Many of the adjustments to be made are minor and easily accomplished with understanding and a little ingenuity. Since, in the camp community, the accepted goal is to meet the individual needs of each camper, stretching to meet the needs of special children adds to the challenge.[6]

SPECIFIC PROGRAM ACTIVITIES

Camps continue to broaden the variety of activities that can be used in the camp setting. There is virtually no limit to that variety, except in the camp's program philosophy and consideration of what can be done in the camp setting that cannot be done easily in the camper's normal environment. Obviously, the fact that most camps are located in a setting with natural environmental resources would indicate that there is an advantage in using those resources wherever possible and in building on them as the core of the program emphasis.

It is not practical to deal with individual activities in detail in this book, and there is a wide variety of resources for those activities in the resource list in Appendix C. However, here are the general areas of activities that most often occur in camps:

Land Sports and Games

- Team sports: baseball, basketball, football, soccer, softball, lacrosse, volleyball
- Individual sports: archery, badminton, horseback riding, horseshoes, riflery, snowboarding, table tennis, tennis

[6]Ibid., pp. 17–20.

- Informal games: tetherball, all sorts of chase and hunt games that have developed in various camps

Water Sports and Games
- Swimming activities: competitive, instructional, recreational, synchronized, water ballet
- Water activities: fishing, water polo, water slides
- Watercraft activities: canoeing, kayaking, rowing, sailing, sailboarding, waterskiing

Arts
- Performing arts: creative writing, dance, drama, music
- Arts and crafts: ceramics, jewelry, leatherwork, metalcraft, nature crafts, painting, photography, weaving, woodwork

Outdoor-Oriented Activities
- Outdoor living skills: overnights, firebuilding, knot tying, orienteering, outdoor cooking, shelter building, tent pitching (see Appendix I for more information on ACA's Outdoor Living Skills Program)
- Physical skills: backpacking, climbing, canoe tripping, cross-country skiing, hiking, mountaineering, ropes courses, snowshoeing, snow skiing
- Nature-oriented activities: animal lore, astronomy, birdwatching, butterfly catching and releasing, conservation activities, gardening, marine life study, nature hikes, rock collecting and painting, weather predicting
- Vehicular activities: biking, go-carts, flying, miniature race cars

Special Events
All-camp events which use a theme are common in camp settings: Christmas in July, Regatta, Paul Bunyan Days, Circus or Carnival Days, Olympics of all sorts, and Pageants. In general, these sorts of events involve campers and staff in planning, preparation, costumes, and performance. Sometimes, the event is tied into a presentation on a Visitors' Day or a Parents' Weekend or a Fourth of July celebration.

International counselors and campers can often be encouraged to do presentations about their home countries, adding a wider dimension to the world of camp. (If you communicate such requests to international staff prior to their arrival, they can come prepared with a program as well as with items representative of their countries.) Preplanned short skits using staff in amusing ways often contribute to the sense of fun and provide opportunities for sharing.

Social Recreation
These events range from quiet games in the living area to all-camp cookouts or banquets. Games such as charades and skits which require no equipment are a staple of campfires and evening social programs. Singing is an important ingredient of many of

these events, and is often a part of campfires and evening programs. Some camps have dances and other coeducational events.

Spiritually-Oriented Activities

These activities range from nonsectarian vespers, chapel services, or bedtime chats to camps where the religious emphasis is a major focus in the program. In the latter, there may be Bible study groups and religious services daily, as well as a strong emphasis upon religious philosophy in all aspects of the living-group experience. Almost all camps develop certain devices that are used to assist participants in character building and the recognition of the spiritual aspect of life and its integration into the physical, mental, emotional, and social elements. Clarice M. Bowman said it well: "Spiritual values are not just another group of desired outcomes; rather they comprise the core of the constellation of all other values, the pulsating heart of the camping program. Very little may be said about spiritual values in words, but they will be communicated if they are present in the spirit of the leaders, in their motives for being at camp, in their vision of the goals, and in their sensitivity for helping campers have worthy goals of their own that may be achieved by engaging in delightful activities."[7]

OPERATING PROCEDURES FOR PROGRAM

Whatever the activity or program event, there are some specific standards that should be applied in preparation for that event. Part of these standards relate to the concern for risk management (see chapter 10), and all of them grow out of the camp's concern for quality in its operation. The camp's operating procedure for each activity should include the following information:

1. Supervisor and activity leaders' qualifications and skill verification procedures
2. Means for controlled access
3. Appropriate equipment availability
4. Eligibility requirements for participation
5. Camper/staff supervision ratios
6. Identification of appropriate protective equipment
7. Safety regulations
8. Emergency procedures
9. Equipment maintenance procedures
10. Identification of safety concerns related to the use area

Leadership

Leadership is the key to any program activity, and the availability and qualifications of staff for an activity are the first considerations. What skills are essential to making this

---

[7]Clarice M. Bowman. 1954. *Spiritual Values in Camping.* New York: Association Press (Y.M.C.A. of the U.S.A.). pp. 39–40.

a quality experience for campers? Is the activity such that it requires some type of documented training (e.g., Red Cross certification) or completion of a given course? If the activity involves teaching a skill, does the person have the ability to teach? (There is considerable difference between being skilled at an activity and being able to teach that skill to others.) What is the camper/staff ratio?

A camper/staff supervision ratio should be established for each activity since the degree of supervision needed and the risk involved will vary for each activity. In addition to the skills related to the activity, the staff member who is to lead the activity must be trained in the safety regulations established by the camp for the activity. He or she should have the maturity to be able to identify hazards that may be present in the environment of the activity or any situation which might arise. It should be clear to the staff person what safety procedures should be observed in the conduct of the activity and what emergencies could occur and what procedures should be in place to deal with them. The staff member leading the activity (or another who is present) should be trained in first aid or related situations that might arise from an accident or health situation during the activity.

Appropriate Equipment

Appropriate equipment, including protective equipment, for the activity, stocked in adequate numbers, is essential so that there are no lengthy waiting periods or safety hazards created for campers. "Appropriate" indicates that, in some cases, the equipment needs to be sized for the age and size of the camper. To use an adult sized PFD (Personal Flotation Device) for a nine-year-old during a boating activity is dangerous and inappropriate. In some cases, such as for riflery and archery, the equipment will need to be stored in such a manner that it is not accessible except when the leader is present. In all cases, such equipment must be checked regularly and well maintained.

Appropriate Skill Level

Participant age and skill for the given activity dictates the level at which the activity is to be conducted. The eligibility requirements for age and skill should be established initially. If there are a limited number of persons competent to supervise and instruct the activity, there should be a limit to the number who can participate. The latter element will require the establishment of camper to staff ratios that will insure quality time with safety for each camper.

In many cases, the resource materials and certification programs developed by various national organizations will provide the guidance and outline needed. However, there are many activities for which there are no national certification programs. There is resource material on most activities which the director or program director can study and there are various experts who can assist in the development of a written curriculum for instruction and supervision.

Safety and Emergency Procedures

Obviously, when one reviews the variety of program activities available there are differing levels of risks and skill involved. These factors should be considered for each and every program and become part of the risk management program of the camp as outlined in chapter 11.

Safety regulations for each program area need to be established. A more detailed approach would obviously be required for rappelling than for an all-camp campfire. Safety concerns about a given program area should be reviewed at the same time. These regulations and concerns should be addressed during staff training, and put into writing and posted where appropriate.

Emergency procedures relating to certain program areas (such as the waterfront) need to be clearly defined in writing and training given to staff and in many cases reviewed with campers.

CHECKPOINTS

1. List all the program activities utilized in your camp last summer.

2. Test the program development guidelines against those activities and see if other program directions arise.

3. Using the modified list of program activities, test each activity against each of the following elements:
   - goals and outcomes
   - experienced and qualified staff
   - adequate and appropriate equipment
   - safety and emergency procedures
   - eligibility and numbers of participants

4. Review the flow of a typical day at camp; consider where there are times for:
   - strenuous physical activity
   - quiet, reflective, relaxed time
   - choosing an activity
   - learning new skills
   - meeting campers from other living groups

5. What special populations does your camp serve and what are their special needs?

Related Standards

Accreditation Standards for Camp Programs and Services: PD-1–24, PA-1–35, PC-1–16, PH-1–13, PT-1–20; "Additional Professional Practices": Items 30–39

Standards for Conference and Retreat Centers: III-1, 8–31

Sickle Cell Disease Research Foundation,
Los Angeles, California

6

Personnel Organization and Recruitment

The quality of the camp staff is of the greatest importance in the successful operation of a camp program. Comparisons of the relative success that different camps have with their programs show that the physical factors, such as size, layout, buildings, and equipment, are also important. But camps with similar or comparable facilities vary considerably in the quality of their programs. The differences are largely explainable by the variations in <u>the ability of the personnel who make up the camp staff.</u>[1]

A lmost fifty years later, that statement stands. The accomplishment of a camp's mission and goals is largely dependent upon the staff who work directly with the participant in that camp.

How qualified, committed, and effective those staff members are is largely dependent upon the camp director and his or her ability to recruit and train that staff. Each and every staff member is important to the accomplishment of those goals and outcomes. One staff member who does not understand and follow the camp's policies and procedures can not only be an impediment but also demonstrate negligence which can trigger a lawsuit.

It is important that every prospective staff member be given a clear picture of the type of situation, and of the staff and camper community in which he or she will work. The ability or willingness of the staff person to be flexible will be as vital to a good experience as the flexibility of the camper and staff community.

Background of a prospective staff member is another factor to consider in hiring. If a person comes from a cultural or ethnic background different from the majority of the staff, he or she can add an exciting dimension to the experience of both campers and staff. These staff members, like all other staff members, should be made aware of the diversity or composition of the camper and staff population.

---

[1]Reuel A. Benson and Jacob A. Goldberg. 1951. *The Camp Counselor*. New York: McGraw-Hill. p. 41.

STAFF ORGANIZATION

It is important to design a staff organization that parallels the camp's mission, goals, and objectives and the resulting program, and matches the camp's philosophy. The camp director now needs to outline the following elements:

1. Specific job responsibilities that will be required by the program design
2. Ratio or the number of each position required to the number of campers
3. Line of supervision of each position
4. Job descriptions for each position

Job Responsibilities

Starting with broad general responsibilities such as food service, health and wellness, facility maintenance, and program, the director needs to identify the overall responsibility the staff member has. For example, the food service responsibility may be to provide healthy meals for campers and staff. The specific responsibilities would be to supervise the kitchen staff, meal preparation, cleanup, etc. Only one person performs this job. On the other hand, some positions, like the living-group counselor, will need to be performed by more than one staff member.

In all camps, there are program areas which require specialists with outside certification. Perhaps the most common is the waterfront, and no other area of camp program has consistently contributed to as many deaths in camps nationwide. Therefore, extreme care needs to be taken in the selection of the person responsible for overseeing the aquatic program, staff, and facilities. That person should be at least twenty-one years of age with previous experience in the supervision of an aquatic area for at least one season. In addition, the person should hold certification from a nationally recognized certifying body such as the American Red Cross or Boy Scouts of America. The director of aquatics needs to be a person with the maturity of judgment to train and supervise other members of the aquatic staff, as well as to recognize any potentially dangerous situations in the specific aquatic environment. Specialized training from the American Red Cross is available for head lifeguards, and from the YMCA for the waterfront director. A list of ACA-approved certifying bodies is listed in the appendix of the *Accreditation Standards for Camp Programs and Services*. See Appendix C for additional organizational resources.

Where recreational swimming is conducted, the lifeguards should hold certification from a nationally recognized certifying body (such as American Red Cross Lifeguard Training, YMCA Lifeguard, Lifeguard Boy Scouts of America, Royal Lifesaving Society). Similarly, swimming instructors should hold a certification from a similar body (YMCA Youth and Adult Instructor I and II, BSA Aquatics Instructor, or Red Cross Water Safety Instructor).

If there is aquatic activity other than swimming, the person supervising each specific activity should have skills specific to that activity. This person should be certified through a nationally recognized certifying organization and have documented experience in the knowledge and skills required to teach and supervise the program, as well as in rescue and emergency procedures specific to the aquatic area and activities. In addition, any staff dealing with boats should be conversant with U.S. Coast Guard Boating Safety Standards and the proper registration labels for recreational boats. Instructor certification programs are available through the American Canoe Association, U.S. SAILING, the American Water Ski Association, and from some chapters of the American Red Cross. Additional training in powerboat operation is available through the U.S. Coast Guard Auxiliary, the U.S. Power Squadrons, and the state boating agencies. Many states have mandatory education requirements for individuals who operate any motor-powered vessel. Courses from these organizations will fulfill those requirements. See Appendix C for contact information.

At each location of aquatic activity, one staff member should be certified in American Red Cross Standard First Aid or its equivalent and must be certified in cardiopulmonary resuscitation (CPR) for the age level served. CPR training that also includes training in the use of breathing devices is highly recommended and is available through the American Red Cross, American Heart Association, and National Safety Council. It is not possible to identify a ratio of lifeguards to swimmers that applies to every situation. Therefore, the camp director, along with the aquatic supervisor, needs to carefully study the various aquatic locations, activities, and participant skill levels and then establish an overall aquatic policy that includes reasonable ratios of lifeguards to swimmers. This policy will determine the number of certified persons the director needs to employ.

Note: The Occupational Safety and Health Administration (OSHA) has defined a lifeguard as someone who has a legal "duty to act" or is a professional rescuer. Where an employee by designation is required to perform a task, it is implied that the employer must provide the appropriate tools for the job. For example, rescues which include mouth-to-mouth resuscitation or treatment of wounds require equipment to protect the rescuer from communicable diseases and bloodborne pathogens. In this case, required tools include protective breathing devices and latex gloves.

Equestrian programs also offer an area of potential danger unless properly staffed and administered. Safety factors and the importance of animal care require persons with experience and instructional skills. Horsemanship training is available at various universities, riding academies, and the U.S. Army, and certification is available through the Camp Horsemanship Association and the Horsemanship Safety Association.

Ratios

Staff to camper ratios are critical in terms of accomplishing goals and objectives as well as health and safety. Some industry ratios are clearer than others. For example, the American Camping Association Standards identify the following minimum ratios of staff on duty with campers in living groups and activities:

Camper Age	Number of Staff	Number of Residential Campers	Number of Day Campers
4–5 years	1	5	6
6–8 years	1	6	8
9–14 years	1	8	10
15–18 years	1	10	12

Even here, the type of program, environment, or the presence of campers with special physical, medical, or behavioral needs may require a higher ratio of staff to campers. There are no standard guidelines concerning the ratio of administrative staff to camper population. However, some general guidelines for ratios can be projected as follows:

- Food Service — one cook and one dish and pan washer for every 50 to 60 campers.
- Health Service — one nurse for the first 125–150 campers and one additional nurse for each 100 campers over 175.
- Each program activity will require analysis of a variety of factors including age group served to determine the ratio of leadership to campers. For example, the ACA Standards ask the camp director to determine the number of lifeguards or lookouts needed for supervision of a given number of campers in a swimming situation. There are many varying factors that help the director determine that ratio: type of swimming area — pool, river, or lake; size of the swimming area; size of the group that will be swimming at one time; design of the swimming area, etc. Each activity needs to be evaluated separately; and once ratios are determined, they should be put in writing and reviewed each year.
- Maintenance ratios are almost impossible to generalize because of the variation from camp to camp in the number and complexity of facilities such as running water, electricity, buildings vs. tents, laundry, and sewer. The employment of a year-round, full-time caretaker or ranger may lessen, to some degree, the number of seasonal employees needed.

Supervisory Lines

At this point, consideration should be given to which position will supervise other positions. Except in the smallest camp, it will become apparent that the camp director cannot supervise everyone. The amount of emphasis placed on various positions will depend on the degree of centralization and structure desired, and the size of the camp will determine the number, experience, and complexity of staff. A generally good rule for supervisory ratios is that one person cannot adequately supervise more than seven persons.

The camp's program philosophy will also affect the number of supervisory personnel needed. A *centralized* program will most often require a number of program department heads such as waterfront, crafts, sports (which can be broken down by individual sports), as well as a unit leader or head counselor who supervises a certain number of living units and their counselors. In a more structured centralized camp, program scheduling and a camper's individual schedules are a function of the director or program director in conjunction with the unit leaders or head counselors and department heads. Counselors usually carry cabin responsibility and assist in a program area.

A *decentralized* program will normally require fewer department heads in specific program areas and more unit leaders or head counselors. Counselors will normally concentrate on the living group and either develop the program or help campers plan their program as part of the ongoing group living process. A program director in a decentralized program serves more as a program resource, supervisor, and coordinator of unit leaders and program areas in which a certified specialist is needed for safety or as a resource. An overall or basic camp schedule may or may not be done depending on whether meals or other "all camp" activities are done together. Some decentralized camps require the counselor or at least the counselors in a unit to carry the program certifications.

Most people find that, in determining supervision patterns, a diagram begins to take form. Endless time can be spent on the best type of diagram. Though symbolism of any design is important, the clarity of the diagram to show the relationship of one position to another is the most important element. The diagram will be primarily used for the director and supervisory staff, but all staff should know the reporting and accountability structures. A general ground rule of organization is that a person should not be supervised by more than one person without careful coordination. Solid lines in an organization chart indicate supervision, enabling a person to follow the solid line up to the next box identifying the supervisor. Dotted lines indicate advisory or consultative relationships. An arrow in the direction of supervision is helpful if a nontraditional diagram is developed; for example, see illustration 6.1.

Several sample organization charts for camp staff are shown in illustrations 6.2 and 6.3.

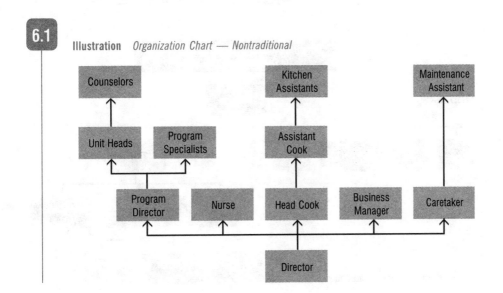

6.1

Illustration   *Organization Chart — Nontraditional*

6.2

Illustration *Camp Staff Organization Charts*

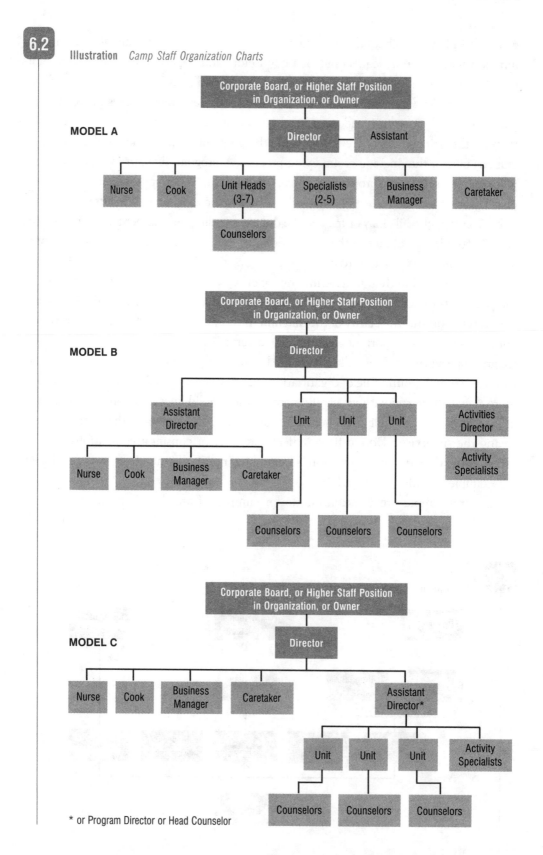

6.3 Illustration *More Staff Organization Charts*

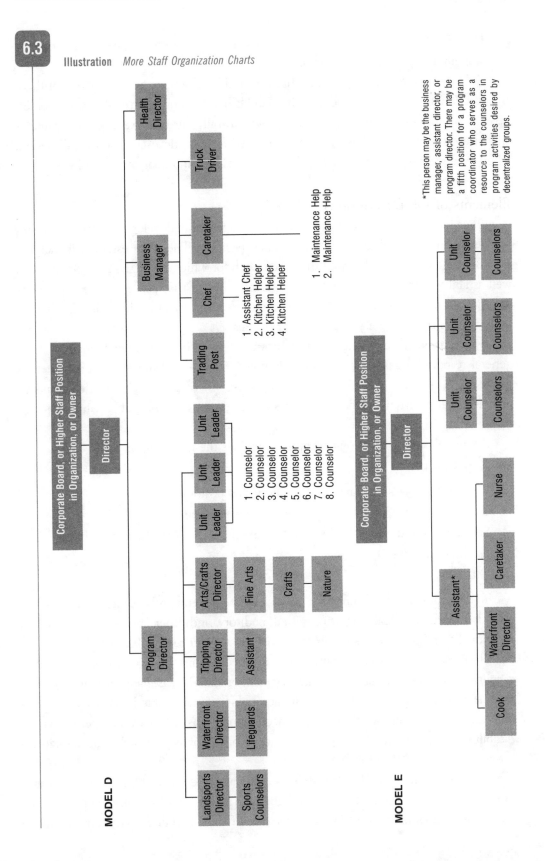

MODEL D

Corporate Board, or Higher Staff Position in Organization, or Owner

Director

- Program Director
  - Landsports Director
    - Sports Counselors
  - Waterfront Director
    - Lifeguards
  - Tripping Director
    - Assistant
  - Arts/Crafts Director
    - Fine Arts
    - Crafts
    - Nature
  - Unit Leader
  - Unit Leader
  - Unit Leader
  - Unit Leader
    1. Counselor
    2. Counselor
    3. Counselor
    4. Counselor
    5. Counselor
    6. Counselor
    7. Counselor
    8. Counselor
- Business Manager
  - Trading Post
  - Chef
    1. Assistant Chef
    2. Kitchen Helper
    3. Kitchen Helper
    4. Kitchen Helper
  - Caretaker
    1. Maintenance Help
    2. Maintenance Help
  - Truck Driver
- Health Director

MODEL E

Corporate Board, or Higher Staff Position in Organization, or Owner

Director

- Assistant*
  - Cook
  - Waterfront Director
  - Caretaker
  - Nurse
- Unit Counselor
  - Counselors
- Unit Counselor
  - Counselors
- Unit Counselor
  - Counselors

*This person may be the business manager, assistant director, or program director. There may be a fifth position for a program coordinator who serves as a resource to the counselors in program activities desired by decentralized groups.

The size of the camper population will determine, to a large degree, the size of various program or support departments.

However, it must be emphasized that it would be unwise to adopt any one of these organizational patterns until the camp has established clear program goals and outcomes/objectives. Staff organizational patterns grow naturally out of these, and the examples shown are meant to be illustrative and adapted for specific uses. The overall design, whether narrative or diagrammatic, should be outlined and analyzed carefully.

Elements of Job Descriptions

Once jobs have been identified and lines of supervision developed, it's time to begin the development of job descriptions for each position. These are essential in helping each staff member to understand the specific job for which he or she is responsible, as well as abilities and skills needed in the performance of that position. A good job description shows how one particular job correlates with others in the staff organization and provides the basis for performance appraisals.

By definition, a job description is a written statement of the minimum qualifications, general responsibilities, specific responsibilities, and essential functions pertinent to a particular position. It also identifies the supervisor by title. A position title should be assigned that clearly identifies to other staff, campers, and the public what the staff member does.

A general outline for a job description includes the following six areas:

1. Position title
2. Responsible to — the name of the supervising position
3. General responsibility — a simple descriptive statement
4. Specific responsibilities — the specifics relating to the general responsibility
5. Essential functions
6. Qualifications

To determine essential functions go back to the general and specific responsibilities and identify the physical, cognitive, visual, auditory, and other abilities *essential* for an individual to fulfill these responsibilities, with or without reasonable accommodations. See illustration 6.4. Does the position, for instance, require the physical ability to lift a certain weight, walk or climb a certain distance, or swim? Reasonable accommodations include making existing facilities readily accessible to and usable by persons with disabilities, restructuring the job or making accommodations in order that a person with a disability can perform the job (e.g., modifications of equipment, providing devices, interpreters, etc.).

Since the Americans With Disabilities Act was passed in 1990, it has brought employers to a new awareness of their responsibility to avoid unlawful discrimination against a qualified individual with a disability because of that disability. "The term 'qualified

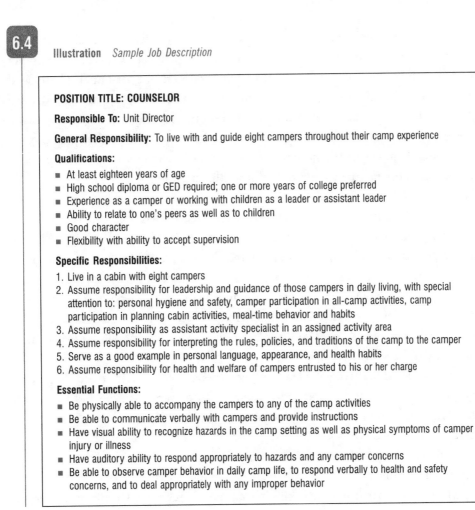

6.4

Illustration *Sample Job Description*

POSITION TITLE: COUNSELOR

Responsible To: Unit Director

General Responsibility: To live with and guide eight campers throughout their camp experience

Qualifications:

- At least eighteen years of age
- High school diploma or GED required; one or more years of college preferred
- Experience as a camper or working with children as a leader or assistant leader
- Ability to relate to one's peers as well as to children
- Good character
- Flexibility with ability to accept supervision

Specific Responsibilities:

1. Live in a cabin with eight campers
2. Assume responsibility for leadership and guidance of those campers in daily living, with special attention to: personal hygiene and safety, camper participation in all-camp activities, camp participation in planning cabin activities, meal-time behavior and habits
3. Assume responsibility as assistant activity specialist in an assigned activity area
4. Assume responsibility for interpreting the rules, policies, and traditions of the camp to the camper
5. Serve as a good example in personal language, appearance, and health habits
6. Assume responsibility for health and welfare of campers entrusted to his or her charge

Essential Functions:

- Be physically able to accompany the campers to any of the camp activities
- Be able to communicate verbally with campers and provide instructions
- Have visual ability to recognize hazards in the camp setting as well as physical symptoms of camper injury or illness
- Have auditory ability to respond appropriately to hazards and any camper concerns
- Be able to observe camper behavior in daily camp life, to respond verbally to health and safety concerns, and to deal appropriately with any improper behavior

individual with a disability' refers to a person with a disability who, with or without reasonable accommodations, can perform the essential functions of the job. All employers must therefore identify the essential functions, as opposed to the marginal functions, of each job."[2] Many camp directors also find it prudent to include in every job description a statement that additional tasks may be assigned at the discretion of the director or supervisor.

In determining the qualifications of the job description, the director must refer to the responsibilities and functions identified in numbers 3, 4, and 5. Qualifications differ from essential functions; this category describes the minimum age, education, experience, and characteristics necessary for an applicant to be considered for the position. Though this category often has been presented immediately after the position title and supervisor, it is difficult to define these qualifications in the writing process until items 3, 4, and 5 have been determined.

[2]Edie Klein. 1992. *It's My Job*. Martinsville, IN: American Camping Association. p. 3.

Age is a primary employment factor which must be considered carefully. Often industry standards, certification criteria, or government regulations will specify minimum ages for certain functions such as drivers of vehicles or waterfront personnel. These need to be researched carefully, even though the director may choose to require an older age or higher skill level if specific responsibilities are beyond the ordinary. For example, the group may be a considerable distance from the central camp support or public assistance, or the individuals in the group may have special characteristics. In both cases, higher skill and more maturity are required from the attending staff.

The accepted age in the industry for camp counselors is eighteen or above. Certainly, age is no guarantee of maturity, but experience has shown that, generally, persons over eighteen tend to be more mature than persons younger. There are also federal labor regulations prohibiting individuals under eighteen years of age from being employed to operate or clean kitchen slicers or mixers or operate vehicles in excess of 6,000 pounds.

It is essential to have a person of legal adult age in certain positions such as in waterfront supervision, supervision of camper groups taken off site for extended tripping or travel, and driving of passenger vehicles. Supervisors should generally be two or more years older than the staff they supervise.

For staff expected to drive vehicles carrying passengers, a current driver's license for the state in which the camp is located is required. If drivers are expected to operate vehicles designed to transport sixteen or more people or vehicles in excess of 26,000 pounds, a commercial driver's license is required. In either case, it would be wise to run a background check of previous driving history through the state police.

Staff in all program areas need to provide documented evidence of their experience and expertise as well as instructional skills in that specific program. Certification is available in the skills of waterfront, archery, boating, riflery, and water-skiing. Though adventure or challenge programs such as ropes courses, rappelling, initiative courses, and climbing have multiplied in recent years, there is no nationally recognized certification of instructors at this time. Authorities in the field feel that accreditation of a site-specific program is more appropriate than certification of individuals in these activities. However, there are several reputable organizations and regional resources that provide training in these skills; twenty hours of such instruction and experience should be the minimum expectation of an applicant to supervise such programs. (See Appendix C.)

Gender appears to be less of a factor in camp employment, except where counselors are assigned to live in the same quarters as campers of the same sex. Some camps with very young campers may not find this a factor. Of course, neither sex nor age can legally be used to discriminate in employment. Where a certain age base or sex is a requirement of a particular position, that should be carefully documented in the job description.

For certain staff positions, it is essential to hire staff with previous experience. Of course, experience is a plus in any position. Obviously, the value of a potential staff member's experience depends upon the situation in which it was acquired. A camp director can best determine the value of such experience from references, though an interview may assist greatly in that evaluation.

The camp director must consider skill as well as experience when hiring staff, especially program specialists. As mentioned earlier, various kinds of skill certifications are available in such areas as aquatics, riflery, health service, campcraft, and horsemanship. In other areas, where certification is not available, the director must go beyond the applicant's statement of experience and skill to talk to or correspond with persons who have actually supervised the applicant in the specific area or who have observed the person in action. If the person is to be an instructor in a skill area, then questions about teaching ability are as important as the person's own technical skills.

If there is a level of education the position demands, this should be spelled out, along with any particular training necessary. Personal qualifications such as flexibility or ability to work with others may be included if they are essential. However, according to equal employment regulations, all qualifications must be *directly* related to the job. In every job description, it is wise to have a statement that identifies that the position has responsibility for the health and welfare of campers.

In starting the process of writing new or revising existing job descriptions, the director can gain insights by asking supervisors and staff to organize a checklist of tasks related to their individual positions. This may also identify some misconceptions as to the actual responsibilities of the position. "Job descriptions require systematic thought and continual revision. They cannot be written in a vacuum; careful consideration of how the camp operates is an integral part of the job description."[3] Changes may have to be made in initial descriptions after persons are employed and the summer staff is in residence but this should be done with the full participation of the staff members concerned. A sample job description format is given in Appendix A.

If you are writing job descriptions for the first time, the most cogent information on the process is available in Edie Klein's book, *It's My Job*. If you are rewriting some of your descriptions and wish to increase their effectiveness and avoid discrimination as defined by the Americans With Disabilities Act, the same book provides efficient guidelines and sample descriptions for more than thirty camp jobs.

Salary and Benefits

In advance of staff recruitment, careful consideration should be given to the camp policy of compensation and benefits for staff. Obviously, the philosophy of the organization will dictate the plan, to some degree. For example, Girl Scout day camps or local church camps may be staffed by volunteers. However, even camps with a predominantly volunteer staff need a policy.

[3]Karla A. Henderson. "Job Descriptions Help Measure Staff Performance." *Camping Magazine* Vol. 62, No. 4, February 1990. p. 24–25.

In addition to wages, benefits can include meals, lodging, transportation, laundry, baby-sitting, insurance, or a camp experience for children of staff members. Each benefit costs the camp money and saves money for or provides the staff member with something of value; such benefits should be clearly identified in a statement of personnel policy. In addition to salary, the camp director should also consider what portion of the benefit has FICA or income tax associated with it. Each situation will be different, so guidelines should be developed before staff recruitment begins. Each benefit has special considerations.

Meals. Most camps that serve meals automatically provide meals to staff members, for the convenience of the camp, at no additional charge. However, meals for the staff member's dependents are a negotiable matter. Some camps charge cost and deduct it from salary; some include meals as a benefit. Others require families to prepare their own meals in separate living quarters, while the camp takes responsibility for the staff member's meals only when he or she eats with the staff and campers.

Lodging. Resident camps generally provide lodging for staff members, most often in multiple-living units. Counselors are usually required to live with campers, although a privacy division or room in the same building may be provided. Lodging for dependents of staff members is sometimes charged against salary or, in other cases, given as a benefit of employment. Many camps provide housing for families in order to secure older or returning staff.

Transportation. Day camps generally require some staff members to ride on camper buses and usually provide space for any staff member at no charge. Resident camps often meet staff at central locations. Some camps provide a transportation allowance, particularly for staff members who travel more than a minimum number of miles to get to camp.

Baby-sitting. Day camps utilizing volunteers often provide a central baby-sitting service for children of staff members or reimburse volunteers for the cost of home baby-sitting.

Insurance. Worker's compensation, automobile, and liability insurance are covered later in this chapter. Many camps provide a health and accident insurance policy to staff members as a benefit of employment or offer it as an option which the staff member may purchase.

Camp Experience. Where a single parent or both parents come as staff members to camp and have camper-age children, it is not unusual for those children to be enrolled as campers in their proper age group, as a credit against wages. Even for volunteers, the value of this benefit may be considered income and be subject to taxes.

Salary. If any amount is agreed upon and paid to a staff member in advance (whether it is called an honorarium, a stipend, a scholarship, or a gift), that remuneration is considered salary. Initially, the director should secure information on the state's minimum-wage laws as well as the applicability of federal minimum-wage laws. It may also be helpful for him or her to visit with camp directors of comparable camps in the area to learn what salaries are being paid in similar circumstances.

If minimum wage is applicable, rooms or other facilities provided by the employer may generally be a part of the minimum-wage calculation. (The rule of thumb for determining the value of these services is to document the average cost of the meals including overhead, labor, and raw food. For lodging, the documentation should include the value of the lodging provided based upon the local community market, with consideration given to whether the lodging is private, semiprivate, or dormitory style.) It is best to check with a human resources expert or your lawyer as federal and state wage-hour laws change frequently.

Increments in salary levels are decided in a variety of ways:

- By number of years on the staff
- By age and experience
- By certain qualifications (cook, nurse, waterfront certification, outdoor living skills certification)
- By position in the organization chart
- By need, i.e., the camp finds that the only way to secure staffers from the inner city is to pay considerably over the going rate because of economic circumstances

The camp director should give careful thought to salary scales, to any increases built into those scales, and to their fairness to staff members. Though most persons do not work in camps solely for the monetary benefit, there is a sensitivity, in such a close community, to differences or unfairness in wages that can interfere with the more important parts of camp life. It is essential that it not be implied that counselors are the lowest point on the scale because there is, potentially, no more important person in terms of health and safety or camper relationships than the counselor. The objectives and program philosophy will emphasize that responsibility more in some camps than in others; but, in every case, it is vital that the nature of the counselor's responsibility be fairly recognized.

Personnel Policies

Although the camp director may be covered by the personnel policies of his or her employer, seasonal staff may not be. It is generally the camp director's responsibility to develop personnel policies that define the guidelines and expectations for seasonal staff. Each staff member should be given a copy of the personnel policies. See illustration 6.5 for a sample of some personnel policies. For further information, see Appendix R in the *Accreditation Standards for Camp Programs and Services*. Ideally, they should be attached to the employment agreement and should be reviewed by the staff member before a contract is signed.

Personnel policies generally cover the following issues:

- Pay periods: dates, deductions, method of payment
- Overall benefits
- Termination: length of notice necessary, termination pay, causes

6.5

Illustration   *Sample Personnel Policies for Seasonal Staff*

SAMPLE PERSONNEL POLICIES FOR SEASONAL STAFF

The camp wishes to make your employment period with us as enjoyable and beneficial as possible. Camp is a community and the actions of each member of that community affects the other members. Certain policies help clarify the expectations of the employee and the employer, and minimize any difficulties within the community.

It should be recognized that employment at camp is "at will." Either party can terminate the relationship at any time, for any or no reason, with or without notice, under the state's "at will" doctrine.

1. Camper Welfare

The first responsibility of each and every staff member is the health and welfare of the campers. Each staff member is expected to take every care to protect the privacy and person of each camper. Physical punishment or any sexual contact between staff and campers is inappropriate, and will be grounds for dismissal. Staff members should never touch campers in any area covered by a bathing suit or show outward signs of affection that could be misinterpreted as sexual abuse.

2. Insurance

Worker's compensation and health insurance is carried by the camp on each employee for work related injuries or illnesses. This insurance does not cover nonwork related injuries or illnesses.

Liability insurance is carried by the camp which covers each employee when carrying out assigned camp responsibilities, as long as the employee is not negligent in carrying out those responsibilities, is following the policies and procedures of the camp, and acting within the authority of their job.

3. Pay Periods

For the convenience of the camp office, the wage agreement is based on a weekly rate. It is impossible to clock the actual work hours in the camp setting for counselors, program personnel, and program supervisors. However, the kitchen and maintenance employees must furnish a daily record of the hours worked on the cards provided. The camp will issue pay checks on the first and fifteenth of each month during contracted time.

4. Time Off

Time-off periods will be scheduled as regularly as possible, but necessarily at the convenience of the camp program. Each week staff can normally expect one twenty-four-hour period free of duties, agreed upon with the employee's supervisor a week ahead. In some cases, days off may be accumulated for a two-week period to provide two successive days off. Days off cannot be accumulated without advance permission.

At least two hours daily will be freed up for persons related to living groups. A plan for coverage of the living group should be worked out with the staff member's supervisor.

5. Sick Leave

If a staff member is sick, a camp director, supervisor, or health director may request that he or she see a doctor or go home to recuperate from an illness or injury without pay.

- Time off: amount to be expected, method of determination, scheduling, sick leave days
- Work rules: use of tobacco, alcohol, controlled substances; a specific sexual harassment policy, etc.
- Other regulations: use of personal automobiles or equipment in conjunction with camp program, etc.
- Equal employment opportunity statement
- Performance appraisal system: discipline, grievance procedures, etc.
- The camp's policy statement concerning the welfare of children and the action to be taken in case of child or sexual abuse

Because of the current litigious climate, the camp director may do well to include in the personnel policies a statement indicating that the policies are designed to clarify,

6. Alcohol/Tobacco/Controlled Substances

Alcohol and controlled substances are not allowed on the camp property. Employees are expected to follow this policy. In addition, employees are not to return to the camp grounds under the influence of alcohol or controlled substances. Breaking this policy is grounds for immediate dismissal.

Smoking and chewing tobacco is discouraged, but is permitted in the staff lounge or the living quarters of staff not living with campers. All employees are asked to refrain from smoking in any areas of camp frequented by campers, as well as in the kitchen.

7. Community Relations

Staff are asked to be sensitive to the people in the communities near the camp. Each staff member represents the camp in his or her dealings with members of the local communities, as well as in behavior off the camp grounds.

8. Tips/Gratuities

Staff members are asked not to accept any tips or gratuities from the parents or relatives of campers.

9. Health Services

A registered nurse is on duty at camp and staff members have access to his or her services as needed. The cost of prescriptions and doctor or hospital visits must be covered under one's personal insurance or that purchased through the camp unless the injury or illness is work related (See 2.)

10. Grievances

Should there be a disagreement over the interpretation of camp policies or a grievance related to one's duties or relationships with fellow staff members, it should be reported to one's supervisor promptly. Should the supervisor be the source of the grievance, the staff member may report the grievance to the supervisor of his or her supervisor or to the camp director.

11. Performance Appraisal

In an effort to help each staff member perform his or her duties at an optimum level, each staff member is evaluated on a regular basis. The employee's supervisor will indicate the frequency of the supervisory conferences, and, at the conclusion of each conference, will share a written evaluation with the employee. The employee and supervisor will both sign the agreed upon evaluation and it will be filed in the staff member's personnel file.

A staff member does not have to wait for a scheduled supervisory conference to seek advice or counsel from his or her supervisor. The primary responsibility of a supervisor is to be available to deal with the day-to-day problems of his or her supervisees.

generally, the employer/employee relationship and should not be considered as a contract nor as a guarantee of employment. It should also be indicated that the employer/employee relationship is an "at will" relationship which may be terminated with appropriate notice by either party at any time. At-will relationships are discussed in more detail later in this chapter.

Termination is a matter that a director seldom considers until he or she is faced with a staff member who is not fulfilling his or her responsibilities. Discussion, prior to the season, with other camp directors concerning their termination practices can be helpful. It is important to recognize that, despite one's concern for the employee as a person, termination of that person may be the most beneficial action for the total camp community. Because of the twenty-four-hour living situation in a residential camp and the short season of many camps, termination becomes necessary where, in other settings, more time could be given to coaching or waiting and seeing whether the problems could be solved. For these same reasons, it may also be better to pay the terminated employee for the notice period and have him or her leave camp immediately rather than to have a disgruntled employee in the living situation for that period.

The camp director should also pay careful attention to a plan and pattern for time off for resident camp staff. The living situation at a resident camp demands twenty-four-hour responsibilities from most personnel; however, because of that continuing day-to-day situation, it is vital that time off be arranged for each staff member. In addition, some free time to pursue personal needs should also be available each day. That time will occur naturally for many staff who work given hours, but program and counseling personnel, in particular, need a plan. For safety reasons, those plans should be coordinated carefully and counselors should always know how their camper-group responsibilities will be supervised in their absence. A minimum of two free hours a day, apart from sleep time or eating with campers, is the accepted norm.

In addition to daily free time, every staff member needs a minimum of twelve consecutive hours free each week (or twenty-four hours every two weeks) so that there is time to get away from the camp community or to find uninterrupted time for personal needs in camp. Obviously, such time has to be scheduled and, in most jobs, personnel replacements arranged. Adequate flexibility in job descriptions and numbers of staff is needed so that other staff can substitute for those who are off duty and still maintain an appropriate camper/staff ratio. Provision for time off is an obligation of the camp as an employer but scheduling may be at the employer's convenience. It is important that the camp director also take a day off, for his or her own good as well as for the benefit of staff.

If the new director begins after staff recruitment has been completed, he or she should make a careful review of the program to determine how it is affected by the individual abilities and skills of the staff. Program plans should then be adjusted accordingly. Of course, it is desirable that the new director have the opportunity to develop an ideal organizational plan for his or her staff before beginning recruitment.

RECRUITMENT

After developing a clear organizational design and job descriptions, the director can effectively begin the recruitment process. A director cannot approach this task lightly, for finding qualified staff in recent years, with the current economy, lower employment rates, and lower population of college-age young people, is a challenge and has taken much time and effort.

The director should organize his or her recruitment materials and examine them for clarity, attractiveness, and appeal. These should include a camp brochure, a job description, an application form, a description of the job benefits and unique aspects of your camp. The materials must compete with those from many other seasonal jobs and camps trying to recruit the same personnel.

Sources

Where does one find staff? Here are a variety of different possibilities.

Through Former and Present Staff. Ask them to participate in the search. Obviously, staff members have a clear understanding of the camp's philosophy, working conditions, and the type of personality that will be most effective in your setting. Beware, however, of primarily staffing with friends; cliques may be formed and newcomers left out.

Colleges and Universities. Find a contact person in the university setting whether it is a former or present staff member or someone in the summer placement office or in the recreation, physical education, or education department. Resident hall assistants often have experiences which prepare them for camp supervision. Explore internships as a possibility of students' gaining credits. Make sure brochures, applications, and job descriptions are given to your contact. Arrange for a day of interviews on campus.

Job Fairs. Take advantage of college and university campus job fairs; plan a tour of fairs in schools in the same state. *Camping Magazine* carries a regular calendar of locations, dates, and contacts for job fairs. Fairs often have so many participating camps and summer employers that it is difficult to attract the attention of students unless you develop an unusual display or graphic and include video or pictures of the camp. Most directors soon find that some college and university profiles better match their camp program, location, and staffing "personality," and concentrate on those fairs.

Directories of Summer Employment. These provide opportunity to draw staff from broader geographical areas. The American Camping Association publishes an annual *Summer Camp Employment Booklet.*

Former Campers. Former campers and particularly past participants in counselor-in-training or leader-in-training programs are already familiar with your camp.

Faculties. Educators and administrators from elementary, middle, and high schools, colleges, universities, and private schools have valuable experience with young participants.

Membership of the Sponsoring Organization. This is the first source of volunteer staff of a camp sponsored by an organization. The local Volunteer Bureau may also be helpful in the search for volunteers.

Placement Services. These offer an opportunity for the director to file a list of positions along with job requirements. These include departments of manpower or employment services in many states as well as some American Camping Association section offices.

International Staff-Placement Organizations. Several excellent agencies screen potential staff applicants at different overseas locations and provide applications and interview information to the camp director. Individuals from other countries can broaden and stimulate the camp experience for campers and staff alike. Addresses of such organizations (Bunacamp, Camp America, Camp Counselors USA, International Camp Counselor Exchange Program, International Camp Counselor Program) are in Appendix D. In addition, the International Camping Fellowship publishes an annual *Resource Directory* which lists individual members who are looking for an international camp experience.

Community Groups. Neighborhood or community centers, block clubs, churches, and youth boards are good sources for staff, especially minority staff.

The Internet. A camp Web site with photos, program descriptions, location, and a list of jobs available will attract the attention of students and others. An application form can even be included on your site.

There are also job directory services on the Internet. For example, the American Camping Association and Peterson's Guides have joined together for an on-line service "Great Summer Jobs." If your camp is accredited by the American Camping Association, your camp's listing in the *Guide to ACA-Accredited Camps* can be linked to your camp's Web page.

Advertise. Advertising is most effective, if you can do so in a publication specific to the skill or type of position needed.

Parents. A parent may be quite willing to take a camp position if his or her child can attend camp at a reduced rate.

Seniors. An alternative source of staff which many camps have found productive is to hire senior adults. Seniors have discovered the joys of being with children in a beautiful setting and of being able to continue to use skills and abilities gained from previous jobs. Camp administrators have discovered among seniors a wealth of practical work experience unmatched by younger staff. "Camps that employ seniors can enrich the camper's experience and provide a great summer for senior adults. This attractive staffing alternative is gaining momentum."[4]

Although these sources may provide most of the program and counseling staff, the camp director will probably need to turn to more specialized sources for cooks and nurses. The state employment agency, schools with cafeterias, and fraternity and sorority houses are good sources for cooks. Similarly, the state nursing association, state employment agency, nursing schools, and school systems can provide leads for camp nurse candidates.

International Staff

In recent years, the number of staff from outside the United States has increased steadily just as the national population in the traditional camp-staff age group (eighteen

---

[4]William A. Becker and Dawn Shelar. "Employing Seniors at Camp." *Camping Magazine* Vol. 63, No. 4, February 1991. p. 49.

to twenty-five) has decreased. There are great advantages to having international staff members, if those persons are well prepared for the particular camp setting, possess the skills for the position for which they are employed, and are used to stimulate international education through the camp program.

Some international exchange organizations, such as the International Camp Counselor Program, are able to sponsor visas for year-round international interns. Environmental education programs and conference centers may find this helpful in maintaining an international presence and program during the fall, winter, and spring seasons.

"Campers and staff from the United States gain valuable insights into other cultures — their language, history, ways of thinking and looking at the world, customs, food, and dress. Learning from staff with whom they interact on a daily basis can be a . . . powerful learning experience . . . International staff members have allowed us to view our program and staff training through fresh eyes," states Nancy Halliday of Hofstra University.[5]

However, to simply employ such staff because it is the easiest way to fill difficult positions is unfair to the camp and to the international applicant. It is critical that information be shared with all applicants so that they understand not only the scope of duties, but also the type of living accommodations, working conditions, and proximity (or lack thereof) to cities. If a personal interview is not available, it is essential that the camp director take extra steps to communicate with the applicant and a former employer, even at the cost of international phone calls. This is particularly true of applicants who would be working directly with campers on a day-to-day basis, where ability to work with children and fluency of the language spoken in camp are both important. Faxes and e-mail have speeded up communication with potential international staff.

As Christy L. Phillips writes, in the recruitment process it is important to "remember that there are good people who are just waiting to work in your camp. Now, all you have to do is find them. Make a staff recruitment calendar and work with camp associations and other camp professionals. With some persistence, your staff recruitment efforts will be successful."[6]

Negligent Hiring

A lawsuit for negligent hiring is based on the theory that the employer is liable for the actions of an employee who was unfit or who created an unreasonable risk of harm.[7] To translate this process to camp vernacular, negligent hiring is an action wherein a

---

[5]Nancy Halliday. "International Flavor — The Value of Including Internationals on Your Staff This Summer." *Christian Camp and Conference Journal* by CCI/USA Vol. 2, No. 1, January/February 1998. p.12. Reprinted with permission.

[6]Christy L. Phillips. "Find the Staff You Need." *Camping Magazine* Vol. 69, No. 2, November/December 1996. p. 4.

[7]Marge Scanlin. "Getting References — The Task of Finding Good Staff." *CampLine* Vol. 2, No. 2, October 1993. p. 1.

parent sues a camp for injuries sustained by a camper that were caused by the careless actions of a staff member or of an unqualified staff member. Camps have been sued for negligent hiring of staff who had previously been convicted of sexually abusing children. Generally, the expectation of the parent is that the director should discover this fact before hiring the person.

Many of the steps described in this chapter are designed to provide protection against such suits: clear job descriptions, complete application forms, references, a thorough screening process, interviews, and documenting each step. All of these steps are equally important for the camp which has a volunteer staff. Though some steps may be more difficult in such a camp where staff often changes from week to week, it is critical that a modified plan be developed which covers the same basic steps.

To help you be consistent in your hiring practices, you may want to "log" all of the steps you take for each person. A sample hiring log is shown in Appendix H.

Applications

Beyond the data ordinarily required for employment, a camp staff application form should emphasize the skills and experience required in the job description. A director should be aware of the importance of eliciting only that information which is needed for a decision about the job and, on the other hand, of requiring all information which is needed to determine if an applicant meets all personnel selection qualifications. For example, it is permissible to ask the applicant's sex or whether the person is at least a certain age only if the job requirements demand a certain sex or minimum age. Asking for that information when the job does not require it may open the camp director to charges of discrimination. Illustration 6.6 shows an application developed by the American Camping Association.

It is also wise to provide enough space on the application form so that every previous job may be listed, enabling the director to check for gaps in employment. Such gaps give the interviewer an opportunity to ask questions about that period in the event that such incidents as convictions of a felony or crime related to abuse were the cause of the lapses of time.

Where a license or certain level of experience is required, a copy of the license or, in the case of experience, outside documentation should be required.

The steps taken after an application is received are critical in the selection of competent and conscientious staff. Careful planning needs to be given to the type of references desired, the format of the interview, and the delineation of the camp's philosophy and policies before implementing these steps. Training and supervision cannot cure the employment of an incompetent and potentially negligent person in a staff position.

Specific questions should be asked about previous convictions for child abuse; however, one should clear those questions with the camp's attorney. For instance, the application might ask: "Have you been previously convicted of a felony or misdemeanor? If

6.6 Illustration *Sample ACA Application FM 10*

Camp Staff Application Form FM 10

Developed by *American Camping Association*®

Return to:

(Please type or print) Date of Application _____

Name_____ Social Security Number _____

Permanent Address _____ Phone _____
Street & Number   City   State   Zip   Area/Number

School or Business Address _____ Phone _____
Street & Number   City   State   Zip   Area/Number

Can you perform the essential functions of the job for which you have applied, with or without reasonable accommodation?
☐ Yes ☐ No

If you are hired would you desire or need housing for any person(s) other than yourself at the camp? ☐ Yes ☐ No

Education

Years	School	Major Subjects	Degree Granted

Past Employment *(Provide a full record of all employment and explain any gaps in employment. Use a separate sheet, if necessary.)*

Dates	Employer	Address & Phone	Nature of Work	Supervisor	Reason for Leaving

Indicate any employer you do not wish us to contact and the reason _____
_____

Camp Experience

Dates	Camp	Director	Address	Camper or Staff

References *(Give names/addresses of 3 persons [not relatives] having knowledge of your character, experience, and ability.)*

Name	Address & City	Phone

What type of position do you want at camp? _____ Salary desired? _____

Dates available From _____ To _____

6.6   **Illustration**   *Sample Sample ACA Application FM 10 continued*

In the following list, put numeral "1" before those activities you can organize and teach as an expert; "2" for those activities in which you can assist in teaching; and, "3" for those which are just your hobby; "C" for those in which you have *current* certification and attach a copy of your certification card.

Adventure/Challenge
- Climbing/Rappelling
- Ropes Course
- Spelunking

Arts and Crafts
- Basketry
- Ceramics
- Electronics
- Ham Radio
- Jewelry
- Leather Work
- Macrame
- Metal Work
- Model Rocketry
- Nature Crafts
- Newspaper
- Painting
- Photography
- Darkroom
- Sketching

- Weaving
- Woodworking

Campcraft/Pioneering
- Campcraft
- OLS Program Leader
- OLS Instructor
- Hiking
- Orienteering
- Outdoor Cooking
- Overnight
- Mountaineering
- Minimum Impact

Dancing
- Ballet
- Folk
- Social
- Square
- Tap
- _____
- _____

Dramatics
- Creative
- Play Directing
- Skits and Stunts

Music
- Lead Singing
- Instruments (list)
  - Accordion
  - Bugle
  - Piano
  - Guitar

Nature
- Animals
- Astronomy
- Birds
- Conservation
- Flowers
- Forestry
- Insects
- Rocks and Minerals

- Trees and Shrubs
- Weather
- Gardening
- Animal Care

Sports
- Archery
- Backpacking
- Badminton
- Baseball
- Basketball
- Bicycling
- Boxing
- Fencing
- Fishing
- Golf
- Gymnastics
- Hockey
- Horseback Riding
- Informal Games
- Ping Pong

- Riflery
- Skating
- Soccer
- Softball
- Tennis
- Track and Field
- Volleyball
- Wilderness Trips
- Wrestling
- _____

Waterfront Activities
- Canoeing/Kayaking
- Diving
- Rowing
- Sailing
- Scuba
- Swimming
- Water Skiing
- Board Sailing
- Rafting

- Lifeguard
- Synchronized Swimming

Miscellaneous
- CPR
- Emergency Care
- First Aid
- Auto Mechanics
- Campfire Programs
- Carpentry
- Electrical
- Evening Programs
- Farming
- Plumbing
- Storytelling
- Word Processing
- Worship Services
- Language

Answer these questions only if applying for a position requiring driving

Do you have a valid driver's license? ☐ Yes ☐ No   State _____

Do you have current chauffeur's-type license? ☐ Yes ☐ No   Do you have a commercial driver's license? ☐ Yes ☐ No

---

What contributions do you think you can make at camp? _____
_____
_____
_____

What contributions do you think a well-run camp can make to children? _____
_____
_____
_____

Write a brief biographical sketch, including specialized training in camping, and experience or training in other fields which might have a bearing on the position(s) for which you are applying. _____
_____
_____
_____
_____
_____

Are you available for an interview? ☐ Yes ☐ No   Where? _____

I authorize investigation of all statements herein and release the camp and all others from liability in connection with same. I understand that, if employed, I will be an at-will employee and that any agreement to the contrary must be in writing and signed by the director of the camp. I also understand that untrue, misleading, or omitted information herein or in other documents completed by the applicant will result in dismissal, regardless of the time of discovery by the camp.

Signature _____

All statements become part of any future employee personnel files.

This form has been drafted to comply with federal employment laws; however, ACA assumes no responsibility or liability for the use of this form.

the answer is yes, please indicate on a separate sheet of paper the convictions, dates, and circumstances," or "Have you been previously charged with any crime related to the abuse, mistreatment, or molestation of children?"

The American Camping Association standards require either a criminal background check or voluntary disclosure statement. The application could request permission for the camp to conduct a criminal background check. A voluntary disclosure statement outlines similar questions as well as requiring residences for the previous five years. See illustration 6.7 for a sample voluntary disclosure statement.

References and Background Checks

In the development of the application form, a director will need to decide the number of references required and how they will be utilized. Generally, of course, applicants request references from persons they know will give favorable recommendations. And it is unusual for persons giving written references to make negative comments. This tendency does not necessarily mean that references are useless, but rather that care should be exercised in requesting them.

If your concern is job performance, you should ask for the names of an applicant's supervisors in the last three jobs, rather than for general references. Here, it is important to ask specific questions about performance as an employee, any dismissal, and if so, the reason for it. If your concern is the applicant's ability to relate to children, then you should ask for the names of persons who have had the opportunity to observe the applicant in a position where he or she taught or led children of specified ages. Here, questions about judgment and disciplinary methods should be included. If your concern is performance in a certain skill area, then you should ask for persons who have observed the applicant as a teacher of that skill or as a member of a team practicing that skill. If you wish simple character references, they should not be from relatives. If you request written references, it is courteous to include a stamped return envelope. A sample reference questionnaire is shown in illustration 6.8.

While it is often difficult to get former employers to be frank about an applicant, it is unwise to employ a person without some check of references. ACA has developed "a legal document the applicant would sign releasing former employers from any liability while providing information about the skills and work habits of former employees."[8] The use of such a release may encourage the person giving references to relate adverse information which one should know about an applicant.

A telephone check of references may be the most effective approach to references, since some people are more willing to make negative observations verbally than in writing. However, if you use telephone references, you should develop a system for recording notes on the conversation that can be filed with the job application. The recorded note should

---

[8]Ibid. p. 2.

6.7

Illustration *Sample ACA Voluntary Disclosure Statement FM 16*

**Voluntary Disclosure Statement
All Camp Staff   FM 16**

Developed and approved by
American Camping Association

Mail this form to the address below by _____ (date)

Name _____ Birth date _____
         Last   *First*   *Middle*
Home address _____
             Street Address   *City*   *State*   *Zip*
Social Security # _____ Other names by which known (e.g., maiden name) _____
Home phone _____ Business phone (if applicable) _____
School or College _____
Address _____
          Street Address   *City*   *State*   *Zip*
Driver's License # _____ State _____ Expiration Date _____

1. Previous residence(s) for last 5 years (include college and home residences):

   City _____ State _____ Years _____

   City _____ State _____ Years _____

   City _____ State _____ Years _____

   City _____ State _____ Years _____

   (Continue on separate sheet if necessary.)

2. Have you ever been convicted of any crime relating in any manner to children and/or your
   conduct with them?   ☐ Yes ☐ No
   If yes, please explain: (Use a separate sheet if necessary.)

   _____

   _____

   _____

   _____

3. Have you ever been convicted of any crime including, but not limited to, those listed below
   and/or any crime similar in any manner to those listed below?   ☐ Yes ☐ No
   - Indecent assault and battery on a child under fourteen
   - Indecent assault and battery on a mentally retarded person
   - Indecent assault and battery on a person who has obtained the age of fourteen
   - Rape
   - Rape of a child under sixteen with force
   - Assault with intent to commit rape
   - Kidnapping of a child under sixteen with intent to commit rape
   - Distribution and trafficking of narcotics or other controlled substances
   - Intent to commit any of the above crimes

   If yes, please explain: (Use a separate sheet if necessary.)

   _____

   _____

   _____

   _____

   _____

6.7

4. Have you ever been adjudged liable for civil penalties or damages involving
   sexual or physical abuse of children?   ☐ Yes   ☐ No
   If yes, please explain: (Use a separate sheet if necessary.)

   _____

   _____

   _____

   _____

   _____

5. Are you now or have you ever been subject to any court order involving sexual or physical
   abuse of a minor, including, but not limited to a domestic order or protection?   ☐ Yes   ☐ No
   If yes, please explain: (Use a separate sheet if necessary.)

   _____

   _____

   _____

   _____

   _____

6. Have your parental rights ever been terminated for reasons involving
   sexual or physical abuse of children?   ☐ Yes   ☐ No
   If yes, please explain:

   _____

   _____

   _____

   _____

   _____

I understand that:

a. The camp may deny employment to any person who answers any of questions numbered 2-5
   above in the affirmative.

b. In applying for a camp position the information which I have furnished on this form is subject
   to verification, which may include a criminal history check and request from any Central
   Registry of child abusers.

c. The camp may terminate employment or volunteer service of any person:

   1) found to have a history of complaints of abuse of a minor and/or
   2) found to have resigned, been terminated or been asked to resign from a position whether
      paid or unpaid, due to complaint(s) of sexual abuse of a minor.

d. This disclosure statement must be updated yearly.

Signature _____ Date _____

Signature of Minor's Parent or Guardian _____ Date _____

be dated and signed by the person making the call. If you have questions about an appli-cant after you have received written references, you should make a final telephone check.

References are more important than ever with the new awareness of the potential of employing child abuse offenders. Questions should be asked to determine whether the applicant may have any proclivity toward child or sexual abuse. See the last two ques-tions in illustration 6.8.

Employment Process and Child Abuse

The camp director should take steps in the employment process to minimize the risk of child abuse. The director should examine job descriptions, application forms, inter-view checklists, reference forms, contract forms, and staff-training outlines to make sure that all opportunities to uncover clues as to past abuse history or the proclivity toward such abuse exist.

This means checking references, doing a background check, investigating for a crimi-nal record, asking questions in the interview about the applicant's experience, and check-ing gaps in employment history. While many states recognize claims for negligent hiring, most courts protect employers who can document a reasonable job of checking prior to employment.

The application form offers an opportunity to document the applicant's own state-ment as to previous convictions, as well as to alert him or her that abuse is a concern of the camp. Specific questions are noted later in this chapter.

Wherever statements are made about the position and the requirements (i.e., on job descriptions, in the interview, and in the staff manual), there should be clear statements that abuse will not be tolerated and that the welfare of the camper is a primary job responsibility of every staff member.

During the interview, questions should be posed that delve into areas that may give clues or danger signals. Robert Ditter, a licensed social worker specializing in adolescent treatment, suggests several such questions to be asked twenty minutes or so into the interview.

"Do you have a best friend? Tell me about them — how long have you known them? What's one thing they've taught or done for you?

Would you say you are most comfortable with people your own age, older or younger? (Explore this.)

How were you punished as a child? What did you think of it then? Now? What do you think works best with children?"[9]

In her book, *For Their Sake*, Becca Cowan Johnson, Ph.D., points out that, while there is no way to determine whether or not a person is a molester from traits alone,

---

[9]Robert Ditter. "Protecting Our Campers: How to Recognize Various Forms of Child Abuse." *Camping Magazine* Vol. 58, No. 3, January 1986. p. 23.

6.8   Illustration   *Reference Questionnaire*

REFERENCE QUESTIONNAIRE   **Confidential**

_____ has applied to work on the staff at Camp _____ for this summer. This person has given your name as a reference who could evaluate his or her past performance as well as potential for the above position. Please give careful consideration to the ratings below.

Objective Rating

Under each general heading, check the phrase which most accurately describes the applicant's HABITUAL behavior with regard to that specific trait. Please remember that it will be the truly exceptional person who ranks high in **all categories.**

1. How well is the applicant able to direct and influence others along definite lines of action?
   - ☐ Poor leader; incapable of directing others
   - ☐ Usually follows the lead of others
   - ☐ Normally successful in directing and controlling others
   - ☐ Very successful in leading others
   - ☐ Exceptional leader: inspires others along desirable lines of action

2. How well does individual work with associates and others for the good of the group?
   - ☐ Cooperates grudgingly: makes trouble — obstructionist
   - ☐ Gives limited cooperation: neglects common good for own interests
   - ☐ Cooperates with others toward accomplishment of common cause
   - ☐ Cooperates willingly and actively regardless of self-benefit: makes things go smoothly
   - ☐ Exceptionally successful in working with others and inspiring confidence

3. How does this person react to suggestions or criticisms by others?
   - ☐ Takes criticism as a personal insult
   - ☐ Resents suggestions
   - ☐ Listens to suggestions but may act without considering them
   - ☐ Follows suggestions willingly
   - ☐ Asks for criticisms and suggestions

4. How responsible is applicant? Able to competently get things done on own?
   - ☐ Irresponsible even under supervision
   - ☐ With constant supervision will do satisfactory work
   - ☐ Usually needs detailed instructions with regular checks of work
   - ☐ Carries out routine activity on own responsibility
   - ☐ Exceptionally able to accomplish work without close supervision

5. How well does individual put his or her principles and convictions into action?
   - ☐ Fails to carry out convictions under adverse circumstances
   - ☐ Acts according to convictions under normal circumstances
   - ☐ Carries out principles and convictions constantly and boldly even in fact of obstacles

6. How well does this person apply energy and persistence in following a job through?
   - ☐ Needs much prodding to complete work
   - ☐ Rather indifferent; does not finish job
   - ☐ Completes assigned tasks of own accord
   - ☐ Industrious, energetic; dependable at all time
   - ☐ Unusual perseverance; does more than expected

7. How well does applicant control emotions?
   - ☐ Easily depressed, irritated, or elated
   - ☐ Tends to be over-emotional
   - ☐ Unresponsive; apathetic
   - ☐ Tends to be unresponsive
   - ☐ Usually well-balanced
   - ☐ Well-balanced
   - ☐ Unusual balance between responsiveness and control

6.8

Illustration   *Reference Questionnaire continued*

Narrative Report

Please briefly state specific instances in which you have observed the applicant's behavior as it applies to any of these items. If you have no knowledge, please say so.

1. Impression of suitability as a camp counselor. Would you be willing to have your children under individual's supervision for a period of weeks in a camp situation? If not, why not? _____

2. Maturity of judgment. How does this person react in situations of stress, i.e., make decisions? _____

3. Ability to lead campers toward spiritual objectives of the camp. Ability to lead devotionals, worship? Influence of life? _____

4. Nature of associates. Describe the types of people with whom individual habitually associates. _____

5. Dependability. Can be relied upon? Does person weaken in absence of authority? _____

6. How long have you known the applicant? _____ How have you observed applicant? _____

7. Have you seen him or her in a leadership role with youngsters? _____ What role? _____

8. To what extent does the individual use drugs or alcohol? _____

9. To your knowledge, does the applicant have any proclivity toward child or sexual abuse? _____

Please return promptly to: Name _____

Address _____

City _____ State _____ Zip _____

Position _____

Employed by _____

there are traits and characteristics which can be used as guidelines for identifying potential abusers. She states that, generally, the abuser will have a negative attitude and a hot temper, and will blame others — either the child or a circumstance. Continuing further, Ms. Johnson provides listings of the traits common to potential physical, emotional, and sexual offenders.[10]

In addition to references, the director must consider the question of background checks. Many states now require criminal background checks on all persons who work with children in child care situations. Where such a check is not required by the state, the camp can require the applicant to obtain a check on himself or herself as a requirement of employment. Such checks are generally not available for minors and interna-

---

[10]Becca Cowan Johnson. *For Their Sake*. Martinsville, IN: American Camping Association. pp. 103–113.

tional counselors. ACA's Voluntary Disclosure Statement form, shown in illustration 6.7, is useful in this regard also.

Criminal background checks generally require the applicant to request such a report to be forwarded from the state police, or to give written permission for the camp to secure it. However, the director needs to check in advance on the promptness with which the individual state responds to the request, to make sure it is timely enough to be useful. The average cost of $15 to $35 per applicant legally should be borne by the camp as a condition of employment. There is a serious question about the usefulness of such checks in the seasonal camp employment situation if most of the staff members are of college age, since they may be only one or two years beyond the age where such a record could be documented.

On the other hand, for persons over twenty-one or employed year-round, such a check can be a valuable precaution. It is also wise to secure an FBI fingerprint check on such employees. Although such checks may not be required by most states, questions of liability can arise if an alleged incident occurs and a camp has not utilized the available service. It is, therefore, important for a camp to make a policy determination about whether such checks and/or voluntary disclosure statements will be required.

The Job Interview

The employment interview is probably the most traditional and widely used method of selecting individuals to fill job openings. It can generally be defined as a purposeful exchange of ideas through the asking and answering of questions. Studies by various management associations have shown that training in interviewing guidelines can effectively increase the ability of the interviewer to select the candidate with the best potential for the job, and that experience in conducting interviews over a period of time increases the accuracy of selection.

A 1995 study conducted by the American Bar Association revealed that personal interviews were perceived as the most effective screening practice by youth development organizations. The second most effective tool was previous-employer reference checks.

Preinterview

A number of things should be done prior to an interview so that the time available can be used to the best advantage. Ideally, there is some information which should be in the hands of the applicant prior to the interview time:

A Job Description. A job description as outlined earlier in this chapter, plus an outline of salary, benefits, starting and closing dates of the position, number of hours of work expected, and time off. If food and housing costs are to be deducted from salary, specific amounts should be noted. In addition, if food and housing are provided as part of a salary, their relative worth should also be noted. Job descriptions are helpful in the interviewing process since they will help to give the applicant a more comprehensive understanding of the position for which he or she may be applying.

Information About the Camp. Brochures, material describing the general focus, general goals and objectives, and pertinent information about the age of campers served, fees, length of sessions, type of program, and copies of recent newsletters.

An Organization Chart. Some means of indicating where in the line-up the position in question falls, the immediate supervising position, and the relation of that position to others on the staff.

Ideally the interviewer can review all the facts available on the candidate through pertinent correspondence, the completed application form, written references received, or the notes from telephone calls made to individuals given as references. These materials will help the interviewer plan for the areas in which he or she wishes more information and will serve to pinpoint trouble or blank spots which need further inquiry. In order to avoid possible charges of discrimination, the questions need to be confined to job-related material.

Under the Americans With Disabilities Act of 1990, it can be viewed as discriminatory if you ask questions about an individual and his or her abilities that are not directly related to abilities necessary to perform job-related functions. Therefore, it is inappropriate to ask whether the applicant has any disability. You may, however, ask a question which takes the focus away from the disability and places it on the completion of essential job functions. For instance, "Are there any reasons you would have difficulty performing any of the essential elements of the job?"[11]

It is well to review some of the questions you may and may not ask in this area:

You May Ask	You May Not Ask
Can you perform the essential functions of this job?	Do you have a disability?
Describe or demonstrate how you would perform this job or function.	Do you need reasonable accommodations to perform functions?
Can you meet attendance requirements?	What number of days were you absent on your last job?
Are you currently using illegal drugs?	Were you ever addicted to drugs or treated for drug addiction or abuse?
Have you had prior illegal drug use?	Do you take legal drugs?
What are your drinking habits?	What is your worker's compensation history?

The Interview Setting

The setting of the interview provides an important background which may help or hinder your efforts. The time set aside should be free from distractions, telephone calls,

---

[11]National Camp Executives Group. 1992. *Camp Director's Primer to the Americans With Disabilities Act of 1990.* Glen Allen, VA: Markel Insurance Company. p. 17.

or interruptions by other people. The room where the interview takes place should have adequate lighting and ventilation and comfortable chairs. Avoid placing the desk between the interviewer and the interviewee to reduce the interviewer's dominant role and help break the ice. Sit side by side in comfortable chairs for a more relaxing and less threatening environment. Privacy is an important factor; the interview should not be held in an area where other people can pass through or look on, or where the conversation can be overheard.

The Interview Plan

After the available information has been organized, a specific plan for the interview should be developed. It is helpful to prepare a list of questions you plan to ask all candidates for a particular job as well as specific questions that relate to the information provided to you by the particular applicant. Generally, there are five basic factors the director needs to explore with applicants:

Intellectual Skills and Aptitudes. Look to both their intellectual capacity (or the ability to solve problems) and to their application or effectiveness (how well the applicant applies and uses intellectual capacity). This information can be obtained from a general survey of a scholastic record, together with pertinent questions on work experience and performance.

Motivational Characteristics. Primarily, these may be evaluated by discovering what a person likes to do or finds satisfaction in doing: interests, activities, best subjects in school. These may well come to light in discussing his or her long-term goals and aspirations and reasons for applying for the position in question.

Personality Strengths and Limitations. Behavior, traits, characteristics, and temperament all reveal how a person interacts with work environments and with people. Questions regarding relationships with people with whom he or she has worked on prior jobs may open this area for more information. Interpersonal relationships indicate what a person is like: shy, confident, aggressive, withdrawn, forceful, arrogant, open, outgoing, passive, or dependent. Occasionally, the interviewer may begin to get vague, negative feelings in this area, along with subtle and nonverbal clues. These should be heeded; if the interviewer reacts negatively to the person, it is possible that others will also.

Knowledge and Experience. From his or her past record, which of the job experiences will be most helpful to him or her in the job which is open? Will any of the past experiences hinder him or her in the current job?

Degree of Comfort with the Philosophy and Approach of the Camp. Rather than seeking acquiescence to the camp's philosophy, questions should be asked which reveal whether the person's individual approach is consistent with the camp's approach. Dr. Richard M. Strean suggests that the director "take advantage of the hiring process as the first, often overlooked step in counselor management, an opportunity to hire people who share the camp's philosophy and understand directors' expectations. . . . Such a candidate is far more likely to do what the director would want done when supervisors are not watching for the simple reason that the candidate would tend to do it anyway."[12]

In the light of these five areas, another look at the application and reference material will aid in blocking out areas where additional conversation is needed. A list of these questions in logical order will serve as a reminder during the interview, and also provide documentation of specific questions used in interviewing candidates.

The General Approach

Note Taking. During the interview, the taking of notes provides an organized way of recording data which may be overlooked, and of insuring that a significant response or reaction not be forgotten. It is difficult to take notes and give attention to what is being said at the same time, and the note taking may serve to distract the person being interviewed. The pad should be placed as unobtrusively as possible, preferably in a position where the interviewee cannot read what is being written. In this way, the process becomes an integral part of the situation and can be more readily accepted by the applicant.

Establishing a Good Climate. Applicants are often ill at ease and apprehensive as well as threatened in the face of authority. If an interviewer can show a friendly and interested acceptance at the beginning, the interviewee may be willing to respond in a frank and open manner. If the applicant seems reluctant to talk, a genuine compliment or sincere praise on some past experience or achievement noted in the application may put the person at ease. If an open, frank, and relatively nonthreatening climate can be established, the desired response on the part of the interviewee will generally follow.

Leading Questions. Questions phrased in such a way as to indicate the response desired should be avoided. The question, "Did you take part in extracurricular activities in college?" indicates to the applicant that this is important and he or she will begin to search his or her experience for a suitable reply. A more general approach might be, "Tell me about your college experience; what did you find particularly helpful?"

Open-Ended Questions. It is good to open each topic area with a broad, open-ended question, for instance, "Would you tell me something about your high school days?" The interviewer will then be free to take notes and observe mannerisms and behavior patterns while the applicant has to determine how much or how little to tell. Questions can be used to guide the direction of the interview, to open areas for discussion, and to encourage participation.

General to Specific Questions. Questions should move gradually from the general to the more specific. From "Would you tell me about your work with the YMCA?" (general question) to "What did you like least and most about that job?" (specific question).

---

[12]Richard M. Strean. "Invisible Counselors — Managing What You Don't See." *Camping Magazine* Vol. 69, No.1, September/October 1996. p. 34.

Self-Appraisal Questions. Questions should be directed to motivating self-appraisal. "Do you feel that you effectively accomplished that particular job?" Or, "If you could repeat that experience, what would you do differently?"

Controlling the Flow. Although the interviewer should be in control of the interview at all times, it is to his or her advantage to listen and to try not to interrupt. Natural pauses can be used to check the sequence of points on the interview plan, to see that facts in each area are adequate, and to keep the communication moving along. While the applicant provides the factual answers, the interviewer can determine the answers to some other intangible questions: How does the applicant communicate ideas? Can he or she conceptualize effectively? Is he or she shallow or superficial in his or her thinking? Is he or she perceptive to the social situation?

Conducting the Interview

An interviewer should remain impartial, neither condemning nor condoning what he or she hears. To provide a positive setting, the person conducting the interview should not react negatively to new ideas or unfamiliar subjects. Opinions should be disassociated from facts; time should not be wasted in disagreeing with an opinion. Time should not be taken up with facts contained on the application, but the emphasis should be on moving in the direction the interview needs to go. Although first impressions are important, it is essential that the interviewer try not to form conclusions too quickly.

If it is necessary to secure information which may not be comfortable for the applicant to reveal (e.g., why a particular job was held for a short period or details on a problem with a particular supervisor), the interviewer should indicate that such discomfort is understandable. Essential questions may be asked more than once in different ways to find out from the reaction how strongly the applicant may feel about a particular topic.

Concluding the Interview

An effective technique for ending the appointment is to summarize the interview. At this point, the applicant may be more relaxed and relay additional information. If it is determined during the interview that the person is not qualified for the position, he or she should be told so at this time. If additional information is needed, the interviewer must be sure that the interviewee understands specifically what is required, and a time should be set for receipt of the information. The applicant should also be told the time at which he or she may expect to hear the decision regarding the position.

Documentation

As soon as the applicant has departed, it would be wise for the interviewer to make any additional notes. If the director is interviewing a number of applicants in close sequence, making notes immediately after each interview will help to crystallize facts and impressions and help distinguish one applicant from another. Answers to critical questions such as those about abuse and discipline are important to record. The notes from the interview should be dated and signed by the interviewer and placed in the personnel file; this provides further documentation in the endless task of showing that every precaution was taken in employing an individual in case there is allegation of a child-abuse incident and subsequent litigation or unfounded litigation. Some interviewers find it useful to review by making a list of positive and negative facts ascertained during the interview and to rate job qualifications against a predetermined list.

Evaluation of the Interview

One effective way of developing and refining skills essential to good interviewing is to make a personal evaluation of the performance immediately after the session. One approach is to take a look at the original interview plan and compare it to the actual interview. Was the general plan followed? Did I miss any important category? Did I succeed in putting the applicant at ease? Did my questions get the responses needed? Did the interview move smoothly and stay on track or was it sporadic and difficult to control?

Another means of evaluating is to work from the personal angle. Did I talk too much? Did my personal prejudices and attitudes come through to the applicant, or did I maintain objectivity? Did I conduct the interview from the point of view of the applicant? Did I respond negatively in any instance? If I could redo the interview, what would I add or delete? What approach would I change? When considering impressions from the interview, it is important to remember that the overall picture is the most important. If you are undecided, you may wish to review your notes and information with a colleague.

These few minutes spent in considering interview performance will pay off in terms of increased perceptiveness and flexibility in handling the next interview and in operating more effectively in the selection process. In the final analysis, of course, the acid test of the interview is whether the result is a successful selection of a staff member who performs well on the job.

As part of an interview evaluation, Robert Ditter, in an article in *Camping Magazine* (January 1986), suggests some warning signs that he terms "red flags" which possibly characterize a personality prone to abuse children.

"Who ran the interview, you or the candidate? If you found that you were answering a lot of questions or being distracted by tangential conversation consistently throughout the interview, raise a red flag. Such behavior should make you wonder what a person might be avoiding. (Such behavior could indicate a 'controlling' or 'insecure' personality.)

"How much of a peer support system does this person have? Is he or she a drifter? Currently, are there significant other adults in his or her life? Are there strong connections to others, besides children, to give a sense of balance and support? If there are a lot of negative answers, raise a red flag.

"Does this person spend too much time with children? Does he or she seem to plan time-off activities which sound too much like work (typical of a physical abuser) or involve more time spent with children? If he or she also has weak peer relationships, this is a serious cause for a red flag alert."[13]

Becca Cowan Johnson, author of *For Their Sake*, would add: "How does this person describe how he or she was disciplined while growing up? Was it strict, appropriate, abusive? That is, does a person report an abusive past? Was the abuse emotional, physical, and/or sexual? Studies indicate a strong tendency toward repetition of experiences."[14]

Employment Agreement

It is accepted practice to provide each staff member with an employment agreement at the time of hire. The formality of the written agreement will vary from situation to situation; but, in any event, the staff member and the director should each have a copy of the document which they have both signed. A signed agreement between a director and a volunteer can also be healthy since it clarifies obligations on both sides and shows the responsibilities assumed by the volunteer.

In many states, employees are regarded to be at-will employees unless there is a written agreement specifying an employment period. The advantage of at-will status is that the employer can release the person earlier than had been anticipated if enrollment is slow or conditions warrant. An employment agreement may specify the dates of expected employment *and* indicate that the employment is at-will. Of course, an employment agreement does not force the employee to remain should he or she decide to terminate. Using the word *contract* instead of *employment agreement* may imply an independent contract or relationship. It is wise to have the format and wording of such an agreement reviewed by the camp's legal counsel, since there are legal implications that may be binding.

A sample employment agreement is shown in illustration 6.9. Such a letter usually contains the following items:

- Dates of employment or time commitment, with expected termination date
- Title of the position and reference to job description
- Remuneration
- A statement that employment is "at will" and may be terminated by either party
- Policy for termination by the staff member or the camp
- A statement of agreement by the staff member that he or she will abide by the personnel policies which are attached, or the specific policies included in the agreement
- Dates of signing
- Signatures of staff member and director (where the staff member is under the state legal adult age, the director may wish to have the letter cosigned by one parent)

---

[13]Robert Ditter. "Protecting Our Campers: How to Recognize Various Forms of Child Abuse." *Camping Magazine* Vol. 58, No.3, January 1986. p.23.

[14]Becca Cowan Johnson. 1992. p.116.

6.9

Illustration *Employment Agreement*

STAFF EMPLOYMENT AGREEMENT

Dear _____:

Camp _____ is happy to offer you a position as a _____ (insert position) on our staff. The position of _____ is described in detail in the attached job description, but do keep in mind that from time to time the administration may assign other duties deemed appropriate.

Your employment will begin on _____, 200___, and we expect that it will terminate on _____, 200___. Your salary will be based on the gross rate of $_____ per week. Deductions from your gross salary will include:

- federal and state withholding tax
- health insurance of $_____
- resulting in a net weekly rate of $_____

It should be noted that all of our employees are employed on an at-will basis.

Attached is a copy of the camp's personnel policies, outlining time off, behavioral expectations, and related matters. Your signature to a copy of this letter indicates your acceptance of the terms of employment and agreement to these personnel policies. Please return no later than *_____ (date).

The camp community provides a unique opportunity for team work, leadership, and service to our participants. We trust you will join us in our endeavor to make this a successful season for our campers, and for you.

Sincerely,

Camp Director

I accept this position as outlined.

Signature _____ Date _____

Personnel Files

Personnel files which include the application, references, contract, and eventual performance appraisal reports are normally kept for each staff member. These are confidential files and should be kept out of reach of all but supervisory personnel. Medical records on staff members should be kept separate from personnel files. It should be noted an employee may request to see his or her file. All of these files should be kept for a lengthy period of time, at least until the youngest camper at the time of that person's employment has reached six to eighteen months beyond the age of majority in the state of operation. Again, this is a matter to be reviewed with legal counsel.

Rehiring

Returning staff are important in the entire recruitment process. A director counts on retaining a significant number of staff from the previous season in order to maintain quality, continuity, and tradition. However, rehiring previous staff must not be done blindly. It must be recognized that often nine months or more has transpired since the last experience with the person. Much can happen during that period to change a person's attitude, experience level, and relationships.

Some directors go as far as to require returning staff to go through the entire employment process again: application, references, background checks, etc. Other directors use a form to ask the person to update the earlier application, perhaps by attaching a photocopy of the face sheet of the previous application and asking once again about driving record or criminal convictions. At the same time, the applicant can share additional experiences relative to the camp setting that would enable him or her to expand his or her duties. Where a state requires a criminal background check, such a check would need to be done annually. In any case, the director has a responsibility for developing a specific plan for assuring his or her confidence in the background, suitability, and fitness of every individual on the staff, including persons returning to the camp staff, however tremendous they may have been the previous year.

Appendix B provides a checklist for risk management in the recruitment and screening of employees.

CHECKPOINTS

1. List the positions which your program design necessitates and to whom each reports.
2. Review present job descriptions for each position. Check them, if possible, with persons who have filled the positions previously.
3. Outline the general responsibilities and specific functions of each position.
4. Outline the qualifications necessary to accomplish the functions as well as those imposed by position or regulations (i.e., age, certificates, degrees).
5. Test the number of counselors against the number of campers at one given time to find your camper/counselor ratio.
6. List all of the various sorts of remuneration you will be giving staff and develop the actual cost for each one. Compare this with line items in the budget.
7. Identify the different steps taken during the staff screening and employment process to prevent employing persons with a proclivity toward child or sexual abuse. Identify the steps taken to protect the camp in case of an incident.
8. Write out a series of questions you would ask in a job interview. Read them aloud to see how they sound. After revision, try them in an interview. Keep adapting them as necessary.
9. Outline the process your camp will use to screen returning staff members.

Related Standards

Accreditation Standards for Camp Programs and Services: HR-1–10, 21; "Additional Professional Practices": Items 25–29

Standards for Conference and Retreat Centers: II-26, 31–37

Camp Golden Valley, Bostic, North Carolina

Staff Orientation and Training

To the camp director falls the task of taking a number of individuals and helping them to achieve this peak of know-how-on-the-job, at the same time welding the total staff into a smoothly functioning team. It is no simple job, but one to which the camp director must turn much of his energy and planning.[1]

Staff training is probably one of the most difficult but potentially productive functions for a camp director who seeks to create a favorable climate and to set the tone for the summer season. The training of staff falls into three general categories:

- Orientation — the period from the signing of the employment agreement to the staff member's arrival at camp.
- Precamp training — the intensive period at camp set aside before the arrival of campers.
- In-service training — during the camp season — ongoing supervisory conferences, day-to-day problem solving, and staff meetings which include in-service training.

ORIENTATION

The preparation of the staff member for his or her job begins with the materials that are presented with the application for employment and the subsequent interview. It is essential that the prospective staff member understands the philosophy and goals of the camp as well as the unique makeup of a camp community since the interplay within that community has much to do with the accomplishments of the camp's goals. The information given a staff member in the interview and in correspondence must cover not only the job functions, but also the living conditions, transportation arrangements, philosophy of operation, and patterns of staff relationships.

During staff recruitment and interviews, the interviewee's concern for securing the job and the director's concern for hiring a staff member often push concerns about the

[1]Catherine T. Hammett. n.d. *A Camp Director Trains His Own Staff*. Martinsville, IN: American Camping Association. p. 7.

details of camp living into the background. The director cannot, therefore, depend on the description given at the interview or in prospective employee materials to thoroughly familiarize the employee with the setting and responsibilities. The time between recruitment and reporting to camp is longer than it is for many other jobs, and provides candidates a long time for second thoughts and opportunities for other jobs. This timing issue, added to the potential for a last-minute vacancy, makes it even more important to use the time between a staff member's hiring and reporting to camp for additional orientation.

If staffers come from within a hundred-mile radius, a number of orientation approaches are possible which cannot normally be used by a camp whose staff comes from across the country. In the former case, two or three meetings can be planned at a central location over the spring — giving new staff an opportunity to meet each other and former staff, to begin developing relationships, and to secure informal orientation. Local authorities or resource persons, who would ordinarily be unable to travel a longer distance or to come for a more extended period to precamp training, can often be recruited for presentations at such meetings.

A winter sport weekend, spring work weekend, or day at the camp can provide orientation to the facilities and property as well as give further opportunity for new employees to get acquainted with returning staff and to experience the camp living situation. These events also give the director a firsthand look at the new staff members and a chance to determine what approaches or content should be included in staff training.

A spring meeting of the local section of the American Camping Association or Christian Camping International usually provides a number of workshops and opportunities for additional certifications that are of interest to newly hired camp staff. In addition to workshops, these section meetings provide the opportunity of interaction with staff from other camps in the area. Such interaction provides a broader insight into the camp profession and, often, as the staff member gets involved, can lead to a commitment beyond the current summer. Many camp directors encourage membership in one or both organizations, and may financially contribute in order for staff to attend workshops or join organization(s).

In the case of camps with geographically scattered staff, orientation will most often depend upon a visit with the director or on printed materials. Frequent newsletters help stimulate interest and familiarize staff members with other staff, place names, and other features of camp. In addition, a staff manual can be a valuable orientation and training device as well as a helpful administrative tool for outlining policy and procedures. It takes a great deal of time, the cooperative assistance from key staff, and constant revision to prepare and maintain the most useful staff manual. "Current employment law emphasizes . . . that a carefully written employee handbook is essential."[2] A staff manual should include the following:

---

[2]"Written Employment Policies." *Trendlines* Vol. VIII, No. 3, January/February 1996.

- A brief history of the camp
- The camp's purpose, goals, and objectives
- A map of the property
- An organization chart of staff, clearly delineating supervisory lines
- A job description for each position
- The personnel policies, including a statement concerning compliance with local, state, and federal nondiscrimination laws
- Other policies and operational procedures:
  - Rules with specific disciplinary actions
  - A description of compensation policies including a statement that all raises, other than uniform or automatic wage increases, are at the discretion of the employer
  - Any laws affecting the duty of the employee
- A description of the operating body (agency, church, corporation)
- A list of items staff members will need to bring to camp
- A bibliography of helpful materials
- General counseling tips*
- Emergency procedures (e.g., for lost campers and natural disasters)*
- A statement that the staff manual/employee handbook does not constitute a contract of employment and that the camp reserves the right to terminate employment at any time

The items with an asterisk (*) and other items of similar nature may be better added to the manual during precamp training, as the matters are discussed.

Some directors use a rotating library of three or four books which best describe the camp's program and counseling philosophy for staff orientation. A book is mailed to a staff member with mailing labels for other staff; after each staffer has read the book, he or she mails it on to the next person. Often, the assignment of certain portions of the books for presentation by individual staff during staff training will focus interest.

Whatever information is sent to new staff before camp, it is vital that it be condensed as much as possible and its importance or value highlighted. If the staff member is a teacher or student, classes will occupy much of his or her attention and only a limited amount of preparation or reading can logically be expected. Therefore, the director should choose material carefully and plan to get it to staff well in advance.

Orientation is equally as important in day camp as in resident camp. Since day camp staff members tend to be from the same community and many times hold full-time jobs, staff sessions on Saturdays or Sundays may provide the orientation and training time needed prior to staff training immediately before camp.

It is important that the camp director plan ahead to ensure that staff members receive needed camp information as early as possible. Students can often use school health service personnel for their physicals if they receive the form early enough. Providing a list of clothing and equipment needed at camp soon after employment will enable the staff member to shop carefully. Other information sent to staff should include: the date and time they are expected at camp, the transportation available, the phone number and address of camp, and directions to camp.

However experienced in camp life a new staff member may be, he or she will always feel a degree of concern about a new site, a new camp community, and a new employer. Every step the director takes to relieve this concern and to help the new employee adjust and feel more confident will better his or her chances of success upon arrival at camp.

PRECAMP TRAINING

A precamp staff training program is one of the most effective forms of staff development and of assuring the camp will fulfill its mission. Basically, the purpose is to bring staff together to develop personal skills and competency for the job, and to mold individuals into a functional team for accomplishing the camp's goals and objectives. Precamp sessions also seek to provide opportunities for personal evaluation and growth.

In order to plan the most productive type of staff training, the camp director should begin early in the year to pull together possible topics and activities and to see what suggestions can be found in evaluations of the preceding year's training. If at all possible, the planning should include members of the program and administrative staff for the coming season; it is often good to add one or two experienced counselors to the group. As the planning begins, there are a number of factors to be considered.

Staff Come from Varied Backgrounds. Many will have had experience in other types of camps and will be prone to making comparisons, while others may not have been exposed to the demands of camp living. Some may come from sections of the country remote to the camp location and will have no knowledge of or familiarity with the natural environment or other resources of the new area.

New Staff and Inexperienced Staff Will Be Trained Together. There are usually some difficulties in planning the training with returning staff and new or inexperienced staff in the same group. Variation in the format and schedule of the training from year to year and the use of experienced staff to share their abilities with the new group can help to alleviate some of the problems. Working in small groups, when possible, gives new staff a chance to integrate more easily into the larger staff.

All Staff Need to Participate in the Training Process. This does not mean that every staff member needs to participate in every session of training, but there are certain sessions which apply to all staff — (i.e., administrative, support, counseling, returning, and new staff). For example, it is very important that kitchen staff or maintenance staff understand the philosophy of the camp and the importance and goals of the program operation, but they may not need the additional sessions related to camper behavior, conflict resolution, etc. All staff need to have a review of personnel policies and practices as well as camp rules so that there can be no misunderstanding.

Training Usually Centers Around Counselors and Staff Who Work Directly with Campers. Because they make up the largest portion of the staff and are primarily responsible for carrying out the camp's goals and outcomes, the training usually centers around counseling staff. The difficulty is that this group is probably composed primarily of individuals whose age and lack of experience may mean that they are at a loss about how to translate such goals or outcomes into everyday activities. The director's task is complicated by the necessity of clarifying for them the connection between the camp's goals and its procedures and policies of operation. Such understanding will, it is hoped, be gained in precamp training.

Experiential Training

Some directors find it helpful to organize the training period, to some degree, after the pattern in which counselors will work with campers. The counselors, in this plan, are divided into small living groups under the supervision of an administrative staff member or experienced counselor acting as counselor or facilitator. Within these groups, they can function as will their camper groups later in the season. They will move through the usual opening schedule: check in at the office, report to the health center with their health examination forms, tour the campsite, eat a meal in the dining hall, clean their cabin, etc. This plan has the potential of orienting the counselor more swiftly and provides a small living group to whom new counselors can more easily relate. This pattern can be continued daily throughout the training time and related to the camper experience in as detailed a manner as is desirable.

In any case, the training needs to be experientially based. Bob Ditter suggests that activities used in staff training "either provide a *shared* experience for counselors or tap into the counselors' *own* experience to make them more sensitive to children." He further quotes Ray Diamond of Camp Kokanda as suggesting, "If my Group Heads and Head Counselors have seen it first and have had a chance to practice it, they are less worried that some activity they might do with staff will be a flop."[3]

During the initial training period, habits will be formed, patterns established, attitudes developed, and relationships with peers and supervisors begun. Regardless of the necessarily high concentration of time on the factors which create a good experience for the campers, the staff member's greatest gain should be in his or her own growth, maturity, and development of potential. The advantage, of course, is that such personal development among staff members results in increased benefit to the campers with whom staffers will live and work.

---

[3]Bob Ditter. "New Direction in Staff Training and Development." *Camping Magazine* Vol. 67, No. 3, January/February 1995. p. 38.

On the practical side, some basic goals and objectives need to be reached during staff training:

- Infusing staff with the basic philosophy, goals, and desired outcomes of the camp and defining their implication for procedures and operations
- Fostering a sense of pride in the camp job and developing a harmonious working relationship among staff
- Teaching and providing practice of necessary program skills
- Developing an understanding of the characteristics of various age groups being served and providing an insight into working with them
- Providing the opportunity for staff to understand working policies and procedures as they relate to individual staff responsibilities and the camp as a whole
- Teaching individual and group skills in working with people

On a more individual and personal level, there are other objectives. There should be opportunities during the training for personal interaction so individuals find it easy to establish personal relationships with peers, immediate supervisors, and administrative staff. The use of experiential training activities can help guide a staff member to an increased self-knowledge and understanding of him or herself.

Scheduling

To deal successfully with all these factors and to accomplish the desired results in the time allotted demands careful planning. The time set aside for training never seems to be sufficient to cover all the priorities; even an experienced director who has worked at staff training over a period of years may not be pleased with the results.

The time allotted to precamp training varies from a minimum of twenty-four hours for day-camp staff and six days for resident and trip or travel staff to as long as two or more weeks depending upon the program and size of staff. A period of six to ten days will usually suffice. Shorter time periods seldom allow sufficient time for building the spirit of camaraderie so important in a camp community. Generally, staff are contracted to arrive for and are paid for this training period.

Before beginning to fill in a time schedule or consider topics, a director may find it helpful to review training schedules and post-camp evaluations from previous years. Discussions with staff who were present for some of those periods may provide insights into the character and effectiveness of the methods used. The evaluations at the end of the previous training sessions and the summer season can add additional data.

Once a block of time is set aside, a director is ready to decide what he or she expects to accomplish during the training period. Setting these intentions and objectives will do much to help choose and prioritize subjects and activities.

As the schedule is developed, the progression of the activities and sessions during the week should be considered. Early get-acquainted activities in the larger group will help put new and old staff at ease and give opportunity for new relationships. From this point, it is easier to move toward team-building activities in smaller groups. As staff members experience various program elements, the flow of camp will become more real. At this point, the group will be more open to child-centered training, and various techniques and approaches can be tied into the camp's program design and goals. The smaller the living or working group (up to five or six persons), the greater the personal involvement and commitment will be.

Child Abuse

One of the topics which should be dealt with during training is child abuse. The topic should be presented in such a way as to reinforce the alliance between the director, staff members, and parents, rather than to create an atmosphere of mistrust or fear. Placing comments about child abuse in the context of the stress or wear and tear that camp life can have on everyone provides an opportunity to talk about the possibility of impatience or unintentional meanness of counselors toward campers. This is one of the chief symptoms of burnout. Including this topic in staff training will send a clear, specific message that you, as a director, are concerned and moving to ensure the quality of care for all campers.

The discussion should include a clear and frank detailing of the basic definitions, tips for helping staff monitor their own level of fatigue, and guidelines for handling a situation which may have the potential for child abuse or child abuse accusations. Legal ramifications should be clearly pointed out, both for the director, who is required by law to report allegations of possible abuse, and for the staff member who may be involved. Ground rules concerning the continued employment of a staff member alleged to have abused a child should be concisely stated.

Practical examples of behavior management should be discussed. Role playing can be helpful as different behavior problems are illustrated and methods of management discussed.

In addition, staff should be alerted to watch for signs of physical or sexual abuse that may have occurred to the child prior to his or her arrival at camp. Symptoms outlined in chapter 4 should be discussed with counselors, and policy concerning notification of the appropriate camp administrators should be outlined. The camp administration has a responsibility to report such alleged abuse if observed at camp. Legal responsibility for reporting suspected child abuse differs from state to state, but almost every state has a reporting requirement today. Make certain that you and your staff are aware of laws and reporting methods in your state. (Some states, such as California, require every staff member in contact with children to sign a form acknowledging their awareness of state laws that mandate them to report any suspected or known incidents of child abuse.)

In her book, *For Their Sake*, Becca Cowan Johnson suggests two different formats which can be used to cover this topic for staff training. Other chapters in the book provide a wealth of reference material and current information which can provide an excellent basis for staff discussion.[4]

Varying Training Sessions

Actual training sessions should be planned for variety and balance. For instance, sessions requiring physical activity should be alternated with sessions requiring sitting and listening. A variety of teaching techniques should be employed to assure maximum attention and comprehension: guest speakers, demonstrations, films, charts, discussions, panels, and human relations games and activities. Variation in numbers can stimulate participation; group sessions where all participate may be alternated with small group gatherings.

In any case, the training needs to provide participation, demonstration, and interaction around the learning. Since many staff people are college students, they will have been exposed to all types of academic techniques and may have some resistance to being bombarded with facts and theories beyond the end of the school year. They may well expect to be far removed from the formal presentation of knowledge and anxious to have physical exercise.

Work sessions, with specific tasks assigned to small groups, can get necessary work done before camp opening and provide an opportunity for small groups of staff to work together. However, the director should avoid the temptation to spend fifty percent or more of the staff training time on the physical tasks required to open camp. The painting, cleanup, and repairs should be completed by a work crew well in advance of staff arrival so that the time set aside for training can be devoted primarily to camp objectives.

In searching for ways to accomplish the training objectives, it is important for the director to assess the needs and feelings of individual staff members. An open-ended discussion early in the period can reveal needs felt by a number of staff. Some directors also use a written needs assessment to identify needs that a staff member may be hesitant to mention early in the camp relationship. The size and experience of the staff will, in part, determine the method the director uses to gain an understanding of staff members' individual needs and objectives. Staff participation can be increased by assigning sessions or topics to individual staff with expertise in a specific area.

Outside resource persons from universities, county health departments, the U.S. Forest Service, or state conservation departments can often provide additional expertise for specific presentations. The involvement of such people will also build relationships in the local area. However, the selection and spacing of such presenters should be carefully scheduled so that they do not interfere with the development of group spirit and the overall thrust of the training.

---

[4]Becca Cowan Johnson. 1992. *For Their Sake*. Martinsville, IN: American Camping Association. pp. 121–128.

Several other processes should be included in the training period. Specialty program directors or department heads should have an opportunity to confer with staff who will be under their immediate supervision. Procedures and responsibilities of each staff member can then be defined before actual operations begin. A tour of the campsite should also be included, along with an orientation about the region in which the camp is located. Health and safety procedures need to be covered in detail, as do rules and procedures regarding the dining room, waterfront, and camp store. There should also be some opportunities for relaxation and fun — and simply for talking together. Appendix G offers a list of training topics suggested to meet ACA standards.

An overnight camping trip (or one slightly longer) can be a productive part of staff training. Such a trip would allow time for practice of camping or outdoor living skills and latitude for working and relaxing together in a more informal setting. This type of overnight or trip is even more important in a day camp where training may be day-only sessions which do not allow the time needed for socialization.

When setting the time schedule for training week, the director should plan a day off for staff between the close of training and the arrival of campers. The intensity of the training period can often be exhausting and staff need the relaxation and perspective of time away from camp as well as an opportunity to purchase any items they did not know to bring with them.

Training for Supervisory Staff

There are some specific areas in which supervisory staff need training that will not be of general interest or profit to other staff. However, since these supervisors are responsible for the staff who carry out the camp's outcomes/objectives directly with the campers, it is important that supervision skills be addressed. A good supervisor with the framework of a well-executed supervisory program can effect changes in staff performance and skills resulting in better experiences for campers, and more personal development and a higher return rate among staff.

As a result of a study of 100 camps and how they train supervisors, Becker and Shepherd state: "In many cases, however, new supervisors are often thrown to the wolves with little or no supervisory training. Camp administrators almost never start a summer without extensive, comprehensive precamp training. So, then, why do many camps skimp on training and orientation for head counselors?"[5]

ACA has a seven and one half hour training resource, *So You Want to Be a Supervisor*, that includes the roles supervisors play, a process for analyzing skills and handling appropriate and inappropriate behaviors as well as an individual supervision plan for each staff member. The curriculum also covers many of the following responsibilities that should be covered in supervisory training:

---

[5]W. A. Becker and Tony Shepard. "Study Suggestions to Improve Camp Supervisory Training." *Camping Magazine* Vol. 61, No. 1, January 1989. pp. 32–35.

- How to oversee staff. What are the specific functions and roles the director expects supervisors to carry out?
- How to treat staff members as individuals. It is important that a supervisor learn early in his or her experience the importance of treating staff as individuals and respecting that individuality. In the beginning, the supervisor ought to learn all the details about his or her staff: likes and dislikes, talents, skills, motivations, and how they react to different situations and to their supervisor.
- How to praise staff. Recognition of work well done has long been known as an important factor in motivating staff. This recognition can be on a personal basis, at staff meetings, or part of a supervisory conference. Public recognition or recognition before one's peers is even more effective as a motivator.
- How to challenge staff. A supervisor who believes in the potential of individuals he or she supervises can inspire them to accomplish a task simply because he or she believes that an individual has the ability to do the job. It is essential that a supervisor always remember to look beyond current job performance to the capacity a person has for achieving.
- How to deal with inappropriate behavior. This is an important function of a supervisor, especially in a camp setting, since staff problems may very quickly exert a negative impact on other staff and campers. The biggest hurdle is to get the staff member to see the problem; if this is accomplished, methods of solving the problem can then be dealt with. An important part of the supervisor's effectiveness with problems is to address the behavior and to be supportive but not to condemn the person.
- How to conduct supervisory conferences. These conferences may be difficult for new supervisors, particularly if there are negative points to be discussed. It is essential that he or she learn how to conduct such conferences with the proper balance of support, praise, and constructive criticism. A supervisor needs to comprehend how to make negative feedback a more positive experience by suggesting ways in which the staff member can improve his or her performance. And, most important, he or she needs to convey that his regard for the staff member has not changed because of problems.
- How to provide on-the-spot supervision. Not all supervisory comments can wait until a supervisory conference. On the other hand, pointing out an improper method or a violation of a procedure in front of other staff or campers at the time of occurrence will likely be embarrassing and difficult and is not appropriate unless the issue is one of immediate health and safety. Supervisors need help in learning the best way to share tips and observations with staff soon after such behavior is observed.
- How to work with the camp director. Supervisors should be able to solve routine camper and staff problems in a consistent manner without having to consult with the director. But there are some problems which should be discussed in full; the dilemma is to identify which is which. The director needs to be kept in the picture

since he or she is usually one step removed from the day-to-day operation, but he or she does not need to be consulted about every detail.

- How to handle framework. A clear understanding of the underlying philosophy and desired outcomes should be discussed so that supervisors know how their responsibilities and the responsibilities of their subordinates fit into the total framework; this allows them to work from a secure base of full understanding of the whys and wherefores.

- How to handle the supervisor's role. It is often difficult for a new supervisor to understand how much his or her role has changed as he or she moves into supervising other staff. To be adequately prepared for this role, he or she must recognize that, with such leadership, comes a difference in the way he or she is viewed by subordinate staff. As the person ultimately responsible for performance of staff, he or she may become the motivating force behind goals and outcomes/objectives that staff may not share.

- How to deal with the alleged abuser. The general rules for reporting an alleged abuse situation and the protection of the abused child are covered earlier in this chapter; however, in most camps, there is a policy about what the process is when an accusation is made. The staff member is usually suspended with or without pay. The director should give advanced thought to any role the supervisor might play with the alleged abuser; e.g., reporting to director, being with the accused until he or she leaves camp, etc. John Durall suggests that "the abusing staff person may feel anxious or depressed. He also may be worried about going to court, being sentenced to jail, handling the effects the incident may have on his future, and facing family and friends. On a deeper level, he may feel shame, guilt, and self-devaluation, as well as hopeless and desperate."[6]

The supervisory and appraisal process is discussed in detail in chapter 8.

Documentation

A schedule of the entire precamp training week with annotations about content and presenters should be kept in the permanent file. It is also wise to have an attendance sheet for each session for staff to sign as they enter the training area. They should be helped to understand that this is a protection for them in the sense that it documents that they have had training in the identified areas, in case their qualifications are challenged after an alleged incident at camp; the director should also document how staff that are new or miss precamp training receive instruction. Again all of this is part of the risk management plan and a protection package that the camp director develops and preserves in case of a lawsuit or alleged abuse incident.

---

[6]John J. Durall. "Encountering Child Abuse at Camp." *Camping Magazine* Vol. 70, No. 6, November/ December 1997.

IN-SERVICE TRAINING

When precamp training concludes and campers arrive, the training of staff does not end. With seasonal staff, training must be continued throughout the season: first, in effort to continually assure a quality experience for the participant, and second, to address issues that come up during camp. Also, many of the staff will return another season and the training will bear further dividends. After precamp training and during supervision, supervisors often have the best handle on what topics need to be covered in such training and can help develop the format. Common problems or voids in performance will appear in a number of staff members as the season goes along. This can occasion a meeting or staff-training module designed to fill that void or deal with a specific problem. Since time is precious and staff is under pressure, such training periods should be planned carefully and developed for a succinct and practical presentation.

A meeting devoted solely to a training problem or concept focuses staff attention on the training without the time competition and attention pressures of a regular staff meeting. However, it is often from the regular staff meeting, supervisory observation, or conference that topics for the special training sessions are derived.

In-service training sessions may also be an extension of topics begun during precamp training, where time or readiness of staff members did not allow more advanced discussion. In fact, many training topics become more meaningful after the staff members have had experience in their program areas or with participants. Because of the experience gained at this point, it is vital that some time in the training module be allowed for discussion and sharing among group members.

The use of outside resource persons is most effective in these in-service training sessions when the topic requires a certain expertise or authority. For example, if abuse is the topic, a psychologist or social worker with experience in the field can add a certain authority to the issue, answering questions from experience. Similarly, a naturalist with knowledge of local flora and fauna can bring expertise to a nature walk or presentation that may not have been possible during precamp.

It is critical that the topics chosen for in-service training events be timely and of practical use by the staff at that point of the season. Staff will be under considerable pressure from ongoing program and relationships and will exhibit impatience and inattention if they do not find the session pertinent to their current day-to-day experiences.

Also, one of the realities of a camp staff group is that there are always some individuals who arrive in the middle of or after staff training. The termination of an employee necessitates a replacement early or midseason. A returning staff member cannot leave university classes until midway through staff training. A weak link is created each time a director assumes that a returning staff understands all of the assigned responsibilities or that a new employee can "pick up" the information he or she needs as he or she goes along. Therefore, it is important to have a plan to make sure that the training topics such a staff member missed are covered before the person assumes assigned duties.

STAFF MEETINGS

In-service training modules are different from administrative staff meetings or all-staff meetings held on a regular basis throughout the season. The purpose of regular administrative staff meetings is the coordination of program events, operational details, personnel, and personal concerns. An opportunity should be given for all staff members to share concerns, to clear up details, or to explain decisions. It is important that matters announced or discussed at all staff meetings be distributed in some fashion to those not present who may be on duty with campers or in other operations. Some immediate behavioral problems may be resolved at such meetings or identified for future in-service training. Staff may learn by leadership behavior modeled by the director or other administrators. These staff meetings can be considered training only in a limited sense.

CHECKPOINTS

1. Have the dates for precamp training been clearly identified to staff at the time of the contract?
2. What are the specific objectives which need to be accomplished during the precamp training period?
3. Have staff applications and interview records been reviewed to determine areas in which particular help or instruction will be needed by individuals?
4. Which staff members with particular expertise can be used during staff training as group leaders, presenters, or instructors?
5. Are there outside resource persons within fifty miles of camp that can be helpful?
6. Are you, as a director, going to assume the leadership role in staff training, or are you collaborating with other key staff or delegating the training to others entirely? How are those roles to differ?
7. Have you involved staff in designing a needs assessment to try to uncover the training needs felt by individual staff?

Related Standards

Accreditation Standards for Camp Programs and Services: HR-11–17, 19; "Additional Professional Practices": Items 26, 27

Standards for Conference and Retreat Centers: II-38–40

Nancy Bland, Patriot's Trail Girl Scout Camps, Boston, Massachusetts

8

Staff Supervision and Performance Appraisal

Supervision is seen to be — first, last, and all the time — a relationship of persons; as such, it calls for deep qualities of heart and mind and spirit, and for acceptance of whatever disciplines and plain hard work are necessary to develop the needed abilities and skills.[1]

Possibly one of the most overlooked and underestimated procedures in general camp administration is a regular system of supervision and performance appraisal for staff. Under the pressures of the summer season, it is difficult to allot sufficient time for supervisory functions unless a plan is developed prior to camp. A regular program of supervisory conferences provides countless opportunities for stimulation of individual growth, for a deepening of supervisor and staff relationships, and, ultimately, for upgraded job performance.

This supervisory process, if carried out in a relationship of mutual trust and respect, can be a major factor in the retention of staff. As staff become conscious of their own personal growth through the supervisory procedure, the usual result is on-the-job satisfaction and a desire to repeat the experience. There are few jobs available to young people today that provide such a climate of interested and productive supervision.

The director has no more valuable asset for ensuring good job performance than his or her personal knowledge and relationship with supervisory staff who assess individuals' job performances. This interplay of relationships provides an opportunity for the director to share in the lives of individuals with a people-oriented commitment to the camp and its programs.

FUNCTIONS OF A SUPERVISOR

A supervisor has been defined as a person who holds the following responsibilities:

- The conduct of others in the achievement of a particular task
- The maintenance of quality standards

---

[1]Margaret Williamson. *Supervision — Principles and Methods.* New York: Women's Press. p. 4.

- The protection and care of materials and people under his or her control
- The rendering of services to those under his or her control

There are numerous ways to categorize functions of supervisors. Writers and trainers generally identify the following functions of supervision.

1. Teaching Staff Their Job
   - Understanding all the tasks required in the job being supervised
   - Teaching skills in a progressive manner (i.e., what has to be learned first, second, etc.)
   - Assessing whether and how well the skill has been learned

2. Delegating Responsibility
   - Assigning staff
   - Delegating tasks (e.g., ordering supplies, planning an event, supervising the wash house, etc.)
   - Determining time off and coverage for staff responsibilities (e.g., days off, rovers, etc.)

3. Evaluating Performance and Accountability
   - Observing performance
   - Writing reviews of staff performance
   - Holding supervisory conferences
   - Providing verbal feedback on a regular basis, both praise and constructive criticism

4. Improving Performance
   - Observing behavior
   - Analyzing skill performance
   - Determining what has to be improved and how to improve it
   - Establishing and maintaining a positive relationship with staff so that they accept instruction
   - Communicating what needs to be changed

5. Dealing with Problems
   - Listening and observing
   - Handling conflict
   - Confronting problems rather than letting them fester
   - Recognizing the difference between a complaint and a real problem

GUIDELINES IN SUPERVISION

There are some further guidelines concerning relationships that may be helpful to a supervisor who has had little experience directing others.

Trust. This factor is basic to establishing a meaningful relationship, both for job performance and for personal interaction. Each staff member needs to know that the supervisor can be trusted to deal objectively and unemotionally with problems and discussions that arise. He or she must also know that the supervisor can deal with matters involving other individuals, seeing several sides of his or her personal problems and concerns. The staff member also must know that his or her job performance and discussions with the supervisor will remain confidential (unless the disclosure must be shared with the camp director, and then the staff member should be informed of the intent to do so). To maintain this trust relationship with staff, the supervisor must show staffers that he or she values and respects them regardless of job performance. It may be difficult, at times, for the supervisor to maintain this attitude, but it should grow out of his or her innate respect for the worth of every individual, a respect which can transcend differences or personality conflicts.

Rapport. The ability of a supervisor to quickly establish communication and a relaxed interaction with staff members who may be unaccustomed to and wary of the supervisory framework is paramount. Along with the belief in individual worth, a genuine liking for all sorts of people and skills in human relations will help create the desired climate.

Sharing. The supervisor should cultivate the habit of sharing with employees, individually and collectively, his or her appreciation of the job being done. Regular commendation of a job well done will also help to prepare the staff member to accept criticism when it is necessary. It is also helpful if the supervisor has a plan to regularly observe the people he or she supervises — "on the job" while with campers, while teaching, while interacting at meals, etc. If staff find that this is done in a benevolent spirit, they will gradually become less self-conscious about observation. A supervisor's support and appreciation may very well not be perceived by others unless it is expressed verbally and backed up by his or her benevolent treatment.

The details of the staff supervision process should be shared with the group during staff training. It is helpful, also, to give an idea of general expectations and the criteria to be used in performance appraisals. If written notes from supervisory conferences and observations are to be added to personnel folders, the staff should be told this.

How Does One Begin?

As preparation for beginning a staff supervision program, time can well be spent in reviewing personnel information folders of returning staff and the application and interview papers of new staff. Acquaintance with staff backgrounds and facts is an asset when meeting the individuals, since it helps establish them in memory. Before the opening of the camp season, the supervisor might well seek opportunities to chat and get personally acquainted with local staff who are new and with returning staff whom he or she may not know well. With out-of-town staff, the chances for beginning a relationship are fewer and perhaps limited to letters but are, nevertheless, important.

With the opening of camp and the beginning of staff training, personal contact can be broadened through discussion sessions, small group activities, human relations training, unstructured social occasions, group work projects, and staff overnights or trips. Any personal interplay which strengthens a relationship between supervisor and staff is a major plus in beginning a supervisory relationship.

LEGAL NEGLIGENCE AND THE SUPERVISORY PROCESS

In court cases where a camp is being sued for negligence in failing to protect a camper against accident or abuse, one of the lines of defense is to show that a plan or process for supervision is in practice consistently for all staff. To be adequate, this plan or process for supervision should include the following points.

1. Each employee must be given information as to who will be his or her immediate supervisor.
2. There should be a definite plan for supervision including observations, formal conferences, informal conferences, written reprimands signed by supervisor, and a performance appraisal system.
3. Supervisors should have a clear understanding of their authority and the options available to them when staff behavior does not match expectations.
4. There must be a specific plan for dealing with an alleged abuser.
5. There must be a system for dealing with alleged harassment, camper to camper, staff to camper, or staff to staff.
6. Special training must be provided for supervisors and should deal with a uniform performance appraisal system, observation and recording methods, appropriate and inappropriate staff behavior, and conference formats, recording, and techniques.
7. There must be a formal plan that includes authority for terminating an employee, documented evidence of events leading to firing, and a plan for the final interview.

Techniques for Supervising Others

The following is a range of possible supervisory techniques that help define the supervisory relationship and the behaviors, attitudes, knowledge, or situations supervisors may encounter. Supervisors need to be able to quickly access factors that are motivating a behavior(s) and select a course of action.

1. **Teaching**

   Teaching assumes the person being supervised lacks knowledge. This may be because information has yet to be presented on the topic, or because the staff member has forgotten the presentation or is unable to apply the knowledge to a different set of facts. The role of the teacher includes:

   - Directing
   - Providing instruction

2. **Coaching**

Coaching assumes the person being supervised lacks experience or confidence in performing appropriately or with high skill. The individual may not have connected the intellectual knowledge he or she has with its application in a given situation. The role of the coach includes:

- Reminding about key principles
- Encouraging where necessary
- Instructing in parts of the skill where necessary
- Indicating confidence that staff will get it right
- Helping staff "walk through" the potential experience and rehearsing the skills

3. **Modeling**

Modeling assumes the supervisor is always being watched and should be constantly demonstrating the skills and attitudes he or she expects of staff members. Staff members will notice if the supervisor says to be consistent in enforcing policies with campers but is not consistent with him or herself in enforcing policies with staff. They will see it if you are not responsive to their problems but you expect them to be responsive to camper problems. The role of the model includes:

- Always demonstrating positive attitudes
- Always demonstrating compliance with camp rules and philosophy
- Always taking problems to the source or to your own supervisor and never gossiping or talking behind people's backs
- Working hard and showing initiative
- Acting in the best interests of the camp and the campers, not in your own best interest

4. **Reinforcing**

Reinforcing assumes you are observing staff frequently enough to find them doing things right! It further assumes that you provide positive feedback when you see appropriate behavior, recognize positive changes the staff member has made, or note a positive attitude in difficult circumstances. Reinforcing good behavior prepares the staff member to hear constructive criticism. They know you are not just looking for the bad, but you willingly praise the good. The role of the reinforcer includes:

- Being a frequent observer of each staff member
- Complimenting and praising each staff member frequently
- Finding things staff members are doing well

5. **Correcting**

Correcting assumes you are observing behaviors that have not changed in spite of teaching, coaching, modeling, and reinforcing. Except in cases where safety requires immediate intervention to correct a behavior, supervisors should generally use one of the first four techniques in dealing with staff behavior prior to correcting or disciplining. Correcting should be done in private, and in a manner that focuses on the behavior rather than the person. More specific training will be provided on this topic later in this chapter. The role of the corrector includes:

- Maintaining the self-esteem of the person being corrected
- Focusing on the behavior, not the person
- Teaching, coaching, reinforcing, and modeling prior to correcting except when safety demands immediate correction

Appendix B provides a checklist for risk management in the recruitment, screening, training, and supervision of employees to help administrators in the area of negligence.

THE SUPERVISORY PROCESS: COUNSELORS

Since counselors are the majority of staff members, a supervisory plan for counselors and the persons supervising them (whether a unit director, head counselor, or the camp director) will be outlined here. However, this program can easily be broadened and adapted to other staff and departments.

In the case of each of the supervisory conferences, written records need to be kept by the supervisor, along with pertinent reports and appraisals, and filed in the individual's personnel folder. This provides a permanent, on-going performance record while the person is employed by the camp; it also becomes a valuable resource during rehiring decisions and when references are requested by future employers. The overall goal is to help all staff members perform their jobs as expected and feel success and appreciation for their work. Waiting until midseason or the end of camp to let people know how they are doing will not help job performance improve quickly and may be interpreted by staff as satisfaction with their job performance on the part of the supervisor. During precamp training, supervisors will want to assess their staff's attitudes and participation to determine if some staff will need additional training in certain areas and to see if they understood the training content.

Post-Staff-Training Interview

It is often effective for the supervisor to schedule twenty- or thirty-minute conferences with each counselor at the end of staff training and before the arrival of campers. There are some specific questions which can help the supervisor increase his or her knowledge of the staff member. Other questions can help get feedback on the training period and, at the same time, assist the staff member in solidifying and expressing his or her own personal reactions. Questions to be included in the appraisal may be:

- What areas of the job, as you see it now, do you feel confident in handling?

- Are there any areas about which you feel apprehensive?
- Are there still areas where you feel less than competent? (If teaching skills, is there an area where you have difficulty with organizing and teaching material?)
- If age groups have not been assigned, is there a particular age group of campers you would prefer and why?
- How do you feel about your relationship with other staff? (Although the counselor's answer here is important, your observations may be necessary to complete the picture.)
- With which areas of staff training did you feel most comfortable?
- Were there sessions of training that were of little or no interest to you?
- What are your goals for the summer? (These goals should be measurable, attainable goals which can be evaluated in an objective manner later. There should be job-related goals as well as personal-growth goals.)

One very positive factor in avoiding a climate which may be favorable to child abuse is to stimulate staff to set personal goals. Another is to encourage staff, at this point, to plan ahead to spend some time each day refreshing and recharging themselves, without neglecting responsibilities, to keep from getting overly drained.

Observation

A planned program of informal observation provides a supervisor with an occasion to observe the counselor in various activities that are a part of his or her performance — in the living situation, in skills teaching, and while participating in program activities with campers and other staff. These observations, which should be carried out informally and on a regular basis, will provide information about the counselor's ability and potential. Concerted efforts should also be made to talk with campers in informal situations, since these contacts may give further indication as to the job the counselor is doing. The frequent presence of the supervisor in daily activities will also provide latitude for interchanges that may not otherwise happen. Although these drop-in practices may cause some anxiety in the beginning, staff and campers will usually come to accept them as part of the routine.

The best feedback to the counselor on his or her performance is that given immediately after the observation. But since the feedback should not be given when others are present, the opportunity may not present itself. In any case, notes should be made of each observation as quickly as possible after leaving the observation area. Such notes can be tucked into the counselor's personnel folder and used at the time of the next supervisory meeting. It is important that these notes include positive feedback as well as criticism, and they should show the date, place, and conditions of the observation (e.g., counselor teaching group canoeing). These notes also provide another link in the protective chain for the counselor and the camp if there should be alleged child abuse or negligence. It may be possible to develop a checklist which can be used in observation of all personnel in similar positions.

In his *Camping Magazine* column, "In the Trenches," Bob Ditter notes that being a good observer includes: watching carefully, waiting to draw conclusions, checking assumptions and appearances, and observing one's own biases. He also suggests that using an observation guide will help keep the observer on track. The guide could include such things as: eye contact, appropriate touch, one-on-one communications, pitching in, and working well with co-counselors.[2]

Periodic Conferences

Depending upon the length of the camp's sessions, another supervisory conference should be scheduled with each counselor after a primary period of working with campers. The conference should come at a logical program point within the first two weeks. This gives an opportunity for mistakes to be corrected or habits changed before the lapse of too much time. This conference should deal with a number of topics such as:

- **The counselor's comments on each camper** in his or her group and the relation of each to the group as a whole. The discussion on this topic has a dual purpose. First, the supervisor receives information helpful in dealing with the individual campers. Second, he or she has a chance to check on the counselor's ability to relate to and observe campers and to articulate understanding both of individuals and the group living process.
- **Any problems or conflicts which arose or currently exist** and whether they have been worked out. This probably will arise naturally out of the first topic; if not, it is good to include it as an indicator of how the counselor interacts and makes decisions concerning campers.
- **The counselor's conclusions** about what things he or she might handle differently if the time could be redone.
- **The counselor's evaluation of his or her personal job performance,** including frustrations and high points, if any.
- **The counselor's assessment of the accomplishment of any goals,** and establishment of new or modified goals for the next period.
- **A brief review of the supervisor's observations of the counselor in action:** Good points should be given first, followed by any problems or suggestions for a more effective performance. It may be a good idea to introduce this area by asking the counselor to evaluate the weaker and stronger points of his or her own performance during the period. This often opens the topic on a more positive note, and sometimes brings up the very areas the supervisor wishes to discuss.

A sociogram (see illustration 8.1) is often used in this type of conference, particularly if the camp's program is focused on small group living and camper relationships. Such a diagram serves as a visual reminder of questions that should be covered during this and subsequent discussions.

---

[2]Bob Ditter. "Skills for Staff Supervisors." *Camping Magazine* Vol. 68, No. 5, May/June 1996. pp. 15–16.

8.1

Illustration   *Sociogram*

LIVING GROUP   Pioneers   COUNSELORS   Smith Levine

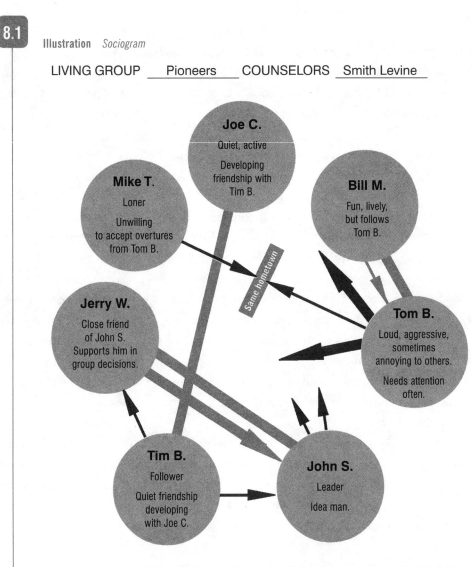

The circles provide a space to detail personal information, observations, or problems of each individual camper. The spaces between circles can be used to indicate relationships with other individuals. The center space can be used to sum up general observations about the group as a whole; how they worked together, attitudes, spirit, etc.

This type of conference can well be repeated at the end of each camp session where there is a change in camper assignments, or on a regular basis if the camper group remains longer. The topics can be adjusted to deal more specifically with problem areas and with progress since the previous conference.

End-of-Season Performance Appraisal

The goal of any good supervisor is to enable the staff member to come to the point of effective self-appraisal followed by appropriate responsive behavior. However, certainly as one nears the end of a summer season or a three to four month period with a year-round employee, the performance appraisal emerges as a responsibility of the supervisor. Any performance appraisal should relate to the employee's job description and especially the essential functions the employee is expected to perform. There may be other areas of evaluation tied to performance which are related to stated job functions, of course.

So far, only the evaluation from the viewpoint of the counselor and his or her immediate supervisor has been pinpointed. This, however, provides only a partial view of the counselor's job performance. In addition, some system should be devised for evaluation of the counselor by supervisory personnel in other departments or areas of camp with whom he or she has had some contact during the summer. Some of these, depending upon the basic staff organization, may be the nurse, the program or unit directors, the assistant director, the business manager, the tripping director, the food service director, and the waterfront director. It is helpful if these evaluations can be devised in such a manner that they can be added together to get a numerical average in various areas of concern which can be readily communicated to the counselor. See illustration 8.2 for a sample staff appraisal form. You will note that the evaluation form is tied to the sample job description shown in illustration 8.3. The performance appraisal refers to specific responsibilities in the job description.

There should be few surprises for the counselor when he or she comes to the end-of-season performance appraisal. Any major performance concern or problems will have been dealt with as the occasion arose during the summer. The final conference of the season should begin with an end-of-period appraisal for the last camper session of the summer. This conference also offers other opportunities to the supervisor:

- To share his or her evaluation of the counselor's performance over the summer along with any comments and evaluations from other staff gained through the evaluations mentioned above
- To hear the counselor's feelings about camp, the experience, and his or her own performance
- To hear the counselor's assessment of his or her accomplishment of job-related and personal goals for the summer

Through this closing conference, the supervisor should seek to guide the counselor in understanding the importance of self-evaluation as a necessary part of growth and development. It is also an occasion for the supervisor to share his or her support of the counselor along with an expression of appreciation for the job carried out.

8.2 **Illustration** *Sample Staff Performance Appraisal Form*

EXPLANATION:

1. Person doing rating studies each square in horizontal row and circles one number (1-10) indicating appropriate level of skill. High numbers indicate a high rating; low numbers indicate less satisfactory performance or areas that need work. Particularly appropriate phrases can be circled and inappropriate phrases can be crossed through.

2. Various persons' ratings are recorded on a central form and a line is drawn through the form connecting the ratings for each row (see bold, vertical line).

3. Employee being evaluated is invited to mark a form on him or herself, with supervisor pointing out the importance of self-evaluation as a growth tool.

4. The employee's evaluation line is marked in a different color on the central form (see dotted line), and the comparison of the two lines is used as a basis of the supervisory conference. Again, emphasis is placed on self-perception in the evaluation process.

PERFORMANCE APPRAISAL FORM

Confidential Appraisal of _____ by _____

Please circle a number in each row which best approximates your position of staff member or skill area noted in the first column. Mark through words or phrases that do not apply.

UNDERSTANDING OF AND RELATIONSHIP WITH CAMPERS *Relates to specific responsibility #2.*	■ limited understanding of groups/individuals ■ communication on basic level only ■ no close relationships with campers	■ beginning comprehension of groups/individuals ■ begins to communicate ■ occasionally develops close relationships with campers	■ basic understanding of group dynamics/personal growth ■ good communication but limited depth ■ develops friendships with campers ■ participates with campers	■ good understanding of group – establishes rapport quickly ■ limited awareness of potential of individuals ■ some close relationships	■ reveals excellent understanding of group/individuals ■ shows real involvement with and respect for campers ■ good communication skills ■ recognizes/develops individual/group potential ■ many close relationships
	1 2	3 4	5 6	7 8	9 10

(continued on next page)

8.2 **Illustration** *Sample Staff Performance Appraisal Form continued*

	1–2	3–4	5–6	7–8	9–10
MANNER/ RESPONSIVENESS *Relates to specific responsibility #2/3.*	■ timid ■ overbearing ■ withdrawn ■ cocky ■ dominates conversations ■ curses, vulgarity	■ quick tempered ■ irritating ■ indifferent ■ does not volunteer information ■ evasive ■ inappropriate language	■ well balanced ■ good listener ■ responds well ■ mature/balanced ■ appropriate language	■ very confident/alert ■ self-assured ■ tactful ■ spontaneous ■ stable ■ appropriate language	■ enthusiastic, warm ■ perceptive ■ imaginative ■ exceptionally self-possessed
MOTIVATION *Relates to specific responsibility #6.*	■ just wanted a job ■ not interested	■ primarily interested in camp life, not campers ■ self-centered	■ willing to work ■ interested in campers ■ considerate	■ genuine interest in/love for campers ■ very industrious	■ primary concern is to work with campers ■ always thoughtful/ considerate of others
APPEARANCE *Relates to specific responsibility #5.*	■ untidy ■ sloppy ■ often dirty ■ disheveled	■ careless in dress/ cleanliness	■ good appearance ■ generally clean/tidy	■ very neat ■ careful in dress/ cleanliness	■ gives evidence of concern/care in cleanliness at all times

8.2

	1 2	3 4	5 6	7 8	9 10
ATTITUDES TOWARD CAMP OPERATION *Relates to specific responsibility #2/3/4.*	■ avoids participating in certain camp activities ■ complains about assignments ■ sees only small part of total operation of camp as important	■ participates but avoids active leadership in activities ■ attitude discourages participation of campers ■ ill at ease before a group – timid, hesitant ■ lacks confidence to secure group's attention	■ leads some activities ■ works in most any assignment without complaint ■ lends support to programs through attitude/participation	■ relaxed/confident in leadership ■ gains enthusiastic response from audience ■ well prepared/organized ■ brings fun to any activity supervised	■ participates in and enjoys activities/group ■ inspires enthusiastic response ■ can handle any situation when leading group
TEACHING OF SPECIFIC SKILL *Relates to specific responsibility #3.*	■ disorganized ■ wordy ■ unsure of self ■ limited ability in skill area	■ ill at ease ■ knows basic skills ■ lacks organization/confidence in teaching	■ comfortable ■ communicates skills well to individuals ■ adept at skill	■ well organized ■ very much at ease ■ varies pace, involves group ■ involves individuals in trying skills	■ exceptional command of organization ■ speaks camper language ■ involves individuals easily ■ expert at skill

Notable strengths _____

Notable weaknesses _____

If you were director, would you employ this person another year?   ☐ Yes   ☐ No

8.3

Illustration *Sample Job Description*

SAMPLE JOB DESCRIPTION

POSITION TITLE: COUNSELOR

Responsible To: Unit Director

Qualifications:
- At least eighteen years of age
- High school diploma or GED required; one or more years of college preferred
- Experience as a camper or working with children as a leader or assistant leader
- Ability to relate to one's peers as well as to children
- Good character
- Flexibility, with ability to accept supervision

General Responsibility: To live with and guide eight campers throughout their camp experience.

Specific Responsibilities:
1. Live in a cabin with eight campers
2. Assume responsibility for leadership and guidance of those campers in daily living, with special attention to:
   - personal hygiene and safety
   - camper participation in all-camp activities
   - camp participation in planning cabin activities
   - meal-time behavior and habits
3. Assume responsibility as assistant activity specialist in an assigned activity area
4. Assume responsibility for interpreting the rules, policies, and traditions of the camp to the camper
5. Serve as a good example in personal language, appearance, and health habits
6. Assume responsibility for health and welfare of campers entrusted to his or her charge

Essential Functions:
- Be physically able to accompany the campers to any of the camp activities
- Be able to communicate verbally with campers, and provide instructions
- Have visual ability to recognize hazards in the camp setting as well as physical symptoms of camper injury or illness
- Have auditory ability to respond appropriately to hazards and any camper concerns
- Be able to observe camper behavior in daily camp life, to respond verbally to health and safety concerns, and to deal appropriately with any improper behavior

THE SUPERVISORY PROCESS: NONCOUNSELING STAFF

A supervisory process similar to that designed for counselors is applicable to noncounseling positions and administrative staff. The supervisor can follow similar principles and steps:

1. Establish initial ground rules and understandings of responsibilities and performance goals with the staff member in a conference at the close of the training period.
2. Observe the staff member at work and make notes of these observations.
3. Establish a scheduled time for periodic conferences to discuss the staff member's concerns, job performance, personal goals, and accuracy of the job description.
4. Hold an end-of-season performance appraisal in which some feedback is given, pointing out improvements over the season and evaluating together the staff member's accomplishment of personal goals. Again, this appraisal of performance should be related to the specific responsibilities and essential functions from the job description

and should not be a surprise to the subordinate. This discussion should open the way for any feedback from the staff member and for his or her self-evaluation of job performance.

For administrative staff, there should also be a plan for securing evaluations from counselors and other staff who work with and for them. A summary of these should be shared at the final performance appraisal at the end of the summer. The form shown in illustration 8.4 gives one example of a form for administrative staff evaluation.

If the camp director does not supervise certain staff directly, he or she can benefit from the supervisor's notes on each appraisal conference that are placed with the employee's personnel record. The director can also learn from administrative staff meetings and written records of the overall individual needs and performance of staff whom he or she may not be able to observe directly.

The supervisory program for full-time, year-round staff can operate under the same framework as that for summer administrative staff. The timing of supervisory appraisals could parallel that of summer administrative staff and then be adjusted to long appraisal periods for the remainder of the year. A yearly performance appraisal should be scheduled according to the organization's personnel policies (e.g., end of year, end of fiscal year, or anniversary date, etc.). Or, if the job description of the full-time staff member does not essentially change during the summer season, evaluation might be more effective on a periodic basis apart from other members of the summer administrative staff.

8.4 Illustration *Evaluation of Administrative Staff by Counselors*

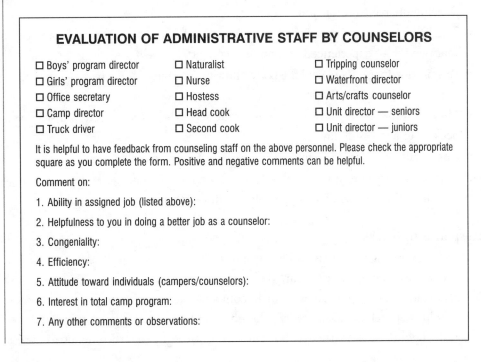

EVALUATION OF ADMINISTRATIVE STAFF BY COUNSELORS

☐ Boys' program director	☐ Naturalist	☐ Tripping counselor
☐ Girls' program director	☐ Nurse	☐ Waterfront director
☐ Office secretary	☐ Hostess	☐ Arts/crafts counselor
☐ Camp director	☐ Head cook	☐ Unit director — seniors
☐ Truck driver	☐ Second cook	☐ Unit director — juniors

It is helpful to have feedback from counseling staff on the above personnel. Please check the appropriate square as you complete the form. Positive and negative comments can be helpful.

Comment on:

1. Ability in assigned job (listed above):

2. Helpfulness to you in doing a better job as a counselor:

3. Congeniality:

4. Efficiency:

5. Attitude toward individuals (campers/counselors):

6. Interest in total camp program:

7. Any other comments or observations:

STRESS AND CAMP STAFF

In any program of supervision at camp, the camp director and department supervisors need to be aware of the potential problems of stress. The intensity of living in the camp community provides its own proclivity to stressful situations. It is essential that the director and all supervisors have a somewhat technical understanding of stress, its symptoms and effects, and how to help alleviate those effects in themselves and the staff they supervise. Stress management in staff has been previously named as one factor in risk management as well as in staff retention. Attention to the symptoms of stress has been shown to decrease the number of accidents/incidents greatly.

Definition of Stress

Stress is a physical, chemical, or emotional reaction that causes bodily or mental tension. Stress results from factors that tend to alter an existing equilibrium. These stressors are external demands or internal attitudes and thoughts that require us to adapt. Stress triggers a response from a complex part of our brains and bodies called the autonomic nervous system. This system creates the fight-or-flight response, which provides for bodily changes that enable humans to fight or flee from physical dangers to their survival. Stress may cause people to experience some of the following symptoms:

- Digestion slows so that blood may be directed to the muscles and brain — experienced as "butterflies in your stomach"
- Breathing gets faster to supply more oxygen for the needed muscles — experienced as being unable to catch your breath
- The heart speeds up, and blood pressure soars, forcing blood to parts of your body that need it — experienced as a pounding heart
- Perspiration increases to cool the body, allowing it to burn more energy — experienced as increased sweating
- Muscles tense in preparation for important action — experienced as a stiff back or neck after a stressful day
- Chemicals are released to make the blood clot more rapidly
- Sugars and fats pour into the blood to provide fuel for quick energy — experienced as a surprising increase in strength and endurance during an emergency

Response to Stress

Camp often triggers stress and its symptoms but provides few outlets for relief. Unlike other jobs where a person can go home and find outlets for relieving stress, the seasonal staff work long hours with little contact from their home or from others who might help them relax. Additionally, when human beings cannot run from anxieties or physically fight their fears, the result is emotional stress. Even if the chemicals produced by emotional stress could be safely burned off, the resulting psychological distress can interfere with productivity, learning, and interpersonal relationships. When stress reactions continue without relief, people become less and less able to handle even minor stress.

Short-Term Stress. In the short term (a period of hours), stress responses often manifest themselves by: a jittery stomach, a lump in the throat, a tight feeling in the chest, a racing pulse and pounding heart, a pain in the neck and shoulders from tension, or a tendency to fly off the handle.

Long-Term Stress. In the long term (a period of weeks), stress responses become chronic and incessant and have much wider implications for the staff member. It is at this point that the supervisor may first become aware of the presence of stress, because the staff member exhibits some of these symptoms. He or she:

- Becomes less productive
- Never has enough time
- Becomes withdrawn and depressed
- Has increased smoking or drinking problems
- Experiences an increase in pain associated with chronic diseases (arthritis, headaches)
- May eat more and gain weight, or eat less and lose weight
- Is subject to day dreaming and has difficulty concentrating
- Experiences sleeplessness or sleepiness
- Has feelings of worthlessness, inadequacy, and rejection
- Has difficulty dealing with campers and other staff

Stress Management

To help the stressed staff member cope with the situation, the supervisor needs a basic understanding of the biological systems related to stress factors. The major system, the autonomic nervous system, has two divisions. The first, called the sympathetic nervous system, is the one that triggers the fight-or-flight response to danger and is responsible for the changes in the physical body. It is the second system, the parasympathetic, that influences the body in ways that are almost the exact opposite of those of the sympathetic. This second division is responsible for conservation and replenishment of energy and modification of the sympathetic nervous system response. There is some evidence to suggest that the parasympathetic nervous system can be activated through relaxation procedures, thus minimizing and negating the physical responses of the sympathetic nervous system.

A supervisor who observes the symptoms of stress can counsel the affected staff member to take practical steps toward managing the stress. Most stress can be divided under three main categories: stress from your situation, stress from your mind, and stress from your body. Within these categories, there are some immediate solutions or ways of handling stress that staff can be educated to use.

Situational Stress

- Assert yourself; say "no" or ask for exactly what you need.
- Remove yourself or escape from the problem.
- Plan specific steps to avoid, reduce, or correct the problem in the future.
- Pace yourself and schedule time to relax.

Mental Stress

- Catch yourself when jumping to conclusions, taking things personally, or attaching much importance to a minor event.
- Mentally yell "stop!"
- Replace negative or anxious thoughts with positive thinking or your happiest memory.
- In your mind's eye, see yourself taking charge in a relaxed and confident way.

Physical Stress

- Breathe in deeply, counting slowly to five; as you exhale completely, count slowly back to one and relax all muscles.
- Imagine you are loose and relaxed from head to toe.
- Avoid caffeine, nicotine, or any stress-causing chemicals; substitute a quick stretch or a brief walk.

However, these solutions are of a temporary, stop-gap, or preventive nature. They may be effective in some cases of short-term stress and may help to alleviate some problems. But in some individual cases, medical or psychiatric assistance may be necessary if symptoms seem severe and if the person is unable to function normally under the day's demands.

Burnout

Some degree of stress is healthy and helps the individual be productive and competitive in the day-to-day situation. However, if stress is unrelieved or moves to long-term stress, burnout can result. Burnout is a condition of emotional and physical collapse brought on by the unchecked escalation of pressure or stress. Particularly in the resident camp situation, where staff members are often with campers twenty-four hours a day, day after day, even with time off a counselor can find him or herself burnt out by the end of the fifth or sixth week of camp. Time off may actually cause additional stress when pressured to be with friends, do laundry, drive distances, etc. There are signals which can alert the supervisor to the potential burnout of a staff member.

People who are over-enthusiastic are prone to burnout. They get so wrapped up in the job and situation that they feel everything is wonderful and do not hesitate to share that with one and all. Antagonism toward others sometimes arises at this point, and the individual often moves away from peers who are less enthusiastic or tire of the individual's enthusiasm. Those who frequent the health center with colds, neck pain, back pain, rashes, and other similar conditions are often actually exhibiting the early signs of burnout.

The individual begins to sense that his or her commitment level is lessening or something is wrong with the assignment. The person may feel that he or she needs something more challenging, indicating that he or she is not enjoying the present assignment as much as in the past. Or a request may be made for more time off to provide a new viewpoint. Days off may be spent in frenzied activity to relieve this feeling or tension. However, the relief of time off does not seem to last; within a day or two, the old symptoms begin to show.

At this point, the individual begins to find it difficult to function as efficiently as in the past, and often tries to cover up inefficiencies or mistakes by making excuses or lying. Relationships seem to deteriorate, and it is difficult to find peers who are willing to help or support the individual. The person may appear nervous, forgetful, or distracted. From this point, burnout can progress to desperate efforts to combat the feeling of defeat and it can resemble depression. Day-to-day tasks become more difficult and the person uses lies or deception to cover up the problem.

A well-developed supervisory process lends itself to helping the potential burnout candidate recognize the problem and the symptoms and develop a program to utilize his or her free time and days off for relaxation rather than for frenzied activities. The supervisor and other staff may try to provide support and nurturing concern for the individual; at the same time, the supervisor should help the individual recognize the importance of opening him or herself to those who are supportive.

Careful attention to providing the adequate time off and days off for all staff is important to prevent burnout and relieve stress in all staff. Though some types of personalities are more prone to burnout than others, the pressure of the camp living situation can bring on burnout in persons who otherwise would not succumb. Therefore, as the season progresses and staff tend to get more tired, relaxing events for groups of staff and careful coaching for individuals can help prevent burnout.

THE SUPERVISOR AND TERMINATION

If a supervisor utilizes all the techniques of supervision and does everything possible to encourage a staff member to function as expected, but the employee still doesn't have the skill or does not cooperate, it may be time to fire him or her. Today's increased awareness of many employment issues such as sexual harassment means that employers must terminate employees as a result of such unacceptable behavior. Failure to do so puts the supervisor, as well as the camp, at risk. Training and supervision, however, are designed to minimize the possibility of having to dismiss staff because of inappropriate behavior or inadequate job performance. A copy of the staff manual (containing the rules for termination) in the hand of each staff member assures that the "no one told me" excuse cannot be used. Most supervisors do not have the authority to fire a staff member without discussing it with the director.

If a supervisor is having difficulty with an employee, the first action is to confront the employee regarding the problem and take steps to correct the behavior. In an article in *The Journal of Christian Camping*, Rob Crawford recommends a three-step process.

1. Sit down with the employee and talk it over. And, what is more important, listen to the employee. Most employees want to do the right thing; it may be that they need more direction or training, which the supervisor needs to provide. Following the conversation, there should be a follow-up memo to the individual, stating the problem and the appropriate action decided upon. If Step 1 has not resolved the problem, go to step 2.

2. The supervisor and the staff member, together, agree upon a more formal process, which is agreeable to both. The agreement must stipulate the objective, measurable behavior which is required. A time line is set, and the consequences clearly set out. The consequence might not be termination; other disciplinary measures might be chosen. Everything should be clearly defined, with a reasonable penalty for failure to comply.

3. Follow through with what was agreed upon in Step 2.

If all else fails and termination is the only answer, do it quickly. Once the supervisor realizes that it is beyond the point of no return, give the employee a final check with a fair severance pay and request that he or she leave the property as soon as possible. To protect against the potential charge of discrimination, the supervisor needs to see to it that all employment policies treat everyone equally. It is also essential that the supervisor refuse to discuss the circumstances of firing with other staff.[3]

Oddly enough, there can be a positive side to firing a staff member. It will confirm to other staff members, who may have witnessed the continuing problem, that the ongoing disruptive behavior brought its own result. In addition, the termination may actually prove to be a new beginning and a more positive move for the employee.

CHECKPOINTS

1. Outline who supervises whom.
2. What is the plan for supervision of staff that you, as director, supervise?
    *   Conferences?
    *   Observation?
    *   Group meetings?

---

[3]Rob Crawford. "The Firing Line." *Journal of Christian Camping* Vol. 27, No. 3, May/June 1995. pp. 16–19. Reprinted by permission from CCI/USA.

3. How does that plan relate to the overall plan of supervision?
4. Outline performance appraisal tools to be used.

Related Standards

Accreditation Standards for Programs and Services: HR-8–9, 18, 19, 20, PD-12, 14; "Additional Professional Practices": Item 26

Standards for Conference and Retreat Centers: II-41

Cheley Colorado Camps,
Estes Park Colorado

9

Selection, Development, and Maintenance of the Site

To guide the orderly development of any camp site, a plan is needed. This will govern the total development that may take place over a period of years. . . . While it may seem a lot easier and much more fun to skip planning more or less completely, such a course . . . can only lead to headaches, trouble, and possibly disaster. Impatience to get the job done and over with and unwillingness to spend money for professional planning services are poor excuses for not using hard won . . . funds to produce the best possible result.[1]

PHYSICAL FACILITY AS AN ASSET

The physical setting of the camp is an important element in the planning of program and, therefore, in meeting the camp's goals and outcomes/objectives. If used to its greatest potential, the setting can make the best experience even better. On the other hand, the neglect of the physical property of a camp can make even the best program a disappointing one for participants and staff.

Whether a camper, a parent, or new staff member, the first impression a person has of a camp is its appearance. A camp director needs to go to camp one day and try to see it as a first-time visitor would. What strikes one: cleanliness and loving care or neglect and disarray?

The most valuable asset a camp owns is its physical site and the buildings on it. With less and less suitable land available for camping and with land values continuing to escalate, the camp director has a tremendous responsibility to protect that asset. Part of the camp director's responsibility is to help safeguard and preserve a physical site and property for future generations of campers, as a camp, conference center, and/or outdoor education facility. Today there are many pressures from outside developers and urban sprawl, and from within financially struggling parent organizations, to use camp properties for other purposes or to gain capital from their sale. The camp director becomes the

---

[1]Julian Harris Salomon. 1959. *Camp Site Development.* New York: Girl Scouts of the United States of America. p. 29. Reprinted by permission.

guardian of this asset, not only from the viewpoint of discouraging the sale of the property, but also for making sure the property is accomplishing its purpose so well that discussion of its sale can be effectively fended off.

SELECTION

Though most camp directors inherit a physical site, other camp directors rent facilities and therefore have the opportunity from time to time to select a site. The most fortunate of all camp directors are those who get to select a site and build a facility from the ground up, but this book is not designed to provide all the steps necessary in that process.

As a camp director reviews a variety of camp facilities in the process of selecting a site, especially in regard to rental, here are some guidelines that may be helpful:

- Check to see if the appropriate local and state permits and licenses are available for review. Have there been appropriate water tests? When were they taken? Is the sanitation system approved and in working order? Has there been an inspection by the fire authorities? States and localities vary in their permitting systems and regulations, and the absence of certain permitting processes or regulations means that the director must be more knowledgeable and more careful in his or her inspections and questions during the selection process.

- Review the camp site for health and safety factors. Are there apparent natural hazards? Are buildings well maintained or does their condition provide hazards? Are those hazards easily corrected or does the condition of a given building require major repair or replacement? What is the swimming facility like in terms of water quality, location, ease of control, and safety? Is the kitchen clean and rodent free? What is the condition of major equipment such as walk-ins, refrigerators, ranges, dishwashers, etc.? Is the camp accredited by the American Camping Association?

- Look at the layout of the property, location of buildings, the natural environment of the camp, and program facilities. Do they complement your program philosophy and goals? How would you have to adapt your program in this setting?

- Check the location. Is it convenient enough for transportation to and from the areas from which you draw campers or from major transportation terminals?

- Determine the distance to the closest medical, fire, and other emergency services.

- Survey the camp's closest neighbors. Do the homes or activities surrounding the camp create potential problems currently? What is the zoning of surrounding properties? What potential development could occur that might affect the camp in the future? Is a major highway or thoroughfare planned?

- Look for security problems. Are there any obvious ones that might endanger campers or staff? How many access points are there into camp? How easy is it to control those access points?

When a site is rented for seasonal use, it should not be assumed that the owner is routinely taking care of maintenance problems. At the time the lease agreement is signed, a careful inspection of facilities and a list of expected repairs and maintenance should be made and incorporated into the lease agreement. An advance understanding between the director and renter about meeting state and local regulations, as well as any standards set by the organization, is vital. A clear understanding about cleaning and other advance preparations should save some frustration later. Be prepared upon leaving to fulfill your part of the agreement.

Before signing a lease agreement, the director should study it carefully to understand the responsibilities of both parties. It is advisable to have it checked by an attorney. Similarly, closer to time of use of property, an informal inspection should be made and reminders given to the owner about items not yet completed.

DEVELOPMENT OF AN OWNED SITE

Most camp properties are in perpetual change, and every camp director is faced with decisions about these changes at some time: building new structures, remodeling and repairing older structures, or constructing roads or sewer lines, etc. This may not be the primary interest or strength of the camp director, and it may seem to be an interruption of the more important aspects of programming and service to people. However, the camp director must develop a plan to effectively deal with those changes, both in the acquisition of funding as well as designating staff to supervise and/or accomplish the changes.

Long-Term Planning

The wise camp director understands that form follows function and will work to help develop a facility that serves and enhances the program functions of the camp. If there is not a master site plan resulting from a long-term look at the camp's philosophy, market, program, finances, and facilities, then this should become the first priority of the director, owner, or volunteer board or committee. To make extensive changes in the property without an overall plan could be both costly and frustrating.

A master site plan requires a commitment to study the overall camp situation and its potential. In most cases, an outside consultant will be most valuable from the beginning of the process. Whether that person is paid or a volunteer, it is critical that he or she be objective, have an understanding of organized camping with some depth of knowledge of camps beyond your camp, and have basic planning skills. Eventually you may also need the expertise of an architect and perhaps a landscape architect. There are professional camp-site planning firms, as well as individual consultants, who offer services in this field.

A comprehensive site plan will encompass a number of procedures:

- A review and evaluation of the camp's purpose and philosophy
- An analysis of the clientele now served and a review of what potential markets the camp may desire to serve in the future

- A careful cost analysis of existing services and programs, as well as a look at potential funding sources
- An inventory of present facilities and property
- An inventory of present uses of each facility and each portion of the property year round
- Statements by the director, owner, and, in nonprofit camps, the committee or board about the purpose, new or existing target markets, overall program of the camp, and desired uses year round
- Evaluation of the accessibility of the buildings and program facilities for staff or campers with disabilities, and the difficulty with which modifications/adaptations can be made
- Development of a schematic site plan that would best use the existing buildings and the natural resources of the property, showing where new buildings or program areas might be constructed
- Development of a time line and plan to accomplish whatever site plan is agreed upon after input and discussion among the planner, the director, the owner, and any volunteer structure

Often the first thought after securing proposals for a master site plan is that the cost of such a plan could easily offset some of the direct expenses of the actual development. Many camp directors may be tempted to short-cut the process and simply do it in-house. Though this may save money initially, most often it will cost a great deal more in the long term due to the lack of objectivity or expertise.

Dan Smith points out that "while there are basic principles of design, arriving at a well-designed solution is not a simple cookbook process. Even though computers have placed the means to draw floor plans within the reach of almost everyone with a keyboard, there is more to good design than a wide selection of fonts and a big assortment of furniture symbols. Good design includes both a knowledge of design principles and an understanding of the concepts behind these principles. Also needed is an 'eye for design.' It is this knowledge, understanding, and 'eye' that consultants in the field bring to the camp."[2]

Short-Term Planning

Though development of a master site plan is ideal, not every director will be able to wait on such a plan before instituting development. However, there are some steps that will assist in making immediate decisions about such development. They will also be invaluable when retaining a planner and starting a master site plan.

First, make sure you have accurate maps of the property, topographical as well as schematic. If there is not a topographical map on file and you cannot afford to have one

---

[2]Dan Smith. "Design — Good or Bad — Influences Your Ministry." *Journal of Christian Camping* Vol. 27, No. 5, September/October 1995. p. 19. Reprinted with permission from CCI/USA.

made, purchase the U.S. Geological Survey map for your area. An aerial map will also prove valuable. There should be a survey map of the property which was secured at the time of purchase of the property; however, that is not always the case. A survey map should indicate property lines, highways or roads, rights-of-way or easements. Major buildings and utility lines should have been added to this map as they were built. If there are questionable property lines which have not been surveyed, this should be a first order of business.

Second, make sure all utility and sanitation lines are correctly drawn on a property map so that water lines, electrical lines, and gas lines (with cutoff points and valves) are clearly identified. Blueprints of buildings should also be gathered in one location.

Third, secure as much information about the land, soil, vegetation, wildlife, and water resources as possible. State or county foresters, fish and wildlife personnel, and conservationists will often be willing to walk the property with you and provide suggestions on reforestation, improving wildlife habitat, protecting and improving the lakes and streams, and other conservation measures that can be undertaken. All of this information will give you clues to areas that should not be developed with buildings or program activity areas, and to other areas where development will do less damage.

Fourth, if you do not have copies of the state, county, and local regulations and building codes that specifically apply to camps, they should be secured now. Obviously, these become the first priority in the development of the site, should the camp not already comply. New development may be required to meet higher standards to come into compliance. Also, state, county, and local health and sanitation officials often can provide guidance to developmental concerns in their areas as well as to the adequacy of your waste disposal system, water system, and related sanitation concerns.

The director should give careful attention to the implications the Americans With Disabilities Act of 1990 (ADA) has for providing accessible facilities.

> *Camps must consider needs of persons with physical disabilities in relation to the site, facilities, and program. A camp is not relieved of its legal responsibility to make "reasonable accommodations" simply because it is not currently serving any persons with disabilities. As public accommodations, all camps must adhere to applicable laws. For the purpose of the ADA, camps must also consider hearing and visual impairments, emotional disturbance, developmental delays, and so forth.*

> *For specific guidance, refer to the "Americans With Disabilities Act Accessibility Guidelines for Buildings and Facilities" (ADAAG) which is available through the U.S. Access Board. [See Appendix G for contact information.] ADAAG standards refer mainly to buildings, toilets, bathing facilities, and parking. . . .*

> *Full compliance with ADAAG is required only for new construction and alterations. Existing facilities can be made more accessible through some "readily achievable" changes in which barriers are removed.*

States will vary on accessibility regulations. Camps must comply with the most stringent requirements (that which provides the greatest access for individuals with disabilities) of the local, state, and federal codes that apply.[3]

Fifth, uncover the inventories of the physical facilities and major equipment. If an updated inventory is not available, then one should be made, noting the years of construction of buildings and acquisition dates and identification numbers for all equipment.

Now that you have this information, you can do more intelligent planning. Take a walk through your camp's property and examine each building and program area. Note where improvements are needed, such as areas with erosion problems or natural hazards, and buildings needing modifications to comply with the ADA, and where additional development may complement program and appearance or provide new opportunities to serve new groups. Divide this list into repairs or corrections that can be done quickly and easily or need to be made immediately to alleviate risks, and those which may require more funding or assistance than is immediately available.

It is the list of repairs which can be made immediately that will start your development plan. These items should be prioritized, with those that affect health or safety receiving earlier priority than those that are cosmetic or programmatic in nature. Each development project should be evaluated against the information you have secured in your earlier surveys to determine its effect on the natural environment, its fit in the overall aesthetics of the camp, its seasonal use, and, as far as possible, its care-free maintenance. With this background, detailed plans should be developed, involving a structural architect, landscape architect, or engineer where necessary. Only then are you able to begin to develop a budget and time line for completion. This process becomes the camp's short-range plan until such time as an overall master site plan can be developed.

MAINTENANCE

A Maintenance Plan

The first list of immediate repairs and corrections will fall under maintenance as opposed to development, and should be resolved as part of an ongoing maintenance plan. This overall plan is one that should be developed in collaboration with the year-round caretaker or ranger who normally supervises camp maintenance. It should include:

- A routine inspection of all facilities after their use by a group, to assess any damages and identify cleaning needs

---

[3]American Camping Association. 1998. *Accreditation Standards for Camp Programs and Services*. Martinsville, IN: American Camping Association. p. 197.

- A regular schedule of painting or application of protective finishes to exteriors and interiors of buildings
- A schedule of draining, unhooking, and connecting water lines if the camp is located in the freeze zone and lines are not winterized
- A plan for checking and correcting erosion throughout the camp grounds that includes a plan for alternating activity areas or traffic patterns to restore a setting to a healthy state
- A routine inspection schedule of all water and sewage systems, including the swimming pool and its maintenance, and a regular testing schedule of drinking water, the swimming pool, and any natural bodies of water used for swimming
- A routine schedule for cleaning, lubricating, and checking each piece of machinery and equipment with moving parts, including tests of smoke detection equipment and replacement of filters
- A schedule for routine inspection, replacement, and repair of screens, windows, railings, steps, docks, and roofs
- An annual inspection of all electrical service and heating systems

When these various routines have been established for cleaning, repairs, and testing, a written record, giving scheduled and completion dates, person responsible, and specifics of what is done, is wise. The keeping of a maintenance logbook will greatly assist other staff and preserve a record of all work done. Preventative maintenance will lengthen the life of buildings and equipment and make the facilities more attractive to guests. Samples of two forms that may be adapted for use in routine inspections are shown in illustrations 9.1 and 9.2.

A daily schedule can then be prepared of the prioritized tasks with specific assignments made to staff who may be assisting. It is to be recognized that emergency repairs will come up on a day-to-day basis, sometimes pushing scheduled projects on to the next day.

As part of the maintenance plan, a strategy should be developed for the cleaning and upkeep of high-traffic areas in camp: bathrooms, the dining hall, meeting areas, pathways, etc. In most camps, the day-to-day cleaning of living areas such as cabins or dorm rooms is left to the camper groups that occupy the areas, through camper assignments or group projects. However, in rental situations with certain types of adult groups, cleaning of rooms may also need to be assigned to staff. Many camps depend on campers to clean the bathrooms, but supplemental cleaning and checks by staff will help. Campers and staff should use rubber gloves and follow procedures for handling bloodborne pathogens when cleaning the bathrooms.

Most camps have a large number of older buildings which require constant maintenance and upgrading to extend their lifespan.

Not enough can be said about the importance of regular annual maintenance of each and every building in camp. Camps in a budget squeeze often look first to see which

9.1

Illustration *General Maintenance Inspection Checklist*

GENERAL MAINTENANCE INSPECTION CHECKLIST

Camp name _____ Date _____

Check as okay, or indicate assigned job card number.

Item	✓	Item	✓	Item	✓	Item	✓
1. UTILITIES		**3. FOOD HANDLING**		Walks		Communication equipment	
Water System		Arrangement		Pool walls			
Well casing		Stoves		Pool floor		Office furniture	
Well cover		Refrigeration		Gutters		Inspected by:	
Spring protection		Freezer		Drainage		Date:	
Intake screen		Mixer		Dressing rooms			
Pump(s)		Ovens		Showers			
Pump motor(s)		Dishwasher		Toilets		**8. PROGRAM AREAS**	
Chlorinator		Sterilization		Filters		*Waterfront*	
Filter		Sinks		Chlorine equipment		Piers	
Control system		Tables/counters		Cleaning equipment		Floats	
Pipe lines		Dishes		Inspected by:		Boat dock	
Storage tank		Dish storage		Date:		Guard tower	
Valves		Utensils				Beach	
Winter drains		Storage space		**6. LAND MANAGEMENT**		Control fence	
Sanitation		Ventilation		*Lakes/Ponds*		Check board	
Sewer lines		Lighting		Silt control		Boats	
Septic tanks		Garbage		Aquatic weeds		Oars	
Seepage pits		Inspected by:		Dam		Canoes	
Disposal field		Date:		Spillway		Paddles	
Garbage disposal				Control gate		Sailboats	
Grease trap		**4. MAINTENANCE**		*Conservation*		Lifesaving equipment	
Electrical		Trucks		Erosion control		PFDs	
Power lines		Tractor		Wildlife management			
Line clearance		Tractor equipment		Stream management		*Tripping/OLS Equipment*	
Telephone		Trailers		Forest management			
Telephone lines		Power tools		Landscaping		Rope	
Line supports		Hand tools		Foot trails		Axes	
Gas/Oil		Spare parts		Soil conservation		Saws	
Gas lines		Standby equipment		Obnoxious plants		Compasses	
Storage tanks		Fire equipment		Conservation equipment		Cooking equipment	
Regulating equipment		Fire extinguishers				Shovels	
Inspected by:		Camp signs		*Public Areas*		Tents	
Date:		Flammable/hazardous material		Picnic area		Packs	
				Boundary fence			
2. ROADS/PARKING		MSD sheets		Lawns		*Other Program Areas*	
Surface		Basic records		Inspected by:		Archery range	
Ditches		Utility maps		Date:		Archery equipment	
Drainage		Mechanical equipment records				Rifle range	
Bridges				**7. OFFICE**		Rifles/guns	
Culverts		Vehicle records		Computers		Fishing gear	
Service roads		Inspected by:		Printer		Ropes course	
Gates		Date:		Copy machines		Ropes course equipment	
Barriers				Phone system			
Inspected by:		**5. SWIMMING POOL**		Answering machine		Inspected by:	
Date:		Fence		Fax machine		Date:	

9.2 Illustration *Building Maintenance Inspection Checklist*

BUILDING MAINTENANCE INSPECTION CHECKLIST

Camp name _____ Date _____

Person making inspections _____

Check as okay, or indicate assigned job card number.

NAME
OF BUILDING
OR STRUCTURE
⇨

Foundation																								
Sills																								
Floors																								
Outside walls																								
Inside walls																								
Doors																								
Windows																								
Screens																								
Roof																								
Steps/rails																								
Chimney																								
Fireplace																								
Wiring																								
Plumbing																								
Fire protection																								
Building																								
Gutters																								
Drainage around bldg.																								
Housekeeping																								

repairs or improvements can be postponed. However, to postpone maintenance whether it is painting, replacing screens or water pipes, or reroofing is "penny-wise and pound-foolish." Delay only increases the wear and tear and the eventual cost, as well as often leaving the camp open for potential accidents or injuries.

In the day-to-day maintenance of a facility with a large number of staff and campers, it is important to have a system for reporting needed repairs. Oral transmission of such requests through the camp director or directly to the maintenance supervisor is unfair since it relies on the memory of a busy person. A form should be available so any staff member can report an item needing repair or attention by placing the form in a given location. See illustration 9.3 for an example of such a form. Providing a tear-off or duplicate copy enables the director or supervisor to keep a copy while forwarding a copy to the person charged with the repair. That person returns the duplicate copy indicating the date of completion and circumstances of the repair. It is wise to maintain a file of such forms for risk management purposes.

Essential to any extensive maintenance program is a building that houses tools, equipment, and vehicles, and provides dry, heated or cooled workshop space with sufficient electric power to conduct repairs and build replacement items as needed. Adequate storage space is needed for supplies and extra beds, mattresses, and other equipment. Scott King points out that "at many facilities, one of the first things a guest sees is the maintenance building and the assorted objects and vehicles around it. Screen this area and other undesirable elements from the guest's view. A pleasing entry to your facility sets the tone for what guests expect when they arrive."[4]

Where the camp director has a supervisor or a volunteer committee off site, it is vital to share information concerning facility needs and problems with the appropriate party on a regular basis. In this situation, it becomes a shared responsibility because the camp director may not be in a position to free the funds needed to undertake certain projects or to make a final decision about location and construction. When supervisors and committees are kept well-informed and involved, they will be more likely to help in finding unbudgeted funds to solve problems or expand facilities.

9.3

Illustration   *Request for Maintenance*

REQUEST FOR MAINTENANCE

Director (copy)

Date _____

Check one: ☐ Building repair   ☐ Equipment repair   ☐ Grounds repair

What building or piece of equipment? _____

Nature of problem _____

_____

_____

                                    Signed _____

- -

For Maintenance Department Use Only

Action taken _____

Date completed _____   By whom _____

---

[4]Scott King. "The ABC's of Facilities and Maintenance." *Journal of Christian Camping* Vol. 20, No. 5, September/October 1988. p. 9. Reprinted by permission from CCI/USA.

Personnel

Careful selection of property management personnel is as important to a camp as the selection of camp counselors. To provide year-round maintenance, it is essential that responsibility be assigned to one individual. That person is most likely the ranger or caretaker who lives on the property and becomes the property or site manager by default. It is important that such a designation carry with it the appropriate job description, level of responsibility, and compensation plan. However, not just any person will possess the skills to do the job. On the other hand, some on-site managers get so accustomed to being in control for nine months that they take on a feeling of ownership and seasonal directors and guests feel as though they are intruding on private land.

As a maintenance plan is developed and scheduled, it should help identify the pressure points where additional part-time or full-time maintenance assistance is needed or where certain contract services will alleviate that necessity. It will also show downtime when maintenance personnel can take time off. Much will depend upon the skills the caretaker or ranger brings to the job, and there may be skills that need to be supplemented by additional help or training.

The director should give some thought to the potential involvement of volunteers in repairs. A work weekend at a resident camp site or a work day on a day camp site can accomplish quite a bit at very little cost, if adequate energy and time has gone into the planning. One of the most important elements is recruitment of skilled parents, organizations, members, staffers, and volunteers as well as campers and less skilled volunteers for general labor.

Thought should be given to who supervises the volunteers. Some property managers may have the skills to work with and supervise volunteers, where others may feel inadequate or uncomfortable in such a role. If the latter is the case, the camp director or another staff or committee member may need to team with the property manager to ease relationships, while the property manager supervises the projects and ensures that projects are completed properly.

Careful organization of the projects, including assignments of teams, proper tools and materials, and clear, written instructions are essential to the success of such volunteer experiences. Some projects are too lengthy or involved to be accomplished in a weekend, and others require licensed personnel and should not be attempted during a volunteer weekend. The food service at such an event may be a volunteer effort where everyone brings a food item and the camp furnishes basic food and supplies, or the camp might provide total food service.

It is always a temptation to leave much of the cleaning and minor repairs for the week when staff arrive for precamp training. Except where certain work projects are used for a one- to three-hour period to build staff teamwork and ownership of the site, it is unwise to use this valuable training period for such routine cleaning and maintenance.

Written Records

Reference has been made to the importance of written plans, records, and reports. The importance of written records will be further commented on in the chapter on risk management. However, aside from alleviating liability concerns, if the property is truly the camp's most valuable asset, then written records to ensure its health and continuance are not too burdensome. These records should include:

- A surveyor's map of the property
- A topographical map of the property
- An aerial map of the property
- A schematic map of the property showing facilities and program areas
- A map of the property showing all utility lines, cutoffs, disconnects, and valves
- The property deed and any related easements or rights-of-way
- The blueprints or construction drawings of buildings
- A record of each structure, its construction date and subsequent repairs
- A master site plan
- Any written reports of land or resource conservation management
- Inventory of all mechanical equipment, including dates acquired, serial numbers, and repairs made
- All warranty information on equipment, along with instructional manuals and manufacturers' catalogs
- The ongoing maintenance schedule, with written checklist showing dates and work completed
- Inventories of supplies and minor equipment

A clear designation of which staff member is responsible for securing, storing, and maintaining these records should be made in job descriptions. A specific location should be identified where these records are maintained.

WINTERIZATION

Since camps have traditionally been summer-only operations, their buildings have often been built without protection of water lines from freezing temperatures and without insulation and heat. In the past three decades camps have steadily moved to operating longer than the summer months. New camp buildings are almost universally being winterized for use in nonsummer months.

The modification of summer-only buildings into winterized facilities is often an expensive and unsatisfactory proposition. An analysis of the types of use that are desired and the nature of possible user groups should be made before any steps are taken toward winterization. A careful assessment should be made to see if the need for such facilities is being met in the area by other camps or conference/retreat centers or a real interest is documented for a new program. A market analysis, as described in chapter 12, is a logical exercise at this point. After this analysis, one is better able to judge the type of facilities that will attract these groups as customers, and to determine whether it is feasible to modify existing buildings or whether the volume of business or service will justify the construction of new winterized facilities.

A camp should carefully consider the distance from the nearest metropolitan area, which is most often the source of extensive nonsummer use, as well as existing competition from other camps or conference/retreat centers in the area. Is there a demand for weekday as well as weekend use? There is no question that year-round operations can spread the cost of maintenance and staff over a larger number of users, allowing better cash flow, broader accomplishment of purpose and goals, and certain savings. However, without the appropriate market or facilities, the opposite may occur. Certain costs will increase with winter use. For example, buildings will need to be kept at a minimum temperature even when not in use, and additional cleaning and maintenance will be necessary, so energy and personnel costs will rise. There will be increased wear and tear as well. Careful study should precede a move toward a four-season facility to make sure that increased usage will more than cover the increased expenses.

Another critical factor in the decision to winterize or expand summer program to other seasons of the year relates to the camp's overall purpose and philosophy. What is the overall mission and how will moving to year-round operation affect that mission? Will changes in the character or design of buildings have any effect on the summer program? Will expansion of program beyond the summer create different demands for the time and skills of staff? Will continuous use of existing buildings or grounds over a year have any detrimental effects for their use during the summer?

CHECKPOINTS

1. Do you have the appropriate maps of the property — topographical, survey, schematic?
2. Do you have a map showing all current buildings with utility lines, cutoffs, disconnects, and valves?
3. Do you have an inventory of all equipment?
4. Do you have a maintenance schedule for all mechanical equipment on the grounds? For all buildings (painting, caulking, repairs)?
5. Do you have a master site plan? If not, are you working toward securing such?
6. Have you made an inspection of all buildings and program areas, listing needed repairs and corrections? Have you prioritized them and outlined a plan for their correction?
7. Have present buildings and program areas been given evaluation to determine what modifications are needed to bring them into compliance with the Americans With Disabilities Act of 1990?

Related Standards

Accreditation Standards for Camp Programs and Services: SF-1–25, 28–30; "Additional Professional Practices": Items 1–8, 14, 19, 22

Standards for Conference and Retreat Centers: I-38, I-46–50, II-2, 5, 6, 9–17, 24, III-18–19, 30–31

Eric Dresser, Camp Easter Seal – West,
New Castle, Virginia

10

Risk Management

Risk management is one of the most important tasks of camp administration. . . . The board must establish risk management policies in conjunction with the director, and the director must work with the staff and campers in implementing the policies. . . . The quality of the camp experience deteriorates in direct proportion to the extent of unreasonable risks to which the camper is subjected. A camper must be able to participate with confidence that the experience will be a safe one in regard to instruction given, the nature of supervision, and in environmental conditions. A safe experience is a primary responsibility in the conduct of a camp. However, fear of legal liability . . . should never be the reason for not having adventurous, challenging activities. Such activities are needed in today's society.[1]

DEFINITIONS

Risk is an uncertainty or probability concerning the loss of resources. The loss of resources, depending on their importance and value, can endanger the very life of an organization. Through a poorly managed risk, camps can potentially suffer such losses as the reputation of the camp, the health and safety of staff, the loss of camp property or financial resources, and ultimately, the loss of the camp as a resource for future generations. Some of those aspects are very tangible, money and property, while others are intangible, such as the camp's reputation and public attitudes.

Although camps have always been concerned about the health and safety of the campers, it is the litigious climate of the past four decades that has caused camps to broaden their understanding of the risks involved in camp and conference center operations. In this process, a term developed that has become a critical facet of camp administration — *risk management*. This term implies an overall integrated plan that seeks to manage the risks that might occur in any and every aspect of camp life.

[1]Betty van der Smissen. 1993. Foreword. *Management of Risks and Emergencies: A Workbook for Program Administrators*. Kansas City, MO: Camp Fire Boys and Girls, Inc. p. v.

A risk management plan is a system to identify a camp's physical, human, operational, and financial resources and to develop a plan to evaluate, reduce, or control the losses that might result from the operation. It is first an attitude, the attitude that risks can be managed and minimized even if they cannot be eliminated. It is impossible to remove all risk from camp life. Therefore, developing a system to identify and handle those risks in a variety of ways in advance of such losses is wise and necessary.

The areas in which camps are exposed to risk are generally categorized as physical assets, human resources (e.g., personnel or participants), operational financial resources, and standard of care or third party liabilities. Physical or property assets can be lost through fire, floods, theft, vandalism, poor maintenance, and negligence. Risks affecting people, whether campers, staff, or the public, include death, injury, abuse (physical, mental, sexual, emotional, or verbal), and loss of their service or property. Operational financial risks involve fidelity and income risk. Fidelity risks involve the loss of financial resources through theft, nonperformance of duties, or mismanagement. Similarly, risks to income include events which close the camp or prevent continuance of a camper period, thus requiring refunds or the nonpayment of fees. Third party liabilities are those imposed by law or assumed under contract (contractual or tort liability).

LEGAL ASPECTS

In each of these areas, the camp may suffer direct loss and may become entangled in litigation. Of course, the goal of good risk management planning is to avoid either. When a suit is brought against a camp, both the corporate entity and an individual can be involved in the legal action.

Litigation has become a byword in today's society, and no camp is exempt from lawsuits. To avoid them, one needs good legal advice as well as advice concerning camp management and public relations. The camp needs regular access to an attorney who has good understanding of the camp program and operation. This goal will require a period of orientation and education of the attorney by the camp director. A good risk management plan is going to require advice from that attorney, among others, about avoiding legal entanglements without hampering the camp program. Regardless of how capable an attorney the camp has, the director also needs some basic understanding of both civil and criminal law. Some legal terms and principles of law need review by the administrator.

Initially, the director needs to understand the *doctrine of respondent superior*, which states that a corporate entity is accountable for the actions of employees (including volunteers) *if* acting within the scope of their responsibility or authority. Understanding this concept gives the corporate chief employed officer and board reason to make sure that the responsibility and authority given employees is clearly identified in job descriptions and training. Similarly, helping an employee understand this concept encourages that employee to carefully carry out his or her responsibilities as outlined in his or her job description, follow camp policies and procedures, and use only the amount of authority so delegated.

Individuals in camps can be guilty of *criminal acts*, where the offender is punished for actions that might include child abuse, using drugs, harassment, theft, etc. However, it is far more likely that camps will get entangled in *civil law*, where an injured party seeks financial compensation for negligent actions of the camp or an individual at the camp. Such litigation is likely to be very costly, even if the camp has not been negligent.

Most litigation in camps involves either *contractual* or *tort liability*. The camp enters into contracts with various businesses, individuals, campers, parents, groups, and employees; some are written and some verbal. Where there is a disagreement concerning the terms of that contract, whether it relates to the refund of a camper fee or the purchase of equipment or service, litigation can develop. The development of language in implied contracts such as camper registrations, staff agreements, and rental agreements needs careful thought by the author and review by legal counsel. Verbal contracts are even more difficult, and clear policy statements should be developed about who can make alterations in written policy or commit the camp to financial or other obligations.

Tort liability involves wrongful acts against a person other than through contracts. Torts may be *intentional or unintentional*. Camps can avoid the intentional torts relatively easily since they include such actions as slander, physical attack, or invasion of privacy. However, camps are exposed to unintentional torts wherever there is an allegation of *negligence*. There must be some evidence of negligence which involves proof that all four of the following occurred:

1. The person in charge had a legal duty to the individual injured.
2. The person in charge violated that duty to prevent an accident or incident that was foreseeable.
3. That breach of that duty was directly related to the incident.
4. There was actual loss or damage resulting from the incident that was caused by the breach (e.g., emotional, physical, mental, etc.).

The term *in loco parentis*, "in place of the parent," applies to camps/conference centers at any time the entity assumes the responsibility for a minor "in place of the parent." The entity, whether the corporation or a cabin counselor, has the responsibility of maintaining the same or better level of care of that minor than would be expected from the minor's parents.

IDENTIFICATION OF RISK EXPOSURES

The camp director should list all the assets he or she can identify that might be exposed to risk before methods of managing those risks can be chosen. Organizing those risks first by category (who or what is exposed) and then within those categories by types of exposure should help in this process. For example, risks can involve:

1. Physical property or equipment (fire, theft, vandalism)
2. Personnel and participant (injury, death, loss of personal property)
3. Operational financial
4. Standard of care or third party liabilities (contractual, tort action)

    Types of exposures within these four areas could be:

- Program activities (swimming, tripping, rappelling)
- Business operations (contracts, tax status and documentation, trademark)
- Natural hazards (poisonous animals or insects, lightning, cliffs near trail, rushing rivers)
- Natural disaster (floods, hurricanes, tornadoes, earthquakes)
- Operation, maintenance, and supervision of facilities and equipment (loose steps, faulty PFDs)
- Behavior of people (campers, staff, visitors, trespassers)
- Preexisting medical conditions (asthma, epilepsy, allergy to bee stings)

A review of accident and insurance reports, health service records, and any history of lawsuits will reveal the frequency with which previous losses from these risks occur. Those which show up most frequently should be noted and analyzed. The analysis should include review of types of injury, locations of accident, times of day, days of week, ages of injured, types of activity, and amounts of supervision in place. Consideration should be given also to how severe various losses might be. For instance, though you have had no record of a drowning or head injury from rappelling, either loss could be quite severe involving lawsuits, negative public relations, and long-term effects upon the participant. Those losses with greatest severity should also be noted and analyzed. Obviously risks which appear in both lists (frequency and severity) provide the areas of first concern.

REGULATIONS

No risk management planning is complete without careful consideration of the laws and regulations governing the camp operation. These laws and regulations arise at the federal, state, county, and local level; and, except for the federal regulations, they vary considerably from state to state.

The first step is to secure a copy of those regulations. If no one in a camp is knowledgeable about them, the director should make an effort to talk with other camp directors or the offices and staff of the local American Camping Association or Christian Camping International section. The department of health or social services and the Occupational Safety and Health Administration (OSHA) will often have regulations affecting camps, including specifics on how health records are maintained and what training is mandated for staff. Some states will require a permit or license to operate: some licenses will require an inspection by state or county personnel and some will not.

Regulations also may be applicable to camps in other jurisdictions: fire, water, pollution, natural resources, building codes, sanitation. Some states have integrated most regulations affecting camp into a single "Camp Safety Act." Most states, however, have regulations affecting camps in areas such as health, labor, child care, human services, agriculture, or even education.

If, after study of the regulations, the director finds some that are unclear or very difficult for the camp to comply with, he or she should call for an appointment with a person in the appropriate office. The role of the state or local official is to help the director know how to comply with regulations and to give some assistance in problem situations. It is wise to check on the pattern of inspections. Some departments require a preopening inspection as well as during-operation inspections; others inspect annually or biannually.

Where a camp has its home office or its incorporated parent organization in one state and the camp's physical location in another, the regulations of both states need to be examined. Although the governmental unit and state in which the camp is physically located may have jurisdiction over health, sanitation, vehicles, fire protection, and pollution control, the state of incorporation may have primary jurisdiction over payroll, employment practices, and tax laws.

MANAGEMENT OF RISKS

Four methods of managing risks have been identified. In general, risks can be avoided, transferred, retained, or reduced. Choices will have to be made as to which method or methods best fit the risk exposure.

Avoiding of Risks

First one should review risks to see if there are unnecessary risks which the camp can simply avoid. One may eliminate an activity that is not essential to the accomplishment of camp goals. A practice such as allowing anyone to ride in the back of an open-bed truck can (and should) be eliminated. An old dilapidated wooden shed that could easily catch fire and spread may be a risk that can be avoided by simply tearing down the shed.

Transfer of Risks

Many of the risks in a camp are transferred to another party through insurance or specific agreements or contracts.

Waivers

The camp attorney may develop "hold harmless" statements which can transfer responsibility for certain actions to the participant or sponsoring group. Leases are one method of transferring certain risks to the lessor. There is some debate in the legal community about "waivers," "hold harmless" statements, or "releases." A minor or even a minor's parents cannot waive the minor's rights. That is one reason a minor may file suit against a camp for a supposedly negligent act some months or years (depending on the state) after the minor reaches the age of his or her majority. However, properly worded permissions and releases can have the parent give informed consent rather than a general overall consent to participate. These *waivers* have been accepted in the courts of all fifty states as showing that the parent was knowledgeable that the minor was participating in a given activity and that there was some risk involved. Releases can be effective tools in helping bar recovery by the parents or guardians when the child is injured.

On the other hand, a waiver by adult participants may be more binding or carry more weight in court. Janna S. Rankin states that "with regard to adult activities in a recreational setting, a release may be upheld if it is carefully worded, concerned with a risk normally associated with that activity, and the recreation service provider has not been clearly negligent."[2]

A general permission to participate and a release or a waiver should both be considered. A signed *permission* form is a consent by the parent or guardian to participate in some activity or activities. The camp enrollment process should provide a full description of the activities, including the nature of risks and potential dangers of any activities that are not commonly known to the average person. The camp should then seek a signed specific parental permission for that activity. In this way the parent is giving informed consent.

Many camps are now requiring releases in addition to permission forms. A signed *release* is an act whereby the participant, parent, or guardian gives up some claim, right, or interest to the persons against whom the claim could be made. A parent may release his or her rights to sue the camp, but the parent may not waive or release the rights of the child. Beyond the permission form and release, some camps are now also using an *indemnity agreement*, which requests the parent or guardian to reimburse the camp for any expenses (e.g., legal, medical, etc.) incurred by the camp as a result of providing services to the camper.[3] Such permissions and releases need to be developed in consultation with the camp's attorney. An example of a permission form used by one camp can be found in illustration 10.1.

Certainly an organization can assume responsibility for its own members or participants when renting a facility, if the contractual responsibilities of both parties are clearly drawn. However, requiring a certificate of insurance from the organization is often a safeguard to the written agreement.

---

[2]Janna S. Rankin. "Waivers." *Camping Magazine* Vol. 58, No. 3, January 1986. p. 24.

[3]Marge Scanlin and Richard Smikle. "Reviewed Your Permission Form Lately?" *CampLine* Vol. 3, No. 2, October 1994. pp. 3–4.

10.1

Illustration *Permission Form*

PERMISSION FORM

I understand and certify that my child's participation in Camp _____ and its activities is completely voluntary and I have familiarized myself with the camp's program and activities in which my child will be participating.

I recognize that certain hazards and dangers are inherent in the Camp _____ events and programs and particularly, but not limited to, the activities of horseback riding, swimming, rock climbing, high ropes course, rappelling, and winter tubing, and I acknowledge that although Camp _____ has taken safety measures to minimize the risk of injury to camp participants, Camp _____ cannot insure nor guarantee that the participants, equipment, premises, and/or activities will be free of hazards, accidents, and/or injuries. I further recognize and have instructed my child in the importance of knowing and abiding by the camp's rules, regulations, and procedures for the safety of camp participants.

Insurance

A critical ingredient of any risk management planning is insurance protection. Insurance can be purchased that will transfer the financial liability of much of the damage to or loss of property. Though some camps may be in a position to self-insure, insurance is used by camp directors to transfer risk. The careful selection of an insurance agent or broker is the first step in securing insurance. If possible, an agent should be found who has some understanding of camps and does not cringe at each program activity which, on the surface, seems to pose a risk. If the agent has the designation CPCU (Chartered Property Casualty Underwriter) or CIC (Certified Insurance Counselor), it indicates the person has taken the time to seek the certification and has acquired a broad background in insurance. However, there are many qualified persons without either of these designations.

It is important also that the director be familiar with the various types of insurance that need to be considered. Here are six general categories or types:

Property Insurance. Property insurance may be purchased for camp buildings and personal property. Coverage options are available for Basic Causes of Loss, Broad Causes of Loss, or Special Causes of Loss. Basic Causes of Loss coverage, previously known as Named Perils Insurance, covers damage from events such as fire, lightning, windstorm, and vandalism. Broad Causes of Loss adds a few additional events to these causes of loss such as collapse due to weight of ice and snow. The most comprehensive coverage for camp property is offered by the Special Causes of Loss form. The difference between the forms is that the Basic and Broad Causes of Loss forms cover only those events named in the form, where the Special Causes of Loss covers all events, except those excluded.

Some directors choose to insure the buildings and contents up to their replacement costs. In years of escalating inflation, building values must be adjusted annually to keep pace with the rising costs of replacement. It has become very expensive to insure all camp buildings at replacement value, and an option to consider is insuring only the most valuable or essential buildings in this fashion. It is well to consider which buildings are the most valuable and without which it would be difficult to operate. In recent years, laws regarding construction have been passed on a local, state, and federal level which increase the cost of reconstructing a building after a loss. The additional cost of reconstruction is not automatically included under Replacement Cost insurance. Optional coverage for application of these building laws, including demolition and increased cost of construction is available. Also factored into this equation should be any disaster, such as a flood or earthquake, which might destroy the entire camp.

The second option is to insure buildings for their actual cash value or depreciated value. If a building is destroyed, then the camp would receive only the value at the time of the incident, and replacement would probably cost considerably more. This option brings a reduction in rates in proportion to the reduction in values. It is also important to note if a building contains particularly valuable contents which would be difficult or expensive to replace. Ed Schirick notes that "factors that reduce depreciation include proper maintenance, renovation and repair practices. While there is some subjectivity in determining depreciation and actual cash value, detailed records of repair, maintenance and improvements help you negotiate successfully on this issue."[4]

In any case, it is important to have a schedule of all buildings and an inventory of their contents with their present replacement value. In this fashion, the risk you are carrying in terms of the difference between value and replacement costs is known. Accurate, up-to-date inventories and pictures of buildings and especially their valuable contents should be kept to document the loss should a fire or loss occur. These records should be stored at an off-site office or in a fire-proof safe. Property should be reappraised from time to time to ensure that the values are current, given inflation or diminished value.

The amount of the deductible the camp assumes will also affect the premium. As premiums for insurance coverage have increased, camps have tended to partially retain the loss (self-insure) through higher deductibles (for example, $1,000, $2,500, $5,000).

Commercial General Liability. A liability policy is designed to provide protection for the camp if lawsuits are brought as a result of alleged negligence. Such allegations may be brought as the result of property damage, bodily injury, advertising injury (e.g., infringement of copyright), or personal injury (e.g., emotional injury, loss of earnings). The insurance company generally evaluates all conditions that increase or decrease risk. For example, the number, experience, and training of horses for horseback riding; the number of motorboats for waterskiing; and the number of staff all affect the risk factors as viewed by the insurance company.

---

[4]Ed Schirick. "Risk Management — Insuring Your Camp's Buildings and Contents." *Camping Magazine* Vol. 70, No. 3, May/June 1997.

It is important that the camp director help the insurance agent understand the camp and its different risk exposures provided in the individual program and setting. It is at this point that your risk management planning will help the agent understand the precautions and steps taken to minimize risks. The agent should also have exposure and understanding of the camp's American Camping Association Camp Accreditation or Conference/Retreat Center Accreditation. Many insurance companies offer reduced rates to camps that hold ACA accreditation.

The camp director should be realistic in setting the limits of coverage to be purchased. In an increasingly litigious environment, camps have to be careful to have enough insurance to cover a major incident. Minimum limits to be expected today are $1 million in general liability and $1 million to $5 million in excess limits (generally called umbrella insurance) depending on degree of risk.

The policy should be checked in detail to see if it provides malpractice insurance for improper medical treatment, product liability coverage for food service, and any type of coverage for independent contractors who may work at camp in construction or program. There also exists today a professional liability policy covering full-time employees that protects the individual against alleged negligence in the performance of professional duties. This is wise coverage to have.

Given the increased awareness of inappropriate sexual behavior in recent years, camps should be sure that their policies provide coverage for sexual misconduct. One must not assume that coverage is provided when contracts are silent on this subject. It is advisable to have an affirmative statement that the policy provides this coverage through an endorsement to the general liability policy. Further, one should question whether this statement covers sexual harassment. An additional coverage, Employment Practice Liability, may be necessary to cover sexual harassment, along with allegations such as discrimination and wrongful termination.

In addition, for camps with several year-round full-time staff who receive employee benefits, consideration should be given to the purchase of Employee Benefits Liability coverage. This covers the camp against mistakes in the administration of their employee benefits plan.

Where there is a governing board, consideration should be given to coverage for directors and officers (D and O insurance). This provides protection to those persons for their actions on behalf of the camp. In addition, if there are volunteers used in any fashion in the camp operation, coverage should be checked to make sure they are included.

Worker's Compensation. Required by law, this policy covers medical and hospitalization costs and loss-of-time (wages) compensation incurred for employees injured at work or suffering a work-related illness. The requirements for worker's compensation limits vary from state to state. The experience rating of a camp can affect the premium in certain situations, so the control of staff accidents is an important part of risk management planning.

Motor Vehicle Insurance. Vehicles, particularly where they carry passengers, are a major risk. It is vital that the vehicles owned or used by the camp be covered by insurance. Coverage should include liability, property damage, medical payments, and uninsured motorist coverage. Collision and comprehensive coverage is available but must be examined in light of the value of the vehicles and the additional premium. If the camp uses staff-owned vehicles for any purpose whatsoever, nonowner coverage should be secured. If the camp hires or leases vehicles, the lessor is normally expected to carry the insurance, but the director should require a certificate or letter of insurance in advance of the use of a leased vehicle.

Health and Accident Insurance. Health and accident insurance is designed to cover the costs of medical services and hospitalization for camper and staff accidents or illnesses occurring or contracted during the camp stay. Various kinds of coverage are available under such policies. Many camps automatically cover campers and offer coverage to staff as a benefit. Other camps offer campers and staff the option of taking the insurance or relying on their own family policy. If the policy covers staff, work-related injuries are still covered first under worker's compensation insurance. Health and accident insurance that covers the cost of treatment may show the camp's concern for the well-being of all persons, reduce costs to parents, and, thus, help minimize the likelihood of a lawsuit.

It is possible to secure a policy which covers the camper in coordination with the family's insurance. The policy pays the deductible on the family policy and anything in excess of the maximum paid by the family policy. Where no family insurance exists, then the policy becomes the primary insurance. This type policy generally costs less than covering all campers directly.

Insurance Binders. The director should request and receive binders on each insurance policy on or before the date the policy takes effect, if the policy is not available on that date. A binder assures the director that the policy is in effect for a given time. It is wise to inquire of the agent as to the Best rating of the insurance companies issuing policies; the rating should be a B++ (Very Good) or higher, if at all possible.

Retention of Risk

Certain risks may be retained in instances where it is not possible to avoid or transfer the total risk. Insurance to completely cover all physical losses is too expensive for most camps, so some risk must be retained by the camp. There are certain activities which are so important to the mission and goals of the camp that one would not consider eliminating them. For example, though drowning may be a severe risk, a camp likely would not eliminate all aquatic activities.

The retention of a risk should be a deliberate decision of the administration and the sponsoring organization, if there is one. Each risk should be identified and outlined with the potential consequences. The potential financial consequences of such risks should be estimated.

Where insurance is used to transfer part of the risk, there is normally a financial deductible or threshold that the camp must retain. The insurance company must pay the costs beyond the amount of the deductible. There should be a reserve or contingency fund set aside that can be tapped if such risks materialize.

Reducing Risks

When a camp retains a risk, then the management of that risk is examined to see how much of the risk can be reduced. Once the camp has identified which risks are to be eliminated or avoided, the balance of risk management planning is developing the policies and practices which will reduce the remaining risks to an acceptable level. The plan for reducing risks examines what can be done before and during the operation of the risk.

Staff other than the director should be involved in identifying risks, for there are others much closer to many risks. "All managers should be given the opportunity to brainstorm ways to reduce risk. They should constantly monitor their staff for behaviors that reduce . . . the opportunity for incidents to occur," states Chris Rollins.[5]

For example, the camp's administration feels that providing a certain activity to every participant in a certain unit is important in attaining certain goals or outcomes in the camp experience. In advance of the activity, several steps are taken to reduce the risk:

1. Leadership is selected on the basis of documented experience and maturity, and on demonstrated ability to work with types of campers being served.
2. Leaders' skills are tested and verified during precamp training.
3. Written operating procedures that include safety regulations and prerequisites for participation or eligibility are followed and used as the basis for all staff training.
4. Participants are given adequate training and tested on the skills essential to their participation in the activity. Leaders are trained to watch for fatigue, over-competitiveness, stress, and other signs that may bring a greater human risk factor to an otherwise safe situation.
5. Equipment that is appropriate and safe is provided for use in the activity.
6. The location where the activity is to take place is examined for potential hazards, such as natural hazards or outside interference from other activities and events.
7. A ratio of leaders to participants that ensures adequate supervision is established and carried out.
8. Leaders are trained to implement a clear action plan for emergencies that might arise in participation in the activity.

It is equally important that during the operation of the activity, the following steps be taken to reduce risk:

---

[5]Chris Rollins. "Train Away Risk." *Camping Magazine* Vol. 71, No. 5, September/October 1998.

1. Supervision of the activity by one or more of the leaders is carried out at all times. Certain activities may require a minimum of two leaders at all times.
2. Appropriate clothing and equipment are required of the participant during the activity.
3. An unsafe practice or violation of operational procedures is stopped immediately upon observation.

The foci of lawsuits in camps over the years have centered on supervision of the activity, the manner in which the activity is conducted, and the availability and condition of facilities or equipment related to the activity. With this knowledge, it is possible to carefully examine program activities, establishing clear policies by the camp administration and regular supervision to see that policies are continually implemented. Since the courts hold camp staff to the standard of care of a "reasonably prudent professional," the recruitment, training, and supervision of staff are critical to help prevent allegations of negligence. Not only is it important that such steps be taken, but there needs to be documentation that appropriate recruitment, training, and supervision of staff occurred.

In addition, clear policies need to be put in writing and in the hands of all staff. A notebook or staff manual which organizes all such policies and procedures in an orderly fashion is perhaps the best method for preservation and annual review. Nothing is as helpful in litigation as producing written documentation that can be attested to as being available and used in an orientation or training process.

However, everything cannot be written. For instance, though there may be a written policy for the supervision of an activity, that does not ensure that the supervision did occur at a particular time and place. Where the risk in question is severe, it is wise to have at least two leaders present so that a second person can attest to the supervision given.

Handling Incidents

However well a plan is put into practice to reduce risks, incidents will occur. Action taken at the time of the incident is as important as the preventive steps taken before the incident. As much as possible, the steps to be taken at the time of an incident should be identified in advance. Bob Schultz speaks of the importance of developing a crisis communication plan "before a crisis strikes and it should outline general procedures that are reviewed with all staff. Ideally, the plan should include the formation of a crisis team from all facets of the camp. The crisis team should consist of an executive leader (the director), counselor staff, camp health professional, board member(s), legal counsel and PR counsel (local, ACA, etc.)."[6]

Staff members in leadership positions should be given training and directions to cover such points as:

- Providing immediate care of the individuals involved in the incident, both injured and uninjured.

---

[6]Bob Schultz. "Does Your Camp Have a Crisis Communication Plan?" *CampLine* Vol. 4, No. 2, October 1995.

- Notifying one's supervisor or designated person as soon as possible.
- Securing outside assistance, if necessary.
- Writing a report of the incident, documenting as many facts as possible (see OSHA requirements later in this chapter).
- If serious, reporting to appropriate persons outside of the camp (e.g., government agencies, parents of the participant, camp's home office).
- Diverting or organizing the persons not involved in the incident into other activities or other areas of the camp.
- Referring media and determining who speaks for the camp/organization. On this point, it should be recognized that media relations can be as critical an element in risk management as notifying parents. Adverse and incorrect publicity can account for long-term damages to the camp. As Dr. Bari S. Dworken points out, "In many cases, reporters and photographers often arrive at camp even before the emergency crew. This can create more than just the initial emergency to deal with."[7]

Some of the incidents will be emergencies and others will not be. It is equally important in nonemergencies to take the above steps where applicable. However, there are certain types of emergencies which can be examined in advance and procedures developed to cover them, e.g., drowning, fire, tornado, injury requiring medical assistance. For each different type of emergency:

- Procedures should be put in writing, reviewed by various experts, and given to staff.
- Procedures should be rehearsed during staff training, where practical.
- Emergency phone numbers and contact information should be posted in critical places, such as the swimming area, maintenance building, kitchen, and office.
- Staff trained in basic first aid/CPR should be assigned to pertinent areas where emergencies might occur.

Thought should be given not only to the first aid for physical injuries, but also to how to deal with the stress brought on by the emergency. Stress in general should be discussed during staff training. Particularly where the participants are children, staff should be helped to understand the signs of mental and emotional stress, the areas where stress can increase the possibility of an accident, the ways stress can manifest itself once an incident is underway, and the appropriate responses.

Where an alleged incident of abuse occurs, the first concern should be for the welfare of the camper(s). Therefore, the accused staff member should be relieved of his or her responsibilities, and a staff member with expertise and experience in dealing with children should be assigned to the camper group. One must not assume that the staff member is guilty just because an accusation has been made. That guideline should be

[7]Bari S. Dworken. "10 Commandments of Risk Management." *Camping Magazine* Vol. 71, No. 5, September/ October 1998.

made clear at the outset to the accused staff member and any other staff involved. However, to protect both the campers, the staff member, and the camp, there should be a separation of the staff member from any camper group.

A clear understanding of the accusation and situation must be secured before making a report. It is important to get the facts but not interrogate the child involved and any other children who are witnesses. Any questions to the child must be kept very low key and witnessed by another staff member. Every effort to ease the child's emotional stress should be taken. Remember, it is not your responsibility to determine whether the abuse occurred; that is the responsibility of trained professionals. If there is an accusation or indicator of some type of physical, emotional, or sexual abuse, the proper authorities should be notified. Reporting allegations of abuse is mandated in all fifty states, though the procedures vary from state to state. Specifics on reporting should be determined before camp and be readily accessible during camp.[8]

From this point on, the role of the director will be related to controlling the impact of the incident by dealing with the parents of the child, the balance of the staff and campers, the owner of the camp or board of directors, the media, and perhaps the parents of other campers in the camp session at the time. Legal advice may be warranted in dealing with parents of other campers in the living group or total camp, as well as with the media. At this point, a written plan for such incidents made prior to camp is extremely valuable to help the director act and react carefully and logically.

RECORDKEEPING

One of the functions for which the camp director must take responsibility is seeing that accurate records are kept of the entire camp operation. As Ed Schirick states, "Defining relationships and responsibilities, as well as terms of agreements with other parties, are examples of responsible risk management and represent good business practice."[9] Though the director will not be able to do this alone, it is important that he or she identify the types of records to be kept, who is to keep them, where they are to be stored and for how long.

Records serve a number of purposes:

- To provide a paper trail that shows what, when, and why things were done
- To provide information about the current financial state of the organization
- To provide information to analyze operations and costs for efficiency, health, safety, and effectiveness
- To show the operation is in compliance with local, state, and federal regulations and America Camping Association standards

---

[8]Becca Cowan Johnson. 1992. *For Their Sake*. Martinsville, IN: American Camping Association. p. 68.
[9]Ed Schirick. "Get It in Writing." *Camping Magazine* Vol. 70, No. 4, July/August 1997. p.12.

- To protect against and be available as evidence in case of litigation
- To maintain a history of the camp

There are certain records and information which are needed so that those who follow the present personnel know what significant events and actions occurred over a period of years.

Health Records

The isolated setting of many camps means that the camp is the primary health care provider for campers and staff. To provide the best health care possible a camp must collect information about each camper's and staff member's health (e.g., health history, medications, allergies, etc.) and inform the appropriate staff of any health considerations in their areas. For example, unit counselors and kitchen staff should be aware of food allergies, unit counselors should be aware of campers who need to receive medications at the health center, and program staff should be aware of campers with illnesses like asthma.

The collection of this information can be difficult because parents and staff don't always understand the significance of providing this information. While the forms may be separate from camper registration forms, the process for collecting this information should be part of registration and follow-up. Forms on which to collect this information should be mailed to parents and staff in advance, accompanied by an explanation of the importance of providing this information. See chapter 11 for an example of the health history and examination form developed by the American Camping Association.

It is important to recognize that information collected about a camper's or staff member's health history is to be used solely to provide accurate and helpful information to those providing health care to the individual and must not be used to refuse the individual a position as a camper or a staff member. In fact, regulations in the Americans With Disabilities Act require that the health information on staff members be collected *after* a position has been offered and before camp begins.

It is also true that most of an individual's health history needs to be maintained confidentially and some of that history need not be known by the camp. For example, knowing an individual's HIV status should not change the health care given at camp because all staff with health care functions should be trained in the use of universal precautions that would protect the staff member from transmission of such a bloodborne disease. Additionally, under the Americans With Disabilities Act, persons who have tested positive for HIV may not be denied enrollment due to their HIV status.

Additionally, any health care provided to campers or staff members while they are in the camp's charge should be recorded. There are various regulations affecting health records and a variety of methods for maintaining the health care given at camp. American Camping Association standards and OSHA require that camper health care records and medical logs be kept separate from staff health care records. Other federal regulations require that health care information on staff be maintained apart from their personnel files.

Incident Reports

It is particularly vital that reports be made of all accidents or incidents and that uniform information be recorded each time an accident or incident occurs. The term *incident* is used deliberately, for there are occurrences in camp which are not accidents but are of such a significant nature that there should be a record in case questions arise at a later date. These questions tend to relate to emotional stress, alleged abuse, or outside intruders breaching security, etc. No form will cover all potential types of incidents, so a narrative identifying witnesses and dates, precautions taken, actions taken, and any specific results will usually suffice.

The American Camping Association has designed an accident/incident report form which serves as a good model (see illustration 10.2). Such reports should be attached to insurance claims where applicable and filed along with all records of treatment of injuries and illnesses until the injured is at least one to four years beyond the age of majority (or for the period of statutory limits in the state where the camp is located, whichever is greater), along with the importance of completing appropriate worker's compensation and OSHA forms recording incidents involving employees. The appropriate recordkeeping of injuries and illnesses is also discussed in chapter 11.

Keeping the records of injuries and incidents is only the first step. One important use of these records is to assist the camp director and health manager in analyzing the frequency and severity of certain types of injuries and the location where those injuries occurred. Between the camper health record (see chapter 11), the accident or incident reports, and insurance claims, the director has a clear source of data which requires tallying and analysis at the end of each season. A comparison of such data after several seasons will be most meaningful in risk management planning.

Record Retention

Recognizing that a minor may sue up to one to four years beyond the age of majority, and therefore a child of the minimum age at the camp (for example, seven years old) would have thirteen years to bring suit, it would be wise to maintain all records concerning campers involved in accidents or incidents for thirteen years (e.g., health records, accident reports, registration forms and permissions signed by the parent, insurance coverage records, witness, etc.). Further information on record retention is found in chapter 13.

There are many different statutes of limitations with time periods which vary from law to law and state to state, especially in regard to tax, and unemployment and worker's compensation records. Therefore, the director should give careful thought to record retention and should obtain legal advice. The policy of the organization or camp on recordkeeping and record retention should be developed on the basis of law, the rule of

10.2 Illustration *ACA Accident/Incident Form FM 01*

Accident/Incident Report Form　　FM 01

Developed by the **American Camping Association**®
(Fill out 1 on each incident or person)

Camp Name _____ Date _____

Address _____
　　　　　Street & Number　　　　　　　　　　　　*City*　　　　　　　　　*State*　　　*Zip*

Name of person involved _____ Age _____ Sex _____ ☐ Camper ☐ Staff ☐ Visitor
　　　　　　　　　　　Last　　　*First*　　*Middle*

Address _____ Phone _____
　　　　　Street & Number　　　　　*City*　　　　*State*　　　*Zip*　　　　　　　　*Area/Number*

Name of Parent/Guardian *(if minor)* _____

Address _____ Phone _____
　　　　　Street & Number　　　　　*City*　　　　*State*　　　*Zip*　　　　　　　　*Area/Number*

Name/Addresses of Witnesses *(You may wish to attach signed statements.)*

1. _____

2. _____

3. _____

Type of incident　☐ Behavioral　☐ Accident　☐ Epidemic illness　☐ Other (describe)

Date of Incident/Accident _____ Hour _____ ☐ a.m. ☐ p.m.
　　　　　　　　　　　　Day of Week　　　*Month*　　　　　*Day*　　　*Year*

Describe the sequence of activity in detail including what the (injured) person was doing at the time _____

_____

_____

_____

_____

_____

_____

Where occurred? *(Specify location, including location of injured and witnesses. Use diagram to locate persons/objects.)*

Was injured participating in an activity at time of injury?　☐ Yes　☐ No　If so, what activity? _____

Any equipment involved in accident?　☐ Yes　☐ No　If so, what kind? _____

What could the injured have done to prevent injury? _____

_____

Emergency procedures followed at time of incident/accident _____

_____

_____

By whom?_____

Submitted by _____ Position _____ Date _____

Phone number_____

Copyright 1983 by American Camping Association, Inc.　Revised 1990, 1992, 1999.
Printed with permission of and under license of American Camping Association, Inc.

10.2   Illustration   *ACA Accident/Incident Form FM 01 continued*

Medical Report of Accident

Were parents notified? ☐ Yes ☐ No   By ☐ Writing ☐ Phone ☐ Other _____

By whom? _____ Title _____ When _____
                                                                          Time   Date
Parent's Response _____

_____

Where was treatment given (check and complete all that apply)?

☐ At Accident Site: Where? _____ By whom? _____

   Treatment given _____ Date _____

☐ Camp Health Service: By whom? _____ Title _____

   Treatment given _____ Date _____

   Released to   ☐ Camp Activities   ☐ Home   ☐ Other _____ Date _____

☐ Doctor's Office: By whom? _____ Title _____

   Treatment given _____ Date _____

   Released to   ☐ Camp Activities   ☐ Camp Health Service   ☐ Home   ☐ Other _____

☐ Hospital: By whom? _____ Title _____

   Was injured retained overnight in hospital?   ☐ Yes   ☐ No   If so, which? _____

   Where? _____ Date _____   ☐ Out-patient   ☐ In-patient

   Name of physician in attendance _____

   Date released from hospital _____

   Released to   ☐ Camp   ☐ Home   ☐ Other _____

Comments _____

_____

_____

Persons notified such as camp owner/sponsor, board of directors, etc.

Name	Position	Date
_____	_____	_____
_____	_____	_____
_____	_____	_____

Describe any contact made with/by the media regarding this situation _____

_____

Signed _____ Position _____ Date _____

Insurance Notification

                                                                  Date

1. ☐ Parent's Insurance   By ☐ Parent ☐ Camp   _____

2. ☐ Camp Health Insurance   _____

3. ☐ Worker's Compensation   _____

4. ☐ Camp Liability Insurance   _____

reason, and the risk involved. Such a policy should be in writing. In many cases, records may be microfilmed and serve as a legal record, but this needs to be checked with an attorney for the specific state ruling.

OSHA regulations require employers with eleven or more employees to maintain OSHA 200 forms, record all employee injuries, and post the summary of the form from February 1 to March 1 each year at a location where employees can read it. In addition, a supplementary record of each individual injury and illness must be kept on the OSHA 101 form and retained for five years. In some cases, a worker's compensation First Report of Injury form may serve both purposes if it covers all information required. An OSH Act poster must also be posted in a location where it can be seen by all employees. Copies of the forms are available directly from the state OSHA office and, in some cases, the state labor department. See chapter 11 for other OSHA requirements.

ACCREDITATION

Accreditation by an outside body has proven to be an invaluable step in all types of institutions across the country, from schools to hospitals. It gives validity to the concern of the camp, in this case, to meet professional standards and to stay abreast of the latest information concerning health and safety in the field. The fact that an outside body comes in to examine all aspects of the operation provides not only a check point for the administrator but also a backup if litigation ever occurs.

The American Camping Association is currently the only national organization with an independent accreditation program for all types of camps and conference centers. Its long history of developing standards in the field as well as its research and constant updating of those standards has led courts and government bodies to hold these standards as *industry standards*. In other words, actions of a camp involved in a lawsuit will be measured against American Camping Association standards whether or not the camp is affiliated with or accredited by the Association. Since ACA Accreditation does not require a camp to meet every standard for accreditation, an ACA Accredited camp may find that in court questions are asked about standards the camp chose not to meet. Therefore, a camp needs to be prepared to provide rationale and documentation for standards not met.

Over 90 percent of the standards relate to risk management, and the paperwork related to those standards would meet many of the suggestions provided in this chapter. Local sections of the American Camping Association offer courses annually that explain the standards and the type of preparation that is needed for an accreditation visit. These courses are invaluable for directors, even if accreditation is not being sought.

The single most effective step a camp can take in risk management planning is to become accredited by the American Camping Association, and to annually update all of the written procedures and policies. Of course, that step is effective only if the camp continues to follow the standards after the accreditation visit.

CHECKPOINTS

1. Which state and local regulations apply to your camp?
2. Prepare a list of the risks that exist in your camp, starring those which appear to happen most frequently and those which carry the highest potential risk.
3. Identify on that list which risks can be avoided or transferred to others.
4. Develop risk reduction steps for all risks to be kept or transferred.
5. Has your camp been accredited or have you checked out what is involved in accreditation?
6. What is your information collection and record retention plan?

Related Standards

Accreditation Standards for Camp Programs and Services: Nearly all of the standards apply to risk management. However, Standards OM-1–21 are not referenced in other chapters and should be considered with the other standards. In fact, the preparation of *The Standards Organizer: Written Documentation Organizer for ACA Accreditation* published by ACA is probably the easiest way to develop risk management planning materials and to keep in one place most of the records necessary for such documentation. "Additional Professional Practices": Items 1–2, 4–5, 7–9, 10, 13–14, 16–23, 25, 30–31, 39

Standards for Conference and Retreat Centers: II-4–20, 30, III-3, 4–31

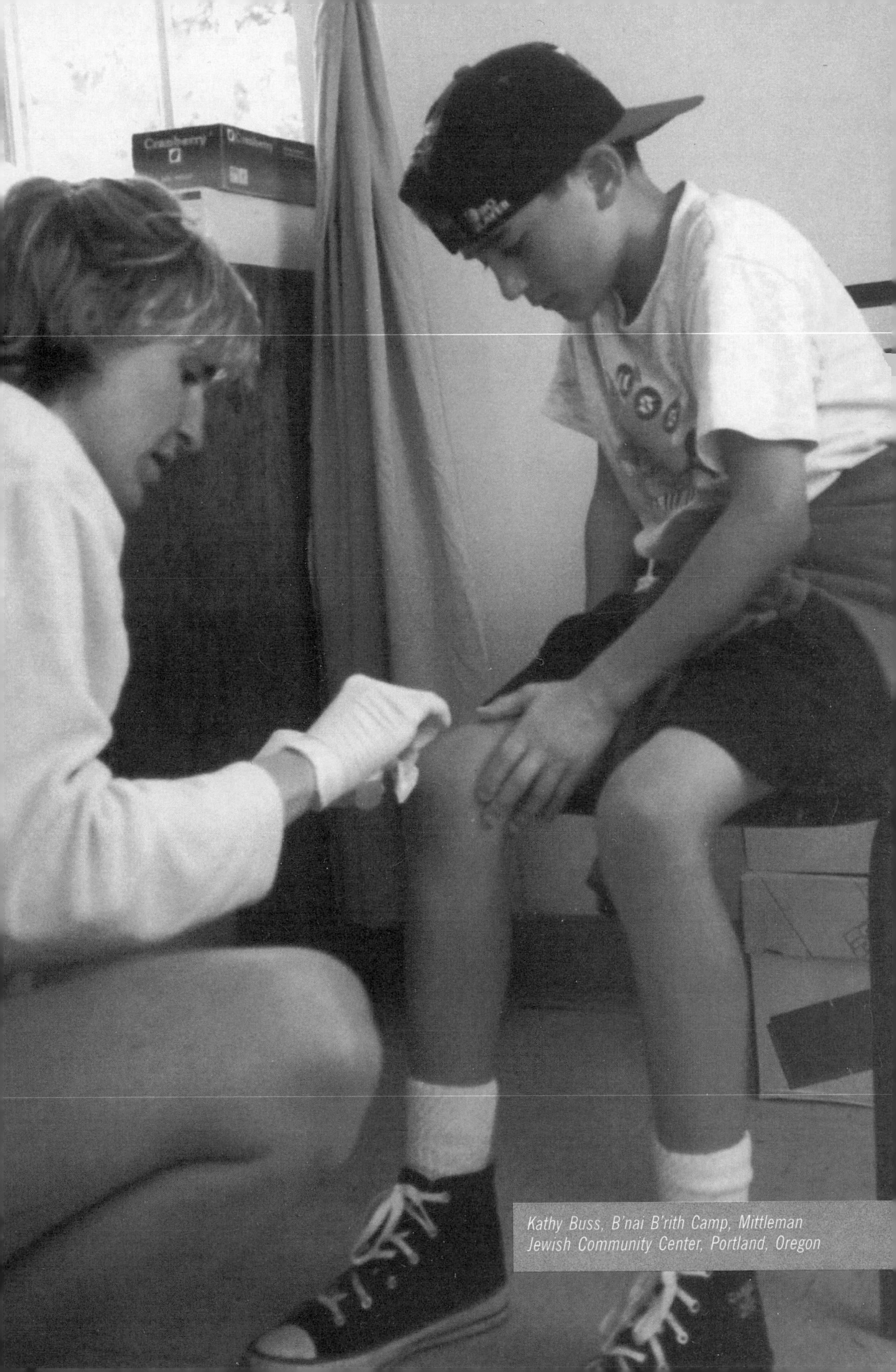

Kathy Buss, B'nai B'rith Camp, Mittleman Jewish Community Center, Portland, Oregon

11

Operation and Supervision: Central Administrative Services

An effective administration relieves program of all nonessential detail . . . . The tracks must be kept clear if program is to operate at its maximum degree of economy and effectiveness. Such matters as health, safety, and sanitation, although vitally important in program considerations are as much the concern of administration as feeding, housing, and transportation. In fact, it is hard to draw the line, when discussing responsibility, as to just what parts of the total camp life are administrative in contrast to those of program.[1]

Though every operation in camp is part of the overall program, certain services tend to be seen in a more supportive role to the direct program operation. The importance of these services in complementing direct program activities, as well as their role in the risk management plan, cannot be overemphasized.

HEALTH SERVICE

There are three broad functions of a camp health service:

1. To manage resources. The purpose of this function is to maintain an effort to promote a healthier, safer camp community and to make policy decisions in the area of camp health. Tasks include defining the scope of health care which the camp will provide, writing job descriptions for health service staff and supervising that group, determining budget, deciding what parents are told about camp health services and how that is communicated, arranging out-of-camp health service, and defining the chain-of-command of health service personnel. This is the function of the *camp health care administrator* most often fulfilled by the camp director; but, in a very large camp, some of the duties may be assigned to the physician or nurse in camp.

2. To provide care. The purpose of this function is to meet the individual health care needs of staff and campers, and to manage the health of the total camp community.

---

[1] Gerald P. Burns. 1954. *Program of the Modern Camp.* New York: Prentice-Hall. p. 59.

Tasks include medication management; screening practices, assessment, care, and evaluation of illness or injury situations; surveillance of the camp community health concerns; collaboration with out-of-camp providers to support recovery of ill or injured people; collaboration with other camp staff to provide a safe and well camp experience; and collaboration with camp administration in an effort to improve camp health practices. This function is often done by the camp nurse or physician, as the *camp health care provider*.

3. To respond to emergencies. The purpose of this function is to develop, implement, and evaluate the camp emergency response system. Tasks include plans to be followed by camp staff for site emergencies and coordinating with external providers. These tasks are usually identified by the camp director and completed by a group of camp staff, including the health care personnel. Persons with CPR and certifications in aquatics and wilderness medicine often are involved in this process.[2]

Personnel

Careful attention to the early selection of a camp physician and the camp health care administrator along with the development of comprehensive health care policies and procedures will save the camp director considerable time and worry later in the season. The director should be totally comfortable with the persons directly responsible for the health care of the campers and staff. Although the camp director can seldom be an expert in medical areas, he or she should be very familiar with this particular part of camp life.

A camp physician should be selected with care and with attention to references, for the director needs the advice of a doctor who has an understanding not only of the medical treatment of children, but also of the unique characteristics of the camp setting. Camps with boards or committees may have a health committee which includes a physician or nurse, but that does *not* substitute for a physician in the camp's local community who is under agreement with the camp to provide medical services. That agreement should be written and may simply be a letter outlining his or her willingness to serve. The camp physician, the director, and, if possible, the principal health care provider should determine several key policies:

- What is the maximum time acceptable between physical examinations by a physician and arrival at camp for staff and campers?
- What are the primary qualifications and responsibilities for the camp health care provider(s)?
- What are the steps to be taken in the health screening of campers and staff upon their arrival and prior to their departure?
- What are the health care policies and procedures to be followed during the camp's operation?

---

[2]Linda Ebner Erceg. Letter. January 1999. Bemidji, MN: Association of Camp Nurses.

- With what external health support resources does the camp need relationships (e.g., emergency room, hospital, dentist, mental health, pharmacy, crisis team, clinic/lab)?

If there is an operating board or committee, it should review the policies established.

It would be ideal if a camp could have a physician and a nurse to retain most of the care of the camp population. However, that is impractical for the majority of camps, except those which have a special health population. Many long-term camps have both a physician and a nurse on their staff. Some camps use several physicians and nurses who are camper parents or former campers or staff who rotate in for a couple of weeks each over the summer. Where there is a turnover of personnel, there need to be clear protocols and established patterns to promote consistency.

Initially, a person needs to be designated as the camp health care administrator who is responsible for the overall administration of the health services of the camp from the development of comprehensive health care policies and procedures to the training of staff in health care concerns and first aid skills. If there is a physician or registered nurse in camp for the entire season, then it is appropriate that he or she perform that role. If the personnel in those positions rotate or if it is a very small camp, the camp director may assume this role.

Where there is a resident camp physician or registered nurse serving as health care administrator, he or she may serve also as a health care provider. There may be other health care providers in camp such as persons certified in first aid and CPR.

American Camping Association standards recommend that, in a day camp, if a physician or registered nurse is not available, the camp should have a previous written arrangement with a physician or registered nurse to provide consultation and daily health care support. In resident camps where such personnel are not available, it is acceptable to make similar arrangements with a nurse or physician who comes to the camp site daily to consult. Of course, in camps that primarily serve persons with special medical needs, it is crucial to have a resident physician or registered nurse.

In addition to these requirements, it is essential to have a person or persons present in camp at all times who have training in first aid and CPR. ACA acknowledges variations in the degree of training needed by the person depending on the proximity of the camp to an emergency medical system. If professional medical help is twenty minutes away or less, first aid and CPR are sufficient. Where the time for access is twenty to sixty minutes, a second level first aid certification plus CPR is required. When the time for access is more than an hour, a person with certification from a nationally recognized provider of training in wilderness first aid and CPR is necessary. The various health certifications are best explained in illustration 11.1.[3] In all cases, previous arrangements with health care personnel and facilities away from the campsite should be made in writing.

---

[3]Linda Ebner Erceg. "Who is Your Camp Healthcare Provider?" *CampLine* Vol. 3, No. 1, May 1994. Martinsville, IN: American Camping Association.

11.1 Illustration *Health Care Providers Comparison*

HEALTH CARE CERTIFICATIONS: A Comparison of Selected Characteristics

Note: Chart information is meant only as a guide; state regulations supersede chart information.

Title of Certifications	Conditions Impacting Ability to Practice	Primary Skill Based on Educational Preparation	Ability to Diagnose/ Prescribe Medication	Ability to Handle Emergencies	Skill with Individual/ Community Health Needs	Equipment Needed to Function in Role
Physician (MD)	Requires license to practice in the state. Works autonomously in medical role.	Diagnosis/treatment of injuries and illnesses.	Priority skill; related to diagnosis/treatment of injury and illness.	Varies with experience. ER ability usually stronger than field work; depends on specialty.	Well-skilled in individual injury or illness needs. Ability in psychosocial and community health domains varies.	Access to lab, x-ray, and routine items; strong physical assessment skill.
Physician's Assistant (PA)	Requires direct supervision of consenting physician. Limits of practice vary by state.	Assists MD with diagnosis and treatment of selected injuries and illness.	Limited to common injuries and illness per directives of supervising MD.	Varies with experience.	Works best with individual injury or illness needs. Community health ability varies.	Varies; some access to lab and x-ray. Physical assessment skill varies with experience.
Registered Nurse (RN)	Requires license to practice in the state. Works autonomously in nursing role.	Diagnosis/treatment of people's responses to health issues, actual or potential.	Provides nursing diagnosis. Does not prescribe meds; gives meds per MD; prescribes treatments.	Varies with experience.	Individual needs; also psychosocial. Community skills, if educated at BSN level.	Minimal/general needs. Physical assessment skill varies with experience and education.
Nurse Practitioner (NP or ARNP)	Varies. Some states don't recognize credential or limit practice (e.g., no prescriptive ability). Check state regs. Need RN license.	Diagnosis/treatment of injuries and illnesses; people's response to health issues; combines RN and PA abilities.	Varies; limited to common injuries and illnesses. State regulations vary; requires prescriptive authority.	Varies with experience.	Individual needs; also psychosocial. Community skills vary based on emphasis during practitioner education.	Varies; some access to lab and x-ray. Physical assessment skill varies with experience.
Licensed Practical Nurse (LPN or LVN)	Licensed to practice in the state. Requires supervision; who defines state regs?	Assists with care of ill or injured.	Limited; gives medication under RN/MD supervision; see state regs.	Limited; usually works under RN/MD direction.	Individual needs; limited psychosocial skills. No community health training.	Minimal/general needs. Minimal assessment skill.
Emergency Medical Tech (EMT)	Varies by state.	Responds to emergency situations.	Recognizes emergency situations; does not prescribe.	Emergency response is a primary skill. Wilderness training needed.	Focused on individual crisis needs. No community health training.	Uses equipment common to emergency work (e.g., ambulance supplies).
First Aider	Usually under Good Samaritan state statute.	Responds to critical situations.	Recognizes critical crisis; does not prescribe.	Limited to scope of training and experience.	Individual life-support needs; no community health training.	"Makes do" with items in the area.

Health Care Planning

In advance of staff training, the camp health administrator and the director should sit down for a lengthy consultation with the camp health care provider and, if possible, the camp physician. The conference should include a review of the previously agreed upon policies and should develop or review the written camp health care plan that includes policies and procedures describing the scope of health services provided by the camp.

Policies. A set of written policies should address the following points.

- Qualifications and authority of the health care administrator, providers, and assistant
- Scope of health care, including emergency care, to be provided at the camp site as opposed to at external health facilities
- External health care resources to be used and how that use is to be determined, including a clear understanding about hospitalization and emergency provisions; arrangements in writing with the hospital chosen by the physician, and with providers of other emergency services, such as dental and mental health services
- Communication to parents about the camp's health service and treatments, and the line of responsibility for that communication

Procedures. A set of written procedures should address the following matters and may comprise a health care manual to serve as a practice guide by the health care provider.

- Name, qualifications, and location on site of all camp health providers, including where first aid and CPR certified personnel are required to be present.
- Supplies and equipment, including a plan for maintaining an inventory of stock medications, supplies, and medical equipment; ordering additional supplies; and storing existing supplies (for example, in a locked cabinet and refrigerator for narcotics and prescription drugs).
- Mealtime procedures for people admitted to the health center, including how to obtain meals from the kitchen, as well as arrangements for special menu requirements.
- Laundering of health center linens and disposal of trash and medical waste, including sharps and biohazard materials.
- Health screening, in resident camps, of campers and staff upon arrival and return (if leaving on extended trips), including what records are kept. In day camps, it is wise to have a routine visual health check for observable evidence of illness, injury, or communicable disease on all campers on the first day, with a plan for daily follow-up thereafter.
- Treatment procedures for routine health care emergencies in situations where health care personnel are not readily available (e.g., out-of-camp trips, camping and canoe trips, etc.). A list of campers with names, home addresses and phone numbers, birth dates, and emergency contact numbers for persons responsible for minors, along with all medical treatment permission forms are to be sent with staff on out-of-camp trips.

- Regular hours for the health center, and how the health care provider(s) are to be reached at night or when not in the health center.
- How campers and staff who have special medical needs are to be assessed for service.
- Management of stock medications kept by the camp and those brought by campers and staff to camp.
- Emergency medical care
  - How life-threatening medical emergencies are to be handled in situations where health care personnel are not readily available (e.g., out-of-camp trips, camping and canoe trips, etc.) as well as when they are available.
  - Emergency transportation, including names of drivers, location of vehicle keys, permission for use of private cars, gas.
- Sanitary procedures to be followed in dealing with medical wastes and bodily fluids.
- Procedures for monitoring health and sanitation — identification of general routines to be followed for monitoring health and sanitation throughout camp, specifying the roles of counselors, kitchen staff, and maintenance staff, and including:
  - A plan for regular inspection of the entire camp, for example, who accompanies health care provider on inspection of living quarters?
  - Daily procedures for living-group counselors to follow in the supervision of camper health, including procedures for regular check-ins at the health center or area.
  - A plan for storage, pick-up, and disposal of trash and garbage throughout the camp.
  - Identification of person(s) to whom the health care provider expresses concerns about observations in area(s) outside his or her supervision.
  - A plan for monitoring the health of staff who handle food and areas used for food preparation.
- Recordkeeping.
  - Type of records to be kept by the camp health care administrator and/or providers including health examination forms, health screening records, a day-to-day bound health log with numbered pages for recording in ink all treatments of campers and staff which cannot be altered or removed, injury/incident reports, and including OSHA forms, any health care documentation required by a state licensing agency, and/or the license held by the camp's health care provider, as well as any other supplementary records.
  - Clear statement of insurance and billing procedures.
  - Review of previous years' injury/illness data for risk-reduction purposes.

These health care policies and procedures and the health care provider's manual are a vital part of the camp's risk management plan and should be maintained with it as well as at the health center. The supervision of these health care policies and procedures is the responsibility of the health care administrator even though specific portions of it may be assigned by the camp director to non-health care personnel, e.g., maintenance or kitchen staff.

This conference of the health administrator, the director, the health care provider, and the camp physician should also include a discussion of the medical protocols or treatment procedures under which the camp health provider will operate. *Medical protocols* are given by the physician so that an RN may carry out certain procedures for the camp population without further consultation, whereas *standing orders* are often provided in the treatment of an individual. Even if camp does not employ an RN, the camp's medical protocols should include procedures and responsibilities in first aid, emergency medical care, routine health care by staff other than the health manager, initial health screening, and professional therapy (if any). These should be discussed carefully, modified as needed, signed by the doctor, and a copy kept by the camp health care administrator, camp health care providers, camp director, and the doctor. Using the camp's previous year's protocols as a sample may make it easier for the physician to review and write them according to his or her viewpoint. Some physicians may be reluctant to sign protocols. Where that is encountered, it is wise for the camp director and camp health manager to develop written health care procedures based upon conversations with the physician and then ask the physician to review and initial them with any corrections.

Staff Training

During the precamp training period for all staff, the camp health administrator and/or the camp health care provider should be assigned a period or periods to work with staff concerning their individual roles in the health care procedures. Everyone should be given a copy of emergency procedures and required to rehearse any drills. All staff should be given some training in basic first aid techniques. Training should include identification of the dangers of bloodborne pathogens and hepatitis B, precautions that should be taken to avoid exposure, and steps to be taken upon exposure. A clear definition should be given staff as to the types of things general staff can care for and what should be referred to the health center.

Staff should be given the impression that the health center is not simply a place for the treatment of serious illness and injury, but a friendly, integrated part of camp life which ministers to many diverse needs in the camp community. Often, the health care provider will deal with homesickness and ailments growing out of stress or other emotional and psychological causes. The involvement of the health personnel in the fun activities of camp, whether as an occasional helper at the waterfront, in the craft shop, or as a participant in skits or stunts at a campfire, can endear the person to the camp as an individual. With the proper attitude, health care personnel can become a listening ear for many of the problems of campers and staff which have little to do with medical treatment.

Living group counselors need additional time with the health provider to better understand their day-to-day role in the health care of the campers entrusted to their care. They should understand how they are to be informed of special health problems of individual campers in their group, when they are to bring campers to the health center, and what symptoms or problems to watch for in their daily living routines, e.g., during dressing, personal hygiene routines, eating, and sleeping. The importance of cabin cleanup, daily inspections, and their relationship to the health of campers and staff should be stressed.

Those daily inspections, the "walk around" along with regular visits to other parts of camp (e.g., the kitchen, maintenance shop, program activity areas, and staff living quarters), are a key part of health supervision. It is important that the health provider not be considered a spy by other departments or counselors. However, the health care administrator should be alert to possible health hazards; when one is spotted, it should be reported immediately to the department supervisor or to the director. Naturally, it is not wise for the health provider or administrator to approach the counselor, kitchen helper, or individual staffer on the spot unless it is an emergency. Rather, the problem should be called to the attention of the person's immediate supervisor.

Staff should also be trained in prevention as well as symptom recognition and first aid or treatment for any health problems specific to the geographic location. This is especially important when staff come from other areas of the country or the world. Topics to cover here might include local poisonous plants or other similar health hazards, such as Lyme Disease. International staff should be given some orientation to the health standards, personal and group, of the country they are visiting.

Staff training should also include information about disease transmittal and precautions to prevent transmission, including hand washing. As employers, camps are now mandated to give training on disease transmission, including bloodborne pathogens, and on universal precautions to prevent their transmission. Specific mention should also be made of AIDS and hepatitis as bloodborne pathogens. In light of having a staff that is conceivably old enough to be sexually active, it would be a serious omission not to also mention sexually transmitted diseases.

OSHA has a number of regulations regarding employee health and safety that staff should receive training on. Certain OSHA regulations require "providing personal protective equipment [for employees]. In the pool area, for example, OSHA requires a respirator, rubber gloves, and eye protection in the filter room. An eye wash station is also needed when chlorine is handled by employees . . . In addition . . . employers are expected to examine workplace conditions to ensure they conform to applicable health and safety requirements," reports Ed Schirick.[4]

Hazards are a key factor in OSHA regulations, which typically require that they be removed or guarded against. A written Hazard Communication Plan is required which includes:

---

[4] Ed Schirick. "What is Your OSHA IQ?" *Camping Magazine* Vol. 71, No. 2, March/April 1998. p. 18.

1. A list of the hazardous chemicals on the site
2. How the staff is trained in the use of such substances
3. The requirements for labeling containers of such substances
4. How the requirement for Material Safety Data Sheets is met

Employers are required to distribute to employees information on any hazardous substances in work areas. Robert Bush indicates that "the OSHA definition of a 'hazardous chemical' is *very* broad" and identifies examples such as: chemicals used in photography, pool cleaning, arts and crafts; and industrial-strength cleaning materials, etc. These substances come with Material Safety Data Sheets (MSDS) which must be kept in a place accessible to employees.

In addition, a safety program should be developed with specific procedures to disable or to prevent inadvertent energization of machines or equipment. These lockout/tagout requirements are designed to prevent the removal of guards or safety devices. The director must be able to show that the plan has been reviewed annually and employees have been trained in the plan.[5]

Role of Principal Health Care Provider

The principal health care provider should be chosen with prudence, and, assuming that credentials are in order, an understanding and love of children should be a primary concern. A physician expecting to have a two-week vacation at camp may find the demands on his or her time far in excess of expectations, if the camper is not the primary reason for the assuming this role. If a health professional is accustomed to the type of support given in a hospital or a medical practice, there may be an adjustment to the autonomous practice at camp.

The camp director has an important role in orienting health care providers, and providing the support that will make their time and work effective. Since a health care provider is often the only person in camp in that profession, opportunities should be sought to put the provider in touch with other camp health care providers by visits to other camps or workshops during the year. The Association of Camp Nurses has proven to be a rich resource for sharing experiences and knowledge among camp nurses across the country.

In selecting a nurse, a careful examination of the nurse's experience and approach is critical if it is to be a good experience for both the camp and the nurse. A nurse who has spent his or her entire nursing career in a hospital or doctor's office may be reluctant to take any step in a camp health center without direct immediate orders from a doctor. Experience in an emergency room, as a school nurse, or in pediatrics is more likely to provide the experience comparable to the camp health situation. The nurse also needs direct experience in first aid, because so many of the minor ailments of camp life require that sort of attention rather than diagnosis or long-term treatment.

---

[5]Robert B. Bush. "A Director's Primer on Selected OSHA Requirements." *The CampLine* Vol. III, No. 2, October 1994.

The role of the nurse in health education with both the camp staff and campers is not to be overlooked. Kris Miller Lishner points out that "the camp nurse is a health education resource person, collaborator, and consultant for the staff . . . Everyone in camp is a health educator and has some responsibility for health teaching. Activity directors, kitchen managers, and administrative staff engage in health education when they point out safe ways to do activities, perform jobs and maintain environmental health and safety. In their daily routines with campers, counselors are their primary health teachers."[6]

If the camp health care provider is to perform the role of overall health, sanitation, and wellness supervision of the camp, careful interpretation of that role must be given to the staff during training. In addition, a clarification of the manner in which the health care provider deals with problems he or she observes in areas outside of his or her direct supervision needs to be determined early on.

Louise Czupryna, a camp nurse, points out that "camp directors can play a vital role in welcoming a nurse to camp, especially newcomers to the field, and giving them the support they need to become a part of the 'camp team.' They often need to be 'helped along a bit.' One of camp nurses' biggest complaints, especially new ones, is the lack of deliberate effort to help them feel a part of the camp operation. Without the interaction and assistance of fellow health professionals that they receive in a hospital or clinic, new camp nurses are apt to feel lonely and disconnected in the rustic camp environment."[7] Camp directors, being in a people-oriented business, should understand the need for this personal attention to someone in a strange setting.

Records

Written documentation is a vital ingredient of good health care as well as for risk management. A variety of types of written records are important.

- Signed permissions for routine health care, for administering prescribed medications, and for seeking or providing emergency medical treatment for all campers and staff who are minors.
- Health examination forms on all resident camp participants, requiring the examination to have been performed within a minimum of two years (or twelve months in some states) prior to their arrival at camp, signed by a licensed physician, specifying date of exam, any current medications, treatments or medical conditions requiring restrictions on participation. A sample health examination form is shown in illustration 11.2.
- Health histories, with names, phone numbers, and addresses of persons to be contacted in case of a medical emergency. A sample health history is shown in illustration 11.3.
- Records of health screening, if resident camp, within twenty-four hours of arrival. A sample health screening record is shown in illustration 11.4.

---

[6]Kris Miller Lishner and Margaret Auld Bruya. *Creating a Healthy Camp Community: a Nurse's Role.* 1994. Martinsville, IN: American Camping Association. p.122.

[7]Louise Czupryna. "Partners on the Health and Safety Team." *Camping Magazine* Vol. 61, No. 5, April 1989. p. 30.

- Health logs with records in ink of the date, time, and name of person ill or injured, general description of injury or illness, description of treatment (if any), administration of routine medications and treatments, and initials of person evaluating and treating patient. A camp director will find a bound health log with numbered and lined pages where records of all patients are recorded on successive lines in ink, the *minimum* requirement for a reassuring record in case of legal defense in a lawsuit. A sample health log sheet is shown in illustration 11.5. This practice does not eliminate or provide a substitute for the recording of the treatment of an individual camper or staff member in a method required by a state licensing agency and/or to the level required by the license held by the camp's health care provider. This separate record goes beyond legal defense to meet certain health care requirements.

  The computer may serve as one source for health care records. However, legal defense depends on having records which cannot be demonstrated as having not been altered. Therefore, in all likelihood, computer records are backup or supplementary records to a written log. The use of passwords and other protections will make whatever computer records are developed more secure and accurate. In any case, the camp director has the ultimate responsibility for being familiar with how records are generated, and making sure there is the appropriate record for legal defense on behalf of the camp.

- Injury/Incident reports completed on all injuries. A sample accident/incident report form is shown in illustration 10.2 in chapter 10. A different form may be required by worker's compensation or OSHA and may substitute for the form used for campers.

- Inventories of medications and supplies at the beginning and end of the season.

- Records, required by OSHA, of all health information and training provided staff in the area of bloodborne pathogens, all treatments rendered to staff concerning bloodborne pathogens, and any incidents in which staff have had exposure to bloodborne pathogens. OSHA requires a written Exposure Control Plan which includes:

  1. Identification of job classes or job tasks with occupational exposure to blood and other potentially infectious materials,
  2. Procedures for evaluating the circumstances surrounding an exposure incident,
  3. A schedule and method for implementing the various parts of the plan, including training of employees.[8]

All of the above records should be placed together and, with the exception of the inventories, kept until one to four years after the youngest participant has reached the age of majority of the state of the camp's location *and* office (be sure to check the statutory limit in your state). They probably need to be immediately accessible during the twelve months following the close of the camp session and could be stored in a fireproof area thereafter.

---

[8]"Camp Health, Bloodborne Pathogens, and OSHA." *CampLine* Vol. 1, No. 1, May 1992.

11.2

Illustration *ACA Health Examination Form FM 12*

Health Examination Form for Children, Youth and Adults Attending Camps FM 12

Developed and approved by
American Camping Association®
with American Academy of Pediatrics

The information on this form is not part of the camper or staff acceptance process, but is gathered to assist us in identifying appropriate care. This form, except for the "Health

Dates of Camp Attendance _____

Mail this form to the address below by _____ (date)

Recommendations of Licensed Medical Personnel," is to be filled in by parents/guardians of minors or by adults themselves.

Name _____ Birth date _____ Age at camp _____
    Last   *First*   *Middle*

Home address _____
    Street address   *City*   *State*   *Zip*

Social Security number of participant _____ Gender: ☐ Male ☐ Female

Custodial parent/guardian _____ Phone _____

Home address _____
(if different from above) *Street address*   *City*   *State*   *Zip*

Business address _____ Phone _____
    Street address *City* *State* *Zip*

Second parent or guardian or emergency contact _____

Address _____ Phone _____
    Street address   *City*   *State* *Zip*

Business address _____ Phone _____

If not available in an emergency, notify _____

Relationship _____ Phone _____

Address _____
    Street address   *City*   *State* *Zip*

Health Care Recommendations by Licensed Medical Personnel

I examined the above camp participant on _____

  BP _____ Weight _____ Height _____

In my opinion, the above applicant ☐ is ☐ is not able to participate in an active camp program.

The applicant is under the care of a physician for the following conditions _____
_____

Current treatment at the time of this report includes _____
_____

Recommendations and Restrictions at Camp

Treatment to be continued at camp _____
_____

Medications to be administered at camp (name, dosage, frequency) _____
_____

Any medically-prescribed meal plan or dietary restrictions _____
_____

Known allergies _____
_____

Description of any limitation or restriction on camp activities _____
_____

Additional information for health care staff at the camp _____
_____

Signature of Licensed Medical Personnel _____

Printed _____ Title _____

Address _____

Phone _____ Date _____

(Left margin labels: Year / Cabin or Group / Name)

11.3

Illustration *ACA Health History Form FM 11*

For Office Use

Health History Form
for Children, Youth and Adults
Attending Camps   FM 11

Developed and approved by
American Camping Association®
American Academy of Pediatrics

Dates of Camp Attendance _____

Mail this form to the address below by _____ (date)

Year

The information on this form is not part of the camper or staff acceptance process, but is gathered to assist us in identifying appropriate care. Any changes to this form should be provided to camp health personnel upon participant's arrival in camp. Provide complete information so that the camp can be aware of your needs.

Name _____ Birth date _____ Age at camp _____
       Last   *First*   *Middle*

Home address _____
              Street address   *City*   *State*   *Zip*

Social Security number of participant _____ Gender: ☐ Male ☐ Female

Custodial parent/guardian _____ Phone _____

Home address _____
(if different from above) *Street address*   *City*   *State*   *Zip*

Business address _____ Phone _____
                  Street address   *City*   *State*   *Zip*

Second parent or guardian or emergency contact _____

Address _____ Phone _____
         Street address   *City*   *State*   *Zip*

Business address _____ Phone _____
                  Street address   *City*   *State*   *Zip*

If not available in an emergency, notify _____

Relationship _____ Phone _____

Address _____
         Street address   *City*   *State*   *Zip*

Insurance Information

Is the participant covered by family medical/hospital insurance? ☐ Yes ☐ No

If so, indicate carrier or plan name _____ Group # _____

Carrier address _____

Name of insured _____ Relationship to participant _____

Social Security number of policy holder or insurance ID number _____

Cabin or Group

Important — These boxes must be complete for attendance*

Parent/Guardian Authorizations: This health history is correct and complete as far as I know, and the person herein described has permission to engage in all camp activities except as noted.

I hereby give permission to the camp to provide routine health care, administer prescribed medications, and seek emergency medical treatment including ordering x-rays or routine tests. I agree to the release of any records necessary for insurance purposes. I give permission to the camp to arrange necessary related transportation for me/my child. In the event I cannot be reached in an emergency, I hereby give permission to the physician selected by the camp to secure and administer treatment, including hospitalization, for the person named above. This completed form may be photocopied for trips out of camp.

Signature of parent or guardian or adult camper/staffer _____
Printed Name _____ Date _____

I also understand and agree to abide by any restrictions placed on my participation in camp activities.
Signature of minor or adult camper/staffer _____ Date _____

If for religious reasons you cannot sign this, contact the camp for a legal waiver which must be signed for attendance.

ALLERGIES List all known.   Describe reaction and management of the reaction.

Medication allergies (list)

_____   _____
_____   _____

Food allergies (list)

_____   _____
_____   _____

Other allergies (list) — include insect stings, hay fever, asthma, animal dander, etc.

_____   _____
_____   _____

Name

11.3

Illustration *ACA Health History Form FM 11 continued*

MEDICATIONS BEING TAKEN

Please list ALL medications (including over-the-counter or nonprescription drugs) taken routinely. Bring enough medication to last the entire time at camp. Keep it in the original packaging/bottle that identifies the prescribing physician (if a prescription drug), the name of the medication, the dosage, and the frequency of administration.

☐ This person **takes NO medications** on a routine basis. OR ☐ This person **takes medications** as follows:

Med #1 _____ Dosage _____ Specific times taken each day _____

Reason for taking_____

Med #2 _____ Dosage _____ Specific times taken each day _____

Reason for taking_____

Attach additional pages for more medications.

Identify any medications taken during the school year that participant does/may not take during the summer: _____

RESTRICTIONS (The following restrictions apply to this individual.)

Does not eat: ☐ Red meat ☐ Pork ☐ Dairy products ☐ Poultry ☐ Seafood ☐ Eggs ☐ Other (describe) _____

Explain any restrictions to activity (e.g. what cannot be done, what adaptations or limitations are necessary)

GENERAL QUESTIONS (Explain "yes" answers below.)

Has/does the participant:

	Yes	No		Yes	No
1. Had any recent injury, illness or infectious disease?	☐	☐	16. Ever had back problems?	☐	☐
2. Have a chronic or recurring illness/condition?	☐	☐	17. Ever had problems with joints (e.g., knees, ankles)?	☐	☐
3. Ever been hospitalized?	☐	☐	18. Have an orthodontic appliance being brought to camp?	☐	☐
4. Ever had surgery?	☐	☐	19. Have any skin problems (e.g., itching, rash, acne)?	☐	☐
5. Have frequent headaches?	☐	☐	20. Have diabetes?	☐	☐
6. Ever had a head injury?	☐	☐	21. Have asthma?	☐	☐
7. Ever been knocked unconscious?	☐	☐	22. Had mononucleosis in the past 12 months?	☐	☐
8. Wear glasses, contacts or protective eye wear?	☐	☐	23. Had problems with diarrhea/constipation?	☐	☐
9. Ever had frequent ear infections?	☐	☐	24. Have problems with sleepwalking?	☐	☐
10. Ever passed out during or after exercise?	☐	☐	25. If female, have an abnormal menstrual history?	☐	☐
11. Ever been dizzy during or after exercise?	☐	☐	26. Have a history of bed-wetting?	☐	☐
12. Ever had seizures?	☐	☐	27. Ever had an eating disorder?	☐	☐
13. Ever had chest pain during or after exercise?	☐	☐	28. Ever had emotional difficulties for which professional help was sought?	☐	☐
14. Ever had high blood pressure?	☐	☐			
15. Ever been diagnosed with a heart murmur?	☐	☐			

Please explain any "yes" answers, noting the number of the questions. _____

Which of the following has the participant had?

☐ Measles
☐ Chicken pox
☐ German measles
☐ Mumps
☐ Hepatitis A
☐ Hepatitis B
☐ Hepatitis C

TB Mantoux Test

Date of last test _____

Result: ☐ Positive ☐ Negative

Please give all dates of immunization for:

Vaccine:	Dates:	Mo/Yr	Mo/Yr	Mo/Yr	Mo/Yr	Mo/Yr	Mo/Yr
DTP		___	___	___	___	___	___
TD (tetanus/diphtheria)		___	___	___	___	___	___
Tetanus		___	___	___	___	___	___
Polio		___	___	___	___		
MMR		___	___				
or Measles		___	___				
or Mumps		___	___				
or Rubella		___	___				
Haemophilus influenza B		___	___	___	___		
Hepatitis B		___	___	___			
Varicella (chicken pox)		___	___				

Use this space to provide any additional information about the participant's behavior and physical, emotional, or mental health about which the camp should be aware. _____

Name of family physician _____ Phone _____

Address _____

Name of family dentist/orthodontist _____ Phone _____

Address _____

Screening Record *(For camp use only)*   Screened by _____

Date screened _____ Time _____ am/pm Updates/additions to health history noted ☐ Yes ☐ No ☐ None required

Meds received _____

Current health needs identified _____

Observational notes _____

11.4   Illustration *Sample Health Screening Records*

Camp Health Record
Individual at Camp   Form FM 02

🏕 Developed and approved by the
American Camping Association®
with the American Academy of Pediatrics

Camp Name

Name _____ Age _____ Sex _____

Entrance Date _____ Departure Date _____

Examination Entrance by_____	Departure by_____	Important Observations to Follow While at Camp
Height		
Weight		
Temperature		
Eyes		
Nose		
Ears		
Throat		
Teeth		
Posture		
Skin		
Feet		

Meds Received_____

Dosage/Interval_____

Copyright 1983 by American Camping Association, Inc.   Revised 1990, 1992, 1996.   (over)

Name · Last · First · Initial · Cabin or Group · Year

Top: Camp Health Record Individual at Camp Form FM 02. Bottom: Excerpted from Health History and Examination Form for Children, Youth and Adults Attending Camps Form FM 08N.

For camp use only

Screening Record

Date screened _____ Time _____ am pm

Meds received _____

Updates/additions to health history noted   ☐ Yes   ☐ No   ☐ None required

Current health needs identified _____

Observational notes _____

Screened by _____

Copyright 1983 by American Camping Association, Inc.   Revised 1990, 1992, 1994, 1995, 1996, 1998.

11.5 Illustration *Sample Page from Health Record Log*

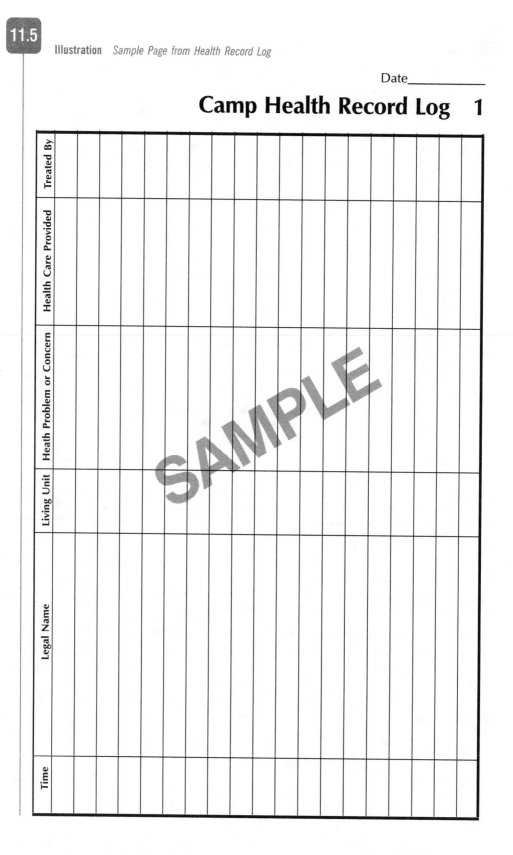

Date_____

Camp Health Record Log   1

FOOD SERVICE

Day Camps

Many day camps do not have the matter of institutional food service as a day-to-day concern. Most often in these camps, campers bring their own sack lunch except on cookout days. However, this does not preclude appropriate planning in the following areas:

- Care and refrigeration of lunches from campers' arrival at site until lunch
- Refrigeration and serving of the drink for the lunch meal (e.g., milk, juice, punch)
- Provision for drinking water throughout the camp day
- Disposal of paper and scraps from the lunch period
- Supplemental snacks for campers who bring inadequate lunches
- Provision of a relaxed community atmosphere during the lunch period to aid good digestion
- Sanitation procedures for food storage and handling for cookout meals, often done with the aid of campers

Some day camps do provide hot meal service for their campers and much of the information that follows is as applicable to such day camps as it is to resident camps.

The Food Service Supervisor

A resident camp travels on its stomach as much as an army does. Therefore, the director should turn his or her attention to the food service early in the planning for the camp season. The early recruitment of a capable food service supervisor is one key to dealing with this important area of camp life.

The qualifications set down for that food service supervisor will depend on the size of the camp and the type of food service desired. A small camp of 25 to 150 campers can seldom afford to employ a trained dietitian or nutritionist as food service supervisor. A cook with experience in a school lunch room or fraternity or sorority house can easily fill the bill, if the menus are carefully planned with a dietitian or nutritionist prior to camp. A camp of 150 or more will require a food service supervisor with more skills in meal planning and staff supervision than will a smaller camp. In fact, the larger camps need food service supervisors whose skills are best in the areas of purchasing, planning, and staff supervision rather than cooking. An experienced first or second cook can provide the cooking ability needed for tasty food. Recent surveys show that 15 to 25 percent of a resident camp's budget is spent on food service, and 25 to 31 percent of that cost is labor.[9] Cutting corners on the salary or living conditions of

---

[9]Armand Ball. "Food Service Cost Survey." *Trendlines*. May/June 1990. p. 1.

the food service supervisor can lead to far greater costs than an increased salary might. Violation of state regulations and standard food service practices can lead to serious health and legal problems.

The development of menus is the first step in purchasing and summer planning. In order to give the food service supervisor (particularly if he or she is new) the best information for developing the summer's menus, the camp director should include the following items in the primary discussion:

1. The previous year's food budget in detail
2. The previous year's menus and any camper or staff feedback
3. A profile of the camp community
4. The style used for serving meals in previous years
5. Whether most preparation is from scratch or from packaged foods
6. The menu cycle, based on camp periods
7. The average daily meal count

The food service supervisor should then revise the proposed menus in light of any suggestions, the current prices of foods, the amount allocated in the camp budget for raw food, personal menu favorites, and the cycle of camp periods. If the camp qualifies for provision of food or financial subsidies from state or federal programs, the food service supervisor should be given appropriate information about these items and any menu requirements prior to preparation of menus and food orders.

Upon completion of the menus, the director should review them and raise questions or concerns he or she has about them. Unless the food service supervisor is a qualified dietitian or nutritionist, menus should now be reviewed by such a person to ensure a balanced diet. Often, a specialist can be found in a district or city school office, or in the home economics department of a nearby college or university, who will be willing to look over the menus for sound nutritional balance. When the menus have been reviewed, the dietitian should be asked to sign the menus and explain his or her suggestions to the director or to the food service supervisor. Ideally, this can be done early in the year so that adequate time is allowed for the purchasing of food. A returning food service supervisor, or one who lives in the area of the camp, may know the best local sources for purchasing various foods. Otherwise, the director should research the best sources.

Food Purchasing

Normally, better prices can be secured on a large initial food order than on a week-by-week delivery. Therefore, there is an advantage in developing a list of the basic canned and dry goods needed for the summer and placing the bulk of that order for delivery at the beginning of the season. If food orders are placed early, companies will often guarantee quoted prices at the time of the order.

Mark J. Brostoff suggests seven factors to be taken into account in the selection of vendors:

- Price
- Quality
- Delivery of product
- Personal relations (with salesperson)

- Service
- Technical assistance
- Competitive position (discounts or rebates)[10]

Before placing an early order, the director should have a relatively stable count of the number of meals to be served during the period for which food is being ordered. To determine the maximum number of meals to be served on a seasonal basis: multiply the maximum number of persons (campers and staff) that can be accommodated by three meals a day, then multiply that result by the number of days feeding each period, including for staff training and days between periods, and add the totals. Dividing the total by the number of days in the particular season provides the *average daily meal count*.

If enrollment is slow or the camp has a variable record of enrollment, then the director should be cautious about the quantities ordered so that there is not a large inventory to carry over beyond the season. If the camp has enrolled only 75 percent of its capacity, it is foolish to order for a full camp until there is evidence that enrollment is climbing to that degree. The same principle follows with nonsummer groups. Where principal nonsummer usage is on the weekend, then food purchases of perishables must be carefully managed to avoid waste and thus higher food costs.

With appropriate food storage areas such as protected dry storage and freezer and refrigeration space, good prices on certain items can often be secured in advance of sudden price increases due to weather or shortage problems. For example, if the summer has been particularly dry and the fruit crop was short, it is wise to check on the availability of the previous summer's canned fruits early in the fall, for there is sure to be a price increase by the next year's season.

Securing bids on food orders can be helpful as a cost-saving device; but, for the director, this process may be an unnecessary burden unless a system of bidding has been established in prior years. On all bids, the grade and type of produce as well as the size container required must be specified or the prices received may not be comparable. In a bid process, the director should secure prices from several firms (if there are multiple delivery sources) on major food items such as milk, bread, meat, and certain canned fruits and vegetables which will be used in larger quantities.

One factor in food purchasing for nonprofit camps in the United States is whether government aid is available in the form of food items or financial reimbursement for part of the cost of meals served to low-income campers. Availability and regulations continue

---

[10]Mark J. Brostoff. "The Dynamics of Camp Food Purchasing." *Camping Magazine* Vol. 61 , No. 4, February 1989. p. 28.

to change in this area both at the federal and state levels. Appendix E gives the information available at the time of publication.

Food Service Staff

When considering the size of food service staff, there are some guidelines which can be used.

Persons per Meal	Staff Required
Up to 70	1 cook, 1 dishwasher
70 to 120	2 cooks, 1 dishwasher
140 +	3 cooks, 2 dishwashers

The employment of staff to assist the food service supervisor is a matter that should be clearly agreed upon between that supervisor and the director. The director and the food service supervisor should discuss expectations about housing arrangements, salaries, the type of skills needed for each position, and expectations for behavior or clothing. Any staff to be hired who will handle food will need to have or be able to secure before arrival at camp a food handler's permit as required by the state or county. It is always an advantage to everyone involved if the supervisor can meet or interview applicants before they are hired.

Though the degree to which food service staff is involved in camp life outside the kitchen varies from camp to camp, it is always an advantage if the food service staff feels a part of the total camp and participates in some of the all-camp program. Food service staff should be made aware that they are part of a much larger team, and that their cooperation and teamwork are essential for a successful camp.

Housing away from the busy and noisy activities of the camp is important for kitchen staff since the schedule in most camps makes it necessary for food service employees to rise early and, therefore, to retire early in the evening. If camper facilities are rustic in nature, the director should give careful thought to the quarters for kitchen staff since they may expect and need some conveniences not provided for campers.

Meal Organization

The type of food service affects the number and type of staff required as well as the quantities to be cooked. Basically, there are two types of service, cafeteria and family style, though camps will often use a buffet for a special occasion or a salad bar in conjunction with one of the types of service. Both of these types of service have advantages and disadvantages. See illustration 11.6.

If the relationship between the counselor and campers is the most important concern and one desires a more intimate, home-like atmosphere, the family type will probably serve the camp better (see chapter 5). Other factors to be considered are:

11.6   Illustration *Food Service Comparison*

CAFETERIA STYLE	
ADVANTAGES	**DISADVANTAGES**
■ Portions are more easily controlled. ■ Quantities served are more easily controlled, as are costs. ■ Table setting is not required prior to the meal. ■ If dining area is too small for the entire community, this style enables persons at the last of the line to fill tables vacated by persons in the first of the line.	■ Some will be completing the meal while others are being served (unless the camp is very small). ■ It is difficult to have any all-camp activity (announcements, singing) at this type meal setting.

FAMILY STYLE	
ADVANTAGES	**DISADVANTAGES**
■ The counselor can better observe how much and what each camper eats. ■ Family atmosphere and group spirit are better. ■ Everyone starts and finishes at the same time — this is helpful if singing and/or any announcements follow the meal and dishes can be cleared before campers leave the table. ■ Provides opportunities for camper groups to share in tasks around the meal service.	■ More food can be wasted unless very careful control is exerted by kitchen staff and the counselor at the table. ■ Tables must be set in advance, requiring more personnel or involvement from campers. ■ More time is generally required for the serving of the meal.

- Who will wait tables, clear tables, clean tables and floor following the meal? Often, campers are used for any or all of these tasks, and their duties are rotated. Other camps employ waiters who set the tables and bring food and refills.

- Who will serve the plates? Food may be passed around the table, each taking the desired amount, or the counselor may serve the plates and pass them down the table. The latter method provides for a more careful check on what the camper does or doesn't eat; this is particularly important with younger campers. Serving the plates for younger campers also can prevent spills of foods and liquids.

- What foods must be apportioned, if any, and what foods may be refilled? This is dependent partially on budget, but also on nutritional desires. It is particularly important for milk, meats, and desserts, which are higher cost items.

- What plan is there for returning dishes and utensils to the kitchen for washing? Some camps have each table group wash its own dishes at the table; in this case, careful sterilization in compliance with state laws is essential. Dishes may be resterilized in the kitchen after table washing to ensure a 180 degree rinse. If dishes are to be scraped, stacked, and returned to the kitchen, this procedure should be established and worked through during staff training.

Cookout Meals

If a camp program calls for cookouts, overnights, or any sort of tripping program that removes campers from the dining room, the director should draw up a plan for notifying the kitchen of changes in meal counts early enough so that the proper amount of food is prepared for those meals. There must also be a plan for those groups cooking out to secure their cooked or raw food. Groups may be required to submit a food service requisition directly to the food service supervisor, or some other staff members working with the food service may be in charge of filling orders. If out-of-camp meals are few in number over the course of the summer, a system can be devised in which menus, established either by the group or the kitchen, can be picked up at the close of the last in-camp meal served to the group. However, as the number of out-of-camp meals increases, the importance of a carefully planned system will become more apparent. Here are some things to consider.

First, the type of experience which the camp wishes to give its campers will dictate the approach to planning menus for such meals. If the objective is to have a camper group do planning and to understand the nutritional elements of menu planning or to have free choice, then it is more important that a food list be developed to assist campers and counselors in planning the menu and the quantities needed. Amounts available per person or per group should be standardized and made known. If the experience of cooking is a more important part of a trip experience, it may be simpler to have them choose between menus or accept predetermined menus.

A stock of food in sizes or types not normally used in institutional cooking should be gathered in one storage and checkout facility and some staff member given responsibility for that area. There is a wide variety of dehydrated and freeze-dried food which will make supply packs much lighter.

Foods to be secured from the kitchen (because of limited quantity or refrigeration needed) should be identified along with a method of securing them.

A checkout plan and amount of advance notice need to be clarified. The group may come with its food list at a specified time and check out the food across a counter so that they may pack and check it for themselves, or staff may accumulate the food from a list and pack it for a group in advance of departure. Careful attention should be given to procedures for keeping refrigerated foods cool and what foods (if any) can be returned to the kitchen.

Some camps operate the out-of-camp meals through a store, providing campers the opportunity not only of planning their menus but also of learning budgeting by purchasing the food items from that store with camp money. This type of learning experience takes preparation — pricing, order sheets, and orientation of staff. The director should also consider the impact of any such program on the food service supervisor, food purchasing, food costs, and nutritional standards before establishing the system.

Sanitation and Health

Camp kitchens range from rather rustic centers where campers take food to their units to cook over wood, charcoal, or gas fires, to fully equipped commercial kitchens with all of the appliances you would find in the finest restaurants. However simple or elaborate, some basic health and sanitation standards need to be followed in food storage, preparation, and serving. The dangers of foodborne illness in a camp setting cannot be underestimated.

To prevent foodborne illness, a food service supervisor should give careful attention to Hazard Analysis Critical Control Points (HACCP), which is a food safety and self-inspection system that looks at the flow of potential hazardous foods though the camp's operation from receiving of food to serving of the food. Hazard Analysis encourages food service staff to ask where the food safety problems are most likely to occur. Critical Control Points suggests what steps are needed to take control of food safety problems and where or when to take them.

A good starting point is to find the sources of dangers of foodborne illness most frequently seen. The North Dakota Department of Public Health identified the following primary sources.[11]

Source	Percentage
Inadequate refrigeration/cooling	63
Preparing food far in advance of service	29
Hot holding at bacterial incubating temperature	27
Infected persons handling food	26
Inadequate reheating	25
Inadequate cleaning of equipment	9
Use of leftovers	7
Cross-contamination	6
Inadequate cooking	5
Storing acid food in toxic metal containers	4
Contaminated raw ingredients in uncooked foods	2
Intentional additives	2
Obtaining food from unsafe sources	1

Storage of all food should be in areas protected from rodents or vermin. Perishable foods should be stored in *refrigerated areas* at 40 degrees Fahrenheit or below. As a safety measure, a clipboard should be mounted beside each walk-in, freezer, or cooler, providing a form with a line for each day for the assigned individual to initial and indicate the temperature at the time of the check. This will ensure that, if the temperature begins to rise in a twenty-four hour period, corrective actions can be taken promptly. The walk-in will fluctuate some during mealtime when it is opened often, but it should quickly return to a safe temperature.

One of the greatest points of danger in food contamination falls in the period of thawing, or cooling after cooking, when pathogenic organisms can multiply more easily. It is best to thaw frozen items in refrigerated areas so that there is no chance the items will sit after thawing in temperatures higher than 40 degrees Fahrenheit.

---

[11]ACN *Compass Point*. Bemidji, MN: Association of Camp Nurses.

A minimum temperature of 140 degrees Fahrenheit should be maintained in *keeping food warm* before a meal or for serving in a cafeteria operation, and it is wise to heat the food to 170 degrees Fahrenheit before placing it in a serving container. The maximum periods in which perishable foods (e.g., meat, fish, eggs, milk, poultry, salads with dressings) should be allowed to sit in 46 to 139 degree range is two hours. Care should be taken that perishable foods be cooked in deep trays or large cooking pots that would take more than two hours to cool the center.

The food service supervisor and health care provider should sit down with all food service staff and discuss the *personal sanitary and hygiene practices* that should be followed, as well as the principles of careful food preparation and serving. Employees should be made aware that, should they have a contagious condition, they should immediately notify both the food service supervisor and the health care provider, so they can be relieved of food service duties. A toilet for use by kitchen employees should be convenient to the kitchen area and display signs reminding employees about washing hands with soap after use of the toilet facilities. Other staff that may be handling foods on a cookout should be trained in food handling and sanitizing dishes, pots, and pans.

A definite system following state regulations for *washing and sanitizing* dishes, pots and pans, and utensils must be established. If there is a mechanical dishwasher, such regulations will require having wash water at least 100 degrees Fahrenheit, and rinse water at least 180 degrees Fahrenheit, or using an approved chemical sanitizing solution. Some camps wash dishes and utensils by hand; however, the temperatures for washing and rinsing should be maintained at 100 degrees Fahrenheit or above and a second rinse should use an approved chemical sanitizer. In both cases, dishes, utensils, and pots and pans should be air dried. As in refrigeration, it is wise to have a clipboard mounted near the dishwashing area where, at least once during the dishwashing process each day, the temperatures are checked, recorded, and initialed.

The cleanliness and sanitation of the kitchen work areas is very important. All work surfaces should be cleaned after use. Special attention should be paid to slicers and can openers which are often overlooked in the daily cleaning. Surfaces in which food comes into contact should be identified to kitchen personnel, and the procedures for cleaning those surfaces before and after every food contact established.

Garbage and rubbish should be promptly removed from the kitchen into leakproof containers with tight-fitting lids. Daily removal and emptying of those containers should be part of the maintenance schedule. Those containers should also be cleaned regularly, even when plastic bags are used inside the containers.

Contracted Services

Many camps have chosen to contract with food service companies to provide the entire food service operation, eliminating the employment and supervision of staff, the purchase of food, and the related bookkeeping chores. Though some control of menus related to what is served or what the camp can afford remains, most of the control and resulting problems become those of the contracted service. Many times the services which contract with colleges and universities find that camps are a natural customer and enable them to retain their staff between school seasons.

The applicability and affordability of such services vary from camp to camp. A careful analysis of the related costs for both types of service should be made. Current customers of the service should be interviewed; and, if at all possible, the food service there observed before making a commitment.

TRANSPORTATION

The transportation of campers and staff provides one of the key areas of potential liability to camps. Careful risk management, including a thorough review of insurance coverage and safety education practices, is essential. In camps, vehicles may include cars, vans, buses, boats, and planes. Transportation issues in a day camp are usually major factors in the program cost and schedule and most likely involve city driving.

The first step is to analyze what transportation is required.

- Do campers have to be transported to and from camp or will parents or the sponsoring group arrange that?
- Do campers have to be transported in groups out of camp for program activities or events?
- Does a camp vehicle haul supplies and equipment into camp?
- What vehicle will be needed within camp for maintenance personnel?
- What vehicle will be needed in an emergency to transport injured individuals to the doctor or hospital?
- Do campers or staff have to be transported to and from transportation terminals?
- Will staff-owned vehicles be used for certain purposes?

The use of staff-owned vehicles should be considered carefully with a review of the camp's insurance coverage for nonowned vehicles and its implications for rates. If a situation warrants the use of a staff-owned vehicle, then a clear agreement should be developed between the director and the staff member concerning insurance, reimbursement for mileage, and periods of use.

Owning, Leasing, or Chartering

Initially, the question of whether the camp purchases and maintains its own vehicles must be answered. Since camp situations vary so greatly, there is no way to suggest that one method is best for every camp. There are some advantages and disadvantages of the three usual methods of securing camp vehicles. See illustration 11.7.

Some advantages can become disadvantages in certain circumstances, so consider carefully the cost, availability of qualified personnel, and the amount of use necessary.

The number and type of vehicles required by the camp program will certainly affect the decision, since the capital investment at one time for purchase may be more difficult than renting, leasing, or chartering annually.

Although some problems are removed by chartering vehicles, it does not relieve the camp of the responsibility of double-checking that the company carries the appropriate insurance, has a regular system of maintenance and vehicle upkeep, and checks on the safety record of its drivers. This should be part of the selection and contract process, and any signs of variance from stated practice should be immediately reported to the charter company.

Drivers

The selection of the drivers for such vehicles is the key to safety and public relations. It is the driver who must regularly check that the maintenance of the vehicle is maintained, be friendly to campers, parents, or vendors, and yet maintain constant surveillance of safety factors. In a day camp, the daily nature of picking up, transporting, and dropping off campers adds an even greater element of responsibility, not only in safety but in the area of public relations.

A careful check of each driver's driving record should be made each year (within four months prior to the camp season or annually for year-round drivers), either by the camp or by the camp's insurance company. The director should also analyze the type of driving experience and how it relates to the particular vehicles to be driven. Experience with the type of vehicle is very important; training should be provided if the person does not have previous experience with that particular type of vehicle.

State licensing laws vary. Some states require a different type of license for drivers of vehicles which carry a certain number of passengers, or where children are transported by a hired firm. State laws should be checked early so that the appropriate license for the vehicle to be driven can be part of the job requirements. Where a vehicle is designed to carry sixteen or more persons or is in excess of 26,000 pounds, federal law requires a special Commercial Driver License issued at the state level. (Note: it is the design and not the number of actual passengers which determines the license requirement.) A Commercial Driver License requires drug/alcohol testing.

Every vehicle carrying campers should have a staff member, which may be the driver, trained to carry out written accident procedures for providing or securing care for any injured, supervising the uninjured, specifying whom to notify in an emergency, and obtaining appropriate accident information at the scene. When a vehicle carries fifteen or more persons, an additional staff member should be assigned to give attention to the campers to manage safety and group behavior. The number of staff members may need to be increased if there are campers younger than nine, or if campers have mental, emotional, or physical disabilities.

Written procedures and policies should be provided to drivers and specific training

11.7

Illustration *Vehicle Chart*

	FACTORS	OWNING	LEASING/RENTING	CHARTERING
ADVANTAGES	Drivers	Camp selects drivers.	Camp selects drivers.	Company provides drivers.
	Cost	Cost may be less.	Some maintenance and repair costs may be covered. No capital investment.	Maintenance covered by company. No capital investment.
	Schedule	Camp controls schedule, employee, and vehicle.	Camp controls schedule, employee, and vehicle.	Contract specifies pickup and/or arrival time and transfers much of risk to company.
	Insurance			Company provides insurance and can add the camp to their policy as "additional insured."
	Other	Can advertise on side of vehicle.	Camp may have newer vehicles earlier than if owned.	
DISADVANTAGES	Drivers	Finding qualified drivers may be a problem.	Finding qualified drivers may be a problem.	No control over selection of drivers.
	Cost	Camp absorbs maintenance and repair costs. Purchase requires a large sum of cash.	Lease contracts vary and can contain much "fine print."	Cost is usually more. Multiple use increases cost.
	Schedule	Camp controls schedule. A careful maintenance schedule is required.	Camp controls schedule. A careful maintenance schedule is required.	No direct control of vehicle.
	Insurance	Insurance may be a problem.	Insurance may be a problem, requiring substantial deductible and offering only state-required minimum limits.	
	Other			

given during the precamp period. All drivers, even those who do not transport campers or staff, should have training in the following areas:

- Use of fire extinguishers and emergency reflectors stored in vehicle.
- Safety inspection of all vehicles he or she is expected to drive.
- Inspection of the vehicle before use and procedures for reporting any needed repairs.
- Importance of not transporting campers in vehicles not designed for passengers, e.g., open-bed trucks or trailers.
- Procedures in case of an accident, including information cards for witnesses to complete, and a camera for accident pictures. Disposable cameras in each vehicle is a good way to handle this.

All drivers who transport campers or staff should have additional training in the following areas:

- Use of the first aid kit kept in vehicles.
- Identification of appropriate behavior for passengers in loading, unloading, and traveling in vehicles.

- Use of seatbelts or, in the case of smaller children (and some persons with disabilities), restraints.
- Maximum seating capacities of various vehicles.
- Availability and location of medical information forms and permission-to-treat forms.
- Procedures for backing up, loading and unloading passengers, dealing with vehicular breakdowns, refueling, and dealing with illnesses of passengers.
- Procedures for rest stops and telephone use during long excursions, i.e., determining when they are needed, choosing locations, and checking to assure everyone is present at the conclusion of the stop.
- Determining when to unload campers or leave them in the vehicle.
- Determining where campers are to be located during refueling of vehicle.
- Division of responsibility of staff other than the driver.
- Maintenance of an appropriate log of trips, including refueling and oil (see illustration 11.8.)

One person on the staff should be responsible for checking out any staff before they are given permission to drive a camp vehicle. This is ordinarily done during the staff training period. In the frenzied pace of camp life, it is too easy to designate any staff member to take a vehicle and run an errand or transport campers. There should be designated drivers, in addition to the regularly assigned drivers, in order to deal with unscheduled trips as well as to allow for time off.

Maintenance of Vehicles

A regular plan of maintenance of vehicles is the second key to good risk management in transportation. Even the best driver is dangerous in a poorly maintained vehicle. A specific staff member should be given the responsibility of maintaining all vehicles, and a system of regular checks should be established. The written maintenance plan should include:

- Written records of all oil changes and repairs, with the mileage and date
- Regular checks to make sure that a fully stocked first aid kit, flares, fire extinguisher, and appropriate tools are kept in each vehicle at all times
- A regular schedule of safety checks of lights, tires, wipers, windshield, emergency warning systems, horn, brakes, and oil and coolant levels
- A quarterly mechanical evaluation of vehicles that carry passengers (or, in the case of a seasonal operation, within three months prior to use)

Camper Education

In addition to all of these precautions, if campers are to be transported, they should be given instructions on appropriate behavior, safety regulations, use of cell phones, evacuation procedures, and use of seat belts.

11.8   Illustration   *Vehicle Record Log*

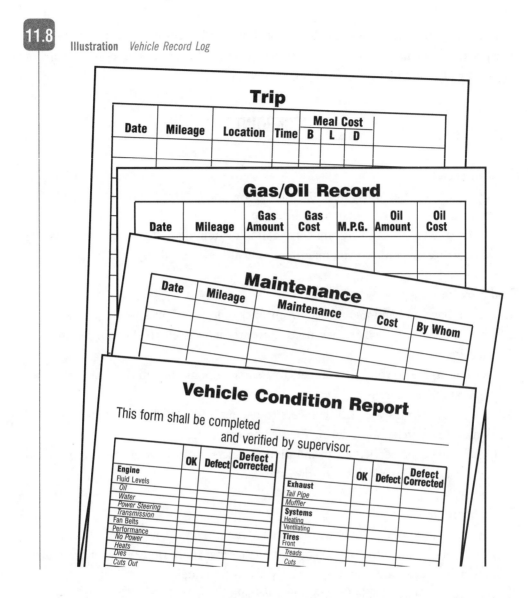

Trip

Date	Mileage	Location	Time	Meal Cost			
				B	L	D	

Gas/Oil Record

Date	Mileage	Gas Amount	Gas Cost	M.P.G.	Oil Amount	Oil Cost

Maintenance

Date	Mileage	Maintenance	Cost	By Whom

Vehicle Condition Report

This form shall be completed _____ and verified by supervisor.

	OK	Defect	Defect Corrected
Engine			
Fluid Levels			
Oil			
Water			
Power Steering			
Transmission			
Fan Belts			
Performance			
No Power			
Heats			
Dies			
Cuts Out			

	OK	Defect	Defect Corrected
Exhaust			
Tail Pipe			
Muffler			
Systems			
Heating			
Ventilating			
Tires			
Front			
Treads			
Cuts			

Day Camps

Day camps which transport campers deal with these sorts of concerns on a daily basis and are generally very sensitive to the issues of safety and transport. Often there are multiple vehicles involved in the transport of campers, and it is vital that a plan for the orderly arrival and departure of vehicles be developed. Areas for loading and unloading, parking, waiting, and moving traffic should be clearly delineated in writing, and staff should be made available to supervise arrival and departure periods.

A written schedule of camper pickup and drop-off times and locations, as well as safety rules and precautions, should be presented to parents along with a telephone number for contacting the central office handling transportation. Even in the well-organized transportation system, all sorts of things will occur which can delay arrival or departure of campers. A system to notify parents of unusual delays in pickups or drop-offs will go a long way toward good public relations.

CHECKPOINTS

Health Service
1. Are there standing orders from the camp physician for the health care provider?
2. Outline the health care plan for your camp.
3. Identify the types of health care certification or training that your staff will need.
4. What written records do you maintain on health care service?

Food Service
1. Do you have on hand menus and inventories of food, supplies, and equipment?
2. Does the type of meal service used currently lend itself to the camp's program philosophy?
3. To what degree do you wish campers to assume responsibility in the dining room for preparation or cleanup?
4. To what degree do you wish campers to assume responsibility for their own meal planning and preparation during their camp experience?
5. Check your food service area sanitation practices against government regulations and American Camping Association standards.

Transportation
1. For what purposes do you need vehicles for camp? How many and what type?
2. Have you examined the options of renting, leasing, chartering, or owning vehicles?
3. In which vehicles are campers currently allowed to ride?
4. Is one person responsible for upkeep of vehicles?
5. Is one person responsible for selecting and checking drivers?
6. If a day camp, is there a plan for the pickup and drop-off of campers, and the notification of parents if plans change?
7. What is your provision for emergency vehicles?

Related Standards and Regulations

Health Service
Accreditation Standards for Camp Programs and Services: HW-1–23; "Self-Assessment Document": Item 16

Standards for Conference and Retreat Centers: II-30, 42–46

Food Service

Accreditation Standards for Camp Programs and Services: SF-22–32; "Self-Assessment Document": Items 6–7, 9–13

Standards for Conference and Retreat Centers: I-24–35

Transportation

Accreditation Standards for Camp Programs and Services: TR-1–19

Standards for Conference and Retreat Centers: I-38–45

Bill Harwood, Camp Counselors U.S.A.,
Palto Alto, California

12

Marketing

Ours is a field where the value is not experienced unless the participant is there. It becomes imperative that we become more aggressive in our advocacy of the camp experience. We cannot wait for the campers to come to us. For all directors this means earlier and more vigorous recruitment of campers. It means more talk about values, outcomes, and specifics in language that can be understood by parents, business people and organization boards.[1]

CUSTOMERS AND CONSUMERS

The simple fact that campers are essential to the operation of a camp is often not considered early enough in camp planning. Nor do camp administrators translate the word *camper* into *customer* often enough; camps have much to learn from the business world in marketing and customer relations.

Marketing is an ongoing year-round process which involves not only the direct recruitment of campers and groups but also the constant interpretation of the values of the camp experience. It is the foundation of all good financial development, public relations, and community relations. It is an attitude that should permeate each and every staff member and be heard in the voices that answer the telephone, seen on the faces of those who greet campers and parents, and sensed in the response to various and sundry complaints.

Marketing involves everything you do, both to attract and to keep customers and consumers of your services. Marketing is all the packaging, not just a single promotional mailing. In camps for youth, it is usually the parent who must be convinced to pay the fee for the child to attend camp. That parent becomes the primary customer. Similarly, in camps that rent facilities, the organization that rents is the primary customer.

In this day, surveys show that children ages seven to seventeen influence their parents' decisions concerning leisure time activities in 74 percent of families.[2] Therefore, the camper

---

[1]Armand Ball. "On the Ball." *Camping Magazine* Vol. 54, No. 3, February 1982. p. 2.
[2]"Parents Are Listening More to Kids." *USA Today.* January 24, 1990.

is not only the consumer of the service in youth camps but also the secondary customer, and must be considered in customer concerns and marketing. The individual participant in the rental situation becomes the secondary customer and consumer.

Since camps are no longer solely summer camps or children's camps, the marketing approach becomes more complex, requiring more market research and strategy if the camp is to attract a variety of potential clientele to fill its beds in all seasons. The customer in a camp may be an adult, a child, a family, an organization, a school, a church or synagogue, or a business. Different segments of the camp operation may have different primary customers, thereby shaping the marketing differently for each segment.

As Edward L. Hayes states, "People form impressions about you and your camp the instant they see you advertised or mentioned in print. Even the way you handle correspondence conveys how you feel about your public. Unanswered inquiries and tardy, poorly typed letters speak worlds to your public."[3]

Early in marketing, one must analyze the boundaries for marketing: What is the present market, target populations, or customer base for the camp and what potential markets exist? Many camps are designed for a particular type of camper based on a specific geographical area, income level, or physical condition and this is usually reflected in the mission or purpose. This focus establishes the parameters of marketing from the outset. In camps which serve broader geographical areas and appeal to campers with no particular physical condition, the potential market is much larger. The fee charged for the camp experience may limit the market to a more specific income level. A camp which operates a conference and retreat program during part of the year may, by mission, be limited to the members of an organization or to churches of the same persuasion. Each of these requirements shapes the ways in which marketing may take place. In other words, understanding the boundaries of the camp market enables you to better design how you package the experience, how much money you spend on marketing, which markets you explore, and how you promote the experience.

MARKET ANALYSIS

A market analysis will be easier if the camp has kept good records previously and if a computer is available in which to record the data. The following eight steps need to be taken.

1. Secure enrollment figures by sessions or type of program and use for the past five years. Compare shifts in total enrollment, types of program and use, and sessions.
2. Break down those enrollment figures for the same period of time, using various factors. The factors will vary, based on the type of programs and length of season. Where

---

[3]Edward L. Hayes. "Positioning Your Ministry in the Market Place." *Journal of Christian Camping* Vol. 22, No. 3, May/June 1989. p. 10. Reprinted with permission from CCI/USA.

there is individual enrollment based on particular programs or different lengths of sessions, break down the enrollment by age, sex, zip code, religious affiliation, school affiliation, ethnic and racial groups, general family income, or any other specification that may affect your situation by each session.

Where the enrollment is by groups, such as schools, churches, social clubs, businesses, break down the enrollment by type of user groups, size groups, age groups, geographical origin, type of camp services used, and seasons attended.

Now, search for patterns or segments of the market where the heaviest and lightest enrollments occur to study further what creates the difference. For example, why do enrollments reflect large numbers from certain neighborhoods and fewer from others. Which types of groups seldom rent the camp facilities? Which are the primary segments being currently served?

Look back at the stated purpose and target market and compare to the camp's existing demographics. Is the targeted audience being served?

3. Examine the return rate. What percentage of campers or user groups return for a second year? A third year? Study evaluations from customers and consumers. Is there a reason for not returning?

4. Look at enrollment dates. When is the earliest registration and what are the dates when the largest number register? What seemingly prompted people to enroll more during a particular three-week period? Who enrolled earliest?

5. Compare enrollment with enrollment in other camps. The American Camping Association, Christian Camping International, and *Trendlines*[4] all run surveys each summer to see what trends are occurring in camp enrollment. Talk with camps in the general area; if the camp is affiliated with an organization that has other camps in your region, seek comparative information. Any significant deviation from the pattern other camps are experiencing may give clues to problems or unique features in your situation which need analysis before recruitment plans are developed.

6. Gather some demographic information about the area served. What is the current population by age groups, socioeconomic groups, ethnic or racial groups? What has been the trend over the past five years? Is there a projection for the next five years? Where is the largest concentration of prospective campers or groups? Has the camp's enrollment followed the trends in the general population?

7. Identify the competition. Competition comes in the form of other types of programs, other camps, schools, sports, and other types of activity that involve the entire family. Competition is not bad; in fact, it is indigenous to our democratic form of government. It is always wise to learn as much as possible about the competition, what they are offering, what fees they charge, and who they are serving.

---

[4] *Trendlines*, a newsletter for camp directors, is published six times a year by Alpha Beta Consultants, 1351-2A Middle Gulf Dr., Sanibel Island, FL 33957.

Dwight Jewson, marketing consultant, states, "the camp competes with other products being marketed to youth . . . . The message or advertisement for the camp thus must be addressed to a specific market or markets . . . . That message exists in the context of many other messages or advertisements for alternatives for the summer, and thus must communicate directly with the needs and concerns of the market segment towards whom it is directed."[5]

8. Once a camp director has all this data in writing and has studied it thoroughly, it should be shared with others. Key staff who have experience with the camp may have insights that will help. If the camp operates with a board or committee, that group should have a presentation of the information and an opportunity to react and discuss it. Another camp director or mentor may be able to offer some observations. Often, outside consultants from the camping field can provide a clearer analysis of this data, and help give guidance to the director and board in developing a marketing plan.

Analysis of Current Market Strategies

Marketing efforts should be motivated by the desire to accomplish the purpose of the camp, meet customer and consumer needs, and provide a quality service that is superior to one's competition or unique in some way. Having already determined the purpose of the camp, time may need to be devoted to analyzing customer needs and the quality of services provided.

Doug Herron reminds camp directors that "headache sufferers don't need aspirin — they need relief from the headache." The benefit is the relief, not the aspirin. He goes on to state, "Benefits are the result customers and consumers derive from satisfactory use of the service. Features (the characteristics we most often talk about) are the distinguishing facts about the service that are true whether the service is ever used or not. Features are easily provable characteristics that are not debatable. They are the elements you can see, taste, touch, smell, and measure."[6]

"Staff who base their selling strategy solely on a description of the program's features are hoping the prospective customer will bridge a conceptual gap and convert all the features into personal benefits. Professional salespeople and marketers know, however, that the typical prospect, no matter how well educated, does not have the time nor inclination to convert all the features into benefits. At the same time they realize that no sale starts without the prospect anticipating some benefits. You must persuade potential customers that use of your service will satisfy their needs and interests."[7]

---

[5]Dwight Jewson. "The Promotional Aspect of Camp Marketing." *Camping Magazine* Vol. 50, No. 6, May 1978. p.17.

[6]Douglas B. Herron. 1997. *Marketing Nonprofit Programs and Services.* San Francisco, CA: Jossey-Bass Publishers. p 34.

[7]Ibid.

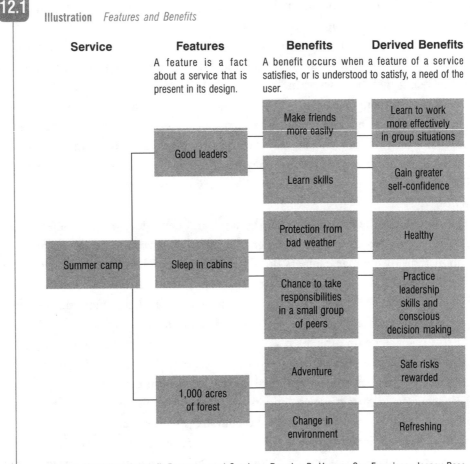

12.1 Illustration *Features and Benefits*

Service	Features	Benefits	Derived Benefits
	A feature is a fact about a service that is present in its design.	A benefit occurs when a feature of a service satisfies, or is understood to satisfy, a need of the user.	

Service: Summer camp

Features:
- Good leaders
- Sleep in cabins
- 1,000 acres of forest

Benefits and Derived Benefits:

Benefits	Derived Benefits
Make friends more easily	Learn to work more effectively in group situations
Learn skills	Gain greater self-confidence
Protection from bad weather	Healthy
Chance to take responsibilities in a small group of peers	Practice leadership skills and conscious decision making
Adventure	Safe risks rewarded
Change in environment	Refreshing

Source: *Marketing Nonprofit Programs and Services*. Douglas B. Herron. San Francisco: Jossey-Bass Publishers, 1997.

Illustration 12.1 helps one understand how the terms features, benefits, and derived benefits apply to the camp setting. The camp's outcome/objectives and the derived benefits should be consistent.

An analysis of the benefits offered by the camp to the potential customer and consumer needs to be made. In chapter 3, some of the generic values of camp were outlined. Those values, or benefits, for the specific camp or programs within the camp need to be outlined. Remember that the benefits outlined in materials describing a camp will be compared by the potential customer/consumer with those outlined by other camps. Benefits need to be clear at the same time they generate excitement.

In a 1990 study by the Maguire Associates, Inc., the five top camp characteristics rated by parents were: caring counselors, enjoyment/fun camper has there, overall quality, safety, and personal attention given to each camper.[8] These were evidently the ben-

---

[8]Report of Maguire Associates, Inc., Concord, MA, for the American Camping Association Private Independent Camps, 1990.

efits perceived by the customers. Compare these with the benefits the camp purports as well as with the benefits campers perceive.

In analyzing customer perceived benefits, an evaluation form that is used with present campers and parents or camper groups can provide some insights into which needs are being met (i.e., what makes them happy) and which are not being met (i.e., what both present and nonreturning campers disliked). The design of the evaluation form is critical and some outside expertise or review will help hone the form to accomplish what you desire. Remember the questions asked of the primary customer (e.g., parent, organization that rents) may be different from the secondary customer or consumer (e.g., camper, participant). This may necessitate more than one questionnaire.

The time when the person is given the form also can affect the outcome. For example, giving it to the leader of a rental group upon their arrival at camp or mailing an evaluation form to summer campers during the Christmas/Hanukkah season may not provide the return rate or information you need. Evaluation needs to be soon enough after the conclusion of the experience to be fresh but not in the moment of unpacking the suitcase. The matter of evaluation is covered more fully in chapter 15.

At this point, a camp director needs to examine current marketing materials and practices. Everything should be examined with care, from the brochures and videos to the schedule of mailings and promotional meetings, with an eye for its target populations, its accuracy, its attractiveness, and its effectiveness in identifying benefits. Make a list of all current marketing strategies and techniques used by the camp.

To deal with a competitive marketplace, a camp must emphasize overall value and differentiate its services from that of other camps. Simply offering more activities than the competition will not necessarily bring campers. Value does not mean necessarily having the fanciest buildings or equipment, but rather relates more directly to having clean and comfortable facilities with capable, mature, caring staff members.

The issue of quality is one that cannot be treated lightly. So much of a camp's reputation depends on word-of-mouth comments that a camp must ensure it provides consistent and continuing service. News of a good camp travels fast, but today's parents are not overly loyal; and when a camp does not produce what it promises, parents are quick to look for another camp.

A specific focus will often stimulate interest on the part of campers and parents. In marketing, this matching of a special focus with a particular group of customers is called "developing a niche." To emphasize a niche, a camp needs to understand the following:

- Concentrate on what the camp does best. Emphasize quality and do not compromise in the area chosen.
- Make sure that the niche chosen is not too narrow, thereby limiting the audience too much.

- Be prepared to give up something else, for example, a less appealing program, staff or equipment in another program area, etc. It is difficult to finance, staff, and ensure quality in every program.
- Choose a name for the program or experience that communicates well. It must mean something to the camper. That may mean using contemporary or classic verbiage.
- Be patient. Success does not come in one summer.
- Provide what is promised. Deliver.

If you are marketing the site to user groups, you still need to determine your competitive niche. Unless you are providing a program that is subsidized from some aspect of your organization, one of your goals is for revenue to exceed cost of service delivery. Your competitive niche includes the qualities of your site and the quality and extent of services you provide for the fee you charge. If you are serving adults, the physical space may be more indoors than outdoors. That space should be physically and emotionally conducive to the program or to meeting goals of the user group. As with any good marketing strategy, you need to match the needs of the user group with the opportunities provided by your product. An outdoor education class or a troop camping experience will have different needs than a college class or an adult training group. The features of the site that are desirable for most adult groups include:

- Quality meeting space
- Indoor bathrooms with privacy
- Comfortable beds and good mattresses
- Comfortable chairs and tables with good writing surfaces
- Good directions to the site and signs or maps of the site
- Hard-surfaced walkways
- Lounge furniture

In addition the following amenities add to the desirability, comfort, and convenience for adult groups:

- Training aids, such as easels, markers, tape, audiovisual equipment, etc.
- Telephones for individual use
- Copier
- Fax machine
- Privacy for meetings
- Flexible mealtimes
- Lounge and deck areas
- Recreation opportunities, including walking paths, game areas, television, etc.

The hosting function is critical in working with user groups. Your interest in meeting their needs from the first phone call to the checkout procedures should be carefully planned and be a part of your marketing strategies. The American Camping Association *Standards for Conference and Retreat Centers* will help you analyze your site against the standards of the field.

DEVELOPING A MARKETING PLAN

Having analyzed the present population served by the camp, examined the demographics of the service area, taken a look at competing services, and evaluated current marketing and services, one should have the necessary information to develop a marketing plan for the coming year. This should be developed in conjunction with the staff and committee members who will carry out the plan.

First, examine what the message is and to whom it is to be communicated. Review the mission or statement of purpose. Is it clear to others? Does it communicate the desired message? Is it concise?

This mission may need to be interpreted in a variety of ways if the camp serves multiple audiences. You may discover that you will need more than one camp brochure or supplemental material to accompany a basic printed piece. In today's market most camps have videos and/or Web sites. Be sure they communicate the mission and desired outcomes and are tailored to the type of use (e.g., camp, conferences and/or retreat centers, small group use, etc.). Often camps are tempted to combine everything into one compartmentalized brochure in order to save dollars, but it is questionable whether such an approach can be effective in attracting multiple audiences (i.e., summer campers, parents, renters, weekend programs, and day and/or resident camps) on the same property. Trying to market messages to a variety of audiences can be confusing. So this step entails actually laying out on paper the audiences to be attracted and the message to be communicated to each of those audiences. If your Web site is for different audiences, be sure they can easily access their specific areas of interest, e.g., campers, parents, user groups, staff, etc.

Determining the camp's desired image is an important step in marketing. Though this certainly relates to the purpose of the camp, it also relates to the setting, staff, and strengths of the camp operation. Some camps are successful at establishing their image as a camp that is general in nature and adept in providing many different activities and programs. Other camps find it better to find a special niche in the marketplace and emphasize that image.

Second, determine the promotional technique you wish to use to communicate your message by reviewing those currently being used and comparing them with techniques used by other camps or similar types of operations, e.g., parks, recreation opportunities, conference centers, etc. Most techniques for communicating your message will fall in four areas: personal interaction, promotional materials, advertising, and public relations. A mix of these techniques will provide a balance of appeal.

Personal Interaction

This technique deserves first consideration because camp is a very personal experience both for the camper and for the parent. In any discussion with camp directors around the country on the topic of marketing, all agree the best way of securing campers is by word of mouth. As in the business world, referral by satisfied customers is the business person's best advertisement.

However effective promotional or advertising materials are, the potential customer will be looking for identification with a person related to the camp. Confidence is instilled by some contact with a caring and informed individual. The following techniques involve some person-to-person contact.

Returning Campers

Except in very unusual camp situations, the primary source of enrollment is returning campers. A national survey of all types of camps shows that the average percentage of campers returning to camps is 50–60 percent. From these percentages, it is apparent that many camps depend upon a much higher return rate. Obviously, the lower the return, the more difficult is the task confronting the director; recruitment of new campers requires considerably more effort, time, and money.

Therefore, the director's first concentration should be on approaching previous campers. An early mailing about the upcoming summer's sessions, dates, and special programs for returning campers is an important step. Follow-up Web site bulletins or newsletters can list the returning campers as they enroll. Many camps find that a regular bulletin or e-mail to campers and staff is a good means of maintaining contact, building spirit, and encouraging a return to camp. It need not be expensive, but it should be attractive and newsy with numerous names mentioned and pictures and memories from the previous summer included. Some camps have set up chat rooms for campers to stay in contact with each other between seasons.

Camper Reunions

A camper reunion often engenders enthusiasm among the previous year's campers and staff. A reunion each year provides an opportunity to share stories, pictures or videos, and fun. The involvement of staff and the showing of a visual presentation from the previous summer are natural elements of a reunion program. Camper reunions can stir memories of the previous summer's experiences and reunite campers who have not been in touch with one another. It is important to have next summer's registration material available at a reunion.

If the majority of campers come from a number of cities or states, then a decentralized plan of reunions or parties may be required. A larger, central reunion provides more excitement and greater contact among campers and staff, but a decentralized plan provides more personal contact between the director and campers as well as a better opportunity to invite prospective campers and parents. Opportunities to share the names of prospective campers (or staffers) can be given for future follow-up. Some camps encourage attendees to bring a friend.

Fun Weekends at Camp

Where the camp property is close enough to a population center, the director can make the property available to groups for their use during the fall, winter, and spring. Day trips or overnight and weekend camping trips on the camp property offer an excellent opportunity for the group leader to describe summer camp experiences. If camp is rented by user groups, explaining other programs open to individuals is an excellent way to promote the summer experience. The director should see that displays, slide shows or videos, and photographs are available which show summer activities.

An "off-season" campsite with all the "in-season" amenities stored, such as canoes, horses, waterfront and archery equipment, does not promote summer sales to visitors. Special care should be taken to have helpful staff, attractive audiovisuals, and a sampling of camp songs, games, and activities to give visitors a taste of the magic of the regular season.

Home Parties

A preplanned visit and presentation in a previous camper's home, where invitations have been issued to friends, is a time-tested method for recruitment. Recruitment parties or events by neighborhoods have proven to be very effective marketing tools when the primary target is youngsters from upper middle income families and above. They are most effective when a parent or several parents invite prospective campers and their parents to a home for a private presentation by the camp director or staff member. An invitation from a neighbor or friend stimulates more interest than an invitation received cold by mail or from someone the person does not know. Where it is difficult to utilize a home, the same method may be used in a school, motel, or church, with several parents of former campers inviting people.

Personal Calls

Once a prospect's name and information has been secured and appropriate information about the camp shared by mail or in person, a follow-up call should be made to answer questions and "close the sale." The personal interest shown, as well as the opportunity to answer even minor questions, can be a determining factor in enrollment. This is no less true of follow-up calls to previous campers who have not enrolled after the initial enrollment periods.

Individualized Responses to E-mail Requests

Though not as personal as the telephone or in-person visits, responses via e-mail to inquiries from the camp's Web page or e-mail address can be individualized. A personal interest and concern can be expressed.

Camp Representatives

Some camps recruit camper representatives, often mothers, in certain cities or neighborhoods to undertake referrals and recruitment. These persons are given training and recruitment tools. In a number of cases, these persons receive a commission from each new camper enrolled who actually attends camp.

Visits to the Camp

It is not unusual for parents to visit a camp the season before their child is anticipating attendance, or for prospective renters to visit the conference/retreat center in advance. In both cases, this is an aspect of marketing that should not be overlooked.

There should be a plan for welcoming visitors who wish to see the camp facility or program in operation. A positive approach is to invite such visits in brochures and newsletters. Signs at the entrance to the property should clearly indicate where visitors are to report upon arrival.

Similarly in recruiting rental or user groups, it is good to invite leaders of prospective groups to visit camp while other groups are in operation. Having them see firsthand the type of facilities in use and services offered can be an effective marketing tool.

It is important that the person assigned the responsibility of showing the visitors around the site be fully familiar with the operation, program, and registration questions. This is not a chore to be done quickly so one can get on with the business of the facility, but an opportunity to interpret and sell. Similarly, when parents arrive with campers for a session or at the end of a session, it is important to provide the opportunity to meet the camper's counselor and to have any remaining questions answered.

Promotional Materials

All materials produced by the camp should be considered promotional materials, and their quality and content should be addressed with this in mind.

Registration Forms

Regardless of whether the camp is enrolling individuals or groups, a registration form will be needed. It should be carefully designed in light of its intended use before, during, and after the campers or groups are at camp. Whether it is a card, a sheet, or a half sheet should be determined by how it is to be filed and how often it will be handled. If the information is to be transferred to a computer file, this will influence the format of the form. It should be remembered that the information gathered on the registration form will provide the beginning of the camp's database of campers and groups. So careful thought should be given to what data will be helpful for comparative purposes a year hence.

Actual information on the *application blank for individual campers* may include:

- Address of camper (zip code sorts may reveal some of your best markets)
- Home phone number
- Birth date
- School and grade (specify whether you wish the grade at the time of enrollment or the following fall)

- Parents' and guardians' names and emergency contacts
- Work address and phone numbers of each parent and guardian
- Height and weight
- Religious affiliation (particularly if special arrangements are made for attending religious services out of camp)
- Name of a friend the camper wishes to have in the same living group
- Where the camper learned about camp
- Other organizational programs or activities in which the camper participates
- Any physical, psychological, or mental disabilities which may require special attention
- Gender
- Any previous camping experience
- Cancellation and refund policy

In addition, there is usually a paragraph which the parent or guardian signs giving permission for the child to be enrolled in camp for the given session, stating that he or she will pay the camper fee. In the case of adult campers there should be a paragraph which the person signs stating the session for enrollment and that he or she will pay the given fee. That paragraph may include:

- A release for the camp to use any photos taken of the camper at camp
- A statement concerning family income, if the child qualifies for financial assistance through any local, county, state, or federal program
- Information about the family's or individual's health insurance carrier (if the camp is not providing health and accident insurance on the camper or if the family's insurance is used as the primary or secondary insurance)
- A medical and surgical release statement (in some communities, this statement must now be notarized as a requirement of the local hospital)
- Information about to whom, if anyone other than the admitting parent, a minor camper is to be released
- Any special dietary requirements

Actual information on the *registration form for groups* may include:

- The name of the organization or group, and its office address and phone number
- The name of the responsible adult who will be in charge of the group at the time of their arrival
- The name, address, and phone number of the person making the reservation
- The number of persons who will be present, including some breakdown by sex and general age grouping
- Where the group learned about the camp
- The planned arrival and departure times
- What services will be covered in the contract (e.g., meals, staff for program, equipment, linens, room setup, special menus)

- The conditions for the use of any equipment and facilities such as swimming area, as well as who is responsible for such items as first aid, supervision, behavior, program
- The rate that the group will be charged
- The amount of deposit required, the minimum fee, and cancellation policies relating to refunds and deadlines
- Any rules which the group leadership must agree to in advance on behalf of the group, such as those concerning alcoholic beverages, controlled substances, or firearms.

Some camps, by their special nature, have rather specific entrance requirements or limitations necessitated by the owner's purpose and program. Those entrance requirements should be clearly spelled out in the promotional materials and on the registration form. The registration form should elicit all the information necessary to determine if an applicant meets those requirements. All camps have some requirements even though they may be only a given sex or minimum age.

The Americans With Disabilities Act of 1990 (ADA) requires that all camps, except those operated by religious groups and private clubs, make their programs and facilities accessible to individuals with disabilities. Religious groups and private clubs are exempted only when serving their own members then and, only if they are not receiving any federal funding or food or milk commodities from the U.S. Department of Agriculture.

To determine appropriate accommodations, it is permissible to ask that disabilities be identified on registration forms. It is important, however, that the information requested about a camper's health and disabilities be used only to identify appropriate health care and to better serve the camper, not to screen out campers. It will be helpful to indicate to parents that the goal of the camp is to provide the best camp experience possible. You may want to add wording to this effect to letters that accompany health forms where parents are asked to identify any disabilities or health problems the prospective camper has.

Some camps may find that they are unable to serve campers with certain disabilities. The Americans With Disabilities Act obligates camps to make reasonable accommodations to include individuals with disabilities in their programs so long as the accommodations are readily achievable and do not create an undue burden on the organization or fundamentally alter the basic experience the camp is designed to provide. "For example, it would appear to fundamentally alter a wilderness backpacking experience conducted in mountainous rocky terrain where there are no paths, if persons in wheelchairs were included on the trip.[9]

Camps must also be concerned with the level of safety provided to the individual and every other camper in the program. "The ADA expressly states that a public accom-

[9]Marge Scanlin. "Better Camping for All: A Beginning Look at the Americans With Disabilities Act." *Camping Magazine* Vol. 64, No. 3, February 1992. p. 31.

modation may exclude an individual, if that individual poses a direct threat to the health or safety of others that cannot be mitigated by appropriate modifications in the camp's policies or procedures, or by the provision of auxiliary aids. [Camp directors] will be permitted to establish objective safety criteria for the operation of their camps. However, any safety standard must be based on objective requirements rather than stereotypes or generalizations about the ability of people with disabilities to participate in an activity."[10] Therefore, decisions about participation should be on an individual basis.

Registration forms may also include an agreement to participate. Ed Schirick, Vice President and Division Manager of Frontier Insurance Group, suggests that "there is a growing trend toward acceptance [of agreements to participate or waivers]. This is especially true when the individuals have been 'properly' informed of the risks and understand what might happen to them if they participate in the activity. The basis of this is a reaffirmation by the courts, in some states, of the common law doctrine of assumption of risk."[11] Obviously, such statements should be developed in consultation with the camp's attorney, but they can never remove the responsibility of the host to the guest. See chapter 10 for more information about waivers and liability releases.

Brochures or Flyers

The most traditional method of telling people about the camp experience is the printed word. The size and quality of printed materials marketing the camp experience varies greatly. Many camps print a high-quality, undated, four-color brochure, which is used for several years in conjunction with a rate and date sheet insert that is updated annually. Other camps print a new brochure annually. Some camps simply have to send out an announcement with an application form — but that happens less and less frequently in this competitive age.

To be effective, a brochure must be targeted to a specific audience and seldom can speak to multiple audiences effectively. If there are a variety of audiences to be reached or significantly different programs to be marketed, several smaller brochures, rather than one extensive one, may be more effective. Each brochure requires careful consideration. For example, type size may not be important in the development of a brochure aimed at youth, but adults prefer at least ten-point type for ease of reading.

A brochure need not be expensive to be attractive and effective, but it does need to look professional. A camp director may not have experience in this area and therefore should seek the help of a volunteer from the design and printing professions, or hire assistance. In the camper recruitment material for parent consumption, there must be clear definition of age and maturity of staff, type of program and instruction, refund policy, health and age requirements, and values; materials directed to the camper will

---

[10]Ibid.

[11]Ed Schirick. "Risk Management." *Camping Magazine* Vol. 62, No. 5, March 1990. p. 9.

deal more with fun, adventure, specific program activities, and peer relationships. On the other hand, a brochure promoting group rental of facilities will emphasize comfort, types of facilities available, the beauty of the setting, appropriate seasonal pictures, good food, and value.

Words should be used sparingly; pictures and open space should make up a large part of content. It is better to use good artwork than poor photographs, though a good picture always speaks best. Although four-color materials are very attractive, a color stock paper with one color ink and the use of screening or reverse techniques can also produce an attractive brochure at a lower cost. In a limited budget situation, one might consider an enrollment card on a page of the brochure and another page as the back cover with space for an address label and postage imprint for a self-mailer.

Prospective Campers and Groups

A brochure, video, or slide presentation, however good, is of little value unless there is a good, qualified prospect to whom it can be presented. Developing lists of qualified prospects requires a system, consistent follow-up, and good planning. With the help of the demographics of your earlier marketing analysis, an interested group can then brainstorm for sources of prospects. As indicated earlier, the best source is previous campers or groups and staff. Next best are personal referrals from previous campers and interested individuals. These are the prime prospects and should be cultivated with care. Therefore, a system of asking for names of friends or children of friends must be devised. A personal contact is most effective. Providing incentives for names and addresses is another approach. The development of a referral slip in each newsletter or mailing may be the first step.

Camps that are operated under the sponsorship of organizations or churches and synagogues have a natural opportunity for getting referrals from other members as well as membership lists in specific age categories. Careful study needs to be given to how members of the organization can be reached for recruitment purposes in the most personal manner. Where members are recruited through troops, clubs, or other neighborhood groups, there is a natural opportunity for interpretation of camp through the troop, club, and group programs and activities; such interpretation of the camp should be part of the ongoing program and emphasis of each group. Many organizations try to get members of a troop, club, or group to come to camp together during the same session. Parents' meetings during the year also offer opportunities to interpret the value of camp for children. Few organizations today can rely solely on their membership for campers or groups, but certainly interpretation and promotion of camp to these organizations is much easier and more effective than to the public at large.

Many camps can cultivate schools or churches and synagogues for the opportunity of presenting a program to an assembly or a class group, or to distribute descriptive material. Though the willingness of a particular public or private body to permit this approach varies, it is worth exploration.

When following up on names received from other individuals, sending materials with a personalized note, indicating "you were recommended by _____," helps make the materials be more meaningful. Of course, individualized follow-ups by telephone or in person will strengthen the chance for enrollment.

A file should be maintained on each prospective camper or group including as much personal data as can be secured: name, address, phone number, name of person referring the prospect, age (if an individual), type (if a group). A file of index cards often suffices, though the more sophisticated operation may computerize the list and develop a system to transfer persons to the enrollment file as individuals or groups are signed up. All inquiries received by telephone or mail, or at events such as camper fairs or slide showings, should be entered into this file.

Incentives

Incentives to returning campers who sign up by a given date and to staff or campers who sign up or recommend new campers can stimulate interest. These incentives range from pennants or T-shirts to cash discounts on camper fees or bonuses on staff salaries. Obviously volunteer referral and genuine enthusiasm are preferable.

Visual Presentations

However good a brochure is, it is impossible to capture the full visual and emotional impact of the camp experience on paper. That is more effectively captured in the voice of a person who has been there along with pictures illustrating the camp experience. Video presentations and color slides are techniques which combine both of those elements. There are advantages as well as disadvantages to each in certain settings.

Again the principle of quality prevails, for it is better to do something simply and do it well than to produce a highly technical video that is done poorly. Therefore, a camp director will do well to start with good slides and either a first-hand, or taped, narration until the time, budget, and expert assistance to move to the next level is possible. With the availability of amateur volunteers with home video cameras, it is difficult not to immediately take advantage of tape offers. To be effective, such filmed efforts need to be carefully planned, scripted, and filmed, and tightly edited. It is better to take the extra time and money and do it right when so much hinges upon telling the story effectively. Try to limit your audiovisual show to eight minutes. That is a short time, but viewers' minds wander when it goes much longer. Supplement the show with ten to fifteen minutes of personal presentation, which may include a camper or staff member presentation. The prospective audience must be determined first, and the presentation designed to address, captivate, and sell that audience.

Though many camps are utilizing video tapes in place of brochures, a live person offering a visual presentation is certainly preferable to achieve a face-to-face sale. Where used as a brochure, the video has the advantage of multiple showings and the potential involvement of many friends and neighbors. On the other hand, however well made such a presentation is, the sales world knows that someone needs to be there to make the sale — to ask the prospect to enroll and sign on the dotted line. Whatever is done should follow good marketing principles.

Outside Referrals

A plan to secure referrals from social agencies, judiciaries, churches, and synagogues can be valuable. Many camps rely on referrals from social workers, agencies, the court system, or their own membership. In these cases, early contacts with the persons responsible for such referrals are important so that the director can establish a good relationship with changing personnel at the agency and develop a plan for working together. A clear understanding of the ability of the camp to serve persons with certain problems and the plan for payment is essential in this arrangement.

Camper Referral Services

These agencies will list a number of camps and refer prospective campers who inquire about a camp or camps which meet the requirements the parents and children have set forth. Some agencies charge the camp a percentage (10 to 15 percent) of the camp fee of children who actually enroll. Other agencies, particularly nonprofit agencies which are there to serve a specific population, will refer campers as a service to the parent, with no charge to the camp.

Public Displays

Displays with quantities of brochures in public locations can stimulate interest in camp. Choose carefully the locations where the demographic profile of the camp's potential customer would shop, stop, or browse. Generally, this cannot be afforded except with a relatively inexpensive brochure. However, an attractive display with pictures or a self-contained slide show and return postcards to request a brochure can lower the cost and narrow the prospects.

Advertising

Camper Fairs

These are events where a large number of camps are invited to set up individual booths to interpret their camp for one day. A fee is normally charged the camp. The event is publicized and advertised broadly and large numbers of people flow through a fair for its duration. A booth must have a lively visual and aggressive but personable staff to distinguish the camp from the many others in the lineup.

Magazines, Newspapers, and Other Media Advertising

This type of advertising requires an attractive, professionally designed ad and, to be effective, must be run on a regular basis during the peak period for enrollments. Advertising on the radio or television certainly requires professional advice and development to be effective. Though many radio stations offer free time for spot announcements to nonprofit organizations, the spots often run at odd hours. In each medium, regular repetition of the ad is vital.

To advertise in any and every publication is not a wise use of funds. Diane Meckler of the *New York Times* states, "An advertising campaign is not an end unto itself in securing enrollments, but a means for securing prospects who can then be turned into enrollments. [When] you have defined the target audience geographically, by your cost and by your specialty, you are ready to choose the right [medium] for your advertising campaign."[12]

Web Pages

A Web page can give basic information about the camp in a fashion to entice the reader to e-mail or call for further information. Since Web pages exist for a variety of camps, it is important to identify the unique characteristics and mission of your camp. Pictures, illustrations, and testimonials will liven up the copy and will appeal to the reader.

Billboards

Attractive, professionally designed billboards can attract attention to the camp. However, location, timing, and duration of exposure are critical ingredients. The cost factor is a consideration. Even if space is donated, the cost of design and printing is significant.

Posters

Posters must be eye-catching and should include tear-off blanks to request more information or the placement of brochures nearby.

Direct Mail

There are businesses which sell lists of names and addresses based upon the specifications given by the customer. For example, a camp may wish to purchase labels for families of 1) a certain income, 2) in certain zip codes, and 3) with children of a certain age range. The camp presents the company with three specifications which they are to meet, and the company provides a set of labels accordingly.

---

[12]Diane Meckler. "Marketing." *Camping Magazine* Vol. 61, No. 1, September/October 1988. p. 23.

At this point, reference to the earlier market analysis will indicate the neighborhoods, schools, zip codes, or organizations from which more campers and groups have previously enrolled. It will usually prove much more effective to market in areas where sales have been made previously than to pioneer totally new territory. It takes less time and budget because of built-in recommendations and contacts, where people have already shown a receptiveness to the camp's message.

With the volume of bulk mail received by the public at large, such a mailing must be eye-catching and have a response gimmick to make it pay for itself. One rule of thumb is that one may expect an inquiry rate of about 4 percent of the number mailed with a 1 percent sign-up.

Publicity and Public Relations

Public Presentations

Various service clubs and community organizations are often looking for a program, and a presentation of the camp's video or slide show along with a verbal interpretation can be a different way of spreading the word about the value of the camp experience. Parents of campers, staff members, and volunteers often have relationships with churches, synagogues, or schools (both public and private) that can make it possible to make presentations to interested persons. Though the presentations may not be designed for camper recruitment, the programs can help others know about the camp.

News Stories

Camp is rich with human interest stories. One need only make sure that a staff member has the responsibility of providing enough details to interest a reporter of a local newspaper or magazine or radio/TV station. Though camp season may offer the most obvious opportunities, special events during the rest of the year may also stimulate stories.

Bringing Groups to the Camp

Arranging a time during the camp season for people in the local community nearest camp to visit the camp can be invaluable in developing strong community understanding and ties.

Though many camps offer facilities for rental in periods other than the summer, the rental groups are often looked upon as a separate program or entity. Actually, if time and energy are spent, these groups can be ideal conduits for camp promotion. These organizations offer a natural marketing target. The nature of a rental group may enable the marketing approach to be tailored in a fashion that may generate interest in specific programs or facilities. Perhaps benefits of individual participation in camp can also benefit the group, thus stimulating the support and interest of the leader of the group.

When rental groups arrive at the camp, there should be a clear plan of check-in and orientation. The orientation should include not only facility locations and directions, but also information about mealtimes, safety regulations, and how to obtain help in case of an emergency. Though much of this information will have been presented to the group in writing, it should still be presented in person, if at all possible. Helping people feel at home and comfortable is the beginning of a good experience, and the continuation of marketing.

Such an orientation provides the opportunity to explain about other camp programs and to indicate that materials are available at a given location. Attractive displays including brochures will stimulate interest on the part of some participants. A self-contained video or slide show could be set up in one corner of the dining hall or a lounge area.

Again it is important that a plan for marketing be developed that selects which of these marketing devices will be used and in what fashion. The selection of the techniques to be used will depend upon many factors: amount of funds available, the number of new campers desired, the camp's philosophy and message, and the audience to be addressed. It is always better to do a few things well than to use many techniques and use them poorly.

Implementation

After identifying the message and selecting the techniques to be used, the third step is to develop a plan of implementation. A plan should outline each of the steps to accomplish the goals, and should place those steps in calendar form for a twelve-month period with a deadline for each.

Joanna Warren Smith recommends that "the best way to convey consistent attention to detail and excellence at every level of your program is to put your ideas on paper and publish a year-round marketing strategy. . . . Plan mailings, phone calls, and newsletters. Be realistic about necessary preparation time. Be clear about the personalized follow-up that every inquiry demands. Through this tracking you can see what is working, what is not, and where you have too much and not enough."[13] The emphasis here is on approaching marketing on a twelve-month basis, calendaring each segment of the plan, and reviewing regularly the progress of the plan.

It is to the director's advantage in planning, buying supplies, and employing staff, to start camper enrollment as early as possible. It takes time to develop a pattern of early enrollment but it can be gradually encouraged. On the other hand, certain weather changes or seasons do encourage thoughts about camp, for example, the arrival of warm days in the spring or a vacation period when the youngsters are around the house a great deal.

---

[13]Joanna Warren Smith. "Out-of-the-Box Marketing Strategies." *Camping Magazine* Vol. 70, No. 5, September/October 1997. p. 25.

The accomplishment of each of these steps is not possible for the camp director to do alone. It is wise to enlist the assistance of staff, former staff, former campers, parents of campers, and committee members. This enlistment will provide a variety of energetic and enthusiastic persons who, given the proper information and training, can spread the camp's story much more effectively than one person can. Most of this process can be accomplished through volunteers, though it may be necessary to employ one or two persons to carry out more time-consuming or specialized portions of the plan. The next step is to implement the plan and to constantly check whether the plan is proceeding on schedule. Even the best volunteers need follow-up calls and pep talks from time to time.

Planning for the succeeding year will require evaluation of how well the plan worked and how it should be changed. There is more on evaluation in chapter 15.

CHECKPOINTS

1. Do a market analysis of your camp.
2. Locate all printed materials previously used for camp promotion. Study them in light of the camp's objectives and of your market analysis. Ask an unbiased outside expert to critique them or check out your competition's marketing materials.
3. List the steps that can be taken in light of your market analysis; arrange them in order of importance.
4. Develop a market plan for your camp, calendared for one year.
5. Implement and follow through.

Related Standards

Accreditation Standards for Camp Programs and Services: OM-12, 19–21 HW-5, 7, 17, 23; "Additional Professional Practices": Item 16

Kathy Buss, B'nai B'rith Camp, Mittleman Jewish Community Center, Portland, Oregon

13

Business and Finance

Continuing success in camping is obviously dependent upon sound business procedures . . . the camp business administration is just as surely a long-term means of accomplishing our camp objectives as are other phases of camp operation, such as program, staff recruiting, and property upkeep.[1]

The fiscal management of the camp is too often the last consideration of many camp directors whose primary concerns lie with campers and program. To others, the bottom line is the starting point and program considerations wait on the financing. Actually, the philosophy, program, marketing, and finances are so interdependent that each one is ineffectual without the other.

Where the camp director chooses to give significant personal attention to the program of the camp when groups are on site, there may need to be a support system in place to oversee the camp's operations and fiscal affairs. Often camp directors retain the direct supervision of program because of their interest and find an assistant who serves as business manager. A business manager typically supervises all or some of the operational systems of the camp, such as: office, business, food service, transportation, property and site management, and health service. Other staffing arrangements may divide functions differently, depending on the interest and skills of the camp director and other personnel, and on camp organizational structure.

The director should assign day-to-day financial responsibilities to one staff person at camp and should provide that person with a precise job description. Lines of responsibility and accountability should be clear to all staff. The maintenance of up-to-date, accurate records is essential, so some training and experience is necessary for this job. A business manager with some accounting experience is ideal; in addition, some camps will have a bookkeeper in the office.

ACCOUNTING PRACTICES

The specific accounting and budgetary practices of camps will vary greatly according to the volume of financial transactions and the sophistication of the operator's or-

[1]John A. Ledlie. 1961. *Managing the YMCA Camp.* New York: Association Press (Y.M.C.A. of the U.S.A.). p. 125.

ganization. Camps which are part of a larger organization will find that systems which the camp is expected to follow are already in place. Other camps will have the opportunity of setting up their own systems; in most cases, those systems will be tied to a computer program. Today even the smallest camps have access to a computer and a simple bookkeeping system. However, with or without a computer, the basic principles are the same and need to be understood from the outset:

- A budget of projected income and expenses should be established.
- All income must be documented and verified.
- All monies (cash receipts, receipts, and income) should be deposited promptly.
- Internal controls should be established.
- Expenditures should be made against approved invoices.
- Regular summaries of financial activity, preferably monthly, should be planned. During more active times, weekly summaries should be scheduled.
- A system should be developed which identifies high and low points of cash flow, so that low points may be adequately planned for.
- The books should be audited annually, by some person not on the staff.

Advice from a certified public accountant or other knowledgeable source should be secured on the following matters (in some cases, a bookkeeping service will be able to answer your questions):

- Choice of a cash or accrual system of bookkeeping.
- Tax reports required by local, state, and federal governments.
- Generally Accepted Accounting Principles (GAAP) as defined by the Financial Accounting Standards Board (FASB).[2]
- Financial records to be kept, including journals and receivables, payables, and payroll, the length of time different records should be kept, and the value of computer records versus paper copy.

Annual Audit

If you are setting up a new financial system or reevaluating a system already in place, an Operational Financial Risks Worksheet (see illustration 13.1) will be of help in identifying office procedures to manage and safeguard financial resources.

Where camps are part of larger organizations, the organization will have already chosen a cash or accrual system of bookkeeping. In an independent camp, that choice is one the director should make in consultation with the accountant. A *cash system* recognizes cash when received and disbursed and treats all monies received and expended in a given period of twelve months as the operating funds. An *accrual system* recognizes income when earned and expenses when incurred regardless of when cash is actually received or paid and seeks to attribute the income and expenses to the actual twelve

---

[2]Financial Accounting Standards Board, P.O. Box 5116, Norwalk, CT 06856-5116.

13.1

Illustration *Operational Financial Risks Worksheet*

OPERATIONAL FINANCIAL RISKS WORKSHEET

Operational financial risks are those where property, equipment, and/or money might be damaged or lost. Considerations to effectively manage and safeguard the financial resources include identifying the financial controls needed and determining procedures to control or reduce the risks.

Oversight of the financial operations includes audits, preparation of financial statements, preparation of and monitoring of the annual budget and cash flow projections, and monitoring of actual cash flow, etc.
Person responsible _____

Petty Cash
1. Amount of cash available _____ Maximum an individual may request _____
2. Person responsible for maintaining _____ Reconciling _____
3. Person with access to petty cash _____ How is cash secured? _____
4. Explain reimbursement requirements from petty cash _____
5. Person authorizing payments _____ How is petty cash replenished? _____

Cash Receipts
1. Person handling checks received by mail _____
   How and when are checks endorsed and recorded (numbered receipts reconciled with cash received)?
   _____
2. How often are deposits made _____ By _____
3. Procedure for giving checks/cash to staff or volunteers _____
4. Person with access to checks/cash _____
5. How are checks/cash secured on-site? _____ Off-site? _____
6. Policy on third-party checks _____

Cash Disbursements
1. Does the procedure include use of prenumbered checks? _____ And a system to secure and account for unused checks? _____
2. Person authorized to sign checks _____
   Is there a limit over which a second signature is required? _____
3. Are purchase orders and receiving documents required for payment? _____
   Person authorizing payment _____ Are invoices canceled after payment? _____
4. Explain the refund policy _____
5. Person with authority to purchase or commit camp funds _____
   Are there limits to this authority? _____
6. Person responsible for entering into a contract on the camp's behalf _____
7. When is bidding required? _____
   What is considered for comparison, (e.g., quantity, quality, delivery availability and time, cost, size or minimum order requirements, etc.)? _____
8. What expenses are reimbursable and at what rate? _____
   Documentation requirements _____

Reconciliation and Analysis
1. Are bank statements reconciled monthly _____ By _____
2. Explain the policy on payroll and benefits accrual _____
   Person responsible for analyzing _____
3. Person responsible for reviewing receivables _____
   Is there a policy on write-offs of accounts receivables? _____
4. Person responsible for generating a monthly list of outstanding unpaid invoices _____

Inventory of Equipment and Supplies
1. Person responsible for program supplies _____ Person with access _____
   How are program supplies secured? _____
2. Person responsible for office supplies _____ Person with access _____
   How are office supplies secured? _____
3. Person responsible for food supplies _____ Person with access _____
   How are food supplies secured? _____
4. Person responsible for sale merchandise _____ Person with access _____
   How is sale merchandise secured? _____

Tax Liability
1. Is sales tax being collected and remitted on selling of supplies? _____ By _____
2. Person responsible for remitting payroll tax forms, filling 990s, paying into unemployment funds, and making provisions for any contingencies that might encumber the future operation _____

13.2

Illustration *Statement of Activities*

ANNUAL NONPROFIT STATEMENT OF ACTIVITIES
AND STATEMENT OF CHANGES IN NET ASSETS

	Unrestricted	Temporarily Restricted	Permanently Restricted	Total
ANNUAL STATEMENT OF ACTIVITIES				
Revenues, Gains, and Other Support				
Contributions				
Fees				
Income on investments				
Other				
Net assets released from restrictions				
Program restrictions				
Equipment acquisition restrictions				
Expired restrictions				
Total revenues, gains, and other support				
Expenses and Losses				
Program A — Summer				
Program B — Environmental Education				
Program C — Rentals				
Management and general office				
Fund raising				
Total expenses and losses				
Change in Net Assets				
ANNUAL STATEMENT OF CHANGES IN NET ASSETS				
Net assets at beginning of year				
Net assets at end of year				

months of operation they affect; thereby, accruing or accumulating and applying income and expense for the next year's operation to the next year's budget.

Financial Statements

There are three important financial statements for camps. The first important statement to be considered is a *statement of activities* or *income statement* which shows the income and expense activity in a given month. This statement should be reviewed on a monthly basis, for management control purposes. The director may want this statement to show columns for that month, and also for the year to date, the budgeted amount, and the actuals for the same month the previous year. This provides a checkpoint for the director (and board, if there is one) to adjust certain expense items if income is not living up to expectations or if some expense accounts are running over expectations. At the end of the year, the nonprofit's statement of activities provides a summary of all income and expenses by accounts for the year and indicates a net gain or loss for the year. For-profit organizations generally call these income statements. See illustration 13.2 for an example of a nonprofit's statement of activities, and illustration 13.3 for an example of a for-profit's income statement.

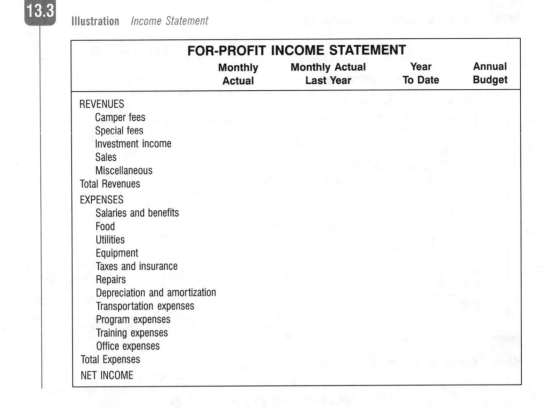

13.3 Illustration *Income Statement*

FOR-PROFIT INCOME STATEMENT				
	Monthly Actual	Monthly Actual Last Year	Year To Date	Annual Budget
REVENUES				
Camper fees				
Special fees				
Investment income				
Sales				
Miscellaneous				
Total Revenues				
EXPENSES				
Salaries and benefits				
Food				
Utilities				
Equipment				
Taxes and insurance				
Repairs				
Depreciation and amortization				
Transportation expenses				
Program expenses				
Training expenses				
Office expenses				
Total Expenses				
NET INCOME				

In addition to a statement of activities, the second important camp financial statement is a *balance sheet* or, under new nonprofit terminology, a *statement of financial position*.[3] This statement summarizes the net assets and liabilities of the camp and is a key to the long-range financial health of the camp. Illustration 13.4 shows a sample nonprofit statement of financial position. Illustration 13.5 provides a sample format for such a balance sheet statement for a for-profit. The annual operations either add to or detract from the positive side of this equation. For instance, a deficit in a year's operation uses any surplus funds that are on hand from previous years or causes obligations against property. The goal of every camp, even the nonprofit operation, is to provide a growth in the assets of the camp to ensure that persons will be served in the future. In the case of the for-profit camp, this investment usually is a good portion of the owner's assets which are to provide income or security at the time of retirement. Both statements identify the actual bottom line of the camp's assets or investments.

The third important financial statement is a *cash flow statement*. Under the new rules of the Financial Accounting Standards Board, nonprofits are required to prepare a cash flow statement as for-profits have done traditionally. These statements identify the changes in cash flow during the year. The cash flow statement shows the difference between the

[3]Kathy J. Tyson. "Accounting Alert." *Camping Magazine* Vol. 66, No. 5, May/June 1994. p. 44.

13.4

NONPROFIT STATEMENT OF FINANCIAL POSITION

ASSETS

Cash and cash equivalents	Assets restricted to investment in land,
Account and interest receivable	buildings, and equipment
Inventories and prepaid expenses	Land, buildings, and equipment
Contributions receivable	Long-term investments
Short-term investments	

Total Assets

LIABILITIES AND NET ASSETS

Accounts payable and accrued expenses	Notes payable
Grants payable	Long-term debt

Total Liabilities

NET ASSETS
Unrestricted
Temporarily restricted
Permanently restricted

Total Net Assets

Total Liabilities and Net Assets

13.5

FOR-PROFIT BALANCE SHEET

ASSETS
Current Assets
    Cash and cash equivalents (investments)
    Accounts receivable
    Inventories
    Prepaid expenses
Total Current Assets
Facilities
    Land
    Building
    Furniture
Subtotal Facilities
Accumulated Depreciation and Amortization (minus)
Total Facilities

Total Assets

LIABILITIES AND OWNER'S EQUITY
Liabilities
    Accounts payable and accrued expenses
    Deferred income
Total Current Liabilities

Long-term Liabilities
    Mortgage payable
Total Long-term Liabilities

Owner's Equity
    Capital stock
    Retained earnings
Total Owner's Equity

Total Liabilities and Owner's Equity

13.6

Illustration *Cash Flow Statements*

ELEMENTS TO INCLUDE IN CASH FLOW STATEMENTS

NONPROFIT	FOR-PROFIT
Cash Flow from Operating Activities	Cash Flow from Operating Activities
Change in Net aAssets	Net Income
Adjustment to reconcile change in net assets to net cash used by operating activities	Adjustments to reconcile net income to cash used by operating activities
Depreciation	Depreciation expense
Increase in accounts and interest receivable	Increase or decrease in accounts receivable
Decrease in inventories and prepaid expenses	Increase or decrease in inventories
Increase in contributions receivable	Increase or decrease in prepaid expense
Increase in accounts payable	Increase or decrease in other current assets
Decrease in grants payable	Increase or decrease in accounts payable
Contributions restricted for long-term investment	Increase or decrease in accrued expenses
Interest and dividends restricted for long-term investment	Increase or decrease in taxes payable
	Increase or decrease in other current liabilities
Total Cash Used by Operating Activities	Total Cash Flow from Operating Activities
Cash Flow from Investment Activities	Cash Flow from Investment Activities
Purchase of equipment	Proceeds from sales of investments
Proceeds from sale of investments	Purchase of investments
Purchase of investments	Purchase of equipment
Net Cash Used by Investment Activities	Total Cash Flow from Investment Activities
Cash Flow from Financing Activities	Cash Flow from Financing Activities
Proceeds from contributions restricted for:	Short-term debt
Investment in endowment	Long-term debt
Investment in plant	Capital stock
Other financing activities	Other equity
Interest and dividends restricted for reinvestment	Total Cash Flow from Financing Activities
Payments of annuity obligations	Net Change in Cash
Payments on notes payable	Cash and Cash Equivalents Beginning of Year
Payments on long-term debt	Cash and Cash Equivalents End of Year
Net Cash Used by Financing Activities	
Net Decrease in Cash and Equivalents	
Cash and Cash Equivalents at Beginning of Year	
Cash and Cash Equivalents at End of Year	

beginning and ending operating accounts. The increases or decreases are shown in the various lines on the statement of financial position, ultimately showing a net change in cash position at year end. Nonprofits should seek the assistance of their own certified public accountant to work out the correct format and records. See illustration 13.6 for a list of elements to include in a cash flow statement.

BUDGETING

As Webster puts it, a budget is simply a statement of the financial position of an administration for a definite period of time based on estimates of expenditures during the period and proposals for financing them.[4] The budget is also a reflection of the

---

[4]*Merriam Webster's College Dictionary*, tenth edition. 1993. Springfield, MA: Merriam-Webster, Inc.

camp's philosophy, since where one secures and spends money indicates the priorities of the operation.

Most budgets cover a twelve-month period, though not all budget cycles follow the calendar year. Some fiscal years or budget years are established differently to parallel the owner's financial and budgetary activity which often follows program operation. Where there is a parent organization involved, the budget will need approval by the operating committee, board, or agency; this necessitates planning and adoption well in advance of the starting date of the fiscal year.

A budget is part of a planning process and reflects the setting of goals such as the number of participants to be recruited, the number of staff to be employed, the number and type of program activities that can be operated, and the ultimate balance sheet position the director desires. Since a budget reflects planning and goal-setting, it has to be adjusted to actual experience as time progresses. If recruitment reports show that there are likely to be fewer campers or groups than budgeted, then not only is the income item for campers lessened but reductions in expenses must be made to the same degree. Where budgets are approved by groups or persons other than the owner and camp director, there should be an established system by which revisions are made and approved.

The Budget Process

The development of a list or chart of accounts, or categories of income and expenses, is the starting point in the budget process. In organizations, those accounts will be given to the camp and the camp will have to fit its income and expenses into those existing descriptions. Where a camp has the opportunity to develop its own set of accounts, it is wise to list all the types of income sources and expenses, grouping them into logical account names. A sample list of accounts is shown in illustration 13.7. Many organizations, including most nonprofits, desire or require that this list of accounts be grouped by different functions or areas of income and expense. This *functional accounting* is demonstrated in illustration 13.8.

Projecting Income and Expense

The safest method of budgeting is to project income conservatively and expenditures more liberally. Ideally, of course, the projections should be as realistic as possible; however, it is better to err on the side of overprojecting expenses than income.

In budgeting, the director should not project income from any more campers or groups than were actually enrolled the previous year unless there is strong reason to believe additional campers will come (e.g., other camps in the area are no longer offering the same programs, your camp has increased promotion efforts, etc.). When increasing fees, and therefore budgeted income, consideration should be given to whether the increase will lead to any reduction in enrollment. Other income accounts should be compared to expenditures for those related activities or services (camp store, transportation

13.7 Illustration *Sample List of Accounts*

SAMPLE LIST OF ACCOUNTS

INCOME

Acct.	Acct. Explanation
110	**Tuition Fees**
111	Camper
112	Environmental education
120	**Fees**
121	Horseback riding
122	Bus transportation
123	Arts/crafts
130	**Rental of Facilities**
131	Summer
132	Fall-Winter-Spring

Acct.	Acct. Explanation
140	**Sales**
141	Camper store (supplies, shirts)
142	Meals to visitors
150	**Miscellaneous**
160	**Contributions**
161	Individuals
162	Government grants
163	United Way
164	Other

EXPENDITURES

Acct.	Acct. Explanation
200	**Wages and Benefits**
210	Full-time employees
220	Part-time/seasonal employees
230	FICA
240	Unemployment compensation/taxes
250	Health/accident insurance
300	**Food Service**
310	Kitchen Food
320	Supplies
330	Campout/trail food
400	**Occupancy**
411	Gas
412	Electricity
413	Telephone
414	Water
415	Sewer
420	Maintenance supplies
430	Equipment repairs
450	Taxes
460	Property/liability insurance
470	Building repairs
480	Building construction
500	**Transportation**
510	Charters or rental/lease
520	Insurance
530	Gas/oil
540	Repairs
550	Licenses

Acct.	Acct. Explanation
600	**Program**
610	Equipment
620	Supplies
700	**Training**
710	Organization dues
720	Books, films, materials
730	Conferences, workshops
740	Training travel
800	**Office**
810	Postage/UPS
820	Printing (stationery, envelopes, etc.)
830	Office supplies
840	Promotional printing
850	Promotional advertising
860	Promotional travel
900	**Board/Committee Expense**
910	Board meeting expense
920	Board training
930	Director/officer insurance
1000	**Designated Contributions**
1010	Campership grants
1020	Special projects

---

to and from camp, special activities) to see if the fees are adequate to provide an acceptable margin of income beyond expenditures in each area. It is vital to include *all* of the related costs of such activity in this comparison; for example, the salary and related costs for the personnel to operate an activity should be added to the cost of materials and facilities when setting an activity's fees.

In projecting expenditures, one should identify the *fixed costs* of operation, or those that will not change as the number of campers or staff changes (e.g., property taxes, base utilities, office space, and salaries and benefits of full-time employees). Expenses that are

ACCOUNTS BY VARIOUS FUNCTIONS

EXPENSES

Administration*

210	Full-time employees
220	Part-time/seasonal employees
230	FICA
240	Unemployment compensation
250	Insurance (health, worker's comp.)
420	Supplies
710	Organization dues
730	Conferences/workshops
810	Postage/UPS
820	Printing (stationery, envelopes, etc.)
830	Office supplies

Food Service

210	Full-time employees
220	Part-time/seasonal employees
230	FICA
240	Unemployment compensation
250	Insurance (health, worker's comp.)
310	Kitchen food
420	Supplies
320	Campout/trail food

Program

210	Full-time employees
220	Part-time/seasonal employees
230	FICA
240	Unemployment compensation
250	Insurance
420	Supplies
610	Equipment
700	Training

Promotion/Marketing

210	Full-time employees
220	Part-time/seasonal employees
230	FICA
240	Unemployment compensation
250	Insurance
413	Telephone — long distance
420	Supplies
810	Postage/UPS
820	Printing
850	Advertising
860	Travel

Fund-Raising**

210	Full-time employees
220	Part-time/seasonal employees
230	FICA
240	Unemployment compensation
250	Insurance (health, worker's comp.)
413	Telephone — long distance
420	Supplies
810	Postage/UPS
820	Printing
910	Campership grants
920	Allowance for uncollectible pledges

Occupancy

210	Full-time employees
220	Part-time/seasonal employees
230	FICA
240	Unemployment compensation
250	Insurance (health, worker's com.)
411	Gas
412	Electricity
413	Telephone
414	Water
415	Sewer
420	Supplies
430	Equipment purchases
440	Equipment repairs
450	Taxes/licenses
460	Insurance (building, liability, etc.)
470	Building repairs
480	Building construction
510	Charters/rental/lease vehicles
520	Insurance — vehicle
530	Fuel — vehicles
540	Repairs — vehicles

Volunteer Leadership

910	Meeting expense
920	Training
930	Director/officer insurance

*Where it is not possible to differentiate functions for certain expenses, a section labeled "administrative" can be added. Those expenses can then be totaled and divided among the other functions on the basis of a percentage based on income, facility, usage, or staff time.

Where camps have substantive operations other than summer camp or conferences (e.g., outdoor education, retreats, etc.), separate functional divisions may be established.

**Nonprofits only.

not fixed are considered *variables* (e.g., food for 50 campers versus 100 campers). Several projections may be necessary with these expenses based upon various levels of camper enrollment. There will be a point when the fixed expenses plus the variable expenses will balance with or exceed the projected income. This becomes the minimum target for budgeting and marketing. The director should always consider the most disastrous thing that could happen, for example, price increases, need for extra staff, equipment breakdown and replacement. Large expenditure items should be carefully documented. Salaries and food often account for as much as 50 to 60 percent of a camp budget and need to be carefully analyzed since a slight change in either item could substantially alter the budgeted expenditures.

Depreciating Buildings and Equipment

Many camps have been slow to include a budget line for appropriate depreciation of camp buildings and equipment. Each building and every piece of major equipment should be depreciated, or have its value reduced, on an agreed-upon schedule, after consultation with the camp's accountant and/or board. Nonprofit camps have often avoided this issue by relying upon campaigns for charitable contributions to replace major structures. However, it is increasingly difficult for many sponsoring organizations to find major capital funds; and, with increasing financial pressures upon nonprofit organizations, camps may have to be aggressive to get the attention of the organization's board for needed capital expenditures.

Final Budget Development

Only when a director has viewed the realistic expectation of income and expenses is he or she in a position to work toward final budget development. It is critical that all of the expenses of camp operation be included in the budget. Particularly in the nonprofit sector, certain expenses may have been covered in other budgets, or allowances may not have been made for depreciation; thus, the budget won't reflect the true cost of camp. For example, in some organizations the salary and related benefits of the year-round professional employee responsible for the camp and/or certain insurance or bookkeeping services may be carried in the overall organizational budget rather than the camp's budget. The accurate amount of any such costs based upon the percentage of time devoted to the camp should be carried in the camp's budget in order to give true costs. All of these issues are important in producing an accurate picture of the camp's state of being for management purposes and for presentation to committees and boards and to the public.

Adjusting Expenses

If, at this point in the budget process, expenses exceed income, the director should review each expense account to see what can be pared down without endangering the program objectives of the camp or the health and safety of the campers. Once the director

13.9

SAMPLE CASH FLOW PLANNING CHART

Accounts	Annual Budget	January	February	March	April	May	June	July	August	September	October	November	December	TOTAL
INCOME														
111 Camper fees	$250,000	$ 5,000	$ 2,000											
112 Environmental education fees	100,000	10,000	8,000											
121 Horseback	10,000													
122 Bus fees	15,000													
until all are listed														
TOTALS	$375,000	$15,000	$10,000											
EXPENDITURES														
210 Full-time employees	$ 75,000	$ 6,250	$ 6,250											
220 Part-time employees	100,000	2,000	1,750											
230 FICA	10,500	490	470											
240 Unemployment compensation taxes	2,000	70	60											
250 Health insurance	8,000	600	600											
until all are listed														
TOTALS	$375,000	$20,200	$ 9,130											
DIFFERENCE	$ -0-	($ 5,200)	$ 870											

(Difference between income and expenses indicates cash excess or cash needed that month.)

has determined the essential expenses, the camper income that can be expected based upon past experience, other self-generated income (such as from the camp store, program and transportation fees), and possible outside funding available (subsidies, foundation grants, camperships funds, contributions), a decision can be made whether any remaining difference should come from increased fees or from reduced expenditures — which may mean decreased program or personnel. Since camper fees need to be set early in the promotional year, decisions related to fees should be completed by early fall.

In determining income from campers' fees in a camp where some campers pay the full fee and others pay a reduced fee or no fee, it is important to show the source of income for the subsidy of camper fees in the income statement. The director must know the actual cost of the camp experience per camper, especially when he or she is seeking supplemental funds for campers who cannot pay the full fee. Donors often respond well to the concept of sending a needy camper to camp but may expect documentation of costs. Outside funding sources, including the United Way and most foundations, require such documentation as well.

Cash Flow

As important as whether one is meeting or exceeding budgetary plans is whether the cash received matches the cash needed to cover the expenses for the same time period. Developing a cash flow planning chart prior to the beginning of the fiscal year will assist the director in planning for cash shortages or overages. A sheet should be completed with the income accounts and descriptions in a vertical column to the left, followed by columns for an estimate of how much will be received or spent in each account for each month, plus a year-end total. See illustration 13.9 for an example of a cash flow planning chart. The income and expense accounts are also totaled separately for a given month, providing a cash position. If there are several months in a row where the cash needs are higher than the income expected, then a plan must be developed to draw cash from reserves or from a bank loan. Similarly, if there are several months where there will be cash excesses, plans should be made for short-term investments during that period to gain interest income. Where there is flexibility, the cash flow planning chart also provides an opportunity to adjust the time table for certain expenditures.

OPERATIONAL SYSTEMS

Purchasing

Once a budget is approved, a plan of purchasing should be adopted, which will give the director control over what is spent against each budgeted account. A purchase order system is the most common approach to purchasing. See illustration 13.10 for one type of purchase order form. The basic principle of a purchase order plan is that a written

13.10

Illustration *Purchase Order Form*

PURCHASE ORDER FORM
Camp Everyone
234 Same Street, Everyplace, NY 12345-6789
123-456-7890 • everyone@camp.com

Purchase Order No. _____ Date _____

To: _____

Ship: ☐ Parcel Post ☐ UPS ☐ Motor Freight ☐ Best Way

Quantity	Item Number	Description	Unit Cost

To arrive by _____ Date _____

Signature _____

---

order (normally in multiple copies) for each purchase is filled out and approved in advance of the purchase: one copy to the vendor from whom merchandise is being purchased, one copy for the bookkeeper (to compare to the invoice when it arrives), and one copy for the person making the purchase. Normally, purchase orders are prenumbered, providing a means of tracking for the purchaser and the vendor. If the purchase order is not given to or mailed to the vendor, the purchase order number is usually given when the purchase is authorized by telephone. The principle of purchase orders can be followed, with some shortcuts, even in a small operation. However this system is implemented, it is vital that the following steps be taken:

- Purchasing be limited to as few people as is possible
- Purchase orders be approved in advance of ordering
- Copies of the purchase orders be written for the vendor and the purchaser
- A secure, agreed-upon price be obtained and included on the purchase order

Purchasing should begin early in the year, and ample time should be given to investigate sources and compare prices and quality for value. The best discounts are secured through advance planning and purchasing. Use of the camp's cash flow planning chart will be invaluable in maximizing potential discounts from suppliers. It is important to order early to ensure delivery of items on time or in advance of the opening date of camp.

Payment System

A system of payment should also be worked out in advance. Most vendors expect payment within thirty days, although some will require payment in advance or on actual delivery. The method of payment should be understood at the time the order is placed and specified on the purchase order. A disbursement system or payment-for-goods system for a camp should include provisions for the following points:

- The time at which the person placing the order, or someone designated by that person, checks to make sure the merchandise or service has been delivered. When the merchandise arrives, each item should be checked as to quantity, type, and condition and all items should be checked against those appearing on the purchase order.
- A careful check of the invoice for mathematical errors and inclusion or exclusion of proper tax and discounts, as well as a check to see that the bill includes only the items received.
- Payment upon receipt of approved invoice which either matches a purchase order already on file or has been approved by an appropriate staff member.
- Payment by check (when payment in cash is necessary, a receipt including all pertinent information and marked "PAID" should be secured).
- Checks should have at least two authorized signatories; checks larger than a predetermined amount should be signed by both persons.

Cash Payments

Due to their rural locations and variety of day-to-day immediate needs, camps generally have more frequent cash payments than do many organizations. A careful procedure for cash expenditures should be worked out. Persons who have custody of cash should be bonded (insured).

A petty cash fund is the most common method of dealing with cash expenditures. A check for a set sum is issued at the beginning of the year, season, or period, and it is cashed. The cash is kept in a locked box in the safe, if there is one, and handled by only one or two authorized and bonded persons. Staff members may make authorized purchases and be reimbursed in cash from the fund upon presentation of a signed receipt, or cash may be advanced for purchases and an accounting made after the purchase. In the case of advances, the amount of cash advanced and the date should be recorded on a slip of paper which is signed by the person taking the cash. See illustration 13.11 for a sample petty cash advance slip. Upon the return of a receipt for the amount spent and the proper change, the advance cash slip is discarded and the change and receipt returned to the cash box.

The receipts and cash should be balanced regularly, depending on the volume of use: daily during periods of heavy cash receipts, weekly during less busy times. When the receipts become significant and available cash is dwindling, receipts should be attached to a written summary, assigned account numbers, and a check written to the cash box caretaker for the total amount, bringing the cash fund back up to the original amount. At the end of the fiscal year or season, any remaining cash should be redeposited in the main camp account.

13.11

Illustration *Petty Cash Advance Slip*

```
┌─────────────────────────────────────────────────────────────┐
│                    PETTY CASH ADVANCE SLIP                    │
│   Date _____                                       │
│   Received $ _____ for _____ │
│                                                               │
│   _____ │
│   Account No. _____ by _____ │
│                                       Signature               │
└─────────────────────────────────────────────────────────────┘
```

Income Documentation

Careful accounting of all funds received is essential for accurate records and good public relations and for the protection of all concerned. A written record should be kept of each payment received. It is wise to be able to provide a receipt to each payee, although many individuals accept their canceled check as a receipt. The camp's record of the receipt is used for two purposes: crediting the payee's account and designating the deposit of that payment to the proper budget account. Receipt records should be maintained for seven years.

Receipts should be deposited with the bank or organizational office at regularly scheduled times. A daily deposit of such funds is preferable; but, in many camps, payments come in cycles (at the beginning of the period, for example). This may necessitate a daily deposit at the beginning of a session, but only a weekly deposit during the balance of the period. By promptly depositing checks and cash, the director can avoid having substantial amounts of money in camp.°

Most camps ask for payment of the entire camper fee in advance or upon arrival at camp. A billing system is usually necessary either to secure the advance payments or to follow up delinquent payments. Bills should specify the amount, the person served, the dates covered, and the services rendered as well as any amounts already paid and the balance due.

Taxes

Although an accountant or an attorney is of great assistance for most financial matters, it is in the area of taxes that such expertise becomes essential. The type of taxes applying to a specific camp will vary not only in the locality of the office and camp location, but also in whether the camp is a for-profit or nonprofit organization. Specific tax areas to be examined are payroll, real estate, personal property, and sales. Always get advice from the camp's CPA.

CAMP STORE AND CAMPER BANK

In most camp situations campers will need certain supplies (e.g., toothpaste, toothbrushes, stationery, stamps) other than those which the camp supplies as part of the fee.

Campers are also anxious to have souvenirs or reminders of their camp experience (e.g., T-shirts, patches, pennants, postcards). The director should consider how such items may be sold to campers in a way which is consistent with the camp's philosophy.

Campers will arrive at camp with varying amounts of cash, whether or not the camp has items for sale. Most camps do not wish to have the camper go to commercial establishments off the campsite. The presence of cash in a camper's duffel or clothing may lead to losses and disputes. A plan to safeguard this cash as well as to disburse it, if items are to be sold to campers, should be developed and announced in advance of camp. Most camps have a plan for campers to deposit funds on arrival, allowing the camper to draw against those funds for necessary expenditures on personal items or for additional activity fees. The following processes should be considered in development of such a plan:

- Suggesting to parents and campers in advance the maximum and minimum amount of cash needed during the camper period.
- Indicating what essential items the campers may need to purchase.
- Listing programs which may require additional expenditures depending on the camper's interests and skill (e.g., craft supplies, trips, horseback riding, ammunition for riflery). If possible, it is best if these can be included initially in the camper fee or identified as an option in the payment of the fee plus extras.
- Identifying what items the camp may wish to make available to campers for purchase.
- Providing the camper with a receipt for cash deposited.
- Setting up a simple plan of accounting: that is, charging against an individual's account for purchases, entering deposits, and providing a refund (if necessary) at the end of the period. Two sample systems are shown in illustration 13.12. The first is a checkbook which the camper uses to write a check for each purchase (providing him or her with a record of expenditures and the experience of keeping his or her own record). The second is a card held by the camp on which deposits and expenditures are recorded at the time the purchase and deposits are recorded.

Where camps serve groups, the problem of dealing with the individual's cash does not arise. However, a system for selling the various supplies should be established and the group leader given information in advance about what is available at camp during the group's stay.

In developing a camp store, careful accounting practices should be established. The store operation should provide income to the camp over and above the cost of merchandise, the cost of labor, and related overhead. It is unrealistic to expect to cover only the cost of the merchandise. Many camps have found this to be a significant source of income. The sale of items with the camp name and logo is also another method of public relations. It advertises the camp wherever that individual goes, and name recognition is important. It can also stimulate others to ask the individual about the camp and his or her experience there. Whether or not to have snacks for sale (e.g., ice cream, candy,

13.12   Illustration   *Expenditure/Deposit Record*

	_____20_____ Check No. _____
Balance forward $_____	
Deposited $_____ **Pay to Camp**	$_____._____
Less Check No. _____ $ _____ Dollars	
for $_____ for _____	
Balance $_____ Signed _____ Cabin_____	

Figure 1. Checkbook Type of Expenditure/Deposit Record

Name _____ Cabin _____

Date	Item Purchased	Cost	Department	Balance

Figure 2. File Card Type of Expenditure/Deposit Record

chips, etc.) will depend on the camp's philosophy, parent desires, etc. The camp may want to limit the number of snacks a camper can buy each day.

An appropriate location which will provide security, accessibility, and appropriate storage needs to be determined. The display of items with clearly marked prices will stimulate sales and save time when campers come to the store. Camp stores are usually open only at certain times that coincide with the program schedule. While one person should have the ongoing responsibility for the store, including the inventory of stock, ordering of additional supplies, and supervising of sales, additional persons may be needed at busy times.

Camp Office

Many camps will have two offices: one in the director's home or city near the home, and another at camp. The camp office should be in a location that is easy to find when arriving at camp, and yet where noisy activities will not be distracting to those at work. Though the office should be the center of efficiency and accuracy in terms of records and administration, it should have a relaxed, congenial atmosphere. It often is the first "people impression" on the camp site, and serves as the reception area for visitors, vendors, and often the parents of campers.

The telephone may serve a similar function of greeting people. Since many of the inquiries and questions from prospective campers and their parents come by telephone, it is important that the person answering the phone reveal a pleasant personality and have many immediate answers to questions.

Staff

The size of the office staff will vary with the size of the camp, with larger camps having a combination receptionist and telephone operator, a bookkeeper, a secretary, and a business manager. Smaller camps may have only one person in addition to the camp director. At times, any camp office may be overly busy and harried, but it is important that people be willing to stop and deal graciously with the public — whether in person or on the phone.

Arrangement of the Office

Several factors should be considered in the construction or arrangement of the office. Sufficient storage for supplies and records is essential. Some privacy for the camp director, other administrators, and program personnel also needs consideration, since conferences with individual staff or campers may be of a confidential nature. A second door with direct access to the outside may provide more privacy. An area near the front door should have some chairs where people may wait. A counter here may assist in separating visitors from the work area and also give a space where it is convenient for a staff member to write or stand and provide information. A more than average number of electrical outlets with adequate power supply will be needed because of the variety and quantity of office equipment and desk lighting. Consideration of controlled access areas should also be made for the security of cash and records. Any desk with computers that need to access the Internet should have a phone line nearby.

Computerization

The computerization of the camp office has changed the way in which many functions are handled. There are computer programs available which allow the entire registration process of individuals or groups to be recorded on the computer, creating not only a registration record, but an accounts receivable, a billing mechanism, labels for mailings, a living group assignment preference, and program group sign-ups. Standard programs are available in the marketplace which can provide accounting, word processing, mailing list maintenance, mail merge, spreadsheets, and desktop publishing. At the same time, several companies have developed special software for camps which provide the program group and living group assignment process, as well as the camp registration format. Christine Z. Howe identifies a variety of applications available as shown in illustration 13.13.[5]

---

[5]Christine Z. Howe. "Change, Computers, and the Camp Administration." *Camping Magazine* Vol. 57, No. 1, September/October 1984. p. 17.

13.13 Illustration   *Selected Applications for Personal Computers*

SELECTED APPLICATIONS FOR PERSONAL COMPUTERS

ADMINISTRATION

Financial
Accounting
General ledger
Investments
Forecasting and decision support
Work load cost tracking
Utility management
Invoices and billing
Budget and revenue and expenditures

Personnel
Recordkeeping and employee rosters
Recordkeeping and volunteer rosters
Recordkeeping and client rosters
Payroll
Insurance
Performance standards and job descriptions

Word Processing — General
Permits and licenses
Mailing labels
Bulk mailing
Manuals and training materials
Printing
Graphics and mapping
Aggregate client data-participation
   and demographics
Monthly reports

Research
Accident studies
Marketing
Long-range planning
Demand studies
Survey tabulation

Maintenance
Custodial cost tracking
Vandalism monitoring
Horticultural and irrigation management
Aquatics scheduling and management

SERVICE DELIVERY

Recordkeeping
Activity registration
Attendance reporting
Facility and site usage
Activity scheduling

Program Planning and Evaluation
Advertising and publicity
Activity master planning
Activity analysis
Activity tracking

Activities
Games — electronic and simulation
Arts and crafts
Music forms
Interactive stories and reading

**LEISURE COUNSELING
AND EDUCATION**

Counseling
Recreational needs assessment
Interest inventories
Problem solving
Values awareness and clarification
Individual demographics
Communication and expression of thoughts
   and feelings

Education
Development of positive self-concept through
   mastery referral systems leisure matching
   systems

On-line computers are now allowing even more convenient information transfer across the country and around the world. The popular on-line services allow access to the Internet. Your camp may receive camper mail or allow registration via this electronic mail (e-mail), or you may be part of the Camp Professional Discussion Group or other groups that discuss current issues. This provides new opportunities to communicate with parents and campers, with other directors, and with other businesses.

It is important that you devise a system to regularly back up your database and other materials maintained on your computer. During registration, a daily backup would be recommended.

Whether investing in a computer for the first time or simply adding new software, it is wise to investigate carefully the variety of options. Technology changes so rapidly and varies so much in applicability to different camp settings that it is wise to examine several hardware and/or software options and compare notes with other camp directors on problems and successes. New software should be implemented program by program, because there will be unforeseen problems that will slow the process and frustrate office personnel. For example, it is best to implement the new accounting system or the word processing system first and get the office staff familiar with the new system rather than to install all programs at once. Henderson and Bialeschki outline several steps to be taken in getting started with computers:

- Review the present operation for sizing. Determine how large your camp enrollments, budgets, and inventories are so you can more accurately decide which computer system you will need and what the benefits might be for its use.
- Set goals and objectives and criteria for what a computer can do for you. . . . Do not buy a computer . . . and then try to decide how to use it. The applications must be determined first.
- Find a vendor and locate software sources. It may be necessary to consult with more than one vendor to determine what the best buy is and who will provide the most support services.
- Design an implementation schedule to determine how you will begin to use the computer and its software. It is impossible to do everything at once, so you must decide systematically how you will begin to use the equipment.
- Begin implementing applications with a continual approach for evaluating and adding potential software.[6]

However, there is no question that, even in the smallest operation, the right computer system can provide a long-term solution to many traditional problems and time-consuming functions in the camp setting. It is critical to have either a very knowledgeable person on the staff who can troubleshoot or a convenient and helpful supplier who makes a commitment to stick with you through the conversion process. In any case, the question of the type of supplier support is critical; the firm's reputation, references, maintenance contract fees, and troubleshooting response should be checked thoroughly.

RECORDKEEPING

The checkbook and bank deposit slips should be balanced with the monthly bank statement upon receipt. If there are multiple staff in the finance office, the appropriate checks and balances between employees need to be established and followed. Records should be kept in a fireproof container and should be retained by the camp or organization

---

[6]Karla Henderson and M. Deborah Bialeschki. "Computer Consciousness." Camping Magazine Vol. 55, No. 7, May 1983. p. 16.

13.14 Illustration *Recommendations for Record Retention*

RECOMMENDATIONS FOR RECORD RETENTION

TYPE OF RECORD	MINIMUM RETENTION
Accident/incident reports	Adults, 7 years
	Minors, 2 years beyond age of majority
Accident/incident reports/claims	30 years
Accounts payable ledgers/schedules	7 years
Accounts receivable ledgers/schedules	7 years
Annual reports*	Indefinitely
Audit reports	Indefinitely
Bank reconciliations	1 year
Camper registration forms*	Adults, 6 years
	Minors, 2 years beyond age of majority
Camper health records (including treatments)*	Adults, 6 years
	Minors, 2 years beyond age of majority
Cash books	Indefinitely
Charters, constitution, bylaws, incorporation records	Indefinitely
Charts of accounts	Indefinitely
Checks (canceled)	4 years
Checks (exceptions: payments such as taxes, property purchases, special contracts, etc.)	Indefinitely
Contracts and leases (expired)	7 years
(current)	Indefinitely
Correspondence (routine)	1 year
(general)	3 years
(legal and important matters)	Indefinitely
Deeds, mortgages, and bills of sale	Indefinitely
Depreciation schedules	Indefinitely
Duplicate deposit slips	1 year
Employee personnel records**	3 years after termination
Employee health records (including treatments)*	30 years
Employment applications (not hired)	3 years
Expense analyses/expense schedules	7 years
Financial statements (end-of-year)	Indefinitely
Fire inspection reports*	6 years
Forms used, dated file copies*	Indefinitely
General and private ledgers with end-of-year trial balances	Indefinitely
Insurance policies (expired)	3 years

for at least five years. Backup computer records can help to reconstruct financial histories but should not be considered equal to or replacements for the primary paper documents.

Record retention requirements vary from state to state; but, in general, the following records should be kept for the minimum time shown (see illustration 13.14).[7] The director should give careful thought to minimum record retention and should obtain legal counsel.

Gerald G. Newborg suggests the "*legal value* adheres to essentially any record which

---

[7]American Society of Association Executives. *Association Management* Vol. 44, No. 9, September 1992, pp. 50–51.

13.14

TYPE OF RECORD	MINIMUM RETENTION
Insurance records (current accident reports, claims, policies, etc.)	Indefinitely
Internal audit reports*	Depends
Internal reports	3 years
Inventories of products, materials, supplies	7 years
Invoices to customers	7 years
Invoices from vendors	7 years
Licenses (federal, state, local)*	Dispose of after receiving new license
Journals	Indefinitely
Minutes of directors', stockholders' meetings	Indefinitely
Notes receivable ledgers/schedules	7 years
Occupational injury/illness records	5 years
Payroll records and summaries	3 years
Petty cash vouchers	3 years
Physical inventory tags	3 years
Property appraisals	Indefinitely
Property records including costs, depreciation reserves, blueprints, and plans	Indefinitely
Purchase orders (except primary copy)*	1 year
(primary copy)*	7 years
Safety inspection reports*	8 years
Securities transactions	3 years
Stock and bond certifications (canceled)	6 years
Stock and bond records	Indefinitely
Subsidiary ledgers	7 years
Tax returns and worksheets	Indefinitely
Time books/records	7 years
Travel expense reports*	3 years
Vouchers for payments	7 years
Withholding tax statements*	4 years

*These record retention timelines are not from the American Society of Association Executives, but from miscellaneous other sources. In many cases, American Society of Association Executives did not offer a suggested retention policy on these items.

**When a minor is involved, records should be kept at least four years beyond the year when the age of majority is reached. This requirement, along with other record retention requirements, should be checked with your state requirements.

provides documentation for a legally enforceable right or obligation. These values may be embodied in state or federal law, state or federal regulations, or in local ordinances."[8]

The policy of the organization or camp on recordkeeping and record retention should be developed on the basis of law, the rule of reason, and the risk involved. Such a policy should be in writing and available to the people who file and maintain these records. In developing a retention policy, the period for retention should be clearly defined by tying the specified retention period to the beginning or end of a calendar or fiscal year.

---

[8]Gerald G. Newborg. 1989. "Record Retention and Disposition Schedules." *Technical Leaflet 107.* Nashville, TN: American Association for State and Local History.

FUND-RAISING

It is the unusual nonprofit camp which does not rely on some contribution income to operate the camp. Many independent camps have moved to nonprofit foundations to ensure the continued operation after the present owners are gone. Other independent camps have utilized an arrangement with the American Camping Association by which friends and parents make contributions to that Association, a 501(c)(3) organization, in the name of a particular camp and the gifts are used to fund campers who cannot afford their full camp fee. This means that almost every camp director is faced with the prospect of mastering another skill — that of fund-raising.

Each state has developed regulations which affect fund-raising. Therefore, it is important to consult with the camp's attorney and accountant to understand the applicable laws and regulations.

Determining the Use of Funds

If funds are to be raised for the camp, their overall use should be carefully evaluated. These funds might be used in the following ways:

- To help alleviate the cost of the camp experience for *every* camper, thus lowering the fee for all
- To lower the cost of the camp experience for particular campers who cannot pay the usual fee
- To cover capital expenditures, such as land development, building facilities, extensive large equipment purchases, or major renovation
- To experiment with new programs which might eventually offer year-round program or diversification
- To improve the wage and benefit package for staff, thus enabling the director to recruit better qualified staff

In other words, the camp director and board (if there is one) must consider carefully the purpose of the fund-raising, for there must be a clearly felt need resulting in a clearly stated purpose. It may be that there are varying needs, ranging from keeping the fees lower than average to replacing buildings or equipment. Before lumping all of the needs together, consideration should be given to the types of fund-raising. It may be helpful at this stage to consider an outside consultant to assist in the creation of a financial development program which provides a foundation and pattern for fund-raising over a period of time.

Basic Principles

Some basic principles should be followed in fund-raising regardless of the type of fund- raising activity:

- Seek professional fund-raising counsel to conduct a feasibility study and conduct the campaign or train the camp director.

- Establish a clearly stated purpose for the funds.
- Recruit capable volunteers to raise the funds.
- Provide a training program for the volunteers.
- Develop attractive, succinct, and clear descriptive materials.
- Acknowledge every gift and recognize the giver in some fashion.
- Use the funds for the purpose for which they are raised, and report back to the giver.
- Maintain careful accounting of all gifts, including pledges. Under new accounting rules, pledges are considered to be income in the year they are made, not the year they are paid.

Annual Giving

Annual giving is one type of fund-raising in which an approach is made annually to one's constituency. In this type of fund-raising activity, a specific period is set aside each year for the effort, and a volunteer leadership secured either from the board, committee, or alumni group. An organization with subchairs and workers is developed similar to the diagram in illustration 13.15. A list of prospective givers is developed from the records of

13.15 Illustration *Campaign Organizational Chart*

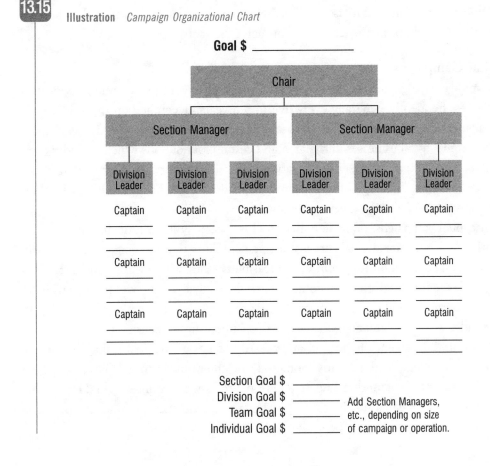

the camp: parents of campers, former campers and staff, foundations, board or committee personnel, and vendors.

The annual giving campaign or event lends itself best to providing funds for the ongoing operating budget of the camp through direct subsidy or the provision of camperships for needy youth. Some camps have used it to replace budgeting depreciation reserves. Once a person has committed to the camp with a charitable gift, it becomes simpler to go back to them each year, as long as a good acknowledgment and information program is in place.

A variety of methods may be used to approach potential annual givers.

- Direct mail — a letter and material describing the needs with an addressed and stamped envelope for returning a contribution.
- Telethon — a group of trained volunteers come together in a location where there are multiple telephone lines, call prospective givers, and take pledges by telephone. A confirmation letter and a return envelope are then sent to those pledging.
- Personal approach — a volunteer approaches a prospective giver, explaining the needs and asking for a contribution. This is always the most effective method.
- Public gathering — a presentation is made at some type of special event sponsored by the camp and return envelopes and pledge cards distributed after a public appeal.
- Fund-raiser — an activity is developed which will render its profits to the cause by the tickets sold or money collected through other activities.

Capital Campaigns

Capital campaigns are another type of fund-raising. In contrast to annual giving, this is done less frequently, generally every five to ten years, depending on the size of each campaign. The constituency to be approached is the same as for annual giving, but also can be extended to businesses in the area and certain foundations which consider capital projects. Again, a volunteer organization is developed, not dissimilar to that of the annual campaign. This type of campaign is dependent upon having individual volunteers approaching potential givers individually.

In capital campaigns, professional counsel is especially important. It is not wise to embark on such a campaign if there is not some certainty that the goal can be reached. A professional consultant may complete a feasibility study which will examine the willingness of potential large givers to contribute to the campaign, uncover persons who are willing to serve in leadership roles, and assess the potential capability of the camp to raise funds. A capital campaign is especially dependent upon securing one or two large gifts equal to 20 percent of the goal and 60–70 percent of the goal from large givers. Therefore, the identification, cultivation, and assessment of potentially large givers is a vital part of this type of fund-raising. In addition, professional counsel should lay out the steps and give advice in a smaller campaign, or be a resident consultant for the period of a major campaign.

Endowment Development

Endowment development is another type of fund-raising, and requires a quite different approach from the capital or annual support campaigns. Though one-time campaigns, similar in organization to the capital campaign, can be run for endowment purposes, they are not as customary for camps as for universities, hospitals, and other organizations. Encouraging supporters to remember the camp in their wills, insurance, or through trusts requires a program of cultivation and education which may not show results immediately, as does the capital campaign format.

While it is possible to approach prospects who have not given to the camp and interest them in planned giving, those persons who have given to the camp through annual support efforts or capital campaigns are usually the best prospects for the endowment effort. Since these persons are known to the camp and the camp reports to them through mailings somewhat regularly, it is possible to begin to develop an awareness of the various instruments used in planned giving without initially asking for a gift. The use of planned-giving instruments affects the estate of a person, and in many cases has helpful tax implications. Therefore, any decision usually requires more consideration, consultation, and often the advice of an attorney, trust officer, or accountant.

A program of endowment development should be carefully charted, with the strong commitment of the committee or board related to the camp. Professional guidance from a person knowledgeable about endowment development efforts should be sought initially. Only nonprofit 501(c)(3) organizations can provide the tax benefits which make this method of fund-raising attractive to many people.

Fund-Raising Personnel

To develop effective fund-raising efforts takes considerable time, training, and expertise. The camp director should carefully evaluate his or her willingness to allot the amount of time from his or her schedule, or another staff member's schedule, for this purpose. Even when an outside consultant is brought in to help with the fund-raising, it will still require time from the camp director. Fund-raising cannot be done effectively if done half-heartedly, poorly, or without professional planning. On the other hand, most nonprofit organizations cannot survive without an effective program of fund-raising.

It may be helpful to seek outside fund-raising counsel to help develop a plan for the total financial development and to actually assist in the fund-raising efforts. The experience and competence of the fund-raising counsel should be explored carefully by checking references with previous or present clients.

CHECKPOINTS

1. Outline the budgeting process for the camp.
2. Describe the three basic types of fund-raising and the principles that affect all good fund-raising.
3. Who may purchase for the camp? By what methods? Who checks the order when it is received and approves payment?
4. Who handles cash at camp? Are they bonded? What check is there on the cash received?
5. Review the insurance of the camp and identify areas that need updating. Is the camp covered with fire and casualty, liability, workman's compensation, vehicle insurance?
6. Is there a study of the expenses and income related to the camp store that shows what margin of income over expenses is being achieved?
7. Describe the steps in moving into a computerized operation.
8. When was your record retention policy last reviewed?

Related Standards

Accreditation Standards for Camp Programs and Services, "Additional Professional Practices": Item 18

Standards for Conference and Retreat Centers: II-3–4

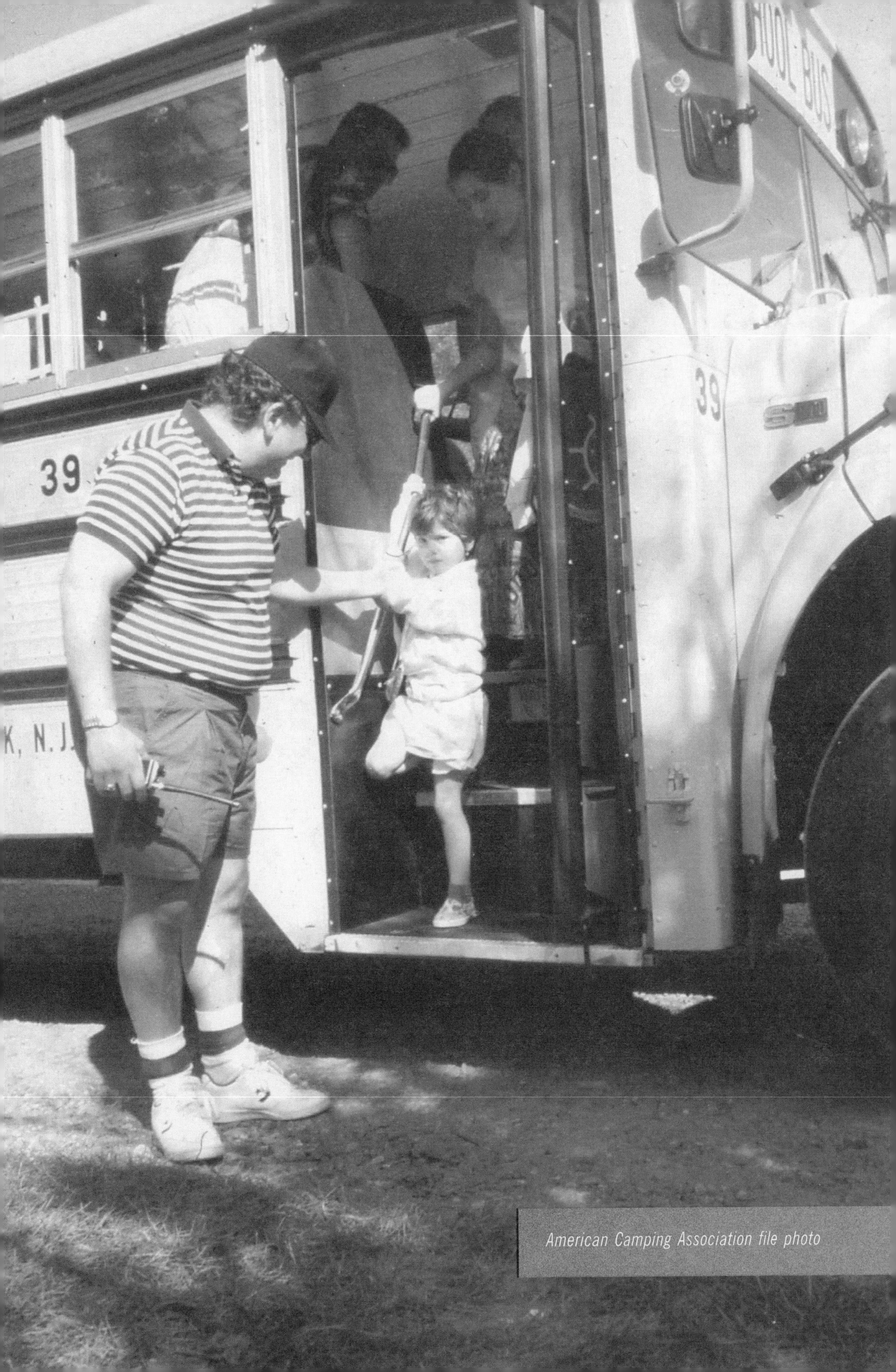

American Camping Association file photo

14

Volunteers

It seems to me that the first and foremost reason that volunteers dedicate so much of their personal lives to chosen projects . . . is that they believe in the organization's mission. In leadership training we call this "alignment" with the mission and vision of the organization.[1]

F ew camps operate without some volunteer assistance — whether it is on the staff, on a board or committee, or former staff, parents, or campers who refer others to the camp. A volunteer is any person who gives his or her services to the camp without any compensation. The growth and nurturing of volunteers is an art that every camp director needs to develop. Volunteers spread and enhance the mission of a camp and stimulate enthusiasm unmatched by staff.

One's first reaction is that volunteers should be cultivated because they save the camp money if they serve as staff members, work around camp, or take on roles ordinarily paid for. Another reaction is that volunteers bring in money because they become fund-raisers or recruiters of campers. Either or both may be true, but first and foremost, volunteers should be cultivated because they are an outgrowth of the spirit and philosophy of the camp. It is a tribute to a camp that former campers or staff and parents of either may wish to share the experience of the camp with others. However, to be most effective and to gain the greatest personal satisfaction from the experience, volunteers also need some structure and professional leadership.

Some principles of any volunteer service should be kept in mind. A need must be perceived by the volunteer. The need may be stimulated or sold by the professional, but it must challenge the volunteer or rekindle earlier positive experiences or felt needs. That need must parallel the individual's motivation, which varies from person to person. Clary, Snyder, and Ridge state that "people volunteer to satisfy personal and social needs and goals . . . . The first step toward successful recruitment is considering the audience

[1]George Burns. "How to Keep Volunteers Coming Back." *Journal of Christian Camping* Vol. 21, No. 5, September 1989. p. 6. Reprinted with permission from CCI/USA.

from which recruiting will take place so that the relevant motivations of potential volunteers can be identified."[2]

Volunteers should be guided to the type of activity in which they will be most effective. Success is important in any task, particularly when one is giving energy, time, and money to accomplish the task. It is not wise to randomly assign or recruit volunteers.

A written job description should be prepared for the task and shared with the volunteer. In a face-to-face interview, the volunteer should be asked if he or she has a problem with any of the functions, as it may be useful to adjust some portions of the task. Along with the job description there should be a targeted time for accomplishment and evaluation.

The volunteer should be informed of the ground rules: personnel policies, limits of authority, budget limitations, or whatever limits there may be.

The volunteer should be given adequate assistance in accomplishing the task — whether it be funds, tools, manpower, or the director's own time to consult.

Supervision should be provided as needed. This includes observation by the supervisor and regular conferences to gain insights into the assigned task.

The performance of the volunteer should be appraised upon completion of the task. There should be public recognition of the volunteer.

LEGAL RAMIFICATIONS

In recent years there have been court cases around the legal definition of volunteerism. *Corpus Juris 2d*, a legal encyclopedia, defines the volunteer as: "one who does or undertakes to that which one is not legally or morally bound to do, and which is not in pursuance or protection of any interest . . . one who enters into service of his own free will; one who gives his service without any express or implied promise of remuneration . . . ; one who has no interest in his work, but nevertheless undertakes to assist therein . . . . "[3]

The definition of a *pure* volunteer is very narrow and somewhat different from a *gratuitous* volunteer. Volunteers may be differentiated by a two-part test concerning whether the person is subject to the control of the organization and whether the person receives any benefit from the job performed. The pure volunteer performs a task when and how he or she prefers for no benefit whatever. The gratuitous volunteer performs the task at a time or in a manner prescribed by the organization and/or receives some benefit from the organization. The pure volunteer may not be able to expect the same sort of legal safeguards that a gratuitous volunteer may expect where the organization

---

[2]E. Gil Clary, Mark Snyder, and Robert Ridge. "Volunteers' Motivations: A Functional Strategy for the Recruitment, Placement, and Retention of Volunteers." *Nonprofit Management & Leadership* Vol. 2, No. 4, Summer 1992. p. 341.

[3]Robert A. Christenson. "What You Should Know About the Legal Definition of a Volunteer." *Voluntary Action Leadership.* Fall 1982. p. 17.

takes on some control or responsibility for the volunteer. Since camps may use both types of volunteers, it is important to understand this difference.

A number of court cases illustrate some of the problems for the organization in gratuitous volunteer service. For example, in *Bond v. Cartwright Little League, Inc.*,[4] the Little League solicited help from volunteers to remove some large lights it had purchased from a municipal baseball field. A volunteer started up one of the 100-foot poles and fell forty feet, injuring himself. The Arizona Supreme Court reasoned that the volunteer was not a pure volunteer because the Little League *set the time and place as well as the manner in which the lights were to be removed and had control over the volunteer.*

In the North Dakota Supreme Court case *Olson v. Kem Temple, Ancient Arabic Order of the Mystic Shrine*, a volunteer was denied financial recovery when he fell off a small stepladder and was injured, because the stepladder is considered a "simple tool."[5] The court reasoned "where the tool or appliance is simple in construction and a defect therein is discernible without special skill or knowledge, and the employee is as well qualified as the employer to detect the defect and appraise the danger resulting therefrom" that there could be no recovery.

In the Washington Court of Appeals case *Baxter v. Morningside, Inc.*,[6] a volunteer driver for a charitable organization was in an accident negligently causing injury to several persons. The court held that the organization was liable for the volunteer driver's actions because it *"controlled or could have controlled the physical conduct and performance of the volunteer driver."*[7]

In 1985 the Supreme Court decided in *Tony and Susan Alamo Foundation v. Secretary of Labor*[8] that workers for the foundation who received room and board were not true volunteers because "they were working with the expectancy of some remuneration." Therefore, the court held that volunteer workers were subject to the provisions of the Fair Labor Standards Act (FLSA), which included the minimum wage. It has been suggested that this decision has "created a new category which might be called the 'quasi-volunteer' who, though functioning like a volunteer, is afforded the 'protection' of the Act, because there is some identifiable expectation of compensation."[9] The Alamo case involved two elements for the nonprofit foundation: a commercial activity and the payment of room and board, both unrelated to its exempt purpose.

---

[4](536 p. 2d 697, 1975) Citations such as this one may be used to look up the complete text of the legal cases mentioned in this chapter. Take the citation to a law library and ask for assistance; law firms and local bar associations often have law libraries.

[5](43 N.W.2d 385, 1950)

[6](521 p. 2d 948, 1974)

[7]Christenson. p. 17.

[8](105 S.Ct.1953, 1985)

[9]George (Chip) R. Grange II and Nancy Oliver LeSourd. "Volunteers: Court Decisions vs. Cost Effective Help." *Journal of Christian Camping* Vol. 21, No. 5, September/October 1989. p. 8. Reprinted with permission from CCI/USA.

So Grange and LeSourd point out that, in a camp setting, the room and board are provided as conditions of employment; that is, because of their job in working with campers and being in the camp setting, it is to the benefit of the camp to provide the meals and lodging. This has yet to be tested in court.

Several principles arise from these cases that should be taken into consideration by camp directors:

- No remuneration should be given that is not for the convenience of the camp. For example, lodging is provided a camp counselor as a convenience to the camp because the person could not effectively do the job without living at the camp. Therefore, it is for the convenience of the employer.
- No remuneration should be given that is not a part of the responsibility undertaken. For example, to provide meals and lodging to a person whose home is a mile down the road from camp and the person only instructs an activity one or two hours a day is really beyond the responsibility undertaken.
- If the camp asks that a specific task be undertaken at a given place and time, then the camp should provide safeguards and give supervision to the activity.
- The same care and training should be required of volunteers as with employees who undertake potentially liable services, such as driving.
- Volunteers should be urged to carefully inspect equipment before using it, though that in no way relieves the camp of ordinary care and upkeep of that equipment.

VOLUNTEERS AS STAFF

Many nonprofit organizations utilize volunteers either as the majority or total of the camp staff. A volunteer director is recruited for a one- or two-week period and then recruits staff to work during that session or sessions. In other camps, the core program staff is employed, and volunteers recruited as counselors or assistants in other functions. Throughout this book no differentiation has been made between the volunteer and employed staff member. Generally speaking, the principles involved in the selection, retention, orientation, training, and supervision of employed staff should also apply to volunteer staff. This means that the camp director or organization should:

- Select volunteer staff carefully, following the same type of screening methods discussed earlier, including an application and references. Where certifications are needed, they should be required of volunteer staff.
- Have a written agreement with those staff members, that states:
  - The person is a volunteer and not a paid employee.
  - Room and board are provided as a convenience of the employer.
  - The camp assigns sleeping space and duties to the volunteer.
  - No fringe benefits provided a regular employee are provided the volunteer.

- Volunteer services can be terminated by either party at any time.
- A training period, before the campers arrive, will be provided.
- Supervision will be provided during the camp periods
- There will be an evaluation and recognition at the end of the period.

There are certainly differences between volunteer-staffed camps and camps with paid staff, and the camp director needs to carefully assess those differences. For example, training may have to occur on several weekends during the spring or early summer, because the volunteers cannot give another week prior to the camp period. More supervision may be needed in certain program areas because of the limited time for training and orientation of volunteers.

It should be pointed out that the practice of giving honorariums or scholarships rather than wages to someone considered a volunteer, and exempting that person from minimum wage or FICA provisions, would probably not hold up under the court definitions of a "pure volunteer" or "gratuitous employee."

VOLUNTEER COMMITTEES AND BOARDS

In nonprofit camps, a governing board or committee of the organization's board works with the employed or volunteer camp director. The relationship between the committee and board and the director can be a most creative and exciting experience or it can deteriorate into a struggle for power. Peter Drucker suggests that the potential for friction between the board and the executive "has forced an increasing number of nonprofits to realize that neither board nor CEO is 'the boss.' They are colleagues, working for the same goal but each having a different task."[10]

Early in his or her employment, the camp director should try to understand the structure of the particular organization for which he or she works. The director should seek answers to the following questions:

- Who is the chief elected officer of the organization?
- What is the elected governing body and its policy function?
- What is the body to which the camp committee or board reports, if any?
- What are the types of policies the camp committee or board has under its jurisdiction?
- What is the organization's staff role as it relates to these committees or boards?
- What is the stated purpose of the organization, especially its "exempt purpose," that is the purpose for which it is granted exemption from certain taxes?
- What are the job descriptions of board members and officers?

Obviously, no two organizations operate in exactly the same way. Therefore, generalizations made in this chapter must be adapted to the specific camp's situation. The

---

[10]Peter F. Drucker. "What Business Can Learn from Nonprofits." *Harvard Business Review* July/August 1989. p. 91.

chart in illustration 14.1 gives an overview of the roles often assumed by committees or boards and by the director of a camp.

There should be a set of bylaws which governs the actions of the board and its subcommittees. This is a legal document that outlines the way in which the organization elects officers and members, and the manner in which meetings of the board and organization must be held. It is an important document to understand, and the employed director has a legal responsibility to help ensure that the elected officials adhere to the bylaws of the organization. Bylaws may be changed, and the method of change is usually specified in the bylaws.

The volunteer support system should never be viewed as an unnecessary step in administration; it can be the greatest advantage the nonprofit organization has. The volunteer committee member can be a vital checkpoint of community or organizational reaction, as well as an additional staff member. However, few volunteers are simply interested in another committee position or in having their names listed. If they commit themselves to membership on a committee or board, they expect to perform useful and meaningful services. To simply be figure heads is degrading and demoralizing and, in the ultimate analysis, deadly to a camp and its sponsoring organization.

John Pearson, former executive director of Christian Camping International/USA, suggests that "the care and feeding of a board member will be much easier if the director can participate in the board member selection process. Camp boards are selected through a variety of election procedures. The alert camp director, however, will request that the nominating committee consult with him before the nominees are recruited."[11]

After the recruitment process is completed, each new board member should be involved in a group or individual orientation session and given a copy of the bylaws, the policy manual, and a job description. When a meeting of the camp committee or board is scheduled, the camp director should make certain that:

- The agenda is developed with the chairperson in advance of the meeting.
- The written reports on subjects to be discussed are clear and concise, and, when possible, have been circulated in advance of the meeting.
- The decisions or actions to be considered are outlined clearly.
- The members who are expected to report have the data or information they need.
- The room and setting are ready for a comfortable and informal meeting.

The director's next step is to involve the volunteer in a task over and above attendance at the committee or board meeting. The assignment of a task by the chairperson to a subgroup often moves that subgroup to action; at this point the camp director should be an aide to that group, helping them outline the steps to be taken and assisting as needed. It is of particular value to have the committee members visit the camp, espe-

[11]John Pearson. n.d. *The Director and The Camp Board: A Creative Partnership*. Wheaton, IL: Christian Camping International, United States Division. p. 39. Reprinted with permission from CCI/USA.

14.1

Illustration *Responsibilities in Volunteer Organizations*

RESPONSIBILITIES WITHIN THE VOLUNTEER ORGANIZATION

Operator Responsibilities	Shared Responsibilities	Camp Director Responsibilities
▪ See that the camp is operated in harmony with the organization's overall mission and goals	▪ Keep minutes of decisions and meetings	▪ Recommend and implement policy
▪ Set policy for the camp	▪ Assist in site development and maintenance	▪ Recruit and train the staff of the camp (full-time, part-time, and volunteer)
▪ Recruit a capable administrator for the camp and provide adequate support services	▪ Raise capital funds	▪ See that the camp site is maintained in good condition and alert board or committee to needs
▪ Provide resources (site, capital, community support)	▪ Raise supplemental (contributed) funds	
▪ Approve an annual operating budget with overall financial policies and direction	▪ Be responsible for meeting the applicable local, state, and federal laws	▪ Develop a budget and provide a careful and honest accounting of income and expenditures
▪ Be responsible for meeting the applicable local, state, and federal laws	▪ Promote the camp and recruit campers	▪ Be responsible for meeting the applicable local, state, and federal laws
▪ Set admission requirements (age, membership, sex)	▪ Monitor good standards of operation in health, safety, and personnel	▪ Recruit campers
▪ Develop overall program goals and direction	▪ Evaluation	▪ Develop, implement, and evaluate camp program
▪ Be responsible to the community		▪ Ensure good standards of operation in health, safety, and personnel
▪ Supervise the administrator		

cially during sessions, so that the program and objectives can be personalized. Work days, weekends, and special program events will also provide opportunities for volunteer leadership and contribution.

A careful and accurate record of committee proceedings, with particular attention to actions taken, should be maintained in the office or headquarters of the camp. Though the secretary may be an elected or appointed position, the camp director has responsibility for assisting and making sure minutes of all meetings are circulated to appropriate persons and kept in a permanent file in the office, preferably bound. The policies adopted by the committee or board should be pulled from minutes and placed in some appropriate sequence or order in a notebook, which is then given each member of the committee or board.

Orientation of new committee or board members should be a part of the ongoing procedures of the committee or board. A regular set of materials, including the policy manual of the group as well as past minutes, should be given each new member, along with a verbal orientation to the way in which the group works.

A plan of volunteer recognition should be established early in the year. The material aspect of the recognition is not as important as the sincerity and public expression of appreciation.

If an award or symbol of recognition is presented, it should be chosen on the basis of its appropriateness to the task and service given, and of a permanent nature. Ordinarily, volunteers should take the public leadership in recognizing other volunteers.

There are also legal ramifications for those volunteers who agree to serve on a managing committee or board of a nonprofit organization. Generally, a board member is not held liable individually for either the directives of the board or the negligence of an employee. If legal action against directors does occur, it is on the basis that the board or an individual failed to take action or that some action taken was inadequate or irresponsible. Although the specific laws in each state may differ, there are three major categories of violations of their fiduciary responsibility. They are: mismanagement, or failure to follow fundamental management principles; nonmanagement, or failure to use existing opportunities for good management; and self-dealing, or personally benefitting from the decisions of the board (not disclosing a conflict of interest). The basic principle is that the board must make sure that its decisions are informed and reasonable.

For the director working with a board, George Webster suggests six guidelines as the result of *Smith v. Van Gordkum* in the Delaware Supreme Court:

1. "Make decisions deliberately and without undue haste or pressure.
2. Be as thoroughly and completely prepared as possible before making a decision. Make sure the board receives and reviews, in advance, materials pertaining to any major decision.
3. Become actively involved in deliberations during the board meeting. Comment as appropriate on written materials.
4. Keep written records of board preparation and deliberation. It is necessary to create a paper trail showing compliance with procedural requirements.
5. In the case of any major transaction, review all basic legal documents and all analyses by experts.
6. Ensure that, at a minimum, in-house experts, and at best, accountants and lawyers, prepare independent evaluations of important issues."[12]

OTHER ROLES

One function that camp committees and boards in today's climate must expect to undertake is that of fund-raising. Fund-raising is a volunteer function, even though it deserves professional leadership and assistance. The actual fund-raising should be made by a volunteer and recognized by the board or committee.

Many camps are fortunate in having volunteers who are also able and willing to be involved directly in program or work events. These volunteers will often organize and

---

[12]George D. Webster and Hugh K. Webster. "Avoiding Personal Liability: How to Minimize the Risks of Board Service." *Association Management*, Leadership. 1994. p. L–57.

lead groups to camp for work or activity weekends, implement much of the promotion of camp and recruitment of campers, and come to camp for a specific work project.

The relationship between the volunteer and staff member can be most creative and satisfying when they share a common purpose and both feel a sense of contribution and worth. As the staff member is an extension of the policy-making group, so may the volunteer become an extension or arm of the staff member.

CHECKPOINTS

1. Does the camp have a written agreement with volunteers?
2. Does the camp have a regular program orientation and training for all volunteers — both at the staff and committee/board level?
3. Is there a diagram or outline of the volunteer structure? If not, develop one for your own understanding and use.
4. Who is the lay person responsible for overall organization direction?
5. What are the specific responsibilities of the camp committee/board and its subgroups?
6. In what ways that are not used now could your camp use volunteers?

Related Standards

Many of the standards and additional professional practices refer to policies, and to the degree that a volunteer board or committee may be responsible for setting policy, those standards would need to be considered.

Accreditation Standards for Camp Programs and Services: HR-1–21, OM-2; "Additional Professional Practices": Items 25–29

Standards for Conference and Retreat Centers: II-34–36

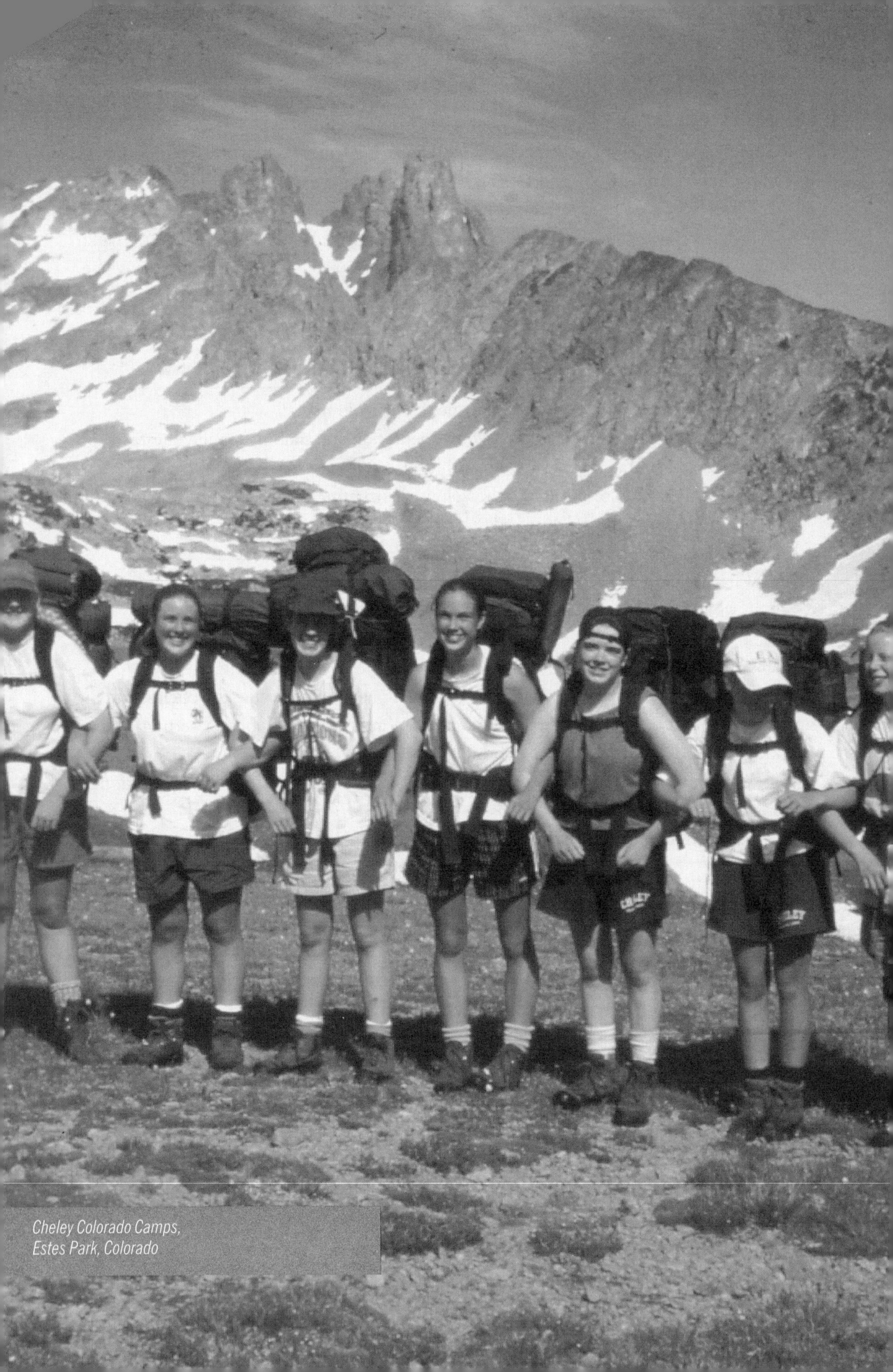

Cheley Colorado Camps,
Estes Park, Colorado

15

Evaluation and Reporting

Evaluation comes at the *end* of the relationships, training and program processes. It is also the *beginning* of new relationships, improved training, and more exciting and purposeful programming. Strategic planning is a circular process which begins and ends with evaluation.

EVALUATION

I n an era when the consumer is demanding more value for money spent, the competition for services in the recreation and education fields continues to grow. Parents are demanding that camps do more to meet expectations concerning their children's experiences. To meet the increasing competition, a camp director can improve quality by establishing a process of evaluation for every part of the camp operation. Dozens of questions need to be asked. Was this a successful season? Did this year's staff do a better job than last year's? Is there a way to improve the food without increasing costs? Which was the most popular program? Did we meet our financial budget this season? How did this season's enrollment compare to last season's? Which staff members should be hired for next season?

Evaluation can be regarded as the process of examining the camp operation to see that every part of the predetermined plan is functioning according to the performance standard necessary for accomplishing established goals. Henderson defines evaluation as the systematic collection and analysis of data to address criteria and make judgments about the worth or improvement of something."[1]

Henderson and Bialeschki further suggest that "evaluation includes all strategies and technologies that are used to determine the value and worth of programs, facilities, administrative procedures, and staff within organizations . . . . The two major reasons for evaluation are accountability and decision making."[2]

[1]Karla A. Henderson with M. Deborah Bialeschki. 1995. *Evaluating Leisure Services: Making Enlightened Decisions*. State College, PA: Venture Publishing, Inc.

[2]Karla A. Henderson and M. Deborah Bialeschki. "Camp Was Great, But the Water Was Too Cold." *Camping Magazine* Vol. 65, No. 5, May/June 1993. pp. 31–32.

One does not wait for a problem to surface before considering an evaluation plan. The advantages of a plan of systematic evaluation of all segments of an operation can be numerous. A comprehensive plan of evaluation can help the director to determine:

- Whether goals and outcomes/objectives have been met
- Whether campers enjoyed camp
- Any shortcomings in various segments of the operation
- The effectiveness of staff performance
- The financial efficiency of the business operation
- The value of various camp program activities
- The effectiveness of administrative staff as well as the director
- What is working and what is not working
- Quality control measures
- Areas to be considered in planning for the future

Determining Criteria

In order to evaluate objectively, the director must establish criteria against which to examine performance. The more precise or specific the criteria the better are the chances for useful information at the end of the evaluation process. There are a variety of sources for establishing the basic performance criteria:

- The goals and desired outcomes/objectives of the organization and/or camp
- Governmental regulations
- Standards of an accrediting body
- Standards of the sponsoring organization, if any
- Expectations of parents, campers, or customers
- A plan of work or strategic planning document

More than one set of criteria may need to be established. For example, to evaluate the camp food service on the basis of governmental regulations or standards and not take into consideration the expectations of parents and campers cannot provide the full information needed.

If the evaluation effort is the result of identification of an existing problem, the focus for evaluation will be more quickly determined and the criteria more easily isolated. Taking the previous example further, if the existing problem relates to too much leftover food after meals, then examination of standards or regulations will be meaningless, whereas the examination of the expectations of campers and staff may reveal useful information.

If the director is following a comprehensive plan of evaluation, all or most of the listed sources may be considered in the development of the criteria. It is recognized that establishing objective criteria will be easier in some areas of operation, for example "a balanced budget," than in others, such as "a camper having fun."

Who administers the evaluation can also affect the outcomes and/or the credibility of the resulting report. Though more costly than internal evaluation, sometimes it is more important to have a completely unbiased evaluation from an outside consultant concerning an operational area where problems are creating significant internal or external concerns. The accreditation visit of the American Camping Association is one example of an external evaluation which carries with it an internal evaluation component. It provides a test against established industry standards and a public recognition of minimum compliance. A consultant may assist in analyzing areas not possible to be covered by standards or regulations or may offer a credibility to the evaluation process that is important only to the immediate camp community (e.g., board, staff, present or potential contributors).

An ongoing plan of evaluation can be accomplished internally with staff and volunteers, as long as objective criteria are set and appropriate methods chosen and administered properly.

Gathering Data

Before beginning to gather data, a director needs to identify the principal areas to be considered in the evaluation process: site and facilities, program, personnel performance, administrative practices, marketing, the camper. Some of these areas, such as personnel performance, require continuous data collection, while others, such as site and facilities, may require only an annual review.

Before selecting methods or instruments, the difference in quantitative and qualitative data should be considered. Quantitative data exists or is converted into numbers from answers such as yes or no. Such data is often most helpful in determining whether goals and outcomes/objectives have been met. Obviously financial records, enrollment statistics, maintenance records, and attendance reports can provide quantitative data by the use of a variety of instruments.

Quantitative data relies most often on:

- Questionnaires — self-administered, or administered in person or by telephone
- Tests — self-administered or in group setting
- Records — financial, maintenance, historical, etc.
- Observations — from predetermined checklists
- Physical evidence — leftovers, wear and tear, etc.

Qualitative data deals most often with words and their meanings in a given context. Here open-ended questions provide clues and new information not easily gained through yes-no answers. The use of qualitative data is most often helpful in looking at processes and describing what happens in given situations.

Qualitative data relies most often on:

- Interviews — open-ended questions, in person or by telephone
- Questionnaires — with open-ended questions

- Focus groups — trained leader asking open-ended questions
- Observation — with field notes
- Records — minutes, historical, publications, etc.
- Experiential — camper logs, narratives, testimonials, letters, etc.

Some expertise is required in the collection and use of both kinds of data, and in the selection and use of various instrument(s) available. It is wise to seek outside guidance in the development of instruments. The very wording of a question, whether open-ended or requiring a yes or no answer, can greatly affect the outcome.

Since quantitative data is most often reduced to yes/no/don't-know answers or numbers relative to degree of agreement (1-2-3-4-5), computer statistical packages can be helpful in sorting the various factors under consideration.[3]

At this point, the director must carefully analyze:

- How will the information desired be secured in statistical format — yes/no, numbers?
- How much manpower is available?
- What is the ease of tally?
- What is the cost?
- What degree of training is required?
- What type of sample — everyone, selective, random?
- How will the data collected be interpreted?
- Who is the information for — public, staff, board, parents?
- Can data be secured without intruding?

Having analyzed these questions, the director is in a position to choose whether qualitative or quantitative data is needed and what instruments will best provide that information.

If for some reason it is not possible or practical to collect information from *all* parties, the type of sample to be used must be examined with a person knowledgeable in statistics and randomization.

To be sure that every part of the operation is included, the director should first develop a list of each component of the camp operation. One way to begin is to list these components, one to a line on the left side of a sheet of lined paper. To the right of these, draw columns and label them: camper, program staff, counselors, administrative board, committee, and so on — whatever groups will participate in the evaluation process. Then each of the components listed should be examined and the appropriate columns on the right checked to indicate the group or groups that participate in each phase of camp life. From this completed chart, the director can then consider the instruments most appropriate to each group and area. (See illustration 15.1.) Particular consideration should be given to the following areas of evaluation.

---

[3]Karla A. Henderson with M. Deborah Bialeschki. *Evaluating Leisure Services.*

15.1 Illustration *Evaluation Checklist*

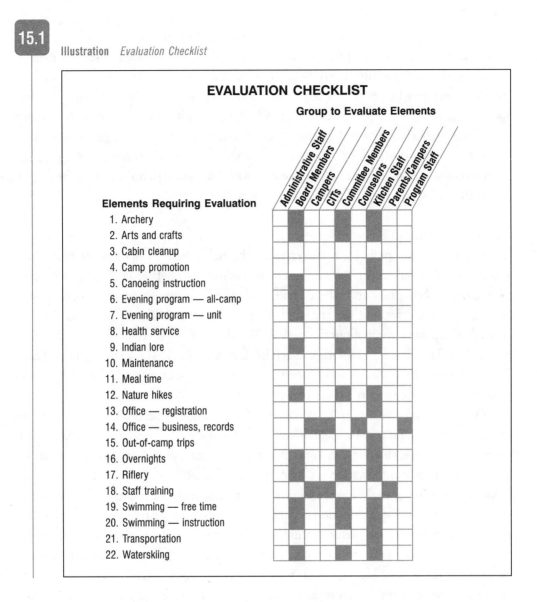

Staff Evaluation of Overall Operation

A questionnaire may provide the most objective information in this situation, but a dialogue with the staff can reveal concerns not easily identified through a questionnaire. A group dialogue by staff should be led by someone who is very objective and has the trust of the group. If the director can establish a reputation for openness to suggestions and ideas throughout the season, staff may be quite willing to respond to questions about the operation. It would be quite natural to set aside an afternoon or a day after campers depart for a group evaluation. The director or discussion leader should give staff members an opportunity to react to each camp area and to make observations about the season and suggestions for the next season. If the director and other administrative staff can keep from being defensive and simply make notes as the discussion moves along, such a meeting may reveal attitudes as well as founded observations.

If the size or departure schedule of the staff make such an approach inadvisable, a questionnaire may be developed. To be most effective, such a form should use a simple method allowing for quick answers, one in which the person can check or circle a choice of answers for each question. It is also effective to include one or two open-ended questions, near the end of the form, which will elicit more extended comments. If signing the form is optional, staff members can be honest without feeling that they might be jeopardizing their chance to return for another season.

Program Evaluation

Since the camp program is the channel through which objectives are realized, it should be subjected to careful assessment to determine whether goals and outcomes/objectives are being met and where changes should be made. Prior to camp, a method should be devised for and specific staff given the responsibility of gathering data on individual programs throughout the period. This data will be used for the end-of-season evaluation. The plan may include a carefully designed checklist for staff to record data on the program from their own observations and from discussions with counselors and campers who participate in a particular program.

Depending on the age and experience of the campers, securing a valid program evaluation from them may be more difficult. If a natural evaluation of an experience can occur informally (such as on an overnight, on a canoe trip, or in a group activity), it can provide qualitative information. A living-group counselor is often the most effective leader of any camper evaluation, except where it deals with the counselor's own performance. If a spontaneous evaluation occurs, there should be a form or some other method of documentation the counselor can use to relay the information to the administration.

Use of video cameras or tape recorders in an evaluation session where campers participate can be a valuable tool. Certainly the group should agree to the use of such devices. However, it takes a very experienced leader to move the group to relaxed and nonself-conscious responses when recording or taping.

Some camper experiences and situations lend themselves to a recounting in personal logs or journals. This activity helps the camper to focus on his or her experiences daily, as well as aiding the camper in understanding the changes during the time frame covered by the experience. This becomes an avenue of self-evaluation for the camper. Sometimes campers will share their journals with the counselor or director. Some camps have had the privilege of publishing excerpts from such journals with the camper's consent.

An evaluation questionnaire may also be helpful. However, handing each camper a form to check off on the last day of camp may diminish the feelings of the moment. Use of a form by the counselor with the living group earlier in the day may be better. Another alternative is to mail the camper a form with a return envelope after the camper returns home.

Alternatively, the director can request evaluations from parents after the camper has returned home. Parents may be able to more effectively voice the camper's feelings as well as evaluate any changes. To encourage responses, the questionnaire needs to be carefully designed and as brief as is consistent with securing the necessary information. Providing a stamped, self-addressed envelope and making a signature on the form optional will probably increase the percentage of return.

Where there are particular program activities run or supervised by particular staff members, these staffers should be provided with an opportunity to evaluate their effectiveness — either orally or by a questionnaire. There should also be opportunity for making recommendations for future changes in the program. Obviously, staff members most closely associated with a particular activity should have the best viewpoint for appraising the procedures and methods used.

There are some general questions about programs or activities that will help staff think about effectiveness. Does the program or activity accomplish the following?

- Consider the needs and interests of the campers as well as their stage of development?
- Provide for individual differences in skill and maturity?
- Stress the values of participation: group loyalty, tolerance, concern for others?
- Allow for self-expression or creativity?
- Enable campers to realize a sense of achievement through participation?
- Promote the development of leadership skills?
- Offer progression to higher skill levels?

In considering the framework of a particular program or activity, there are some organizational factors which should be assessed. Was there consideration given to the optimal size and makeup of the program group? Was the area where the activity took place adequate? Was the equipment adequate, in good repair, and available in sufficient numbers for the group size? Was the activity conducted within safe guidelines?

Administrative Services Evaluation

All administrative services should be appraised throughout the season and reviewed not only by those responsible for the operation but by other staff outside each operation.

Camp property, facilities, and equipment need to be reviewed not only for purposes of safety and good maintenance, but with an eye to possible improvements. The suggestions of participants, parents, and staff regarding changes should be considered.

The food service operation should be examined regarding factors such as food quality, cost per meal, sanitation, efficiency of management and organization, and the maintenance of happy relationships with campers and staff as they move in and out of the dining area during mealtimes.

The health and safety and risk management program should be measured. Can the daily routine for treating persons at the health center be improved? Are there some activities which have a high accident rate? How can injuries be reduced? On out-of-camp trips, are all health and safety precautions taken? Can the procedures at the waterfront be improved to offer a better check on swimmers?

Hospitality Services Evaluation

In a conference/retreat center or where a camp rents facilities to others, questionnaires should be devised to enable guests, group leaders, and staff to comment on housing, equipment, food, staff, hospitality, service, health and safety concerns, grounds, and facilities. Different questions should be asked of the secondary customers (i.e., guests) from those asked the primary customer (i.e., organizations or leaders). Responses can prove to be a valuable tool in marketing, as well as in improving services.

Staff Performance Appraisal

A major part of the evaluation process is the appraisal, at all levels, of employed and volunteer camp staff. This process is discussed in full in chapter 8.

Evaluation of the Director

Often the camp director has the most difficult time getting a direct critique of his or her job performance. There should be a way devised for staff and volunteers to share reactions to the director's performance. Sometimes direct verbal feedback is a possibility; but, most often, a questionnaire (which does not have to be signed) is given to staff and volunteers to be returned to a neutral person. Open-ended questions usually elicit the most helpful comments. A sample form is shown in illustration 15.2. The use of such a form may be helpful to the director's supervisor which could be an agency executive director, camp administrator, owner, or personnel committee of an operating board, since such an annual evaluation and feedback is beneficial to a director.

Evaluation of Boards or Committees

In camps that have governing committees or boards, it is important both to the director/administrator and the chief elected officer to have regular times to check the effectiveness of their work with that body. It is also important for the volunteer governing body to evaluate its own operation. Sometimes this can be done in an informal dialogue in a retreat setting, where time is not as pressed as in regular meetings and methods can be used to secure qualitative input. Where such an approach is not possible, a checklist, such as that shown in illustration 15.3, may provide a more objective evaluation.

Similarly, volunteers need feedback as to their performance and participation. Performance appraisal of volunteer staff members is covered in chapter 8.

15.2 Illustration *Director Evaluation Form*

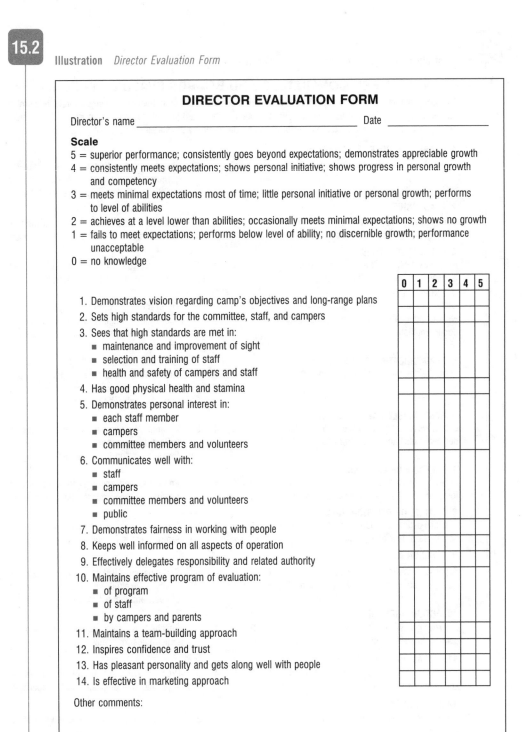

DIRECTOR EVALUATION FORM

Director's name _____ Date _____

Scale

5 = superior performance; consistently goes beyond expectations; demonstrates appreciable growth

4 = consistently meets expectations; shows personal initiative; shows progress in personal growth and competency

3 = meets minimal expectations most of time; little personal initiative or personal growth; performs to level of abilities

2 = achieves at a level lower than abilities; occasionally meets minimal expectations; shows no growth

1 = fails to meet expectations; performs below level of ability; no discernible growth; performance unacceptable

0 = no knowledge

	0	1	2	3	4	5
1. Demonstrates vision regarding camp's objectives and long-range plans						
2. Sets high standards for the committee, staff, and campers						
3. Sees that high standards are met in:						
■ maintenance and improvement of sight						
■ selection and training of staff						
■ health and safety of campers and staff						
4. Has good physical health and stamina						
5. Demonstrates personal interest in:						
■ each staff member						
■ campers						
■ committee members and volunteers						
6. Communicates well with:						
■ staff						
■ campers						
■ committee members and volunteers						
■ public						
7. Demonstrates fairness in working with people						
8. Keeps well informed on all aspects of operation						
9. Effectively delegates responsibility and related authority						
10. Maintains effective program of evaluation:						
■ of program						
■ of staff						
■ by campers and parents						
11. Maintains a team-building approach						
12. Inspires confidence and trust						
13. Has pleasant personality and gets along well with people						
14. Is effective in marketing approach						

Other comments:

Signed _____

15.3

VOLUNTEER COMMITTEES AND BOARDS EVALUATION FORM

This document is designed to obtain your evaluation of our board's (committee) effectiveness. Circle the number on the rating scale that corresponds to your evaluation of the board in each category. Number 1 indicates poor performance and number 5 excellent performance as illustrated by the statements nearest those numbers.

1. CLARITY OF ROLE AND FUNCTION

Lacks. We're fuzzy about our responsibilities.　　1　2　3　4　5　　Present. We distinguish clearly between policy determination and management functions. We know what we are about.

2. LEADERSHIP

Dominated by one or a few persons. Other resources within the board are never used.　　1　2　3　4　5　　Shared among members according to abilities and insights. All resources are used.

3. IMPORTANT ISSUES

Not addressed, but "swept under the rug" or dealt with outside of the board.　　1　2　3　4　5　　Consistently on the agenda for open consideration, debate, and decision.

4. PREPARATION

Lacks. We're consistently caught off guard without adequate information, facts, and documentation.　　1　2　3　4　5　　Outstanding. Committees and staff do excellent preliminary work. Members are well informed and understand the pros and cons of all decisions.

5. COMMUNICATION OF IDEAS

Poor. We don't listen. Ideas are ignored.　　1　2　3　4　5　　Good. We listen and try to understand one another's ideas. Ideas are well presented and acknowledged.

6. RESPONSIBLE PARTICIPATION

Lacks. We reflect our own biases. We "grind our own axes" and watch from "outside."　　1　2　3　4　5　　Present. We're sensitive to the need to reflect for our camp and its clientele. Everyone is "on the inside participating."

7. FREEDOM OF PERSONS

Stifled. Conformity is explicitly or implicitly fostered. Members are often manipulated.　　1　2　3　4　5　　Enhanced and encouraged. Creativity of persons and their individuality is respected.

8. CLIMATE OF RELATIONSHIPS

One of hostility or suspicion or indulgent politeness or fear of anxiety.　　1　2　3　4　5　　One of mutual trust and genuineness. Atmosphere is relaxed and friendly.

9. DECISION MAKING

Superficial. We're a "rubber stamp" body. Decisions are crammed down our throats.　　1　2　3　4　5　　Participative. All data is available and all opinions are aired, with resultant ownership of decisions that are made.

10. ACTION AGREEMENTS

Not reached. We don't set target dates or plan for follow through.　　1　2　3　4　5　　Reached. We agree on next steps and set target dates for review.

11. FISCAL ACCOUNTABILITY

Lacks. We don't consider the cost of an action before it is taken.　　1　2　3　4　5　　Present. We carefully consider financial implications of proposals before approval.

12. CONTINUITY

Lacks. Each meeting seems to "start from scratch."　　1　2　3　4　5　　Present. We build on previous work in an efficient manner.

13. PRODUCTIVITY

Low. We're proud and happy, just coasting along. Meetings are irrelevant and a waste of time and money.　　1　2　3　4　5　　High. We are digging hard and earnestly at work in important tasks. We create and achieve at each meeting.

Please list any additional suggestions or ideas you have for increasing the effectiveness of this board. Particular attention to items you rated 1 or 2 is greatly appreciated.

Evaluation of Campers

The evaluation of campers varies greatly from camp to camp. Many camps keep careful records of each child's program participation and relationship to peers. This information is often helpful in placing the camper in a living group another year and may be useful in planning activities at the beginning of the next season.

Ideally, the evaluation of campers should go back to the developmental goals of the age group served and the outcomes directed to those developmental goals. At the end of the season the degree to which the camp experience has met those outcomes is one true test of the camp experience. Having focused staff on those developmental goals during staff training and referred staff back to them during supervisory conferences, it is logical that the level of achievement of those outcomes be measured. These results can be most helpful in responding to parents and also in assessing changes needed in program operations for the next season.

Two day camps participated in a research project, using established pretest and posttest assessment forms. "Changes in the behaviors of campers, their knowledge of community resources, and their observed enjoyment of camp was [sic] noted," report Saunders, Welch, and Glass.[4] Such programs require involving a professor or staff person skilled in program evaluation techniques to help design the instrument and plan for evaluation in addition to clarifying program outcome objectives and involving the approval of the governing organization, if there is one.

In keeping parents in touch with the camper's progress, some camps use a regular report form for parents at the end of the season, while others require counselors to write progress reports to parents at regular intervals. Camps with shorter sessions require the progress reports at the end of the session the camper attended. Whatever the form or time frame, the evaluation should be approached with concern for objectivity and balance. Counselors need to understand that they see the camper in isolation from his or her familiar environment, which means that their observations may be one-sided or limited in scope. In addition, these records are sometimes necessary for reports to an agency which referred the camper or which has an ongoing relationship to the camper.

In many instances, the most effective form of evaluation is that done in one-on-one conversation with the camper. Helping a camper see him or herself through the eyes of others is an important objective for many camps. If that is a goal, then it can only be reached in an open and trusting living situation. Counselors need careful training and sensitivity in order to give campers a positive experience of self-evaluation. The process should begin with discussing with each individual camper, as well as with the group, individual goals for the camp period. Their conversations with campers should begin on a positive note and emphasize positive achievements toward that camper's

[4]Edward Saunders, Suz Welch, and DD Glass. "Evaluating Your Camp Program." *Camping Magazine* Vol. 70, No. 6, November/December 1997. pp. 20–23.

15.4 Illustration   *Applicable Tools to Various Areas of Evaluation*

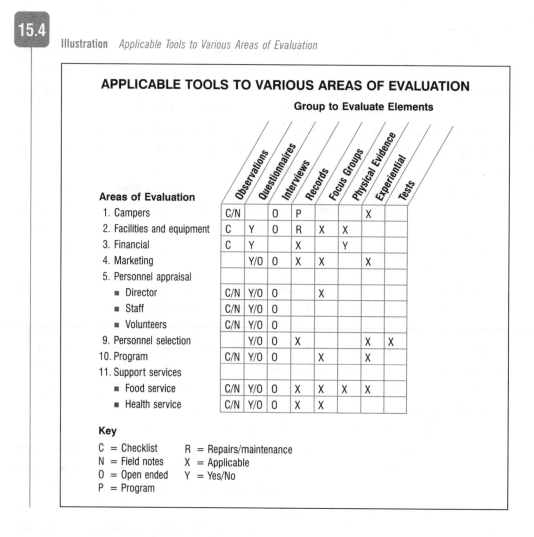

APPLICABLE TOOLS TO VARIOUS AREAS OF EVALUATION

Group to Evaluate Elements

Areas of Evaluation	Observations	Questionnaires	Interviews	Records	Focus Groups	Physical Evidence	Experiential	Tests
1. Campers	C/N		O	P			X	
2. Facilities and equipment	C	Y	O	R	X	X		
3. Financial	C	Y		X	Y			
4. Marketing		Y/O	O	X	X		X	
5. Personnel appraisal								
■ Director	C/N	Y/O	O		X			
■ Staff	C/N	Y/O	O					
■ Volunteers	C/N	Y/O	O					
9. Personnel selection		Y/O	O	X			X	X
10. Program	C/N	Y/O	O		X		X	
11. Support services								
■ Food service	C/N	Y/O	O	X	X	X	X	
■ Health service	C/N	Y/O	O	X	X			

Key

C	= Checklist	R	= Repairs/maintenance
N	= Field notes	X	= Applicable
O	= Open ended	Y	= Yes/No
P	= Program		

goals, but the areas in which a camper can improve should also be pointed out honestly and discussed.

The best evaluation of a camper happens when the camper can be led into a realistic self-evaluation. If the focus of conversations and observations can be on how the camper perceives his or her achievement, skill level, behavior, or response to others, it is more likely to become a part of his or her ongoing life experience.

Accreditation

The program of accreditation pioneered by the American Camping Association is designed to measure the performance of a particular camp or conference center against a list of standards of operation in many areas. The accreditation program features a visit by trained professionals. Preparation for the visit may extend over a period of months. The ACA standards, developed over a period of more than sixty years and now accepted nationally as industry standards, can also be used as a tool for self-evaluation. A great deal is said for having a pattern against which the director can measure the camp. Involvement of administrative staff, as well as any operating committee or board, can also be most useful.

Finances

Though monthly financial reports give a clue to the financial operation, the year-end report provides an opportunity for a variety of evaluations. These will be of the greatest interest to the camp director, business manager, and a governing board. These should include: cost per meal served, cost per camper day, cost-effectiveness analysis, cost-benefit analysis by specific services or program activities, comparison of income and expenditures by category over a five-year period.

Illustration 15.4 provides a chart showing the instruments most applicable to the various areas of evaluation covered above. Though other instruments are available, these are the most commonly used in the camp operation.

REPORTING — THE JUDGMENT PHASE

The final step, once the criteria has been determined and the data gathered, is to make judgments about the meaning of the data in relationship to the camp operation. In a single proprietorship, the data gathered lands on one desk and the judgments are made there. In most cases, however, there are multiple persons involved in the judgment process; this will require reports describing the data and conclusions.

In interpreting quantitative data, the director must not be too quick to simply assume that the highest numerical sums necessarily provide the proper judgment. Rather, the frequencies must be examined to see if there are particular portions of the data which skew the results in some fashion. Establishing a mean or average and a median (the position at which there is an equal number above and below) in the data will help the director discover if the two are relatively close. If there is a substantial difference, the data may need to be examined more closely for anything unusual that is skewing the results. If the quantitative data becomes this complex, many camp directors may wish to consult with someone who has training in statistical analysis for assistance in interpreting the data.

In interpreting qualitative data, Henderson suggests that early, in the organization of data, the director will "continually reexamine the data. 'Negative evidence,' which means you will be trying to make sure everything fits your categories, will be sought." Here the evaluator looks to see whether there is any evidence that does not fit. Further, she suggests the director look "for multiple sources of evidence to draw conclusions . . . that interpretations come from being intimately familiar with the data. Therefore, the evaluator . . . read(s) the data over and over."[5]

---

[5]Henderson with Bialeschki. *Evaluating Leisure Services.*

The director must carefully examine the data for information that he or she did not necessarily seek since there are often unexpected insights that come from evaluation. This information may be more valuable than much of the data that was sought. Look for negative impacts as well as positive experiences.

Once the data has been examined again and again and basic conclusions and inconclusive areas identified, the director writes the report outlining the areas studied, criteria identified, the sample used, the instruments chosen, the data collected, and resulting conclusions and recommendations for action. The use of this report will vary with the audience to whom it is addressed, with considerably more detail offered to the decision makers than to parents or campers. Each audience requires a different approach.

Reporting to the Corporate Board

Most camps have a governing group which expects reports at the conclusion of the camp season. These reports can take many forms but are most often directed to the camp director's supervisor or a governing committee or board. This report should certainly highlight the events of the summer, giving the group a sense of the program and values derived from the experience. The use of comments from camper logs or parental letters can be helpful in sharing this feeling.

In addition to communicating the programmatic aspects of camp, it is vital that the results of the evaluation process be shared with the governing group. Summaries of the data with comparative data from previous summers will give perspective to the facts. Furthermore, the director may wish to make recommendations for improvements and steps for the next season growing out of the evaluation process. This approach helps the governing body focus discussion on the major concerns and alternatives to the recommendations.

Such a report should summarize the criteria, the methods used to collect the data, any instrument used in the process, and the resulting data. Following this narrative, a list of conclusions and resulting recommendations may be presented. If the report is quite long, an executive summary plus the conclusions and recommendations may be used for wider distribution. These reports should be retained in the camp's files, along with the raw materials collected in the process.

Reporting to Parents and Participants

The report to the parents and participants often emphasizes the overview of the season with comments on camper activities and projects. Pictures and stories will make such reports more interesting and readable. It should be kept in mind that the report parents receive is an important tool in developing loyalty and interest in camp for another season, and many times developing a case for future contributions of money or services.

Many camps publish a yearbook or annual calendar which tells the season's story in pictures and words for the campers and staff. Here emphasis is given to the good times had by all, with pictures of as many different campers and staff as possible. Not only is this an instrument for next year's recruitment, but it also provides a tool that might be shared with friends.

The size and layout of the camp's report will depend partially on the funds available. In any case, the report should be designed to be an attractive, interpretative tool.

Reporting to Alumni

Developing an updated list of camper and staff alumni is valuable for sharing information about the camp. Certainly a report of each season should be shared with the alumni group. This report goes beyond the sort of report sent to parents and is not as detailed as the report to the governing body. The report for alumni might be a summary of the major events of the camp season with an enclosure concerning the major decisions the camp is facing in the near future.

Here the report is designed to maintain the interest of the alumni, assuring them of the continuing allegiance to the philosophy of the camp and stimulating interest in ways the alumni can further serve the camp through contributions of money and services.

CHECKPOINTS

1. Were there evaluations done in previous seasons? If so, have you found copies in the files?
2. What type of evaluations would have been helpful to you as you began planning for your first season?
3. Using illustration 15.1 as a basis, develop your own chart listing the areas of the camp program and the people who should be involved in the evaluation of each area.
4. Develop an overall evaluation plan that will provide information identified in question two.
5. What information would your governing committee or board like to have at the end of the season?
6. Review your evaluation plan to see if it will provide that information.
7. What sort of evaluation from your staff will be most helpful?
8. How do you help your campers begin the process of self-evaluation?
9. Have you set up a system to evaluate the camp program against the developmental goals of the each age group? If not, how do you do so?

Related Standards

Accreditation Standards for Camp Programs and Services: OM-2, 3, 5; "Additional Professional Practices": 15, 23

Standards for Conference and Retreat Centers: II-29–30

16

Becoming a Professional

The impetus for an educational experience naturally should come from camp directors. This would not only be the best guarantee of its productiveness, but would also reflect a high degree of genuinely professional consciousness on the part of camp directors.[1]

Ａll the answers are not in this volume because no one can give you all those answers. Many answers will have to be found by the camp director on his or her own — through experience, through peer relationships, through research, through study, through workshops and conferences. The quotation from Hedley Dimock at the beginning of this chapter is as true today as when it was written over fifty years ago.

CAMPING AS A PROFESSION

The subject of the camp director as a professional has been an issue since the early part of this century, but has intensified during the past four decades. In our society, the term *professional* has been so greatly overused that, at times, the only commonality among its many uses is that it differentiates between a paid and an unpaid person — though today we have coined the expression "professional volunteers." Originally the word was used to talk about law, medicine, and religious vocations, but it has been broadened in modern times.

It is recognized that many persons come into the camping and conference/retreat center field for a few years only, before taking other positions in other human service organizations. Many persons in other professions, such as education, spend their summers as well as part of the school year involved in the camp field. However, a significant number of directors are individuals who spend their lives in the camp field — as camp directors, administrators, consultants, and teachers. To these people, there is a strong feeling that being a camp or conference/retreat center director is a profession worthy of note.

---

[1]Hedley S. Dimock. 1948. "Camping and the Future." IX in a series, *Character Education in the Summer Camp*. New York: Association Press. p. 59.

A work group at the ninth Character Education in Camping Seminar at George Williams College identified seven marks of a profession. These are paraphrased here but are taken from that seminar report:[2]

1. A profession rests upon "*a social function, distinct from other functions, that is basic, important and relatively permanent.*" This is most obvious in medicine, the ministry, engineering, and law. Camping is so young, as compared to these professions, that it is a bit premature to espouse our social function, much less equate 130 plus years as permanency.

2. A profession has a "*distinctive or specialized body of knowledge,*" a theory that ties together many disciplines that represent a unique body apart from other fields. As identified in this text, many disciplines have to be mastered in this field, but what makes that body of knowledge unique from education, perhaps the closest profession to camping?

3. A profession "*demands a specialized or professional preparation, in addition to general education, for its practitioners.*" This means that the body of knowledge is so complex and large that it cannot be mastered on the job as in a craft. This is one of the differences between a carpenter and an architect. Standards for specialized education are set, and only those individuals who meet them are eligible for admission to that profession. An effort was made, in this regard, through an American Camping Association Certified Professional program, but after a number of years of granting certification it became apparent that the field was far from accepting this as an eligibility requirement to practice in the field, and the program was discontinued.

4. A profession functions collectively through people "*joining together for mutual betterment and growth and to provide a service to the public.*" These were once called guilds or societies but today are known as associations. The functions include:

   - Formulating the conditions for entrance into the profession, as mentioned in number one.

   - Developing a code governing ethical practices of those in the field, as it relates to the "relationships between the practitioner and the other practitioners, and the practitioner and the public." The American Camping Association has established a code for camp directors, which does set some basic ethical practices for the field. This code is included in Appendix F and deserves study by every camp director, for it does contain the basic ethical practices.

   - Stimulating the "discovery of new knowledge and practice pertinent to the profession." Researching and publishing articles on various aspects of the field's practice is a recognized way of advancing the body of knowledge in a field and one's professional contribution. Dr. Betty van der Smissen and Judy Brookhiser

---

[2]Ibid., pp. 24–26.

developed a bibliography of research in the field in 1982.[3] Other research has occurred since then without further updating a comprehensive bibliography of research. In 1999, Paul Marsh did a meta-analysis of twenty-two studies completed on the influence of camp experiences on youth self constructs.[4]

- "Facilitating the interchange and dissemination of" knowledge in the field throughout the entire profession. This function is the obligation and effort to continually update the field and provide new input into the body of knowledge. It is being done today by camp directors who write for such journals as *Camping Magazine*, the *Journal of Christian Camping*, and the *Journal of Experiential Education*, and who author books in the field. Such interchange and dissemination of knowledge have happened in both Christian Camping International, the American Camping Association, and the International Association of Conference Center Administrators. It follows that, when the camp director becomes part of one or all of those bodies, he or she moves toward being a professional.

5. A profession "*formulates and applies standards that govern the practice of the profession in the community.*" This goal has been met in our field through the standards of the American Camping Association, which have been developed over more than sixty years and are now the accepted standards for the industry in the United States. However, we are still some distance from having all camps or conference/retreat centers meet those standards, or having all states recognize accreditation as essential for licensing.

6. A profession is "*motivated by a social spirit and purpose. Social values presumably transcend individual and economic values in a profession.*" In other words, the reason for camps to exist is to serve the public, and that becomes an essential ingredient of any professional organization or association that brings together camp directors. The challenge, therefore, is to keep individual directors and their associations focused on growth of the camp director and service to the public, rather than mutual protection societies. There will always be pressures to move toward the mutual protection society rather than toward the protection of the public, and the voices of professionals in the field will have to keep their associations on course.

7. A profession "*implies a personal standard of workmanship characterized by both sincerity and intellectual integrity. The professional person seeks to maintain high standards of competence, to keep abreast of changing conditions and of new knowledge and techniques, and to embody the new learnings in his practice.*" This requirement means that a professional has an obligation to continually update his or her knowledge in the field. A professional holds oneself out to the public as being up to date on the current

[3]Betty van der Smissen and Judy Brookhiser, Editors. 1982. *Bibliography of Research in Organized Camping, Environmental Education, Adventure Education, and Interpretative Services.* Martinsville, IN: American Camping Association.

[4]Paul Marsh, "*What Does Camp Do for Kids? A meta-analysis of the influence of the organized camping experience on the self-constructs of youth*" (Master's thesis, Indiana University, 1999).

and best practices in one's field. Herein, the director has to move beyond his or her own camp or organization to exchange information and to dialogue with fellow professionals around key issues and development.

An examination of the seven marks of a profession gives us evidence that some requirements have been fulfilled while others have not. Therein is the challenge for the future. Hedley S. Dimock, in speaking to this issue, wrote: "A professional . . . will submit himself to the rigid discipline of straight thinking, to a constant search for new knowledge and better techniques that should be embodied in practice. In this quest for higher standards of workmanship, he will ally himself with other camp directors and personnel through camping associations or similar organizations. He will accept his share of collective responsibility to discover and disseminate knowledge through research and publications, to raise the standards of camping generally, and to interpret to the public the objectives and standards of the modern camp. He will work within the planning structure of the community to make camping experience available for the larger number of persons who need this experience."[5]

EXPANDING ONE'S EDUCATION

There are at least six areas of educational endeavor that will enable a camp director to gain more knowledge and keep current with developments in the field.

For camp directors, the American Camping Association has devised a Professional Development Plan which is depicted in illustration 16.1. The first course in the plan is a New Director's Orientation which gives an overview of all aspects of the job for new seasonal and assistant directors, as well as late hires, and is offered at the local section level.

The second course is the Basic Camp Director's Course (BCDC), which is the best comprehensive introduction to the management of camps and covers thirteen of the fourteen core areas. Primarily designed for camp directors with less than six years of experience, the course is offered annually, prior to the American Camping Association National Conference, and at other times during the year regionally. Selected resource lists targeted to each core area are available in Appendix J.

Camp Director Institutes are designed for experienced directors who have completed the BCDC and have at least three years of experience as a director with overall responsibility for the operation and management of a camp or conference center or six years of experience as a director.

Christian Camping International, the American Camping Association, and the International Association of Conference Center Directors offer a variety of workshops, courses, and conferences, which will assist the camp director in areas in which he or she

---

[5]Hedley S. Dimock. 1948. *Administration of the Modern Camp.* New York: Association Press (Y.M.C.A. of the U.S.A.). p. 269.

16.1

Illustration *ACA Professional Development Plan*

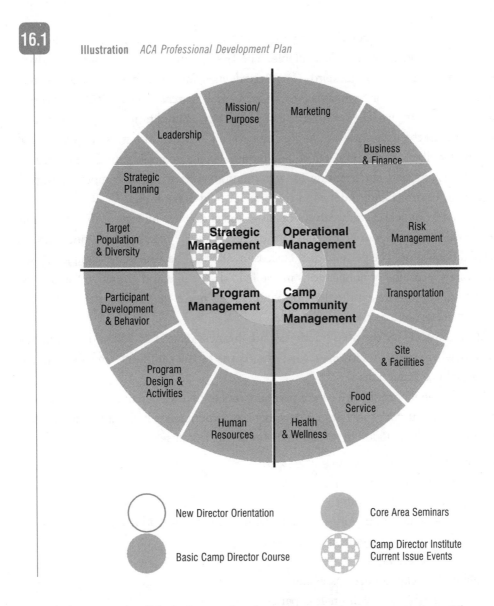

feels deficient and will help him or her keep abreast of current practices. The annual conferences of the organizations provide a wealth of such information. A variety of other organizations offer courses, workshops, and conferences that will benefit camp directors in certain areas. Many of these organizations are listed in Appendix C. In addition, a number of colleges and universities offer courses in camp administration or related subjects through their schools of physical education or recreation and leisure studies.

Participation in a local section of American Camping Association and/or the Christian Camping International provides an opportunity to meet fellow camp directors and to develop relationships that will allow sharing and problem solving together. The American Camping Association's Web site (www.ACAcamps.org/education/calendar.htm) provides details regarding local section educational opportunities.

Participation in the accreditation process of the American Camping Association is one of the best educational tools available. The Basic Standards Course and a study of one or both of the books of standards (i.e., *Accreditation Standards for Camp Programs and Services*, 1998 edition, or *Standards for Conference and Retreat Centers*, 1993 edition) is an ideal way to start, whether or not the camp is seeking accreditation. Of course, actual participation in the accreditation of one's camp is an exciting and grueling educational experience, well worth the time, effort, and money. Further, completion of the course for standards visitors and participating in accreditation visits to other camps is a way to expand your horizons and understand the broader field of camping.

Personal reading and study cannot be dismissed as any less important than the items listed above. The professional journals in the field should be read regularly, and journals in related fields should be perused as the occasion allows. The American Camping Association offers a catalog of publications in the field that is updated annually. You may be distant from conferences and workshops and able to make them only every few years, but books are as close as the bedside table.

All of the costs for the above activities are business related and should be borne by the camp, where possible. However, where not borne by the camp, they may be itemized for personal tax deductions.

A professional portfolio is a career planning tool to help you analyze your competencies and document your professional development experiences. It should contain information commonly included in a resume including such items as:

- career goals
- previous job experience
- completed degree programs
- courses, seminars, and workshops specific to the camping industry
- participation in other educational events
- self-study experiences
- a regularly updated needs assessment
- ACA leadership and volunteer experiences
- other experiences relevant to the profession

Finally, there is an opportunity for every camp director to add to the body of knowledge of the field of camping. One of the exciting aspects of the camping field is that there is an opportunity to experiment and explore more efficient ways of operating camps and conference/retreat centers as well as to develop new methods of helping people grow outdoors. As a director, you can be one who studies, experiments, documents, and adds to that body of knowledge. But whatever you do, may your work in the camping field aid not only those participants and staff in your program, but also insure that future generations will continue to benefit from this unique human experience.

CHECKPOINTS

1. Which of the seven marks of a profession do you feel accurately reflects the camping profession?
2. How does the Code of Ethics apply to your work or your camp?
3. What is your plan for professional development?

Related Standards

Accreditation Standards for Camp Programs and Services: HR-1

Standards for Conference and Retreat Centers: II – 31–33

Sample Job Descriptions

POSITION TITLE: PROGRAM DIRECTOR

Responsible to: Camp Director

General Responsibility: To be responsible for the camp program and to assist in staff training

Qualifications:

- At least twenty-one years of age, preferably at least twenty-five years of age
- At least two years of college, preferably a graduate
- Extensive experience as a group counselor or staff member in camp setting; experience at programming in a camp setting preferred
- Emotionally mature and willing to accept responsibility
- Of good character
- Believe in the individual worth of the camper
- Able to work with a minimum of supervision

Specific Responsibilities:

- Assist the camp director in planning and carrying out precamp and in-service staff training
- Be responsible for all camp programs provided for the camper
- Directly supervise and appraise the unit counselors, nature specialist, arts and crafts specialist, aquatics specialist, equine specialist, and tripping specialist
- Maintain proper records as required by the camp director
- Coordinate, with assistant director and maintenance supervisor, matters of interest in areas of overlapping responsibility while always seeking the best solution for campers and the camp
- Review program budget and search for ways to increase services offered within budgetary constraints; be prepared to defend proposed programming budget changes
- Be responsible for the health and welfare of campers

Essential Functions:

- Be able to train the staff
- Visually observe the assigned staff in performance of their duties, as well as the behavior of campers in their care, and be able to provide guidance as needed
- Visually identify hazards in the camp operation and respond appropriately
- Be able to work and communicate well with a variety of age groups

POSITION TITLE: SITE MANAGER

Responsible to: Camp Director

General Responsibility: To oversee and maintain all properties of the camp

Qualifications:

- High school diploma required, with some college or technical school work beyond high school preferred
- Experience in carpentry, plumbing, electrical, and general maintenance repairs
- Experience in supervising work of others
- Ability to get along well with people

Specific Responsibilities:

- Oversee and maintain all properties according to annual work plans and schedules
- Live on the camp site and act as site manager of camp property
- Hire occasional helpers and subcontractors for projects and ongoing maintenance
- Supervise any employee assigned to maintenance area of camp
- Make recommendations for budgeted repairs and maintenance during budget preparation period; outline costs and detail
- Recommend maintenance and improvements that are beyond budgeted amounts; develop cost figures and details
- Direct volunteer groups who come to camp for work weekends and projects
- See that all major equipment and vehicles are maintained and housed appropriately
- Order maintenance supplies and check delivery; forward approved invoices to the camp director
- Welcome rental groups when asked by camp director and check them out at time of departure; check facilities for damage or unusual disarray
- See that all repair requests are completed or responded to within 48 hours
- Be responsible for the health and welfare of campers

Essential Functions:

- Be able to drive all camp owned vehicles
- Have the necessary physical strength to carry out maintenance and repairs (e.g., to lift heavy objects, to dig, to load and unload trucks, to carry out assigned repairs)

- Visually identify hazards throughout the camp property, and respond appropriately
- Visually identify repairs and cleaning that need to be accomplished throughout the camp property
- Be able to make the appropriate repairs

POSITION TITLE: FOOD SERVICE SUPERVISOR

Responsible to: Camp Director

General Responsibility: To oversee the food service and dining area of the camp

Qualifications:

- A minimum of two years documented experience and training in food service management; previous camp experience preferable
- Emotionally mature
- Of good moral character
- Ability to manage and supervise subordinates
- Ability to relate well to children and other adults

Specific Responsibilities:

- Supervise all kitchen activities
- Enforce all health standards and regulations established by the Department of Health plus those deemed necessary by the camp director
- Supervise the serving of all meals
- Plan all menus according to healthful nutrition standards two weeks in advance for checking by the camp director
- Order all food and kitchen supplies; maintain costs within the prescribed budget
- Provide for special food needs such as cookouts, snacks, and special events, as well as for persons with special needs
- Participate in the total camp program when appropriate and as long as primary duties are not neglected
- Be responsible for the health and welfare of campers

Essential Functions:

- Ability to operate gas, electrical, and mechanical equipment in the food service area
- Maintain accurate records (e.g., menus, food orders, inventories)
- Visual ability to determine the cleanliness of the entire kitchen and dining room, and ability to supervise corrective action as needed
- Physical strength to lift heavy pots and pans and to move food and supplies
- Ability to assess the condition of food upon preparation and in storage
- Ability to provide supervision to kitchen staff

Risk Management Checklist for Camp Personnel

Staff Recruitment

- ☐ Clear organizational chart showing who supervises whom
- ☐ Established ratios (in writing) for
  - ☐ supervisor to supervisee
  - ☐ counselor to campers
  - ☐ program leaders to campers (may vary due to risks)
- ☐ Job description in writing
  - ☐ general responsibilities
  - ☐ specific responsibilities
  - ☐ essential functions
  - ☐ qualifications
  - ☐ revised (in writing) any time duties change or at least annually
- ☐ Written policies on remuneration
  - ☐ time off
  - ☐ insurance coverage
  - ☐ meals/lodging credit toward minimum wage, if any
  - ☐ minimum wage
  - ☐ wages
- ☐ Written job performance and appraisal processes

Screening

- ☐ Application
  - ☐ no gender questions
  - ☐ no marital status questions
  - ☐ no race or national origin questions
  - ☐ no religion questions
  - ☐ no disability questions (unless basis of essential functions of job)
  - ☐ no specific age questions (may ask if over age of majority)

☐ references (at least three)
  ☐ specific to position skills   ☐ volunteer supervisors
  ☐ specific to work with children   ☐ employers
☐ criminal background check
  and/or
☐ volunteer disclosure statement
☐ application updated by returning staff

☐ References checked
  ☐ form includes reference to work with children (if applicable)
  ☐ form includes reference to child abuse
  ☐ form includes reference to specific skill required for position
  ☐ mailed to each reference
  ☐ telephone call to references not received or questionable with written notes on call

☐ Interviews
  ☐ face-to-face
  ☐ telephone, when face-to-face not possible
    or
  ☐ second hand, when face-to-face not possible
  ☐ questions outlined for interview in advance
  ☐ notes taken during interview
  ☐ specific questions around child abuse
  ☐ specific questions around drug use
  ☐ specific questions around discipline

☐ Employment agreement
  ☐ reviewed by legal counsel

Training

☐ Staff or employee manual
  ☐ statement of philosophy, mission, goals
  ☐ personnel policies
  ☐ sexual harassment policy

☐ Precamp training
  ☐ written schedule
  ☐ specific sessions on
    ☐ human development relative to age groups
    ☐ risk management
    ☐ disciplinary policy and practice
    ☐ rules and regulations
    ☐ training specific to each job's functions

☐ hazards and known risks

☐ abuse identification

☐ abuse of camper to camper, staff to camper

☐ abuse prevention

☐ Documented

    ☐ as to who led sessions

    ☐ content of sessions

    ☐ length of sessions

    ☐ who attended (sign-up sheet)

☐ Training provided for late hires or late arrivals (documented)

☐ Tools required by job

    ☐ provided

    ☐ training given in use and care

    ☐ protective devices, with training given in use of

☐ In-service training

    ☐ documented

        ☐ dates   ☐ who led

        ☐ material covered   ☐ who attended

        ☐ length of sessions

Supervision

☐ Each employee given information as to supervisor

☐ Plan for supervision

    ☐ observation   ☐ written reprimands signed by supervisor

    ☐ formal conferences   ☐ performance appraisal system

    ☐ informal conferences

☐ Training provided supervisors

    ☐ uniform performance appraisal system

    ☐ observation methods and recording

    ☐ appropriate/inappropriate staff behavior and consequences

    ☐ conference formats, recording, techniques

☐ Plan for termination

    ☐ documented   ☐ exit interview

Other

☐ OSHA

    ☐ OSHA 101 form   ☐ OSHA poster

    ☐ OSHA 200 form   ☐ MSDS sheets

☐ Personnel files
    ☐ application
    ☐ interview notes
    ☐ notes on references contacted by telephone
    ☐ voluntary disclosure statement
      or
    ☐ criminal background check
    ☐ exit interview, if terminated
    ☐ job description, plus any documented changes
    ☐ employment agreement
    ☐ time cards, if applicable
    ☐ attendance record
    ☐ references
    ☐ supervisory notes
    ☐ any written reprimands

☐ Master file for each year of
    ☐ staff/employee manual
    ☐ staff training outline/documentation
    ☐ supplemental training
    ☐ list of staff by positions
    ☐ counselor/camper housing assignments
    ☐ health records
    ☐ incident reports
    ☐ health and safety bulletins
    ☐ emergency plans
    ☐ completed OSHA forms

☐ Staff health and accident records kept separate from personnel files

Source: *Trendlines* Vol. IX, No. 3, January/February 1999. Alpha Beta Consultants, 1351-2A Middle Gulf Dr., Sanibel Island, FL 33957.

Organizational Resources

Adventure/Challenge

Association for Challenge Course Technology
P.O. Box 970
Purcellville, VA 22132
e-mail acct@net-link.net

Association for Experiential Education
2305 Canyon Boulevard, Suite 100
Boulder, CO 80302
303-440-8844
fax 303-440-9581
www.princeton-edu/~curtis/aee
(journal, conferences, publications, accreditation program, and manual)

Cradlerock Outdoor Network
P.O. Box 1431
Princeton, NJ 08542
609-924-2919
609-466-0234
(publications, assistance in ropes/challenge courses)

National Outdoor Leadership School (NOLS)
288 Main Street
Lander, WY 82520
307-332-1220
fax 307-332-1220
www.nols.edu
(training programs)

Outward Bound National Office
Route 9D
R 2 Box 280
Garrison, NY 10524-9757
914-424-4000
800-243-8520

Project Adventure
P.O. Box 100
Hamilton, MA 01936
(publications, training, ropes courses)

Signature Research and Marketing
P.O. Box 825233
Douglasville, GA 30135
770-577-8048
fax 770-577-8085
(assistance in ropes/challenge courses)

Aquatics

American Canoe Association
7432 Alban Station Boulevard,
    Suite B232
Springfield, VA 22150-2311
705-451-0141
fax 703-451-2245
www.aca-paddler.org
(journal, newsletter, books, maps, certification programs)

American Red Cross
8111 Gatehouse Road
Falls Church, VA 22042
703-206-7120
fax 703-206-7673
www.redcross.org
*(certification, publications in swimming,
boating, and first aid)*

American Water Ski Association
799 Overlook Drive
Winter Haven, FL 33884
941-324-4341
fax 941-325-8259
e-mail usawaterski@worldnet.att.net
www.usawaterski.org
(magazine, certification)

**Boy Scouts of America
(National Office)**
1325 Walnut Hill Lane
P.O. Box 152079
Irving, TX 75015-2079
972-580-2000

**Council for National Cooperation
in Aquatics**
901 West New York Street
Indianapolis, IN 46202
(journal, conferences, publications)

Ellis and Associates, Inc.
3506 Spruce Park Circle
Kingwood, TX 77345
281-360-0606
800-742-8720
www.jellis.com
*(safety inspections, lifeguard training, design
and safety consultation for new aquatic
facilities)*

Lifesaving Society — Canada
322 Consumers Road
North York, Ontario
M2J 1P8
416-490-8844
fax 416-490-8766
e-mail experts@lifeguarding.com

**National Association of Underwater
Instructors (NAUI)**
9942 Currie Davis Drive, Suite H
Tampa, FL 33619-2667
813-628-6284
fax 813-628-8253
e-mail nauihq@naui.ww.org
www.scuba-life.com
(training programs, certification)

**National Organization for River
Sports**
212 West Cheyenne Mountain Road
Colorado Springs, CO 80906
(magazine, publications)

National Water Ski Association
P.O. Box 141
Odessa, FL 33556
813-920-2160

**Professional Association of Diving
Instructors (PADI)**
1251 East Dyer Road, Suite 100
Santa Ana, CA 92705
714-540-7234
fax 714-540-2609
www.padi.com
(training programs, certification)

**Royal Life Saving Society (RLSS) —
Australia**
National Branch
31 Victoria Street
McMahons Point
NSW 2060
61-2-957-4799
fax 61-2-929-5726
www.rlssa.org.au
(water-safety education, instructor manuals)

**Royal Life Saving Society (RLSS) —
United Kingdom**
River House, High Street
Broom Warwickshire B50 4HN
44-1-789-773994
fax 44-1-789-773995
e-mail mail@rlss.org.uk
(water-safety education, instructor manuals)

Spectrum Safety
P.O. Box 11525
St. Paul, MN 55111-0525
612-869-3744
fax 612-869-6261
e-mail ssc@pconline.com

U.S. Coast Guard
2100 2nd Street Southwest
Washington D.C. 20593-0001
202-267-2229

U.S. Coast Guard
Office of Boating Safety
800-368-5647
TTY 800-689-0816
e-mail infoline@navcen.uscg.mil
www.uscgboating.org
(magazine, publications)

U.S. SAILING Association
15 Maritime Drive
P.O. Box 1260
Portsmouth, RI 02871
401-683-0800
fax 401-683-0840
e-mail 104700.3624@compuserve.com

U.S.A. Water Ski Headquarters
(American Water Ski Association)
799 Overlook Drive
Winter Haven, FL 33884
941-342-4341
fax 941-325-8259
e-mail usawaterski@worldnet.att.net
www.usawaterski.org
(coaching clinics, nationwide clubs, waterski kids' club)

YMCA of the U.S.A.
101 North Wacker Drive, 14th Floor
Chicago, IL 60606
312-977-0031
fax 312-977-9063
www.ymca.net

First Aid/CPR

American Heart Association
7272 Greenville Avenue
Dallas, TX 75231-4596
214-706-1136
fax 214-373-0268
www.amhrt.org
(publications, research, courses)

American Red Cross
8111 Gatehouse Road
Falls Church, VA 22042
703-206-7120
fax 703-206-7673
www.redcross.org
(certification, publications in swimming, boating, and first aid)

National Safety Council
1121 Spring Lake Drive
Itasca, IL 60143-3201
630-285-1121
fax 630-285-1315
www.nsc.org
(publications)

Wilderness Medical Society
Box 2463
Indianapolis, IN 46206
317-631-1745

Wilderness Medicine Institute, Inc.
413 Main Street
P.O. Box 9
Pitkin, CO 81241
970-641-3572
fax 970-641-0882
e-mail wildmed@rmi.net
www.wildernessmed.com
(education; search and rescue, outdoor leadership, pre-hospital medicine)

Health and Wellness

American Academy of Pediatrics
141 Northwest Point Boulevard
Elk Grove Village, IL 60007-1098
847-228-5005
fax 847-228-5097
www.aap.org
(professional association, advocacy, research, publications)

American Alliance for Health Physical Education, Recreation, and Dance
1900 Association Drive
Reston, VA 20191
(journal, publications, conferences)

American Diabetes Association
1660 Duke Street
Alexandria, VA 22314
800-232-3172

Association of Camp Nurses
8504 Thorsonveien Northeast
Bemidji, MN 56601
218-586-2633
fax 218-586-3630
e-mail acn@campnurse.org
www.campnurse.org
(workshops, conferences, publications, research)

Centers for Disease Control (CDC)
1600 Clifton Road Northeast
Atlanta, GA 30333
404-488-5080
www.cdc.gov
(publications, research, statistics, training)

President's Council on Physical Fitness
HHH Building, Room 738H
200 Independence Avenue Southwest
Washington D.C. 20201
202-690-9000
fax 202-690-5211
(awards)

Horseback Riding

American Association for Horsemanship Safety
Headquarters and Training Center
Drawer 39
Fentress, TX 78622
512-488-2128
fax 512-488-2319
www.utexas.edu/dawson
(certifications, seminars, workshops)

Association for Horsemanship Safety and Education
5318 Bullard Road
Tyler, TX 75703-3612
800-399-0138
fax 903-509-2474
e-mail horsesafety@aol.com
www.cha-ahse.org
(certification, job placement, insurance program, group buying program, camp riding program guidelines)

Horsemanship Safety Association, Inc.
P.O. Box 2710
Lake Placid, FL 33862-2710
941-465-0289
800-789-8106
(publications, certification)

U.S. Pony Clubs, Inc.
Kentucky Horse Park
4071 Iron Works Pike
Lexington, KY 40511-8462
606-254-7669
fax 606-233-4652
e-mail uspc@ponyclub.org
www.uspc.org
(newsletter, publications, clinics)

Target Sports

American Archery Council
604 Forest Avenue
Park Rapids, MN 56470
218-732-2879
(youth archery program for camps)

Junior Shooting Sports/USA
P.O. Box 3207
Brentwood, TN 37024-3207
phone/fax 615-831-0485

National Field Archery Association
31407 Outer I-10
Redlands, CA 92373
(magazine, youth archery program)

National Rifle Association of America
11250 Waples Mill Road
Fairfax, VA 22030
(range operations, safety standards, teaching marksmanship, activities)

Youth Organizations

Boy Scouts of America (National Office)
1325 Walnut Hill Lane
P.O. Box 152079
Irving, TX 75015-2079
972-580-2000
(educational programs, character building)

Camp Fire Boys and Girls
4601 Madison Avenue
Kansas City, MO 64112-1278
816-756-1950, ext. 247
fax 816-756-0258

Girl Scouts of the U.S.A.
420 Fifth Avenue
New York, NY 10018-2702
800-223-0624

JCC Association
15 East 26th Street
New York, NY 10010
212-532-4949

Pioneer Ministries
55 Greenmeadow Court
Deer Park, NY 11729
516-463-5811
fax 516-463-4810
e-mail hprneh@hofstra.edu

YMCA of the U.S.A.
101 North Wacker Drive
Chicago, IL 60606
312-269-1123
fax 312-977-9063
e-mail telleen@ymcausa.org

Other Resources

American Camping Association, Inc.
5000 State Road 67 North
Martinsville, IN 46151-7902
765-342-8456
fax 765-342-2065
e-mail bookstore@aca-camps.org
www.ACAcamps.org
(Camping Magazine, catalog of publications, accreditation, conferences)

Canadian Camping Association
P.O. Box 74030
Peppertree P.O.
Edmonton, AB T5K257
877-427-6958
(journal, provincial conferences, accreditation)

Christian Camping International/USA
P.O. Box 62189
Colorado Springs, CO 80962-2189
719-260-9400
fax 719-260-6398
e-mail cciusa@cciusa.org
www.cciusa.org
(journal, newsletter, conferences, publications)

Environmental Protection Agency
Washington D.C. 20640
(President's Environmental Youth Awards)

International Association of Conference Center Administrators
9482 Glengarriff Drive
Brewerton, NY 13029-9529
315-676-4130
fax 315-676-2598
e-mail alfriacca@aol.com
www.iacca.org
(conference, publications, personnel referral)

International Association of Conference Centers
243 North Lindbergh Boulevard
St. Louis, MO 63141-7851
(magazine, directory, workshops, conference)

National Audubon Society
700 Broadway
New York, NY 10003
(magazine)

National Consortium on Alternatives for Youth at Risk, Inc.
5250 17th Street, Suite 107
Sarasota, FL 34235
813-378-4793
(newsletter)

National Fire Protection Association
P.O. Box 9101
Quincy, MA 02269-9101
617-770-3000
fax 617-770-0700
e-mail library@nfpa.org
www.nfpa.org
(publications)

National Recreation and Parks Association
22377 Belmont Ridge Road
Ashburn, VA 20148
703-858-0784
fax 703-858-0794
(journal, conventions, publications)

National Sanitation Foundation
P.O. Box 130140
Ann Arbor, MI 48102
(food service, swimming pool, and water system maintenance publications)

National Wildlife Federation
8925 Leesburg Pike
Vienna, VA 22184-0001
703-790-4000
www.nwf.org
(magazines, publications)

OBIS (Outdoor Biology Instruction Strategies)
Delta Education, Inc.
P.O. Box 915
Nashua, NH 03061
800-258-1302
(publications)

Wilderness Education Association
1160 Otter Creek Road
Nashville, TN 37220
e-mail wea@edge.net
www.ebl.org/wea
(training, certification)

International Resources

These agencies currently provide assistance to camps desiring international counselors for summer programs. For specific information, communicate directly with the agencies.

BUNACAMP
P.O. Box 430
Southbury, CT 06488
203-264-0901
800-GO-BUNAC

Camp America
102 Greenwich Avenue
Greenwich, CT 06830
203-869-9090
800-72-STAFF

Camp Counselors U.S.A.
2330 Marinship Way, Suite 250
Sausalito, CA 94865
415-339-2728
415-617-8390
800-999-CAMP (2267)

International Camp Counselor Exchange Program
38 West 88th Street
New York, NY 10025
212-787-7706

International Camping Fellowship, Inc.
Camp Tawingo
Rural Route 1
Huntsville P1H 2J2 Canada
705-789-5612
fax 705-789-6624
e-mail tawingo@tawingo.net
www.tawingo.net/icf.htm

YMCA International Camp Counselor Program
71 West 23rd Street, Suite 1904
New York, NY 10010
212-727-8814
888-477-9622
e-mail ips@ymcanyc.org

Appendix E

Governmental Resources

The following topics often arise in the operation of camps. In each case, the applicable federal, state, and local agencies most often related to the topic are indicated.

These tables are to serve as a general guide. In each case, it is important to check the exact provisions of the regulation and its applicability by contacting the appropriate agency or camping association.

KEY

\# Occasionally county/city ordinances may cover this area. It is best to check.

(L) Indicates that program is implemented through local offices.

(R) Indicates that the best source of information is the department's regional office.

(S) Indicates that program is implemented through state offices.

( ) Indicates alternate names used by some governmental units.

TOPIC	FEDERAL	STATE
Accommodations 　housing 　　restrooms 　　program 　　dining facility	Department of Justice, Civil Rights Division, Office of American Disabilities Act; Department of Transportation; Federal Communications Commission; Architectural and Transportation Barriers Compliance Board	Civil Rights
Boat 　operator's license 　　inspections 　　licenses	Coast Guard (if on water under jurisdiction of USCG)	Department of Natural Resources
Building 　plumbing 　codes 　electrical 　inspections	—	State Building Commissioner
Child Labor 　regulations 　work permits	Department of Labor	Labor
Camper Assistance Funds	Department of Health and Human Services (HHS) (S)	Public Welfare
Employment Practices	Department of Justice, Civil Rights Division, Equal Employment Opportunity Commission Office of American Disabilities Act	Civil Rights
Employment Services	Department of Labor (S)	Labor, Employment Security
FICA (Social Security)	Department of HHS, Social Security Administration	Employment Security

LOCAL	REGULATIONS	SERVICES
—	"Reasonable accommodation" for persons with disabilities must be provided in existing central facilities, some housing and restrooms, and in program. New construction must take disabled into consideration.	—
#	Many states are developing legislation mandating personal flotation devices.	Training programs for boat safety. Rescue services on federal waters.
Building (engineer)	Permits to build new structures or remodel existing structures generally required locally. Certain specifications may have to be met in building or remodeling. There may be regulations for licensed electricians or plumbers in some locales. New construction cannot use lead solder.	—
#	Hours, wages, working conditions, machinery operation (e.g., slicers, deep-fat fryers).	—
Public Welfare	—	Various programs provide fees for clients to attend camp (title xx, ADC, etc.). Block grants to states.
Human Rights Commission (Civil Rights)	Must not discriminate because of disability, race, color, religion, national origin, or sex. In some locales, includes sexual preference. Must provide "reasonable accommodation" to employees with disabilities. Restricts how health information on employees is gathered and maintained.	—
—	Required to report social security number and address on new hires to state. Must give employee written notice if credit bureau retained to do background check.	Lists job openings and persons with qualifications seeking employment.
—	Employers must withhold percentage of employees' wages and also pay percentage tax on wages. International staff exempt from social security withholding, but question about needing social security number.	—

TOPIC	FEDERAL	STATE
Fire	—	Fire Marshall
Fish	Department of Interior, Fish and Wildlife Services	Natural Resources (Fish and Game)
Forestry	Department of Agriculture, Forest Service (R)	Natural Resources (Forestry)
Game	Department of Interior, Fish and Wildlife Services	Natural Resources (Fish and Game)
Health	Department of HHS, Centers for Disease Control	Health (Environmental Resources, Environmental Health, Health and Sanitation, etc.)
International Staff	Department of Justice, Information Agency	—
Lands	Department of Interior, National Parks Service	Department of State Parks
	Department of Agriculture, Forest Service	Department of Forestry (Natural Resources)
	Corps of Engineers	—
	Department of Interior, Bureau of Land Management	—

LOCAL	REGULATIONS	SERVICES
Fire Departments	Inspections and certain protective equipment often required.	Inspections; advice.
—	Licenses to fish (S).	Advice on stocking waterways; resource persons.
—	—	Advice on reforesting lands; often seedlings available at low cost; resource persons.
—	Licenses to hunt or permits to keep "wild" animals/birds (S).	Advice on game management; resource persons.
Health and Sanitation	All but four states* cover camps under this department.	Water testing required; inspection required in some states, voluntary in others; chlorination required; advice on food service, sanitation, health services.
—	International students studying in the U.S.A. must have an F Visa. International students coming from outside U.S.A. to work in camps must have a J-1 Visa, normally secured through a sponsoring organization (see Appendix D). Q Visa is also available. There are certain requirements to qualify for a visa, as well as insurance. See *CampLine* 2:1, May 1993; and 2:3, February 1994. Cannot hire nurses due to INS, USIA regulations.	—
City/County Park Department	Applications for use of land for trips or campsites. User fees apply.	Visitor centers; park naturalists; campsites; campground sites; camp leases. Permits required.
City/County Forest Preserves	Applicable for use of land for trips or camp.	Use permits for tripping, harvesting, permanent camps, overnight camping in certain areas. Forest personnel excellent resource persons.
—	Applications for use of land for trips or camp. Diversion of water from waterways under USCE jurisdiction requires permit.	Land adjoins water impoundments and provides overnight campsites or permanent camp locations in certain areas. Resource for development of dams, waterway diversion.
—	Applicable for use of land for trips or camp.	—

TOPIC	FEDERAL	STATE
Loans	Small Business Administration (R)	—
Minimum Wage	Department of Labor, Labor, Wage and Hour Division	Labor
OSHA (Occupational Safety and Health Administration)	Department of Labor (OSHA)	Labor, OSHA

LOCAL	REGULATIONS	SERVICES
—	—	Low-cost loans to small for-profit businesses. Publications also available.
—	All employees of an organized camp or a religious/nonprofit educational conference center are exempt if open to the public and operating seven months or less a year. For information on federal exemption, see *CampLine* 2:1, May 1993. However, some states cover camps under their minimum wage law, and that law exceeds the federal exemption. Some states only exempt counselors/ program staff, and others specify a minimum wage or percentage of minimum wage.	Publications; telephone advice without identifying your organization.
—	Safety practices as they affect the employee in the camp work setting. Applies to all parts of work setting (e.g., ladders, hard hats, exits, floor surfaces, stairs). Requires poster in prominent place (GP08126-235) and on file a record of injuries/illnesses of employees which grew out of work conditions. Requires bloodborne pathogens precautions and lock out/tag out for power equipment/ tools (OSHA Code Federal Regulations; Title 29, Parts 10-1.1 to 1901.441) (Gen. Indus. Pt. 1 s/n 869-00109-2). MSDS sheets must be accessible; protection for closed spaces. Camps are required to provide: copy of regulations, copies of forms/ posters, health log of injuries/ illnesses, universal precautions (equipment/supplies, gowns, gloves, masks, etc.), testing for Hepatitis B, exposure control plan, offer vaccination for Hepatitis B to employees who primarily provide first aid. See *CampLine* 1:2, May 1992; 2:2, October 1993; 3:2, October 1994.	Provide copy of regulations and copies of forms/posters.

TOPIC	FEDERAL	STATE
Overtime	Department of Labor: Labor, Wage and Hour Division (camps generally exempt)	Labor
Soil Conservation and Erosion	Department of Agriculture, Forest Service, Soil Conservation Services (L)	Natural Resources
Special Milk Program	Department of Agriculture, Food and Nutrition Service (R)	Education
Summer Feeding Program	Department of Agriculture, Food and Nutrition Service (R)	Education**
Surplus Commodities	Department of Agriculture (R)	Education — except Kansas

Taxes
    real estate
    bed
    recreation
    nonprofit
	—	Revenue (Taxation, Assessor) Some states

income	Internal Revenue Service	Revenue (Taxation, Assessor)
Sales	—	Revenue (Taxation)
Unemployment Compensation (FUTA and SUTA)	Department of Labor	Labor, Employment Security

LOCAL	REGULATIONS	SERVICES
See Minimum Wage	—	—
Soil Conservation District Office	—	Soil survey; water and soil conservation. Advice on use of land for recreation purposes.
—	Camp must be 501(c)(3).	Offers reimbursement to camp for a portion of cost of each half pint of milk served campers under 18.
—	Camp must be 501(c)(3).	Offers reimbursement to camp for meals served to eligible campers. Check current eligibility requirements.
—	Camp must be 501(c)(3).	Various commodities (e.g., flour, rice) are available to camps at beginning of camp season. Items and quantity are diminishing in availability.
#	State and local real estate taxes are usual. Some states provide exemption for certain nonprofit groups.	
#	All camps must withhold federal/state income taxes for employees and submit payment regularly. Individuals must file income tax returns. All corporations must file income tax returns, even if corporation is tax exempt. Counselors and international staff usually exempt from withholding due to being under minimum income.	—
#	Some states and/or local units have sales tax applicable to lodging and/or meals and/or items sold in camp.	—
—	Camps are exempt from paying federal unemployment compensation taxes on employees who are full-time students. All camps must pay state unemployment compensation taxes unless specifically exempted by state law or state follows federal law.	—

TOPIC	FEDERAL	STATE

Vehicles
    registration
    licenses
    operator's licenses
    inspections
	Department of Transportation (L),
	National Highway Traffic Safety
	Administration
		Motor Vehicle Bureau

Water	Environmental Protection Agency	Health
Worker's Compensation	Department of Labor	Industrial Board (Labor)

*Colorado and Michigan (Social Services), New Hampshire (Water Supply and Pollution), and New Mexico (Environmental Improvement Agency).

**Some states do not administer the program directly, and the Regional USDA, Food and Nutrition Service office works with camps in those states.

LOCAL	REGULATIONS	SERVICES
#	Regulations vary from state to state, and with type vehicle. All states require commercial driver's license of drivers of vehicles designed to seat 16 persons including driver. Check other requirements in your state. New buses or passenger vans used to transport children to/from schools require special protection package.	—
Health or Sanitation	Clean Water Act; Safe Drinking Water Act. Licenses for operators of water systems required; water tests are often required; sewer systems are regulated; filtration and treatment of water sources regulated as well as wellhead protection.	Safe Drinking Water/Clean Water Acts. Telephone hotline is available to answer questions. See *CampLine* 2:3, February 1994 and 3:1, May 1995.
—	Insurance is required. International counselors with J-1 visas are employees unless state specifically exempts.	—

ACA Code of Ethics

CODE OF ETHICS FOR ALL MEMBERS
OF THE AMERICAN CAMPING ASSOCIATION

1. I shall conduct myself in a manner consistent with the association's mission to serve organized camps, affiliated programs, and the public by promoting better camping for all.

   To accomplish this mission, ACA:

   - Educates camp personnel to create positive growth experiences for children, teens, and adults, using the outdoors responsibly as a program environment;
   - Protects the public by promoting health and safety practices and effective management through accreditation, certification, and education programs;
   - Promotes advocacy of issues affecting camps; and
   - Communicates the value of camp experiences to the public and encourages camp opportunities for all.

2. I shall recognize my responsibility for the welfare of others in my care.

3. I shall abide by and comply with the relevant laws of the community.

4. I shall be a member in the proper ACA classification as currently defined by the ACA National Board of Directors; and I shall disclose my affiliation with ACA only in a manner specifically permitted by the association.

5. I shall make a clear distinction of any statement or action as to whether I speak as an individual member or a representative of this association.

6. I shall respect the confidences of ACA members, camps, and other constituents within the camp community; however, I shall accept responsibility to pass on to the appropriate ACA official, information I deem reliable that will help protect the camp community against unethical practices by any individual.

7. I shall be truthful and fair to all in representations I make regarding any camp.

EXEMPLARY ETHICAL PRACTICES
FOR CAMP OWNERS, DIRECTORS, AND EXECUTIVES

The association recognizes the camp owner, director, and executive as the primary professional persons assuming the greatest responsibility for actual camp practices. Therefore, in addition to the Code of Ethics for all members, any member or nonmember operating a camp accredited by the American Camping Association agrees to subscribe to the following **Exemplary Ethical Practices for Camp Owners, Directors, and Executives**.

8. I shall endeavor to provide an environment conducive to promoting and protecting the physical and emotional well-being of the campers and staff.

9. I shall seek to instill in my staff and campers a reverence for the land and its waters and all living things, and an ecological conscience which reflects the conviction of individual responsibility for the health of that environment.

10. I shall follow equal opportunity practices in employment and camper enrollment.

11. I shall endeavor to employ persons based upon factors necessary to the performance of the job and the operation of the camp.

12. I shall be truthful and fair in securing and dealing with campers, parents/guardians, and staff.

13. I shall provide a written enrollment policy for all camper/family applicants including fees, payment schedules, discounts, dates of arrival and departure, together with a clearly stated refund policy.

14. I shall provide for each staff member a written job description and employment agreement including period of employment, compensation, benefits, and exceptions.

15. I shall promptly consult with parents or guardians of any camper or minor staff member as to the advisability of removing him/her from camp should it be clear that he/she is not benefiting from the camp experience or the camper's or minor staff member's actions have created this need.

16. I shall make arrangements with the parents or guardians for the return of their camper(s) or minor-age staff member(s).

17. I shall pay the correct national and section service fees as established by the ACA National Board of Directors and the ACA Section Board of Directors.

Adopted 2-26-95, ACA Council of Delegates
Revised 3-2-97, ACA Council of Delegates

Precamp Training Topics

The codes following each topic refer to specific ACA-Accredited Standards for Camp Programs and Services.

Site and Food Service

- Proper handling and use of power tools — SF-11
- Proper handling of flammable or poisonous materials, e.g., kerosene, cleaning agents — *SF-2
- Required general maintenance routines, e.g., cleaning, reporting maintenance problems — SF -8 written
- Food preparation, storage, and handling procedures (as applicable) — SF-22 through SF-25 and SF-27 through SF-30

Transportation

- Bus safety procedures and group management — TR-9 and TR-10 written
- Orientation of safety regulations and procedures in vehicles provided for passengers — TR-11
- Procedures in case of accident during transportation — TR-8 written
- Safety procedures for orderly arrival and departure and for loading and unloading of vehicles — TR-3
- Training for vehicle drivers — TR-18 and TR-19 written
- Transportation of persons in nonpassenger vehicles — TR-4
- Transportation policies that specify supervision ratios of staff to campers, availability and location of health information, and permission-to-treat forms — TR-7 written

Health and Wellness

- Procedures for informing staff of special needs of campers — HW-9
- Responsibilities of staff for camper health care — HW-12 written
- Providing health care and emergency treatment when out of camp — HW-13
- How prescription and nonprescription drugs are stored at camp — HW-18, 1–2

- Records kept in health log and incident reports filed — HW-19, A and B

Operational Management

- Camper release procedures — OM-19
- Emergency communications plan — OM-17
- General camp safety regulations and rules — OM-8 written, OM-9 written, OM-10, and OM-14
- Completing incident and accident reports — OM-15
- Missing persons procedures — OM-16
- Policy and procedures covering: personal property — OM-12
- Smoking policy — OM-13
- Procedures for dealing with possible intruders — OM-7 written

Human Resources

- Behavior management — HR-16 written
- Camper/staff ratios — HR-9 written
- Personnel policies — HR-8 written
- Sensitive issue policy — HR-17
- Staff/camper interaction — HR-15
- Staff training in diversity — HR-5
- Supervision of campers — HR-14 written
- Supervision of staff — HR-18 written
- Supervisor training — HR-19 written
- Training for their particular job — HR-7

Program Design and Activities

- Competency demonstration — PD-19
- Details for designated person left in camp — PD-11
- Emergency information — PD-10
- Environmental activities — PD-9
- Equipment availability — PD-16
- Operating procedures for each specialized activity — PD-17
- Procedures for controlled access of activity areas — PD-15
- Procedures for overnights and trips — PD-1
- Program goals and outcomes — PD-6
- Safety orientation for participants — PD-18
- Use of program equipment — PD-4

In addition, staff leading special activities such as archery, boating, etc., will provide training/orientation to general staff and campers before use.

Sample Personnel Hiring Log

SAMPLE PERSONNEL HIRING LOG

Applicant's name _____

Position sought _____

Application Information

Date application received _____

Certifications Received   Date

_____   _____

_____   _____

_____   _____

_____   _____

_____   _____

Criminal Background Checks

Date criminal background records check requested from:

Local _____   State _____   Federal _____

Date criminal background information received from:

Local _____   State _____   Federal _____

and/or Volunteer Disclosure Form received _____

References and Employment

Date requests for references sent _____   Dates references received:

Reference #1 _____

Reference #2 _____

Reference #3 _____

	Date Past Employment Requested	Verification Received
Employer #1	_____	_____
Employer #2	_____	_____
Employer #3	_____	_____
Employer #4	_____	_____

Personal Interview

Person doing interview_____

Date interview completed _____

Job Offer

Date employment agreement sent _____
Date signed agreement received _____

Other Information Requested After Hire

Date health records received _____
Date I-9 received _____
Date W-2 received _____
Reasonable accommodations requested _____

_____

Other Notes

_____
_____
_____
_____
_____

Outdoor Living Skills

Be a Part of Shaping the Future

As camping professionals and outdoor educators, do your campcraft, hiking, and nature awareness programs and practices measure up to current concerns about the environment? Are the campers bored? Then take those blues away and make them green. With the OLS program, campers learn to make responsible decisions while participating in activities such as hiking, cookouts, overnights, games, and nature exploration. They also learn to understand the impact of such activities on the environment.

Great Outdoor Program for Youth

- Customize the program for your campers; earn patches in a few days or over several summers.
- Build a sense of accomplishment and keep your campers coming back.
- Start where you'll be challenged — this well-organized program allows you to begin at any level.

Level-One Participant Requirements

(This is a sample of the requirements for level one; most include group planning and interaction.)

- Plan a half-day hike. Know what to wear and what to take.
- Pack for and go on a half-day hike.
- Plan a lunch that won't spoil. Properly dispose of your trash.
- Play a game that helps you understand ecology.
- Do an activity using your senses.

An Excellent Resource for Precamp Training

- Plan your staff training.
- Learn how to work with all ages of campers.
- Update your nature program with current environmental concerns.
- Learn methods and tips for working with groups.

- Use sample training modules.
- Meet U.S. Forest Service guidelines for minimum-impact camping.

Adult Cards Document Skills

Program Leader Course is for staff or volunteers who work directly with campers. The course will include minimum-impact camping and outdoor skills needed to offer the OLS program to campers. Program Leader cards provide documented training in outdoor living skills activities. This course addresses ACA 1999 standards PD-1, PD-2, PD-3, PD-7, and PD-9.

Instructors Course is for ACA members and nonmembers who are 18 years old or older, with camping experience and outdoor skills. The course covers adult education and training methods, and has a complete session-by-session curriculum for training Program Leaders and counselors. The manual also explains how to administer the OLS program in a camp.

Training

The OLS program can be used by any group. If you would like more information on training, check out the OLS Workshops on the Professional Development Calendar at ACA's Web site: www.ACAcamps.org. Training schedules can be found in section newsletters and *Camping Magazine*; or contact an ACA section or the ACA national office, 765-342-8456, ext. 320, or e-mail aca@aca-camps.org.

Appendix J

Selected Resources

HUMAN RESOURCES/STAFFING

Books

Brandwein, Michael. 1999. *Training Traffic Staff*. Lincolnshire, IL: Michael Brandwein.

Coutellier, Connie and Henchey. Kathleen. 2000. *Camp is for Campers: A Counselor's Guide to Youth Development*. Martinsville, IN: American Camping Association.

Ditter, Bob. 1997. *Trail Signs and Compass Points*. Boston, MA: Little Fox Productions.

Eitington, Julius E. 1996. *The Winning Trainer*. Houston, TX: Gulf Publishing.

Johnson, Becca Cowan and For Kids Sake, Inc. 1992. *For Their Sake: Recognizing, Responding to, and Reporting Child Abuse*. Martinsville, IN: American Camping Association.

Klein, Edie. 1992. *It's My Job: Job Descriptions for Over 30 Camp Jobs*. Martinsville, IN: American Camping Association.

Patterson, John C. 1998. *Staff Screening Tool Kit: Keeping the Bad Apples Out of Your Organization*. Washington, DC: Nonprofit Risk Management Center.

Videos

American Camping Association. *So You Want to Be a Supervisor: An Educational Package to Train Camp Supervisory Staff*. 1996. Martinsville, IN: American Camping Association.

Ditter, Bob. *To Tell the Truth*. 1990. Martinsville, IN: American Camping Association.

SITE AND FACILITIES

Books

Burch, Monte. *Pole Building Projects*.1993. Pownal, VT: Storey Books.

Forster, Gary. *This Old Camp: Camp Property Management*. 1994.Colebrook, CT: Camp Jewell YMCA.

Goltsman, Gilbert, Wohlford and Kirk. *The Accessibility Checklist: An Evaluation System for Buildings and Outdoor Settings*. Berkeley, CA: MIG Communications.

338

Lucchetti, Robert C. *Lightly on the Land: The SCA Trail-Building Maintenance Manual.* 1996. Seattle, WA: The Mountaineers.

MARKETING

Books

Bade, Nicholas E. *Marketing Without Money for Small and Midsize Businesses.* 1999. Willoughby, OH: Halle House Publishers.

Clark, Silvanna. *Taming the Recreation Jungle: 100 Ways to Improve the Quality of Recreation Programs.* 1993. Seattle, WA: Book Partners, Inc.

Herron, Douglas B. *Marketing Nonprofit Programs and Services.* 1997. San Francisco, CA: Jossey-Bass, Inc., Publishers.

RISK MANAGEMENT

Books

American Camping Association. *Standards for Day and Resident Camps.* 1998. Martinsville, IN: American Camping Association.

American Camping Association. *The Resource Pack.* 1998. Martinsville, IN: American Camping Association.

American Camping Association. *Resource Pack II.* 1998. Martinsville, IN: American Camping Association.

Coutellier, Connie. *Management of Risks and Emergencies.* 1993. Kansas City, MI: Camp Fire, Inc.

Jackson, Peggy M.; White, Leslie T.; and Herman, Melanie L. *Mission Accomplished: A Practical Guide To Risk Management for Nonprofits.* 1997. Washington, DC: Nonprofit Risk Management Center.

Videos

American Camping Association. *Camp White Cloud Goes to Court–Video and Leader's Guide.* 1994. Martinsville, IN: American Camping Association.

American Camping Association. *So You Want to Be a Supervisor?* 1996. Martinsville, IN: American Camping Association.

HEALTH AND WELLNESS

Books

Forgey, William. *Wilderness Medicine: Beyond First Aid, Fifth Edition.* 2000. Guilford,
   CT: Globe Pequot.

Lishner, Kris Miller and Bruya, Margaret Auld. *Creating A Healthy Camp Community.*
   1994. Martinsville, IN: American Camping Association.

LEADERSHIP

Books

Covey, Stephen R. *Seven Habits of Highly Effective People.* 1989. New York, NY: Simon
   and Schuster.

Graham, John. *Outdoor Leadership: Techniques, Common Sense and Self-Confidence.*
   1997. Seattle, WA: The Mountaineers.

Hunsacker, Phillip L. and Alessandra, Anthony J. *The Art of Managing People.* 1986.
   New York: Simon and Schuster, Inc.

Game

   American Camping Association. *S'Mores and Other Sticky Stuff.* 1998. Martinsville,
      IN: American Camping Association.

BUSINESS AND FINANCE

Books

American Camping Association. *1999 Salary Study.*1998. Martinsville, IN: American
   Camping Association.

Finney, Robert G. *Essentials of Business Budgeting.* 1995. New York, NY: American
   Management Association.

Tyson, Eric and Schell, Jim. *Small Business for Dummies.* 1998. Foster City, CA: IDG
   Books Worldwide.

FOOD SERVICE

Books

Reath, Jim. *A Recipe File for Camps.* 1998. Muskegan, MI: Jim Reath.

Shugart, Grace and Molt, Mary. *Food for Fifty.* 1997. Upper Saddle River, NJ: Prentice-
   Hall.

Spain, Viki Kappel. *The Camp Kitchen Guidebook.* 1996. Angelus Oaks, CA: Viki
   Kappel Spain.

TRANSPORTATION

Books

Rypkema, Pam. *Avoiding a Crash Course: Auto Liability. Insurance, and Safety for Nonprofits.* 1995. Washington, DC: Nonprofit Risk Management Center.

MISSION/PHILOSOPHY

Books

Hill, Amie and Herman, Richard. *The Interlocken Differences: Four Decades of Experiential Learning and Community.* 1998. Dubuque, IA: Kendall/Hunt Publishing Company.

Nolan, Timothy; Goldstein, Leonard; and Pfeiffer, William. *Plan or Die: 10 Keys to Organizational Success.* 1993. San Diego, CA: Pfieffer and Company.

YOUTH DEVELOPMENT/BEHAVIOR

Books

Beker, Jerome; Magnuson, Doug; Magnuson, Connie; and Beker, David. *What Do I Do Now?* 1996. Martinsville, IN: American Camping Association.

Ditter, Bob. *Life-Lines and Safety-Nets, A Staff Resource and Training Booklet.* 1994. Boston, MA: Little Fox Productions, Ltd.

Nagel, Myra. *What To Do Instead of Screaming.* 1980. Benton, AR: Galleon Press.

Pastore, Michael. *Dynamite Counselors Don't Explode.* 1993. Dayville, CT: Zorba Press.

Pipher, Mary. *Reviving Ophelia: Saving the Selves of Adolescent Girls.* 1995. New York, NY: Ballantine Books.

Pollack, William. *Real Boys.* 1998. New York, NY: Henry Holt & Company.

TARGET POPULATIONS/DIVERSITY

Books

Barbarash, Lorraine. *Multicultural Games.* 1997. Champaign, IL: Human Kinetics.

Chappelle, Sharon; Bigman, Lisa; and Hillyer, Francesca. *Diversity in Action.* 1998. Covington, GA: Adventure, Inc.

Kasser, Susan L. *Inclusive Games.* 1995. Champaign, IL: Human Kinetics.

Roswal, Glenn; Dowd, Karen J.; and Bynum, Jerry. *Including People with Disabilities in Camp Programs: A Resource for Camp Directors.* 1997. Martinsville, IN: American Camping Association.

STRATEGIC PLANNING

Books

Allison, Michael and Kaye, Jude. *Strategic Planning for Nonprofit Organizations.* 1997. New York, NY: John Wiley & Sons.

Bryson, John. *Strategic Planning for Public and Nonprofit Organizations: A Guide to Strengthening and Sustaining Organizational Achievement.* 1995. San Francisco, CA: Jossey-Bass Publishers.

PROGRAM DESIGN AND ACTIVITIES

Books

American Camping Association. *The Outdoor Living Skills Instructor's Manual.* Martinsville, IN: American Camping Association.

Ford, Phyllis M. *Take A New Bearing.* 1995. Martinsville, IN: American Camping Association.

Henderson, Karla A. and Bialeschki, M. Deborah. *Evaluating Leisure Services: Making Enlighted Decisions.* 1995. State College, PA: Venture Publishing, Inc.

Kasser, Susan L. *Inclusive Games.* 1995. Champaign, IL: Human Kinetics.

Milford, Susan. *Kids' Nature Book: 365 Indoor/Outdoor Activities and Experiences.* 1996. Charlotte, VT: Williamson Publishing.

Morton, Annie; Prosser, Angie; and Spangler, Sue. *Great Special Events.* 1991. State College, PA: Venture Publishing, Inc.

Priest, Simon and Gass, Micheal A. *Effective Leadership in Adventure Programming.* 1997. Champaign, IL: Human Kinetics.

VOLUNTEERS

Books

Carner, John. *Boards that Make a Difference.* 1990. San Francisco, CA: Jossey-Bass Publishers.

Isley, Paul J. *Enhancing the Volunteer Experience.* 1990. San Francisco, CA: Jossey-Bass Publishers.

Levin, Mark. *The Gift of Leadership.* 1997. Columbia, MD: B.A.I., Inc.

Index

A

AAHPERD (American Association of Health, Physical Education, Recreation and Dance), 4–5
abuse. *See* **child abuse; sexual abuse; substance abuse**
abusive behavior, 44
accommodations for disabled persons, 69
accounting practices, 241–253
  annual audit, 241–244
accounts list, 249
accreditation, x, 7, 292–293
  risk management and, 183
Accreditation Standards for Camp Programs and Services, personnel policies and, 87–88
activities, 70
  age appropriateness, 64–65
  all-camp, 62–63
  bedtime and, 63
  early camps, 2
  evening, resident camps, 63
  narrow ranges, 64–66
  nature-oriented, 70
  outdoor-oriented, 69
  pacing/flow, 63
  physical skills, 70
  precamp training topics, 333
  program development and, 54–55
  scheduled, varying, 63
  small-group, 55–56
  social recreation, 70–71
  specific program activities, 69–71
  spiritually-oriented, 71
  supervision, liability and, 176
  total-group, 55–56
  vehicular, 70
  visitors and, 70
activities and special concerns
  eight to ten year olds, 37
  eleven to thirteen year olds, 38

five to seven year olds, 36
fourteen to seventeen year olds, 39
ADHD (Attention Deficit Hyperactivity Disorder), 44
adjudicated youth, Outward Bound and, 5
administrative roles of camp director, 15
administrative services, 187–216
  computer software, 259–261
  evaluation, 287–288
  food service, 203–211
  health services, 187–202
  staff, 140–141
  transportation, 211–216
adult education groups, 6
adults and senior citizens, 39, 67
adventure/challenge resources, 312
advertising
  billboards, 236
  camper fairs, 235
  direct mail, 236–237
  posters, 236
  print ads, 236
  recruiting and, 92
  Web page, 236
AEE (Association for Experiential Education), 5
age appropriateness
  activities, 64–65
  equipment, 72
age ranges served by camp, 40
age, employment and, 84
aggression, 44, 45
  increased, 44
AIDS, 45
alcohol, 47
  staff and, 88
all-camp activities, 62–63
alumni, reporting to, 295
American Camping Association, 4
  Code of Ethics, 330–331
  membership, 114

American Canoe Association, 77
American Heart Association, 77
American Red Cross, 76
American Red Cross Standard First Aid, 77
American Water Ski Association, 77
Americans With Disabilities Act of 1990 (ADA), 40
annual audit, 241–244
annual giving, 265–266
Anorexia Nervosa, 45–46
applications for employment, 94–97
aquatic activity, 76–77
  organizations, 312–314
  staff requirements, 76–77
arrangement of office, 259
articles of incorporation, 23
arts, 69
arts and crafts, 69
assessments, program development and, 54–55
assets, physical facility as, 149–150
at will employment, 89, 109
audits, 241–244
Australia, expansion to, 3
auto insurance, 174
avoiding risks, 169

B

baby-sitting service, staff benefits, 86
background checks, hiring and, 94–97
background, hiring and, 75
balance sheet, 245
Balch, Ernest, 2
bank, camper bank, 256–261
bath facility, group living and, 66
bed-wetting, 44, 46
Bedini, Leandra, 68
bedtime, activities and, 63
behavior management, 41–48
  abusive behavior, 44

changing unacceptable
behavior, 43
imitating behavior, 42
medical conditions and, 44–48
praise and, 42
psychological conditions and,
44–48
benefits, 85–87
benefits to consumer, 222–225
benevolent autocratic leadership, 17
Benson, Reuel A., 75
Bialeschki, M. Deborah, 68
Bible study groups, 71
billboards, 236
Binge (BED), 45–46
bloodborne pathogens, lifeguards
and, 77
Blue Lake & Rocky Shore, 1
blueprints of buildings, 153
boards
evaluation, 288–290
volunteers, 275–278
Boy Scouts of America, 3, 76
boys camps, 3–4
brochures, 23, 232–233
recruitment and, 90–111
budgeting, 247
cash flow and, 253
expense projections, 248–251
expenses, adjusting, 251–253
final budget development, 251
income projections, 248–251
building codes, physical facility, 153
buildings, depreciation, 251
Bulimia, 45–46
burnout, 144–145
child abuse and, 119
bus programs, 63
business executives, Outward
Bound and, 5

C

cafeteria style meals, 207
Camp Arey, 2
camp as community, 18
Camp Chocorua, 2
Camp Director's Primer, disabled
persons and, 68
camp director. See director, 13
Camp Directors Association
of America, 3–4, 4
Camp Horsemanship
Association, 77
camp office. See office
Camp Professional Discussion
Group, Internet, 260
camp store, 256–261
camp visits, marketing and, 229
camper bank, 256–261

camper-to-camper abuse, 44
campers
as customers, 219–220
cash and, 256–261
evaluation, 291–292
fees, 256
reporting to, 294–295
returning, 221
staff children as, 86
Camping magazine, 4
camping professionals, 297–303
camping, values of, 8–9
camps
day, 5
defined, ix
description, 7–11
increases in, 4–5
objectives, 4–5
resident, 5
specialty, 4
types, 5–7
Canada, 1
Canadian Camping Association, 4
capital campaigns, fund-raising, 266
Carlson, Reynold E., 9
cash flow
budgeting and, 253
planning chart, 252
cash flow statement, 245
cash payments, 255–256
cash, campers and, 256–261
CCI (Christian Camping
International), 5
centralized programs, 56–59
individuals and, 61
living groups, 60–61
supervisory lines, 78–79
certification, employment and, 84
certifying bodies, 76–77
Character Education in Camping
Seminar, 298
chartering vehicles, 211–212
checklist for risk management,
308–311
child abuse
interview notes and, 107–108
preventing, 100–103
risk management and, 177–178
training and, 119–120
warning signs, 108–109
children influencing parents,
219–220
Christian Camping International
membership, 114
church affiliated camps, 3
CIC (Certified Insurance
Counselor), 171
citizenship, 9
civil law, 167
civil war interest, camping and, 1

cleanup, mealtimes, 206–207
clientele, specialized, 67–69
climate of interview, 106
clothing lists, 49
coaching leadership, 17, 131
Code of Ethics, 330–331
colleges and universities, recruiting
from, 91
Commercial Driver License,
212–214
commercial general liability
insurance, 172–173
committees
evaluation, 288–290
volunteers, 275–278
community groups, recruitment
and, 92
community relations, staff and, 89
compensation, 85–87
competition
market analysis and, 221
target population and, 33
computers, camp office, 259–261
conceptual skills, director and, 17
concluding interview, 107
conference groups, 6
conference/retreat center, ix, 9–11
hospitality services, 10
conferences, counselors and
supervisor, 134–135
consultative leadership, 17
contracted services, food service,
210–211
contractual liability, 167
contribution income.
See fund-raising
controlling flow of interview, 107
cookout meals, 207–208
core areas, x
corporate board, reporting to, 294
correcting, supervision and,
131–132
counselor-in-training programs, 91
counselors. See also staff
end-of-season performance
appraisal, 135–140
supervising, 132–141
CPCU (Chartered Property
Casualty Underwriter), 171
CPR (cardiopulmonary
resuscitation), 77, 189
criminal acts, 167
crisis management, 176–178
criteria for evaluations, 282–283
cultural differences, development
and, 35
current societal trends or issues,
development and, 35
customer interest, program
development and, 54

D

D and O insurance (directors and officers), 173
data gathering, evaluations, 283–285
day camps, 5, 50
  food service, 203
  orientation, staff, 115–116
  transportation, 215–216
decentralized programs, 56–59
  individuals and, 61
  living groups, 60–61
  supervisory lines, 78–79
decision-making skills, 9
democracy, camping and, 8–9
democratic leadership, 17
demographic information, 32
depreciation, 251
developmental characteristics by age group, 36–39
developmental needs
  of participants, 35–40
  emphasis of program and, 65
Dimock, Hedley S., definition of camp, 7
direct mail, 236–237
  fund-raising, 266
director
  administrative roles, 15
  defined, ix
  enablers, 18
  evaluation, 288
  job description, 13–19
  leadership styles, 15–18
  nonprofit camps, 14
  ultimate responsibilities, 18–19
directories of summer employment, recruiting and, 91
disabled persons, 2, 40–41, 67–68, 231–232
  accommodations, 69
  Camp Director's Primer and, 68
  physical facility and, 153–154
discipline, 41–48
  interviewees, child abuse and, 109
discrimination, employment and, 84
  interview, 104
dishwashing, 207
Ditter, Bob, 35
diversity of camp, 33
doctrine of respondent superior, 166–167
documentation
  health service, 196–202
  income, operational system and, 256
  maintenance concerns, 160
  observational supervision, 133
  training, 123
documenting interview, 107–108
driver's licenses, job requirements, 84
drivers, selecting, 212–214
Drucker, Peter, 6–7
drugs, 47
Dudley, Sumner F., 2

E

e-mail, 50, 260
  responses to, 228
eating disorders, 44, 45–46
economic situations, development and, 35
education
  professionals in camping, 300–302
  staff hiring and, 85
education movement, 3
Eells, Eleanor, 1
Elkind, David, 47
emergency procedures, 73
  medical care, 191–193
  waterfront, 76–77
emotional development characteristics
  eight to ten year olds, 37
  eleven to thirteen year olds, 38
  five to seven year olds, 36
  fourteen to seventeen year olds, 38–39
employment agreement, 109–110
employment. See also interviews; recruiting; staff
  background checks, 94–97
  child abusers and, 100–103
  health care provider, 188–189
  negligent hiring, 93–94
  references, 94–97
  returning staff, 110–111
  sample hiring log, 334–335
  second thoughts, 114
enablers, directors as, 18
Encopresis (inappropriate bowel movements), 46
endowment development, fund-raising, 267
enrollment
  interviews, 49
  market analysis and, 220–221
  target population and, 33
Enuresis (bed-wetting), 46
environmental concern, 9
environmental conditions, development and, 35
equal employment opportunity statement, 88
equestrian programs
  organizations, 315
staffing, 77
equipment
  age appropriate, 72
  depreciation, 251
  disabled persons and, 69
essential functions, job description, 82–85
evaluating interviews, 108–109
evaluations, 281
  administration, 287–288
  boards, 288–290
  campers, 291–292
  checklist, 285
  committees, 288–290
  criteria for, 282–283
  data gathering, 283–285
  director, 288
  finances, 293
  hospitality services, 288
  overall operation, staff, 285–286
  program, 286–287
  qualitative data, 283–284
  questionnaires, 283
  staff, 89
  staff performance, 288
evening activities, resident camps, 63
expansion, international, 3
expectations of camp, parents and, 35
expenses
  adjusting, budgeting and, 251–253
  contributions and, 264
  projecting, 248–251
experience
  interview, 105
  staff and, 85
experiential training, precamp, 117–118
exposures to risk, 167–168

F

facility. See physical facility
family style meals, 207
Farley, Elizabeth, Dr., 35
fax number, 50
fear, 44
fees, 6
  contributions and, 264
field trips, 63
final budget development, 251
finances
  accounting practices, 241–253
  budgeting, 247–253
  depreciation, 251
  evaluation, 293
  statement of activities, 244
financial statements

balance sheet, 245
cash flow, 245
income statement, 244
statement of activities, 244
statement of financial position,
    245
first aid, 177, 189
    organizations, 314
first impressions of site, 149–150
fixed costs of operation, 249
flyers, 232–233
Folkerth, Jean E., 35
food service. *See also* mealtimes,
    203–211
    contracted services, 210–211
    cookouts, 207–208
    day camps, 203
    evaluation, 287
    food storage, 208–210
    HACCP, 208–210
    meal organization, 206–207
    personal sanitary and hygiene
        practices, food and, 210
    precamp training topics, 332
    purchasing food, 204–205
    ratios, 78
    sanitation and, 208–210
    staff, 206
    supervisor, 203–204
    supervisor, job description, 307
foodborne illness, 208–210
for-profit camps, 6
former campers, recruiting
    as staff, 91
forms, financial
    operational financial risks
    worksheet, 243
    statement of activities, 244
France, expansion to, 3
free time
    individuals and, 61
    pacing/flow and, 63
    staff's personal, 90
Fresh Air Camps, 2
fund-raising
    annual giving, 265–266
    basics, 264–265
    capital campaigns, 266
    endowment development, 267
    personnel, 267
    use of funds, 264
    volunteers and, 271
funding for nonprofit camps, 6

G

GAAP (Generally Accepted
    Accounting Principles), 242
games
    informal, 69

land, 69–70
    water, 69
gender of staff, 84
general approach to interviews,
    106–107
general to specific questions,
    interview, 106
Generally Accepted Accounting
    Principles (GAAP), 242
Girl Scouts, 3
girls and camping, 2
girls camps, 3–4
goals, 22, 25–26
    evaluation, 28–29
goals and objectives, director
    and, 15
Goldberg, Jacob A, 75
Goodrich, Lois, 53
governmental resources, 319–329
gratuitous volunteers, 272
grievances, staff, 89
group living, 2, 8
    bath facility, 66
    decentralized programs, 57
    mealtimes and, 65–66
    summer camp emphases, 65–66
group tours, marketing
    and, 237–238
groups, 50–51
growth and development, 9
guidance, 9
Guide to ACA-Accredited Camps, 92
Gunn, Frederick William, 1
Gunnery School for Boys, 1

H

HACCP (Hazard Analysis Critical
    Control Points), food and,
    208–210
Hammett, Catherine, 113
health, 4
    insurance, 50
    medical history, 50
    medications, 50
    organizations, 314–315
health and accident insurance, 174
health and safety, 9
    physical facility, 150
health care administrator, 187–188
    role of, 195–196
health care planning, 191–193
health services, 187–202
    documentation, 196–202
    evaluation, 287
    health examinations, 49, 196
    health histories, 196
    health logs, 197
    health records, 179–180
    health screening, 197

injury reports, 197
    medications, 197
    planning, 191–193
    precamp training topics, 332
    ratios, 78
    staff and, 89
    staff training, 193–195
    supplies, 197
    types of workers, 190
health-related associations,
    nonprofit camps, 6
Henderson, 68
hiring log, 334–335
hiring. *See* recruitment; staff
history of organized camping, 1–5
*History of Organized Camping: The
    First 100 Years*, 1
HIV status, 179
Hogg's Hollow, 1
hold harmless, risk management
    and, 169–170
homesickness, 46–47
    visiting days and, 50
Horsemanship Safety Association,
    77
hospitality services
    conference/retreat centers, 10
    evaluation, 288
    outcomes/objectives and, 26
Howe, Christine Z., 259–261
human growth and development,
    34–48
    competencies or attributes
        essential to healthy
        development, 41
    program emphasis and, 64–65
human resources precamp training
    topics, 333

I

in loco parentis, 167
In the Trenches, 35
in-service training, staff, 113, 124
incentives to returning campers, 234
incident reports, 180, 197
income documentation, 256
income projections, budgeting and,
    248–251
income statement, 244
increases in camps, 4–5
indemnity agreements, 170
independent camps, x , 6
individuals
    centralized programs, 61
    free time and, 61
    skills, 56–57
    sports, 69–70
industry standards, 183
infantile behavior, 44

informal games, 69
information packets, 49
  interview and, 104
injuries, volunteers and, 273
injury reports, 197
inner-city youths, Fresh Air
  Camps, 2
inspections, 150
  maintenance, 156–157
instruction, 62
insurance, 171–178
  activity supervision and, 176
  automobile, 174
  binders, 174
  commercial general liability
    insurance, 172–173
  D and O (directors and
    officers), 173
  health, 50
  health and accident, 174
  liability, 172–173
  property insurance, 171–172
  staff benefits, 86
  worker's compensation, 173
intellectual development
  characteristics
    eight to ten year olds, 37
    eleven to thirteen year olds, 38
    five to seven year olds, 36
    fourteen to seventeen year
      olds, 39
intellectual skills and aptitudes,
  interview and, 105
interest groups, 61–62
International Camp Counselor
  Program, 92–96
international camping
  associations, 5
International Camping Congress, 5
International Camping Fellowship, 5
international expansion, 3
international organizations, 318
international staff, 92–96
international staff-placement
  organizations, recruiting
    and, 91–92
Internet
  office, 260
  recruiting and, 92
interpersonal relations, 9
interpersonal skills, directors
  and, 16
interviews
  child abuse warning signs,
    108–109
  concluding, 107
  controlling flow, 107
  documentation, 107–108
  enrollment and, 49
  evaluating, 108–109

general approach, 106–107
general to specific questions, 106
information packets, 104
intellectual skills and aptitudes,
  105
leading questions, 106
motivational characteristics, 105
open-ended questions, 106
organization chart, 104
personality, 105
plan, 105–106
post-staff-training interview,
  132–133
preinterview, 103–104
self-appraisal questions, 107
setting, 104–105

J

Japan, expansion to, 3
job descriptions
  certification, 84
  director, 13–19
  elements of, 82–85
  food service, 307
  preinterview, 103–104
  program director, 305–306
  recruitment and, 90–111
  site manager, 306–307
  writing, 85
job fairs, recruiting from, 91
job responsibilities, 76–77
Johnson, Becca Cowan, 109
Jordan, Debra, 17
Journal of Christian Camping, The,
  146

K

KALEIDOSCOPE, Inc., 10
Keewaydin Camps, 2
Keewaydin Foundation, 2
Kehonka, 2
Kellogg Foundation, 4–5
Klein, Edie, 83
Konopka, Gisela, 18

L

laissez-faire leadership, 17
land sports, 69–70
laundry information, 49
leader-in-training program, 91
leadership
  operating procedures and, 71–72
  styles, directors, 15–18
leading questions in interview, 106
leasing vehicles, 211–212
Ledlie, John A., 13
legal issues, 166–167
  volunteers and, 272–274

legal value, records, 262
length of sessions, 5
liability insurance, 172–173
liability issues, 93–94
licenses, 150
Life Camps, 2
life guards, training and, 76
lifeguards
  bloodborne pathogens and, 77
  OSHA and, 77
  ratio to swimmers, 77
living groups, 56, 60–61
  supervisory lines and, 78–79
lodging, staff benefits and, 86
logs, health logs, 197
long-term planning, site
  development, 151–152
long-term stress, 143
Lyle, Betty, 8–9

M

mailing address, 50
main office. *See* office
maintenance
  inspection checklist, 156–157
  personnel, 159
  physical facility, 154–160
  ratios, 78
  Request for Maintenance form,
    157–158
  vehicles, 214
  winterization, 160–161
managers *versus* leaders, 17
manuals, staff, 115–116
market analysis, 220–225
  competition and, 221
  enrollment and, 220–221
  returning campers, 221
marketing, 32
  advertising
    billboards, 236
    camper fairs, 235
    direct mail, 236–237
    posters, 236
    print ads, 236
    Web page, 236
  benefits to consumer, 222–225
  campers as customers, 219–220
  children influencing parents
    and, 219–220
  current strategies, 222–225
  implementation, 238–239
  personal interaction
    camp visits, 229
    personal calls, 228
    recruiting parties, 228
    referrals, 233–234, 235
    representatives, personal calls,
      228–229

responding to e-mail, 228
returning campers and, 227
reunions and, 227
weekend groups, 228
plan, developing, 226–239
promotional materials, 229
    brochures, 232–233
    flyers, 232–233
    incentives, returning campers,
        234
    prospective campers/groups,
        233–234
    public displays, 235
    registration forms, 229–232
    visual presentations, 234–235
public relations, 237–238
publicity, 237–238
Mason, Bernard, 1, 8
master site plan, 151–154
mealtimes
    cafeteria style, 207
    clean up, 206–207
    cookouts, 207–208
    dishwashing, 207
    family style, 207
    group living and, 65–66
    organization, 206–207
    staff benefits, 86
medical history, 50
medications, 50
    inventories, 197
mental stress, 144
menu planning, 204
minimum wage, 87
minutes of meetings, purpose
    and, 23
mission/purpose of camp, 7, 21
missionaries, 3
mobility, restricted, 67
modeling, supervision and, 131
motivational characteristics,
    interview and, 105

N

National Association of Girls'
    Private Camps, 4
National Safety Council, 77
natural sciences, 3
natural world learning, 8
nature-oriented activities, 70
negligent hiring, 93–94
new stories, marketing and, 237
Newborg, Gerald G., 262
nightmares, 47
nonprofit camps, x, 6
    directors, 14
    funding for, 6

O

objectives of camps, 4, 21–29
    spiritual, 5
observation of counselor training,
    133–134
office, 258–259
    arrangement of, 259
    computers, 259–261
    recordkeeping, 260–263
    staff, 259
oldest camp continuously
    operating, 2
on-line computers, 260
Ontario Camping Association, 1, 4
open-ended questions, interview,
    106
operating procedures, 56, 71–73
    leadership and, 71–72
    safety and emergencies, 73
operation, 187–216
    evaluation by staff, 285–286
    fixed costs, 249
    months of, 6
    outcomes/objectives and, 26
    precamp training topics,
        332–333
operational financial risks
    worksheet, 243
operational systems, 253–256
    income documentation, 256
    payment system, 254–255
    purchase order system, 253–254
    taxes, 256
operator/owner, ix
organization
    director and, 15
    program, 59–63
    staff, 7690
organizational chart, 78–81
    interview, 104
organizations, 312–317
    adventure/challenge, 312
    aquatic, 312–314
    equestrian, 315
    first aid, 314
    health and wellness, 314–315
    international, 318
    target sports, 315
    youth organizations, 316
orientation, staff, 113–116
OSHA (Occupational Safety
    and Health Administration
    lifeguards and, 77
    regulations, 168–169
Ott, Elmer, 31
outcomes/objectives, 21–29, 26–29
    program development and, 54
outdoor education, 4–5, 8
outdoor living skills, 70, 336–337

outdoor/oriented activities, 70
Outward Bound, 5
owner/operator, ix
owning vehicles, 211–212

P

pacing/flow of activities, 63
parental consent, 170
parents
    as staff members, 92
    expectations of camp, 35
    reporting to, 294–295
participants, 31
    developmental needs, 35–40
    preparation, 49–51
participate leadership, 17
pay periods, 87–88
payment system, operations and,
    254–255
    cash payments, 255–256
peer pressure, discipline and, 43
performance appraisal, staff. See also
    evaluation, 88
    counselors' end-of-season,
        135–140
performing arts, 69
perishable food, 208–210
permissions, 170
    health care, 196
permits, 150
personal calls, 228
    fund-raising, 266
personal interaction, marketing and,
    226–227
personal possessions, marking, 49
personal sanitary and hygiene
    practices, food and, 210
personality, interview, 105
personnel files, 110
personnel policies, 87–90
personnel. See staff
petty cash, 256
Phillips, Christy L., 92–96
philosophy, 21
    candidates comfort with,
        105–106
    developing, 22
    program development and, 54
physical abuse, 44
physical activity, pacing/flow and, 63
physical conditions, development
    and, 35
physical development characteristics
    eight to ten year olds, 36
    eleven to thirteen year olds, 37
    five to seven year olds, 36
    fourteen to seventeen
        year olds, 38
physical facility, 149–150

blueprints of buildings, 153
building codes, 153
development of, 151–154
disabled persons and, 153–154
evaluation, 287
inspections, 150
maintenance, 154–160
master site plan, 151–154
precamp training topics, 332
sanitation lines, 153
site selection, 150–151
utility lines, 153
written records, 160
physical skills, 70
physical stress, 144
Pinelands, 2
placement services, recruiting
and, 91
planning, director and, 15
policies and procedures
health care, 191–192
personnel policies, 87–90
staff hiring and, 75
post-staff-training interview,
132–133
posters, 236
praise, positive behavior and, 42
precamp training, 113, 116–123
experiential, 117–118
preinterview, 103–104
preparing participants, 49–51
groups, 50–51
information packets, 49
interviews, 49
transportation to camp, 50
visiting days, 50
primitive processes, 7
print ads, advertising and, 236
privacy in office, 259
procedures, disabled persons and, 69
professional associations, 3–4
professional development, 5
professional practices, x
professionals, 297–303
program design
centralized vs decentralized,
56–59
operating procedures, 71–73
pacing/flow of activities, 63
philosophy, 58–59
precamp training topics, 333
short-term, 66–67
specialized clientele, 67–69
specific activities, 69–71
program development, 53
activities and, 54–55
assessments and, 54–55
customer interest, 54
organization, 59–63
outcomes/objectives, 54

philosophy and, 54
refinement, 55
resources, 55
program director, job description,
305–306
program emphases
age appropriateness, 64–65
summer camp, 64–66
program evaluation, 286–287
program participation, 9
program schedule, 60
program specialists, 58
Project REACH Camp Staff
Training Series, 35
projections, income/expenses,
248–251
promotional materials, 229
property insurance, 171–172
public presentations, 237
public relations, 237–238
publications
Blue Lake & Rocky Shore, 1
Camping, 4
History of Organized Camping:
The First 100 Years, 1
publicity, 237–238
punishment, 43
purchase order system, 253–254
pure volunteer, 272
purpose of camp, 7, 24–25
statements of purpose, 23–24

Q

qualitative data, evaluations,
283–284
questionnaires, evaluations and, 283
questions for interview, 106–107

R

rapport, supervision and, 129
ratio of staff to campers, 76–77
food service, 78
health service, 78
maintenance crew, 78
recordkeeping
health service, 192
legal value, 262
office, 260–263
retention of records, 260–263
retention rules, 180, 183
risk management and, 178–183
records, physical facility, 160
recruiting. *See also* employment;
staff, 90–111
international staff, 92–96
interviews, 103–109
parties, campers, 228
returning staff, 110–111
sources, 91–92

staff, 75–77
reducing risks, 175–176
references, hiring and, 94–97
referrals, 233–234, 235
registration forms, 229–232
computers and, 259–261
regulations of camp operation,
168–169
rehiring staff, 110–111
reinforcing, supervision and, 131
religious entities, nonprofit camps, 6
religious services, 50
rental groups, 50–51, 237–238
short-term sessions and, 66–67
reporting, 293–295
alumni, 295
campers, 294–295
corporate board, 294
director and, 15
incident reports, 180
parents, 294–295
Request for Maintenance form,
157–158
resident camps, 5
evening activities, 63
food service supervisor, 203–204
orientation, staff, 115–116
resource management, 15
resources
organizations, 312–317
program development and, 55
responding to e-mail, 228
responsibility, 9
restricted mobility, 67
retention of risk, 174–175
retreat groups, 6
retreats, ix
returning campers, 221
incentives, 234
marketing and, 227
recruiting parties, 228
returning staff, 110–111
reunions, marketing and, 227
risk management, 165–184
accreditation and, 183
avoiding risks, 169
checklist, 308–311
evaluation, 287
exposures to risk, 167–168
handling incidents, 176–178
hold harmless, 169–170
indemnity agreements, 170
insurance, 171–178
parental consent, 170
permissions, 170
recordkeeping and, 178–183
reducing risk, 175–176
retention of risk, 174–175
transfer of risks, 169
waivers, 169–170

Rothrock, Joseph, 2
Royal Lifesaving Society, 76
rudeness, 44
rules, disabled persons and, 69
Russia, expansion to, 3

S

safety
    equestrian programs, 77
    procedures, 73
salary and benefits, 85–87
    baby-sitting service, 86
    children of staff, 86
    insurance, 86
    lodging, 86
    meals, 86
    recruitment and, 90–111
    transportation, 86
sanitation lines, physical facility, 153
sanitation, food and, 208–210
scheduled activities, varying, 63
scheduling maintenance, 155–156
scheduling training, 118–119
school camping, 4–5
second thoughts about employment,
    114
sections, 62
self-appraisal questions, interview,
    107
self-concept, 9
senior adults, 67
    recruiting as staff, 92
session length, 5
settlement houses
    nonprofit camps, 6
    urban centers and, 2
sexual abuse, 44
    negligent hiring and, 93–94
sexual activity, 47
    inappropriate, abuse and, 44
sexual harassment, staff and, 88
sharing, supervision and, 129
Sharpe, L.B., 57
short-term planning, site
    development, 152–154
short-term sessions, program design
    and, 66–67
short-term stress, 143
site manager, job description,
    306–307
site selection, 150–151
situational stress, 144
skill building, 9
    disabled persons and, 69
    levels, appropriateness, 72
    outdoor living skills, 70
    physical skills, 70
sleeping problems, 47
small-group activities, 55–56

So You Want to Be a Supervisor,
    121–123
social development characteristics
    eight to ten year olds, 36
    eleven to thirteen year olds, 37–38
    five to seven year olds, 36
    fourteen to seventeen year olds,
        38
*Social Group Work: A Helping
    Process,* 18
social recreation, 70–71
social service organizations, 3
sociogram, 134–135
software for administration,
    259–261
sources for recruitment, 91–92
special events, 70
specialized clientele, 67–69
specialty camps, 4
specific program activities, 69–71
specific threats, discipline and, 43
spiritual attainment, 3, 9
spiritual objectives, 5
spiritually oriented activities, 71
sports, 64–66
    individuals, 69–70
    land, 69–70
    team, 69–70
    water, 69
staff, 6, 75–111
    age, 84
    alcohol use, 88
    at-will employment, 89
    background and, 75
    background checks, 94–97
    camp liability, 93–94
    certification requirements, 76–77
    community relations and, 89
    discrimination, 84
    doctrine of respondent superior,
        166–167
    education, 85
    evaluations, 89
    experience, 85
    food service, 206
    free time, personal, 90
    gender, 84
    grievances, 89
    health care providers, 188–189
    health services, 89
        training, 193–195
    in-service training, 113
    job responsibilities, 76–77
    maintenance, 159
    negligent hiring, 93–94
    office, 259
    organization, 7690
    orientation, 113–116
    overall operation evaluation,
        285–286

pay periods, 88
performance appraisal, 88
performance evaluations, 288
personnel files, 110
ratio of staff to campers, 76
ratio to campers, 72
ratios to campers, 77–78
references, 94–97
returning, 110–111
sexual harassment, 88
supervisory lines, 78–82
termination, 88
time off, 88
tobacco use, 88
training, precamp, 332–333
volunteers, 274–275
staff manuals, 23, 115–116
staff meetings, 125
statement of activities, 244
statement of financial position, 245
statements of purpose, 23–24
statutes of limitation, records and,
    180
stealing, 47
Stone, James C., 9
store, camp store, 256–261
strategic planning, 22
stress, 47, 142–145
    child abuse and, 119
substance abuse, 47
suicidal behavior, 48
Summer Camp Employment Booklet,
    91
summer camp, program emphases,
    64–66
supervision of staff, 76
    counselors, 132–141
    conferences, 134–135
    observation, 133–134
    performance appraisal, 135–140
    post-staff-training interview,
        132–133
    food service supervisor, 203–204
    functions of supervisor, 127–128
    guidelines, 128–130
    legal issues, 130–132
    noncounseling staff, 140–141
    rapport and, 129
    sharing and, 129
    techniques, 130–132
    termination, 145–146
    training for, 121–123
    trust, 128–129
supervision ratio, 72
supervisory lines, 78–82
    centralized programs, 78–79
    decentralized programs, 78–79
    living groups and, 78–79
    organizational charts, 78–81

T

target population, 31–34
target sports, organizations, 315
taxes, 256
teacher education, college courses,
    4–5
teaching, supervision and, 130
team sports, 69–70
technical skills, directors and, 16
telephone, 50
telethon, fund-raising and, 266
temperature of food, 209–210
termination, staff, 87–88, 145–146
The Hurried Child, 47
theft, 47
time off, staff, 88
tobacco use, staff and, 88
tort liability, 167
total-group activities, 55–56
training, staff
    child abuse, 119–120
    documentation, 123
    experiential, 117–118
    goals and objectives, 118
    health service, 193–195
    in-service sessions, 113, 124
    precamp, 113, 116–123,
        332–333
    Project REACH Camp Staff
    Training Series, 35
    scheduling, 118–119
    supervisory, 121–123
    varying sessions, 120–121
transfer of risks, 169
transportation
    precamp training topics, 332
    staff benefits and, 86
    to camp, 50
transportation staff, 211–216
    camper education, 214–215

driver selection, 212–214
    vehicle maintenance, 214
trip camps, 63
Trotter, Kathleen, 10
trust, supervision and, 128–129
types of camps, 5–7

U

U.S., Coast Guard Boating Safety
    Standards, 77
U.S., Power Squadrons, 77
U.S., SAILING, 77
ultimate responsibilities of director,
    18–19
units, 62
urban centers, settlement houses, 2
utility lines, physical facility, 153

V

values, 21
van der Smissen, Betty, 165
Van Krevelen, Alice, 21
vandalism, 48
variables, cost of operation, 251
vehicle maintenance, 214
vehicular activities, 70
vendors
    food, 205–206
    payment system, 254–255
Victorian attitudes, girls camping
    and, 2
violence in participants, 45
vision, 21
visiting camps, marketing and, 229
visitor times, 50
    activities and, 70
visual presentations, marketing,
    234–235
Voluntary Disclosure Statement,
    98–99

volunteers, 271–278
    as staff, 274–275
    committees and boards, 275–278
    gratuitous, 272
    injuries, 273
    legal issues, 272–274
    pure, 272

W

wages, 86–87
    contributions and, 264
waivers, risk management and,
    169–170
water skiing, 77
water sports, 69
waterfront, staff requirements,
    76–77
Web pages, 236
weekend groups, 228
Weiters, Nelson, 4
White House Conference on Child
    Health and Protection, 4
winterization, 160–161
worker's compensation, 173
Wyonegonic Camp, 2

Y

YMCA
    camp in Newburgh, NY, 2
    lifeguards and, 76
York Mills, 1
youth organizations, 316
    emergence of, 3
youth-at-risk, 67
    Outward Bound and, 5
YWCA, 2

Z

zoning issues, 150